# FLUENCY INSTRUCTION

# FLUENCY INSTRUCTION
## *Research-Based Best Practices*

SECOND EDITION

*Edited by*

Timothy Rasinski
Camille Blachowicz
Kristin Lems

THE GUILFORD PRESS
New York          London

©2012 The Guilford Press
A Division of Guilford Publications, Inc.
72 Spring Street, New York, NY 10012
www.guilford.com

Printed in the United States of America

This book is printed on acid-free paper.

Last digit is print number: 9 8 7 6 5 4 3 2 1

**Library of Congress Cataloging-in-Publication Data**

Fluency instruction : research-based best practices / edited by Timothy Rasinski,
Camille L. Z. Blachowicz, Kristin Lems. — 2nd ed.
    p. cm.
Includes bibliographical references and index.
  ISBN 978-1-4625-0430-5 (pbk.) — ISBN 978-1-4625-0441-1 (hardcover)
 1. Reading.  2. Reading—Remedial teaching.  I. Rasinski, Timothy V.
II. Blachowicz, Camille L. Z.  III. Lems, Kristin.
 LB1050.F58 2012
 372.41—dc23
                                                          2012007099

11/26/12

# About the Editors

**Timothy Rasinski, PhD,** is Professor of Literacy Education at Kent State University. He has written over 200 articles and has authored, coauthored, or edited more than 50 books or curriculum programs on reading education, including the best-selling books *The Fluent Reader* (second edition) and *The Fluent Reader in Action.* Dr. Rasinski's scholarly interests include reading fluency and word study, reading in the elementary and middle grades, and readers who struggle. His research on reading has been cited by the National Reading Panel and has been published in journals such as *Reading Research Quarterly, The Reading Teacher, Reading Psychology,* and the *Journal of Educational Research.* In 2006 he completed a 3-year term on the Board of Directors of the International Reading Association; from 1992 to 1999 he was coeditor of *The Reading Teacher,* the world's most widely read journal of literacy education; and he served as coeditor of the *Journal of Literacy Research.* Dr. Rasinski is past president of the College Reading Association and a recipient of the Association's A. B. Herr and Laureate Awards for his scholarly contributions to literacy education. In 2010 he was elected to the International Reading Hall of Fame.

**Camille Blachowicz, PhD,** is Research Professor at National Louis University, where she has directed the Reading Specialist Program and the Reading Center. She is the author of six books and more than a hundred chapters, monographs, and articles on vocabulary and comprehension instruction and on working with at-risk readers. Dr. Blachowicz was a Fulbright Scholar in Italy and is co-principal investigator of the federally funded Multiphase Comprehensive Vocabulary Instruction Project. She is also active in professional organizations and staff development nationally and internationally.

**Kristin Lems, EdD,** is Professor of English as a Second Language/Bilingual Education at National Louis University, where she teaches graduate courses for practicing teachers. She has authored, coauthored, or edited a number of books, chapters, and articles in both the ESL and reading fields, including articles in *The Reading Teacher, Writing Systems Research,* and *English Teaching Forum* and the books *Teaching Reading to English Language Learners: Insights from Linguistics* and *The Fluent Reader in Action: PreK–4: A Rich Collection of Research-Based, Classroom-Tested Lessons and Strategies for Improving Fluency and Comprehension.* She directs a National Professional Development Grant with the Office of English Language Acquisition, U.S. Department of Education, her second such grant. Dr. Lems was a Fulbright Scholar teaching TEFL theory and practice in Algeria for 2 years. She wrote a teaching methods book for the Peace Corps and is an English Language Specialist with the Office of English Language Programs at the U.S. State Department.

# Contributors

**Richard L. Allington, PhD,** Department of Theory and Practice in Teacher Education, College of Education, University of Tennessee, Knoxville, Tennessee

**Gwynne E. Ash, PhD,** Department of Curriculum and Instruction, Texas State University, San Marcos, Texas

**Rebekah George Benjamin, MA,** Department of Educational Psychology, University of Georgia, Athens, Georgia

**Camille L. Z. Blachowicz, PhD,** Department of Reading and Language, National College of Education, National Louis University, Evanston, Illinois

**Dana Butler, MA,** Irma C. Ruiz Elementary School, Chicago, Illinois

**Elsa Carmona, MA,** Little Village Elementary School, Chicago, Illinois

**David J. Chard, PhD,** Simmons School of Education and Human Development, Southern Methodist University, Dallas, Texas

**Danielle V. Dennis, PhD,** College of Education, University of South Florida, Tampa, Florida

**Randal Donelson, PhD,** Department of Education, The Ohio State University at Mansfield, Mansfield, Ohio

**Peter Fisher, PhD,** Department of Reading and Language, National College of Education, National Louis University, Evanston, Illinois

**Ellen Fogelberg, MS,** Evanston–Skokie School District 65, Evanston, Illinois

**Greta Gorsuch, EdD,** Department of Classical and Modern Languages and Literatures, Texas Tech University, Lubbock, Texas

**Megan Gregory, EdM,** Literacy and Language Education, Department of Developmental Studies, Boston University, Boston, Massachusetts

**Elfrieda H. Hiebert, PhD,** School of Education, University of California, Santa Cruz, Santa Cruz, California

**Melanie R. Kuhn, PhD,** Department of Curriculum and Teaching, Boston University, Boston, Massachusetts

**Kristin Lems, EdD,** ESL/Bilingual Education, Department of Curriculum and Instruction, National Louis University, Chicago, Illinois

**Jessica Mangelson, PhD,** Department of Education, Benedictine University, Lisle, Illinois

**Jennifer R. Massarelli, MEd,** National College of Education, National Louis University, Evanston, Illinois

**Sarah H. McDonagh, PhD,** School of Teacher Education, Charles Sturt University, Bathurst, New South Wales, Australia

**Becky McTague, EdD,** Department of Language and Literacy, Roosevelt University, Chicago, Illinois

**Kouider Mokhtari, PhD,** School of Education, University of Texas at Tyler, Tyler, Texas

**Mary Kay Moskal, EdD,** School of Education, Saint Mary's College of California, Moraga, California

**Connie M. Obrochta, MEd,** Evanston–Skokie School District 65, Evanston, Illinois

**Nancy Padak, EdD,** The Ohio Literacy Resource Center, Kent State University, Kent, Ohio

**David D. Paige, EdD,** Department of Education, Bellarmine University, Louisville, Kentucky

**John J. Pikulski, PhD,** Department of Education, University of Delaware, Newark, Delaware

**Meryl-Lynn Pluck, MPhil,** Rainbow Reading Program, Nelson, New Zealand

**Timothy Rasinski, PhD,** Department of Teaching, Leadership, and Curriculum Studies, Kent State University, Kent, Ohio

**D. Ray Reutzel, PhD,** Emma Eccles Jones Center for Early Childhood Education, Utah State University, Logan, Utah

**S. Jay Samuels, EdD,** Department of Educational Psychology, University of Minnesota, Minneapolis, Minnesota

**Stephan Sargent, EdD,** Department of Curriculum and Instruction, Northeastern State University, Broken Arrow, Oklahoma

**Paula J. Schwanenflugel, PhD,** Department of Educational Psychology, University of Georgia, Athens, Georgia

**Timothy Shanahan, PhD,** College of Education, University of Illinois at Chicago, Chicago, Illinois

**Kathryn L. Solic, PhD,** The Benchmark School, Media, Pennsylvania

**Bruce Stevenson, PhD,** Worthington City Schools, Worthington, Ohio

**Etsuo Taguchi, PhD,** Department of Japanese, Faculty of Foreign Languages, Daito Bunka University, Tokyo, Japan

**Patsy Todt, MEd,** Department of Teacher Education, Shawnee State University, Portsmouth, Ohio

**Keith J. Topping, PhD,** Department of Education and Social Research, School of Education, University of Dundee, Dundee, Scotland

**Barbara J. Walker, PhD,** College of Education, Oklahoma State University, Tulsa, Oklahoma

**Belinda Zimmerman, PhD,** Department of Literacy and Early Childhood Education, Kent State University, Kent, Ohio

**Jerry Zutell, PhD,** School of Teaching and Learning, College of Education, The Ohio State University, Columbus, Ohio

# Preface

Until recently, reading fluency had not been a priority in reading instruction in the United States. Despite periodic calls for a reexamination of reading fluency (e.g., Allington, 1983; Zutell & Rasinski, 1991), fluency was not able to capture the attention or imagination of most reading educators. This may have been due to the way that fluency was defined. For many educators, fluency was nothing more than reading fast or with good oral expression. Neither of these seemed even remotely connected to the well-accepted goal of reading: comprehension.

Things began to change when reading researchers demonstrated that reading fluency is necessary for good comprehension (e.g., LaBerge & Samuels, 1974; Stanovich, 1980). Reviews of research have concluded that reading fluency is indeed an important component of the reading process and it is essential that it be taught to developing readers (National Reading Panel, 2000; Rasinski, Reutzel, Chard, & Linan-Thompson, 2011). Thus, reading fluency has now taken its place with phonemic awareness, word decoding, vocabulary, and comprehension as a critical component of effective reading instruction.

Yet, despite research that recognizes the importance of reading fluency, many teachers do not have an accurate idea of what fluency is or how it can best be taught. In too many classrooms, reading fluency has become instruction in how to read fast. This is most definitely not fluency. As a result of such misconceptions, fluency has been identified as a "not hot" topic in a recent survey of reading experts (Cassidy, Ortlieb, & Shettel, 2011).

With this second edition of *Fluency Instruction*, we hope to clarify what fluency truly is and how it can best be taught. We have assembled some of the best known scholars in reading fluency and have asked them to share with readers their thoughts on fluency and fluency instruction.

We have also asked practitioner colleagues who are conducting innovative, research-based work with fluency programs in real classrooms to share their perspectives on fluency instruction and assessment. Finally, we have invited diverse educators to look at some specific populations in greater detail.

The book is divided into three sections. The first focuses on some of the ways in which fluency has come to be understood and the educational areas in which it has become situated. The second section highlights some instructional programs and classroom practices that are widely varied in their approach but all built on a deep understanding of how fluency works. Finally, the third section explores the applications of fluency research and practice to some populations not typically associated with fluency instruction.

The book fittingly opens with a historical overview of fluency by S. Jay Samuels, who first brought the issue into literacy education and continues to be one of its most articulate voices. Several new features in this edition are worth mentioning here. Chapters by Becky McTague, Kristin Lems, and colleagues and by Etsuo Taguchi and Greta Gorsuch, and a new chapter by Kristin Lems explore the role of fluency with English language learners. New chapters by Melanie R. Kuhn and colleagues and by Paula J. Schwanenflugel and Rebekah George Benjamin ask readers to consider how prosody or expressiveness plays an important role in reading fluency. Elfrieda H. Hiebert's new chapter considers the importance of matching texts to readers in order to develop fluency, especially among beginning readers. In his chapter, new to this edition, David D. Paige points out that reading fluency is not an issue only for the elementary grades. Indeed, it may be a key to reading success in the middle and secondary grades, especially for struggling readers. And, in another chapter new to this volume, Belinda Zimmerman and Timothy Rasinski report on the implementation of a model of fluency instruction called the Fluency Development Lesson with struggling readers.

We believe that this book represents a significant advance in our understanding of reading fluency and its instruction. Readers will come away with a better understanding of reading fluency and some of the problematic issues in both its conceptualization and application in the classroom. Developing this book has been a labor of love and a marvel of modern technology as we have collaborated, long distance, with some of the finest minds in reading fluency across several continents. We hope our readers will enjoy this new journey into the complex realm of fluency as much as we have enjoyed preparing the paths to guide you on your way.

TIMOTHY RASINSKI
CAMILLE BLACHOWICZ
KRISTIN LEMS

# REFERENCES

Allington, R. L. (1983). Fluency: The neglected reading goal. *Reading Teacher, 36,* 556–561.

Cassidy, J., Ortlieb, E., & Shettel, J. (2011). What's hot for 2011. *Reading Today, 28*(3), 1, 6, 7, 8.

LaBerge, D., & Samuels, S. A. (1974). Toward a theory of automatic information processing in reading. *Cognitive Psychology, 6,* 293–323.

National Reading Panel. (2000). *Teaching children to read: An evidence-based assessment of the scientific research literature on reading and its implications for reading instruction. Reports of the subgroups.* Washington, DC: National Institute of Child Health and Human Development.

Rasinski, T. V., Reutzel, C. R., Chard, D., & Linan-Thompson, S. (2011). Reading fluency. In M. L. Kamil, P. D. Pearson, B. Moje, & P. Afflerbach (Eds.), *Handbook of reading research* (vol. IV, pp. 286–319). New York: Routledge.

Stanovich, K. E. (1980). Toward an interactive—compensatory model of individual differences in the development of reading fluency. *Reading Research Quarterly, 16,* 32–71.

Zutell, J., & Rasinski, T. V. (1991). Training teachers to attend to their students' oral reading fluency. *Theory into Practice, 30,* 211–217.

# Contents

# PART I

# FLUENCY THEORY, FLUENCY RESEARCH

# 1

# Reading Fluency

*Its Past, Present, and Future*

S. Jay Samuels

In the last few years, reading fluency has become a topic of great interest to teachers. An article by Cassidy and Cassidy (2003/2004) that appeared in the International Reading Association publication *Reading Today* was entitled "What's Hot, What's Not for 2004." For this article, numerous reading experts were asked their views about what is "in" and what is "out" in reading instruction. For the first time, reading fluency was added to the list of terms that were evaluated by these experts. This field of experts was of the opinion that not only was fluency a hot topic, but that it also *deserved* to be a hot topic.

With its new popularity, however, fluency is going through a period of what may be thought of as "growing pains." One problem has to do with the definition of fluency and another with how it is measured, and both are interrelated. Because both problems are part of the history of fluency, I begin this chapter by defining it. Then I describe the evolution of fluency from a century ago, from the 1900s to about the 1970s. Using the year 1970 as a benchmark leading to the present, I explain what has been happening with regard to developing and measuring fluency. Finally, I gaze into my crystal ball and attempt to predict some future developments in reading fluency.

## DEFINITION OF FLUENCY

Automaticity theory attempts to explain how people become highly skilled at difficult tasks such as driving a car, typing on a computer keyboard, or reading a book. If we examine the developmental stages in learning a complex skill, we usually find that good instructors break the complex skill into subskills, and the student is given instruction in how to perform each of the subskills. During the beginning phase, while learning to perform to the level of accuracy, the student has to put so much effort and attention into the task that only one task can be performed at a time. For example, beginning drivers find that when driving in traffic, they usually dislike taking on another task such as talking to another person or listening to a talk radio show. This focus on one task at a time is somewhat reminiscent of President Theodore Roosevelt's comments about running the country or taking care of his daughter, who was giving her family some problems. The President said, "I can either run the country, or I can take care of Alice, but I cannot do both."

While it is true that in the beginning stages of learning a complex task the student can perform only one task at a time, with practice that situation changes. With practice the mechanics of driving a car becomes easier, and tasks such as using lane-change signals, watching for traffic lights, steering to avoid accidents, and choosing routes to one's destination can be done with speed, accuracy, and little attention. As the student becomes automatic at the mechanics of driving, he or she finds it is possible to do two things simultaneously. For example, the person can drive the car through traffic and at the same time engage in conversation with another person or listen to talk shows on the radio. In other words, skilled drivers can do two or more things at the same time, whereas novice drivers cannot.

In order to explain the transition from beginner to expert, automaticity theory makes certain assumptions. For example, it assumes that the human mind has only a limited capacity to perform difficult tasks. Second, it assumes that in order to perform difficult tasks such as recognizing words in a text or understanding their meaning, mental effort must be expended, and this effort consumes some of the limited capacity of the mind. Third, with continued practice over time, the amount of effort required to perform these tasks becomes less and less. Finally, when the amount of effort used in performing a task drops sufficiently, that person can then take on a new task *at the same time*. These few simple rules allow us to describe fluent reading.

The reading process requires that two tasks get done. The first task the student must perform is to recognize the printed words (i.e., decode). The second task for the student is to construct meaning for the words that were decoded (i.e., comprehend). For a beginning reader, the decoding task is so difficult that all of the student's mental capacity is used up in the word recognition process. When the entire capacity of the mind is used for decoding, the student cannot construct meaning. However, having decoded the words, the student can then switch attention to getting meaning. So, for beginners, the reading process is one of switching attention back and forth from decoding to meaning. This process is slow, effortful, and hard on memory.

When the student has had lots of practice at reading high-frequency common words found in easy reading material, the decoding process becomes easier and easier, to the point where we can say that decoding is automatic. By "automatic" we simply mean that the words in the text can be decoded with ease, speed, and accuracy. Because the decoding task has become so easy and has not consumed all of the processing capacity of the mind, the student can then direct the unused portion of the mind toward constructing meaning. In other words, the most important characteristic of the fluent reader is the ability to decode and to comprehend the text at the same time. Of course, there are other characteristics of fluency such as accuracy of word recognition, speed of reading, and the ability to read orally with expression, but these are simply indicators of fluency. These indicators of fluency are like the temperature readings in a thermometer when administered to a sick person. The high temperature on the thermometer is not the disease itself, but only an indicator that a person is sick. Reading speed and proper expression in oral reading are indicators of fluency. The essence of fluency is not reading speed or oral reading expression but rather the ability to decode and comprehend text at the same time.

## READING FLUENCY: 1900–1970

About a century ago, a truly remarkable book about reading was written by Edmund Burke Huey (1908/1968), entitled *The Psychology and Pedagogy of Reading*. The book was so extraordinary that the Massachusetts Institute of Technology, one of the leading universities in the world, reissued it in 1968 with a foreword by John B. Carroll and an introduction by Paul A. Kolers, both of whom were early pioneers in the field of cognitive psychology. One of the remarkable aspects of Huey's book was his keen insight into what would later become automaticity theory. For example, on page 104 of the MIT publication, we find Huey's description of how students become fluent readers:

> Perceiving being an act, it is, like all other things that we do, performed more easily with each repetition of the act. To perceive an entirely new word or other combination of strokes requires considerable time, close attention, and

is likely to be imperfectly done, just as when we attempt some new combination of movements, some new trick in the gymnasium or new serve in tennis. In either case, repetition progressively frees the mind from attention to details, makes facile the total act, shortens the time, and reduces the extent to which consciousness must concern itself with the process.

Without invoking what would later become automaticity theory, Huey described the student's progress from beginner, where close attention to the details of words was required for recognition, to the fluency stage, where words could be recognized automatically, with speed and accuracy.

Huey even described how the fluent reader had available a number of options with regard to what unit of word recognition to use in recognizing a word (p. 81). For example, a person can recognize a word letter by letter, in which case the unit of word recognition is the letter. Or a person can recognize a word as a holistic unit, in which case the unit is the entire word. There is evidence that for beginning readers the letter is the unit used in word recognition, whereas the unit of word recognition for fluent readers is the word itself (Samuels, LaBerge, & Bremer, 1978). With prescience, Huey wrote (p. 81) that

> The more unfamiliar the sequence of letters may be, the more the perception of it proceeds by letters. With increase of familiarity, fewer and fewer clues suffice to touch off the recognition of the word or phrase, the tendency being toward reading in word-wholes. So reading is now by letters, now by groups of letters or by syllables, now by word-wholes, all in the same sentence sometimes, or even in the same word, as the reader may most quickly attain his purpose.

What Huey was actually describing was how fluent readers read a text. Fluent readers have the option of using a variety of units as the need arises, ranging from the whole word to the single letter. Beginning readers, on the other hand, do not have these options and are limited to the single letter, at least in the beginning stage of reading development.

Until recently, many texts on reading instruction failed to have an entry in their index for "fluency" or "reading fluency." As Allington (1983) stated some years ago, reading fluency was one of the most neglected areas of the reading curriculum. However, in Huey's 1908 book, there is an entry for "fluent reading" (p. 292). Turning to this page of the book, one finds a description of a technique that is reminiscent of a famous experiment designed to find out how chess masters were different from the run-of-the-mill chess player. In this experiment, de Groot (1965) had chess experts and nonexperts look at a chessboard in which the chess pieces were placed in well-established positions commonly used by experienced players. After allowing the people in the experiment to view the board for a few moments with the pieces in patterns commonly used in chess, the pieces were knocked off the board, and the task was to re-create the positions as they were originally.

The chess expert was able to re-create the original position, but the nonexpert could not. At first it was thought that the expert had superior memory, but then the second part of the study was done. The same number of pieces was put on the chessboard, only now the pieces were placed in a random order. Again, the two groups were asked to re-create the chess positions. However, now the expert and the nonexpert did equally poorly. The interpretation for these findings was that chess masters did not have superior memory. Chess has a structure that the experts had learned but the novice players had not learned. Similarly, English spelling of words has a structure, and sentences in a text follow grammatical patterns and rules. Through the practice of reading and learning how to spell words, the skilled readers have learned the structure of our words, whereas the beginner has not. In addition, English grammar itself has a structure, so that we are comfortable when we read "green grass" and uncomfortable if we read "grass green."

Huey described an exercise in which students were shown a phrase in a book for a brief exposure period and then were asked either to re-create on paper what they had seen or to recite orally what they had seen. This is precisely what de Groot did with his chess players. After a brief exposure to the pieces on the board, the players were asked to re-create their positions, whereas in reading the students were asked to reproduce what they had seen. Huey thought this exercise might help students become fluent readers. This might well be the case, but with the advantage of a century of research on our side, it is more likely that Huey had discovered a good way to determine which students were fluent and which were not. With Huey's task, only fluent readers could perform well.

At about the same time that Huey was writing his book on reading, Bryan and Harter (1897, 1899) began their investigations of how telegraph operators became skilled at sending and receiving Morse code. In many respects, learning Morse code is like learning to read. They found that, when faced with the task of receiving the code and making sense of it, beginning Morse code operators were like beginning readers in that they were slow and inaccurate and had to place all their attention on the task at hand. In fact, beginning Morse code operators found they could only do one task at a time. First, the letters had to be received and made into a word. Second, the meanings could only be constructed after the first task was completed. One of the problems encountered was that if the code came in at a rapid pace, the novice operator could not tell one letter from another, much less one word from another.

Bryan and Harter (1897, 1899) found that with considerable time and practice, the Morse code operators became so automatic at receiving messages that they were able to do this task quickly, accurately, and with little attention. Consequently, they were able to get the meaning of the message at the same time. In other words, they had become "fluent" at the task of reading Morse code. In a remarkable way, the stages of becoming skilled at receiving Morse code paralleled the stages of reading and fluency development described by Ehri (1991) and Chall (1983).

Tim Rasinski's (2003) excellent book on fluency has a section devoted to the history of oral reading. He describes how oral reading was as important as silent reading from the time of the birth of our nation to the beginning of the 1900s, at which time it began to decline in importance. From a historical perspective, oral reading was important, and for good reason. Before the 1900s, often only one person in a family could read, and that person had the responsibility of reading to the others. Oral reading took on the role of entertainment. So the person who did the oral reading had to do it with skill. Reading out loud had to sound natural. It had to sound like conversational speech. In order to achieve these goals, the person who read out loud had to meet the criteria we currently use as indicators of fluency; that is, the oral reading had to be accurate and reasonably fast, and it had to be done with expression. Furthermore, one of the most important reading researchers of his day, William S. Gray, developed the Gray Oral Reading Test. This test had students read orally, and, as they read, they were scored for word recognition, accuracy, and speed, but in addition they were tested for their ability to understand what they had been reading. In essence, this test developed about 80 years ago utilized a technique that measures fluency as we would advocate that it be done today. The test, originally developed by Gray in the 1920s, has gone through four revisions and is still in use today.

Despite the important contributions made by scholars of the past to our understanding of how fluency develops and can be measured, it did not develop as an important research topic from the 1900s until very recently. Exactly why fluency failed to become an important part of the reading curriculum is not clear. One possibility is that other reading-related problems had priority over fluency. For example, the major psychological paradigm from the 1900s until the late 1950s was behaviorism. This paradigm limited what reading researchers could study to what we could classify as outside-the-head topics, such as word recognition or test development. The investigation of inside-the-head topics, such as comprehension, was discouraged during behaviorism. So when the paradigm shifted from behaviorism to cognitive psychology during the late 1950s and early 1960s, there was a rush by some of the best minds in psychology to study the long-neglected topic of comprehension.

Like comprehension, the underlying mechanism for fluency is an inside-the-head phenomenon and, under the rules of behaviorism, fluency was neglected. It was only with the birth of the new paradigm, cognitive psychology, that the work on fluency emerged. In addition, by the mid-1960s, Professors Ken Goodman and Frank Smith had begun their attacks on the reading curriculum, and with the coming years their whole-language philosophy became one of the most powerful approaches to instruction. The reading wars were in full swing. There seemed to have been three different groups represented in the wars: the whole-language group, the skills-based group, and those who advocated a balanced approach. It is now apparent that the whole-language emphasis is on a downward trajectory and the balanced approach is winning favor. Those who are working on reading fluency are seeing a new interest in fluency as part of a balanced reading approach. As we see in the next section, there were new factors emerging that brought fluency to the forefront.

## READING FLUENCY: 1970–PRESENT

In the mid-1960s the University of Minnesota started a research institute called the Human Learning Center, which brought together professors from related disciplines such as psychology, educational psychology, and child development, and encouraged them to collaborate on research. That was how I met Professor David LaBerge, a member of the Psychology Department faculty. LaBerge had developed a machine that presented words on a screen, and when "yes" or "no" buttons were pushed, the machine could measure accuracy and the reaction time of response. He thought the machine could be used in reading instruction, so we began our collaboration with discussions of the reading process.

These discussions lasted for hours each week, and at the end of the year, we realized that we had developed a theory of reading that focused upon the development of automaticity in word recognition. Our theory stated that if the student was not automatic at word recognition, the important job of reading for meaning had to be done in two stages. First, the student had to attend to the task of decoding the words in the text. Because the word recognition task was not automatic, all of the available cognitive resources were used in the decoding task. Second, the student had to switch attention to comprehension. This two-step process was relatively slow and placed heavy demands on the memory systems. However, over a period that typically lasted for two or three grades, during which time the student had practiced reading books that were in his or her zone of reading ability, the student became automatic at the decoding task. Now, the two tasks, decoding and comprehending, could be done together. We wrote up our ideas, and our article was accepted for publication in *Cognitive Psychology*

(LaBerge & Samuels, 1974). Following our notification of its acceptance, a most unusual thing happened. Word had apparently gone out to the research community that a new theory describing automatic information processing in reading was about to be published, and LaBerge and I began to get three, four, or five requests each week for copies of our unpublished manuscript, more requests than we had ever received for any of our other research reports. Our theory on automaticity was readily accepted by the research and educational communities, and has been viewed as one of the harbingers of what would become a new interest in reading fluency.

There was a problem with LaBerge and Samuels's automaticity theory, however. Our article on automaticity was only a theory, with no practical suggestions in it, and I had always thought that a good theory should have some practical aspects. Following the publication of our article, I struggled for 2 years with the problem of what could be derived from our automaticity theory that would have some useful aspects to it. One day, as I was running around the city lakes near my home, I asked myself two important questions: Who are the most highly skilled people in our society, and what kind of training did they get? I came up with two categories of highly skilled people: athletes and musicians. Alpine skiers, for example, who could ski down a mountain without killing themselves had to be highly trained. And jazz piano players who could play a complex melodic line and hold a conversation with me at the same time always impressed me with their skill.

What was most exciting to me was the fact that athletes and musicians usually got the same kind of training. What the athletic coach or music teacher did was take these very complex activities and break each one into subskills. For example, in music, the teacher might take a very simple song and show the student how to play it. Then the student takes the sheet music home and practice it for a week, until it could be played to the teacher's satisfaction, with accuracy, appropriate speed, and expression. In wrestling, the coach might take a move and demonstrate how to do each part in sequence. The students would then practice the move until it could be done automatically, with no thought as to its execution. A college wrestling match is like a game of chess. For each move, there is a countermove, and for each counter there is a countermove to the previous one. However, unlike chess, in which there is ample time to think, the wrestling moves often take place so quickly that there is no time to think. Wrestlers who have to think about their next move usually lose the match. To reach this level of skill in wrestling, where moves have to be executed automatically with speed and accuracy, considerable time must be devoted to practicing the same moves over and over again.

When I compared the way we taught reading with the way that athletes and musicians were taught, I realized that there were some important differences. In sports and music, students practice until they "get it right."

I had been a classroom teacher for 10 years and knew about the pressures placed on teachers to cover a year's work in a year's time. For most kids, the pace of instruction was fine, but for students with below-average intelligence or those with reading disabilities, the pace was too fast. For kids with special needs, every day of school was another day of frustration and failure because they were being pushed through the curriculum too fast and failed to master their work.

What would happen, I asked myself, if we modified reading instruction so that it resembled how we train athletes and musicians? To do this, I got permission from the Minneapolis public schools to work with mentally challenged beginning reading students. I asked the students how one becomes good at a sport, and they all said that one had to practice to become good at it. I then explained that getting to be a good reader was like getting good at a sport, and that we were going to practice at getting good at reading stories. Before meeting with the children, I had taken a short children's story and had broken it into passages about 150 words in length. Each student in the class was given a copy of the passages that covered the short story. As the students held the copy of the beginning of the story and looked at the words, I read the 150-word passage to them. Then the students practiced at their desks, and each student read the short passage to their teacher, who recorded the words-per-minute reading rate for the story as well as the number of word recognition errors. The students reread the 150-word passage a number of times, until each one reached a criterion rate of 85 words a minute. When the criterion rate of reading was reached, the student was given the next passage to practice.

With each rereading of a passage, the students found they made fewer errors, and their reading rate got faster. Before long, the students realized that as they reread the same passage a number of times, they began to sound like good readers. Sounding good was an exciting realization for students who had a history of failure. We had charts for these poor readers that showed their progress, and they liked to see how they were improving. Some of the students asked their parents for stopwatches so they could practice at home on their own. I described the method of repeated reading in an article for *The Reading Teacher* (1979), and it was later reissued as a classic study in reading (1997).

This was the birth of repeated reading, an offshoot of automaticity theory, and the start of numerous studies by others investigating a technique that helps to build fluency. Unknown to me, work similar to my own was being done by Carol Chomsky at Harvard's School of Education. Chomsky's work was in response to teachers' wanting a new technique for helping students who failed to make adequate progress in reading. What Chomsky did that was different from my repeated reading method was to tape-record a children's story, and the students who were having trouble learning to read listened to the tape while they looked at the words in their storybook. When they had listened to the tape enough times that they could read the story on their own, they did so. Chomsky and I independently had come upon similar methods for helping struggling readers. After learning about Chomsky's work, and its similarity to mine, I invited her to write a chapter for the first edition of *What Research Has to Say about Reading Instruction* (Chomsky, 1978).

The method of repeated reading became a popular method of instruction, especially with students who were having difficulty learning to read. Although the method was effective for helping students become more fluent in reading, there was an important problem with the method, especially as it was first introduced. It was labor intensive, requiring a teacher, or aide, to hear each student read orally to determine if the word-per-minute goal was reached. A research discovery was made, however, that overcame the need for computing reading speed. O'Shea, Sindelar, and O'Shea (1985) found four rereadings to be the most efficient number of times to read the passage, and although more rereadings led to gains, they were too small to be worth the extra time and effort. Thus, one way to do repeated readings is simply have students reread a passage four times. There are many variations of the method of repeated reading as it is now used in the classroom. Children, for example, are paired up and they read to each other, or they reread poems and plays.

The method of repeated reading has even been programmed onto computers (Renaissance Learning, 2005). The student using the fluency development program is tested by computer to determine his or her zone of current reading ability; then numerous selections of graded passages at the student's zone of reading development are stored in the computer program and can be used for repeated reading practice. When the time comes for the student to move to a more advanced level, there are passages that increase in difficulty, so that he or she can practice rereading more difficult texts. For each passage the student selects for practice, a model teacher reads the passage to the student. Then the student reads the passage silently for 1 minute and, based on the initial reading speed for the selection, the computer program automatically selects a target speed for the student. The computer program even determines when the student's word-per-minute reading rate has reached the target speed. Although the program frees up the teacher to work in other ways with students, the teacher is called upon to decide when the student is ready to advance to a higher text readability level.

There were other developments that had significant impact upon fluency. Stanley Deno, a professor of special education, had developed a method to help teachers evaluate the week-by-week rate of improvement among students learning to read. The reasoning behind this method was that many evaluations were conducted only after months of instruction, wasting valuable time for those students identified as not making progress. Deno wanted a method that would be fast and easy to use. He devised a system based on 1-minute time samplings of student reading speed. The student was asked to read for 1 minute from a text typical of that used in his or her regular instruction. The number of words read in 1 minute was the test score, which was entered onto a chart. One week later, the student was tested again on a similar passage, and the score recorded. If progress was being made, the rate of reading should increase and the curve on the chart should go upward. Deno's method—curriculum-based measurement (CBM)—has caught on as a means to evaluate progress in reading, because it is fast, easy to administer, and reliable (Deno, 1985; Deno, Mirkin, & Chiang, 1982).

Still other developments helped to elevate reading fluency to the important status it enjoys today. Two highly prestigious reports emphasized fluency. The National Research Council report *Preventing Reading Difficulties in Young Children* (Snow, Burns, & Griffin, 1998) emphasized that reading fluency should be an important goal of the reading curriculum. This was followed by the National Reading Panel (2000) report, research for which was mandated by the U.S. Congress. Congress was aware of the reading wars and wanted to know what reading practices were supported by research. The report had an entire section on automaticity theory and repeated reading. In addition, it presented a statistical analysis of some of the best repeated reading studies in the research literature to determine whether this method was effective. The panel concluded that repeated reading was an effective method for improving word recognition, fluency, and comprehension across grade levels.

To conclude this section on the state of reading fluency in the United States today, it is clear that more and more educators view fluency as an important goal of reading instruction. The routes to fluency development seem reasonably clear. One route is to give students extensive practice reading books that are at their zone of reading development. By encountering high-frequency, common words in a variety of meaningful contexts, students acquire the ability to recognize the words automatically. The other route for building fluency is to use the many varieties of repeated reading. While the routes to developing fluency are clear, the routes to the measurement of fluency are in a state of flux. A commonly used method for assessing fluency is to give students a CBM test of reading speed. This method measures only one aspect of fluency: that is, the ability to read words rapidly and accurately. As reading teachers have discovered, there are students who have adequate oral reading speed, but poor comprehension of what they have read. Another route to fluency measurement is to find out whether students can decode and comprehend at the same time. This is done by simply informing students at the time of testing that they will be asked to read a passage orally and, when they are finished, will be tested for comprehension with questions or by having to recall as much as possible about what they read. This method is a good match for the definition of fluency used in this chapter. Furthermore, one test developer already has a test on the market that can determine whether a student can simultaneously decode and comprehend, and a second company is developing a computerized version of such a test.

## READING FLUENCY: ITS FUTURE

The discovery of alphabetic writing and reading, now about 4,000 years old, ranks in importance with the discovery of how to harness fire and to use the wheel. Although alphabetic reading has a solid future, many of the methods used to teach reading have a short life cycle. For example, whole language, once considered to be an important methodology, has significantly dropped in popularity. While reading fluency is now considered to be an important aspect of the reading curriculum, its future is tied to what will happen in the area of measurement of fluency. To the extent that experts in the field can design valid instruments that measure the ability of students to decode and comprehend texts simultaneously, the topic will enjoy a longer life cycle than if they cannot design such instruments. One of the attractive aspects to American reading instruction is the willingness of teachers to try different approaches. What works, they keep, and what fails to work, they discard.

If one traces the course of the history of fluency, one notices that it has varied repeatedly from hot to not hot and back again. A number of factors account for this fluctuation. For example, soon after Huey (1908/1968), in his brilliant book on the psychology of reading, began to describe how fluency occurs, we entered a period of behaviorism in which psychologists steered clear of reading factors such as comprehension and fluency, and little was done during this rather long period. More recently, the topic of fluency has become muddied by the fact that, as a scientific field, we seem unable to agree on a definition of it. The definition that seems to make the most sense is derived from automaticity theory. This theory states that a person is fluent, or automatic, if he or she can do two difficult things at the same time, whereas before training the person could only do one task at a time. In dealing with a definition of fluency, we need to distinguish between the essential characteristics of fluency and its secondary characteristics. The essential characteristic of fluency is the ability to decode and comprehend at the same time. The less important characteristics are accuracy and speed.

Unfortunately, all of the tests (Good & Kaminski, 2002) measure only accuracy and speed, otherwise known as the Diagnostic Indicators of Basic

Early Literacy Skills (DIBELS) method. Indeed, accuracy and speed correlate with the critical definition of fluency, but unless we use a test that assess whether the student can decode and comprehend simultaneously, we do not know for sure if the student is fluent. Students learn early on that the name of the game is speed and that comprehension will never be tested. Unless the student can understand what is being decoded, can we really call that fluent reading? I can read Spanish orally with accuracy and speed, but I do not understand what I am reading. Can I consider myself to be fluent in Spanish? I do not think so. Neither can we consider a student to be a fluent reader if he or she has not been given a test that simultaneously measures decoding and comprehension.

Let me use an analogy to explain just one of the problems of using DIBELS on a national scale as we seem to be doing. I have a car with an engine that provides power. I also have wheels and gears on my car. I can start my car and get the engine to spin at very high speeds. But if I do not shift the gears and get the engine to engage, the wheels on the car will not move. In order to get my car to move, I need to engage the spinning engine with the gears and the wheels. The students who only decode quickly and accurately are, likewise, just getting the engine to spin. We need to engage the gears so the engine can move the wheels if we want the car to move. We have a nation of kids who can get the engine to spin quickly, but that is not enough. It is essential that students be able to decode *and* to comprehend.

The proponents of DIBELS claim that they have validated the tests, but the validation procedures are improperly done. The validation procedures used on DIBELS mimic what beginning readers do, not what fluent readers do. I urge readers to read the article I wrote in *Reading Research Quarterly* (Samuels, 2007) for a detailed explanation of why the validation procedures used with DIBELS are faulty. Ken Goodman and I have not always agreed, but we concur that the time has come to abandon DIBELS. P. David Pearson and Mike Pressley also have taken aim and blasted the use of the tests.

In summary, regarding the future of reading fluency, much will hinge on the ability of our field to agree on a definition of fluency and find tests that incorporate our definition.

## REFERENCES

Allington, R. L. (1983). Fluency: The neglected reading goal. *The Reading Teacher, 36*(6), 556–561.

Bryan, W. L., & Harter, N. (1897). Studies in the physiology and psychology of the telegraphic language. *Psychological Review, 4*, 27–53.

Bryan, W. L., & Harter, N. (1899). Studies on the telegraphic language: The acquisition of a hierarchy of habits. *Psychological Review, 6*, 345–375.

Cassidy, J., & Cassidy, D. (December 2003/January 2004). What's hot, what's not for 2004. *Reading Today, 21,* 3.

Chall, J. S. (1983). *Stages in reading development.* New York: McGraw-Hill.

Chomsky, C. (1978). When you still can't read in third grade: After decoding, what? In S. J. Samuels (Ed.), *What research has to say about reading instruction.* Newark, DE: International Reading Association.

de Groot, A. D. (1965). *Thought and choice in chess.* The Hague: Mouton.

Deno, S. L. (1985). Curriculum-based measurement: The emerging alternative. *Exceptional Children, 52,* 219–232.

Deno, S. L., Mirkin, P. K., & Chiang, B. (1982). Identifying valid measures of reading. *Exceptional Children, 49*(1), 36–45.

Ehri, L. C. (1991). Development of the ability to read words: Update. In P. D. Pearson (Ed.), *Handbook of reading research* (Vol. II). New York: Longman.

Good, R., & Kaminski, R. (2002). *DIBELS oral reading fluency passages for first through third grades* (Technical Report No. 10). Eugene: University of Oregon.

Huey, E. B. (1968). *The psychology and pedagogy of reading.* Cambridge, MA: MIT Press. (Original work published 1908)

LaBerge, D., & Samuels, S. J. (1974). Toward a theory of automatic information processing in reading. *Cognitive Psychology, 6,* 293–323.

National Reading Panel. (2000). *Teaching children to read: An evidence-based assessment of the scientific research literature on reading and its implications for reading instruction* (NIH Publication No. 00-4769). Washington, DC: National Institute of Child Health and Human Development.

O'Shea, L. J., Sindelar, P. T., & O'Shea, D. J. (1985). The effects of repeated readings and attentional cues on reading fluency and comprehension. *Journal of Reading Behavior, 17,* 129–142.

Rasinski, T. V. (2003). *The fluent reader: Oral reading strategies for building word recognition, fluency, and comprehension.* New York: Scholastic.

Renaissance Learning. (2005). *Fluent reader.* Madison, WI: Author.

Samuels, S. J. (1997). The method of repeated readings. *The Reading Teacher, 50*(5), 376–381. (Original work published 1979)

Samuels, S. J. (2007). The DIBELS tests: Is speed of barking at print what we mean by reading fluency? *Reading Research Quarterly, 42*(4), 563–565.

Samuels, S. J., LaBerge, D., & Bremer, C. (1978). Units of word recognition: Evidence for developmental changes. *Journal of Verbal Learning and Verbal Behavior, 17,* 715–720.

Snow, C. E., Burns, M. S., & Griffin, P. (1998). *Preventing reading difficulties in young children.* Washington, DC: National Academy Press.

# 2

## Developing Fluency in the Context of Effective Literacy Instruction

Timothy Shanahan

**S**ince the early 1990s, I have spent considerable time encouraging teachers to teach fluency. In this work, I have employed a framework I developed to guide the improvement of PreK–12th-grade literacy achievement, and that framework (the Chicago Reading Framework)—more than any other—places great emphasis on the teaching of fluency (Shanahan, 2001). As Director of Reading for the Chicago Public Schools, I mandated that all 600 of our schools teach fluency on a daily basis. I even coauthored the fluency section of the National Reading Panel (2000) report, which found that fluency could be taught, and that such teaching improved reading achievement, including reading comprehension, and later I developed a program to help primary grade teachers to teach fluency (Shanahan, 2004).

Yes, my credentials on fluency instruction are impeccable. Yet my role in this volume is less to promote fluency instruction (there are more than enough excellent chapters that do this) than to put fluency into a fitting instructional context. To explain the reason for this, let me relate something from my experience as a consultant to school districts. Over the years, I gained a reputation as an effective staff developer. This meant two things: Teachers liked my presentations and often adopted the ideas I shared at the institute or workshop into their classroom routines. If I was brought in to do a workshop on vocabulary instruction, the teachers would start to teach vocabulary or would change how they were teaching it.

As good as I was at that kind of work, sadly, I rarely helped raise achievement. How could that be? I was showing teachers how to teach vocabulary—or comprehension, writing, and so on—in ways proven successful in research. The teachers were adopting these effective practices, and the results in terms of children's learning were ... well, less than gratifying. What was happening? The scenario that played out was usually something like this: I would encourage teaching an essential part of reading in sound ways; teachers would consequently drop some of the other essentials they were already addressing to accommodate the new stuff that I shared, and *voilà*, no improvement in reading. I assumed they would add vocabulary to their otherwise successful teaching routine. The teachers assumed they were supposed to do vocabulary *instead* of the terrific comprehension strategies they were teaching and ... well, you can see how the results of that would be a wash.

I stopped conducting those kinds of workshops long ago, and I'm glad, because now when I work with teachers and schools, reading achievement often does rise. In Chicago, 75% of the public schools—schools that serve 85% low-income students in a minority–majority district—improved in reading, and the lowest performing elementary schools in the district improved in reading as much as the higher performing schools for the first time in history. Fluency teaching was part of that, because fluency is part of the Chicago Reading Framework, but it was not the whole story. Fluency—or any other aspect of literacy that we teach—is not the whole story. Fluency is essential, but it is not a magic bullet. The success of fluency instruction depends not only on the quality of the teaching, but also on the degree to which quality teaching is *embedded in a full agenda* of other sound literacy instruction. A teacher—confident that fluency is *the* key to success—who drops phonics to clear space for fluency in the daily teaching schedule is making a bad trade.

The key to adding fluency, or any other important element, to a classroom routine is to ensure that all the other essentials are addressed, too. For me, an "essential" is an aspect of instruction that has been proven to make a difference in children's reading achievement. I am talking here about "scientific research-based reading" teaching, but that term is bandied about a lot these days, and my standards are high for determining which practices fit this description (Shanahan, 2002; Shavelson & Towne, 2002). Before I'm willing to endorse a practice as essential, it must have certain kinds of evidence behind it. There must be, for instance, studies that show that kids who get this kind of teaching do better than kids who don't. There must be evidence drawn from experimental studies in which some teachers adopt the new practice in their classrooms, while other, similar teachers continue as usual. The classrooms in the study must be roughly equal in reading achievement at the start, but they have to be different in the end. There are standards of quality for such studies, and I expect this evidence to come from investigations that meet these quality standards. Finally, I don't think it is enough that a study or two support a particular finding. There should be many independent investigators who tried this practice in different places, but with consistent results (unlike in the physical sciences, this kind of replication does not "prove" that a particular approach "works," but it does show that many people were able to make it work under varied conditions—thus, my thinking is that if they can make it work, so can we).

The Chicago Reading Framework emphasizes three critical steps schools can take to improve achievement, and these steps help ensure the existence of the kind of instructional context in which fluency teaching should be embedded. These critical steps include (1) securing adequate amounts of instructional time for the teaching of reading and writing, (2) ensuring the teaching of all essential aspects of literacy, and (3) providing ongoing monitoring of student learning to allow for appropriate adjustments to teaching. Yes, fluency is an essential aspect of literacy and it should be taught, but the teaching of fluency will be most productive when teachers devote an appropriate amount of time to the teaching of literacy, when that time is divided among fluency and other essential elements of literacy that must be fostered, and when teachers are evaluating the adequacy of student progress along the way.

## THE ROLE OF INSTRUCTIONAL TIME

One thing that leaps out of the literature as being beneficial to literacy learning is sufficient amounts of instructional time (Fielding, Kerr, & Rosier, 2007; Fisher & Berliner, 1985; Meyer, Linn, & Hastings, 1991; Pressley, Wharton-McDonald, Mistretta-Hapston, & Echevarria, 1998). National surveys of teaching suggest that we fail to spend sufficient time teaching kids how to read and write well (Baumann, Hoffman, Duffy-Hester, & Ro, 2000). However, over the past decade, the 90-minute "reading block" has been widely adopted, particularly in the primary grades; teacher and principal surveys indicate that this arrangement is now used in more than 90% of Title I schools (U.S. Department of Education, Office of Planning, Evaluation and Policy Development, Policy and Program Studies Service, 2008). Unfortunately, observations of classroom reading instruction in such schools are not encouraging. Although Title I teachers schedule 90 minutes or more of daily reading instruction, much of this time is devoted to activities that are unlikely to improve reading or writing ability; primary grade children are commonly receiving less than 60 minutes per day of potentially productive reading instruction, and only about 5 minutes of that time is aimed specifically at fluency instruction (Gamse, Jacob, Horst, Boulay, & Unlu, 2008). We've simply allowed lots of wonderful activities that have little to do with children's learning to encroach on reading and language arts time. In my schools, I require 2–3 hours per day of reading and writing instruction. That is a lot more time for learning than most teachers provide, and increasing the amount of instruction is a proven way to enhance achievement.

## ESSENTIAL CONTENT COVERAGE

As important as time might be, its value can only be realized through teaching. But teaching what? It is important to teach children to know or do those things that constitute literacy proficiency. In large-scale analyses of educational research, content coverage or curriculum focus stands out as the second most important factor, right after amount of instruction (Walberg, 1986; Wang, Haertel, & Walberg, 1990, 1993). Reading instruction is most effective when it focuses on those skills and abilities that give kids an advantage in learning to read (Barr, Dreeben, & Wiratchai, 1983; Fry & Lagomarsino, 1982; Roehler, 1992). That might seem like a no-brainer, but far too often I visit schools that neglect or barely touch upon some of these key areas of learning.

In the Chicago Reading Framework, I organize what needs to be taught into four categories and require equal amounts of teaching for each category. The amount of teaching doesn't necessarily have to balance each day, but each element should receive roughly equal attention over a week or two. There are four areas that I am convinced require regular teaching: word knowledge, fluency, comprehension, and writing. Teachers in my schools must teach each of these for 30–45 minutes per day.

Given that the purpose of this book is to explain fluency instruction, and that the purpose of this chapter is to put fluency into the larger instructional context, I detail each of these four categories, but with greater attention to fluency (not because it is most important—they are all equally important). Before turning to each component, let me explain why these particular components merit this much concentrated and continued instructional attention. Although all four components meet the selection standards I set, all of my examples here deal with how fluency satisfies these criteria.

## CRITERIA FOR INCLUSION IN THE MODEL

To be included in this model, a component had to meet five basic requirements. First, it had to be a learning outcome and not an instructional practice. Too many instructional schemes emphasize teaching routines over learning outcomes, and this is a big mistake. Research shows how difficult it is for teachers to keep focused on learning within the complexity of classroom life (Doyle, 1983). Good teachers manage to focus on learning, and less effective ones get wrapped up in the activities themselves. It is sort of like the old joke: When you are up to your neck in alligators, it is hard to remember that your purpose was to drain the swamp. With all the "alligators" out there in a challenging classroom, ineffective teachers often lose sight of the purpose. I don't want teachers aimed at guided reading, shared reading, the Whiz Bang ABC Reading Program, or at any other technique, practice, program, or approach. The research is pretty clear: Methods of teaching don't make that much difference if the content covered is equivalent (Bond & Dykstra, 1967). I don't want my teachers setting aside a certain amount of time each day to do a particular *activity*. I want them to set aside a certain amount of time each day to teach children to do particular things. Learning—not teaching—is the point.

Second, to be included, research studies had to demonstrate the *teachability* of a component. This means that there had to be several research studies showing that teaching could improve performance in that outcome. For example, the National Reading Panel (2000) examined 16 independent studies in which having students practice oral rereading of a text with some kind of feedback led to improved fluency in reading those texts. Furthermore, several other studies found that this kind of teaching led students to be more fluent, that is, to read texts aloud more accurately or quickly. It only makes sense to focus our instruction upon outcomes that can actually be taught.

Third, to be included as an essential outcome, research had to reveal the *generalizability* of a component. This means that there had to be several research studies proving that if one taught this particular aspect of literacy, overall reading achievement would improve. It is not enough to teach fluency, even if that instruction would result in better fluency, if this improvement doesn't, consequently, translate into better overall reading achievement. The National Reading Panel (2000) examined 16 independent studies in which fluency instruction not only improved fluency performance but also actually translated into higher reading achievement on silent reading comprehension tests.

Fourth, in order for a learning outcome to be essential in this model, it had to fit together in a coherent manner with the other components in the model. It had to be *combinable* with the other parts of the model, so there was a chance that the combination of components would lead to even better performance than would be obtained by attending to any one of the components alone. What this means is that, statistically, each component had to correlate positively and significantly with the others and with overall reading achievement as well. Student fluency performance has just that kind of pattern of relationship with other reading achievement variables (Fuchs, Fuchs, Hosp, & Jenkins, 2001).

Fifth, despite the correlations just noted, each outcome had to be an *independent* entity to justify inclusion in the framework. Instruction in one component should not necessarily lead to growth in all of the components. Evidence for independence could include case studies of children with learning disabilities and brain injuries who may excel in one or another component without commensurate levels of performance in the others (Coslett, 2000). In the case of fluency, many experts have assumed that it is simply the result of high-proficiency word recognition. If that were true, then the best way to teach fluency would be to put more time into teaching word recognition. In fact, research shows that although fluency is closely aligned with word recognition, it is also—at least in certain cases—a somewhat independent outcome. For instance, Carol Chomsky (1975) identified a sample of children high in decoding skills but low in fluency. Also, clinical studies have identified students who can read text fluently but without commensurate levels of comprehension (Kennedy, 2003). Independence matters, because it argues for the value of direct teaching of a specific outcome. Since phonics instruction doesn't lead to fluency for all kids, we teach phonics and fluency. Since fluency proficiency does not result in higher comprehension for all students, we teach fluency and comprehension. The surest way to success is to leave nothing to chance in children's learning.

The four key components that satisfy all five of these requirements are word knowledge, reading comprehension, writing, and fluency. And it is to each of these that I now turn.

## Word Knowledge

Word knowledge emphasizes two very different instructional goals. We need to teach children both to recognize written words and to expand their knowledge of word meanings. In most discussions of reading instruction, word meanings are categorized as part of reading comprehension, which makes sense, since both vocabulary and comprehension are focused on meaning. The reason I make such a different choice of organization is threefold. First, everything that we teach in reading, from the lowliest phonic skill to the loftiest interpretive strategy, should ultimately be connected to meaning. This suggests that there is nothing special about vocabulary in that particular regard that justifies categorizing it with reading comprehension. Second, I wanted there to be a consistent plan of instruction—in terms of amounts of time and areas of emphasis in my framework—across the grade levels. By putting word recognition together with word meaning, I have established a routine in which upper grade teachers spend similar amounts and proportions of time on word learning as primary grade teachers, albeit the emphasis of this word work does shift. Third, this plan requires a lot more vocabulary teaching than is accomplished in most instructional programs. When vocabulary is just a part of comprehension, there isn't a great deal of time devoted to its teaching. In this framework, once adequate word recognition proficiency is accomplished (in second or third grade for most kids), more substantial work with word meanings has to be provided.

In the primary grades, it is imperative that teachers give children substantial amounts of word recognition instruction, including phonemic awareness, phonics, and sight vocabulary teaching (National Reading Panel, 2000). Phonemic awareness instruction teaches children to hear and manipulate the separable sounds in words. Most kids benefit from approximately 18 hours of phonemic awareness instruction (about 15 minutes per day for a semester). Of course, some children don't need this much, and others may need more. In any event, phonemic awareness instruction should begin by kindergarten and continue until students can fully segment simple words (e.g., dividing the word *cat* into its separate sounds: /k/ /a/ /t/). Children who can hear the sounds within words are at a great advantage in figuring out the relationship between speech and print.

In addition to phonemic awareness, children should get daily phonics instruction. Phonics teaching aims to impart three kinds of knowledge: It should help children master the letter names and sounds, including the sounds related to common letter combinations such as *sh, ch, th,* and *ng*; it should help them to recognize and pronounce common spelling patterns, such as *ain, tion,* and *ight*; and it should guide children to use this information to decode and spell new words (that means reading and spelling practice should be regular parts of phonics instruction).

Additionally, there needs to be an emphasis on teaching children sight vocabulary; that is, they must learn to recognize some words immediately, without sounding out or any other obvious mediation. English uses some words with great frequency (words such as *the, of, was, can, saw, there, to,* and *for*), and if children can recognize these words easily and accurately, they will be better able to focus on the meaning of text.

It is perfectly appropriate to provide some direct instruction in word meaning during these early years, but the time devoted to this will need to be limited because of the decoding needs. That means most of the vocabulary teaching will be incidental during the earliest years of school (e.g., talking about words during read-alouds). However, as the phonics skills and sight vocabulary are mastered, all or most of the word teaching should shift to a more thorough, formal, and academic emphasis on vocabulary building or word meaning (Blachowicz & Fisher, 2000). Many approaches to the teaching of vocabulary have proven effective. The best instructional efforts require students to use new vocabulary in a wide variety of ways (speaking, listening, reading, writing), and guide them to analyze and explore rich, contextualized meanings of words and the interrelationships among words. Effective vocabulary instruction also includes small amounts of drill and practice and a considerable amount of review.

Finally, spelling instruction can be part of the word component as well. Such teaching should aim to help students spell in a conventional way, and can provide them with an opportunity to think systematically about how words are structured. Spelling instruction necessarily must be kept brief and is probably best accomplished in conjunction with the word recognition and word-meaning teaching that are the major instructional emphases within word knowledge.

Word knowledge is obviously complex. There are multiple aspects of word teaching, and the relative importance of the parts changes over time as children advance through the grades—with relatively less attention devoted to word recognition and more to word meaning over time. Word knowledge is central to reading achievement and is closely allied with fluency performance (Perfetti, Finger, & Hogaboam, 1978; Stanovich, 1981). Children who cannot recognize words quickly and easily—who lack strong decoding skills or extensive sight vocabularies—struggle when they try to read a text. They make lots of errors, and instead of moving along quickly and smoothly, they labor through a text, impelled more by their efforts to decode each word than by the flow of the author's ideas. Using the time devoted to word knowledge to develop expertise in the quick decoding and automatic recognition of words should ultimately contribute to fluency. And this appears to be a two-way street. Research shows that fluency instruction for poorer readers typically results in much improved word recognition abilities (National Reading Panel, 2000).

Vocabulary knowledge also has a role to play in fluency development. Fluency by its very nature is part rapid sequential decoding and part on-the-fly initial text interpretation. To read a text aloud successfully, a student not only has to recognize the words quickly and easily enough to be accurate but also has to have sufficient sense of the meaning of the message to make it sound like language. Vocabulary instruction generally helps in initial interpretation by familiarizing students with the meanings of a broad range of words, but it works, more specifically, in helping students correctly interpret homographs (words with one spelling but different pronunciations, depending on meaning), such as *read, minute, wind, bass, sow, does,* and *tear* (Plaut, 1996).

## Reading Comprehension

A second instructional component in my framework is the teaching of reading comprehension. Students need to be taught to achieve a deep understanding of text on their own, and this instruction has three major goals. We need to teach students to seek particular types of information when they read a text. We need to teach them how texts are organized or structured and how to use these organizational plans to remember or understand information effectively. Last, we need to teach children a variety of thinking strategies or procedures they can use on their own before, during, and after reading to improve understanding and recall.

For young children, learning what kind of information is important—which needs to be attended to and remembered—entails some fairly general notions, such as the idea that both explicit information and inferential information are important (Raphael & Wonnacott, 1985). With development, text demands become more complex and tied to the disciplines, so instruction needs to emphasize the kinds of information that are important within the various disciplinary fields (i.e., history, science, mathematics, and literature) (Shanahan & Shanahan, 2008). It is not just type of information that matters either, because these disciplines differ as to how precise or approximate a reader's understanding has to be ("gist," for instance, is not well thought of in science or math texts).

Narrative and expository texts differ greatly in their organization, vocabulary, and even the reasons why someone might read them. Students benefit from experience and instruction in dealing with both of these text types. Some of the instruction should guide students to think about how these texts are organized. For narratives, that means teaching about plot structure (including, e.g., characters, problems, solutions, outcomes, time sequencing). Students need to learn analogous information about how expository texts are structured (e.g., problem–solution, cause–effect, comparison–contrast) as well as what types of information are likely to appear in particular types of texts. Social studies books, for example, usually provide information on the geography, economics, culture, and history of each major topic being discussed; knowing that allows a reader to analyze the text in those terms.

There is also a plethora of techniques or procedures that can be used by kids to guide their thinking about text more effectively on their own (National Reading Panel, 2000). Teaching students to monitor their reading (to make sure that they understand and know what to do about it when they do not), to ask their own questions, to summarize, and to translate text into graphic form are just a few of the techniques that have been found to improve reading comprehension.

It is important to remember that students benefit from comprehension instruction—not just comprehension practice. Too many teachers give assignments that require reading comprehension but do nothing to improve students' capacity to comprehend. Practice alone is insufficient. Children should be taught how to comprehend, and, in the Chicago Reading Framework, time is regularly devoted to this.

As has already been noted, fluency is closely connected to reading comprehension. Fluency instruction improves reading comprehension scores, and studies with proficient readers show that, even for them, rereading a text improves interpretation, and improvement is first obvious in the fluency changes that take place. Fluency at its base is a kind of integration of word recognition and initial sentence interpretation (Young & Bowers, 1995).

## Writing

Children need to be able to write their own texts. Reading and writing depend on much of the same information (including, e.g., knowledge of spelling patterns, text organization, vocabulary), and learning to read and write simultaneously can give children an advantage (Shanahan, 2005). Writing instruction should teach children to compose for a variety of purposes and audiences, using strategies that help them to solve various writing problems. The compositions that children write should make sense and effectively communicate their ideas.

Children need to know how to retell events (narrative writing), explain and analyze information (exposition), and argue a position (persuasion), and good instruction should show them how to do these effectively. Children need to know how to adjust their voice and message to meet the needs of an audience. They need to know how to write compositions that are appropriately elaborated, focused, and organized and that reflect proper mechanics, usage, grammar, and spelling. And students should have at their command a variety of techniques or strategies that can be used effectively and independently to prepare for writing and to revise and edit what they have drafted.

Writing is less obviously connected to fluency. I know of no study that looks at correlations between writing achievement and reading fluency, and I know of no experimental studies that look at the effects of writing instruction on reading fluency or reading fluency instruction on writing. It is evident that spelling accuracy within writing is closely connected to fluency, but this is more likely due to connections between word knowledge and fluency rather than a more general composition–fluency connection (Zutell & Rasinski, 1986). Nevertheless, writing proficiency in composing words and sentences has been found to be connected to reading achievement generally, and this likely means that regular attention to writing instruction could benefit fluency.

## Fluency

Fluency refers to the ability to read text aloud with sufficient speed, accuracy, and expression. Although fluency is important to both silent and oral reading, research suggests that oral reading practice and instruction are most effective for developing this ability (National Reading Panel, 2000). Activities such as paired or assisted reading, in which students take turns reading portions of a text aloud to each other and give each other feedback and rereading the text multiple times until it can be done well, have been found to be effective practices from the primary grades through high school. These practices have some commonalities: They all require oral reading, provide the reader with feedback and help, and require repetition of the reading until the text can be read well.

If a student is fluent with a particular text, the teacher has two choices. First, if the teacher believes the student is placed in an appropriate level of text reading, he or she only has to continue to monitor the child's reading (by listening), and—in my framework—the amount of fluency instruction for this student can be reduced (fluency is the only component of the framework that can be reduced in terms of time coverage, and this should only be done if the student is fluent at an appropriate level). Second, if the teacher thinks the student should be working on more difficult materials, he or she can have the child practice fluency in more difficult texts, including social studies or science books.

Students who are fluent with a text can usually read it with only about one mistake per 100 words, and they can read the text smoothly and quickly. Young children (through second grade) should strive to read a text at about 60–80 words per minute, while for older children reading should proceed at 100+ words per minute. Students also need to pay attention to punctuation and pause appropriately so that the text sounds like language.

What about round robin reading, in which a child reads a portion of text aloud with everyone else listening? It really has no place here. It is not that the oral reading practice provided by round robin is so bad—being really no different than what is provided in other kinds of oral reading activity—but that it is so brief (Stallings & Krasavage, 1986). Let's say the teacher is requiring 30 minutes per day of fluency work and has 30 children in class. Using round robin, the teacher would only be able to provide about 1 minute per day of reading per child under the best circumstances and only about 3 hours of practice per child across an entire school year. Using paired reading, in which children take turns reading and giving feedback to each other, that same teacher would be able to provide 15 times the amount of reading practice—15 minutes per day and 45 hours of individual practice per year!

It has often been asserted that fluency develops from silent reading practice and not just the kinds of oral reading practice lauded here. Accordingly, some teachers (and programs) include sustained silent reading in place of the fluency time. It should be noted that despite the logic of having students simply reading more, research doesn't actually support it, and without a credible research base, it seems unwise to replace a procedure that we know works (oral reading practice) with one of which we are uncertain (National Reading Panel, 2000).

Some teachers, of course, are afraid to turn their classes loose with something like paired reading, wary that the result will be mayhem rather than fluency. These teachers are correct that they should not turn their classes loose, because paired-reading time is very involving for both the children and the teacher—after all, this is teaching time. If the teacher has the class organized into pairs and those pairs are all reading to each other, the teacher needs to move among the pairs giving additional guidance and feedback. In one pair, the teacher might intervene by giving one of the partners some direction ("How well did Jimmy do? Should Jimmy read it again?"). In another case, he or she may explain the meaning of a word or help the children to decode a word that they find challenging. In still another, the teacher may listen to a child's reading to evaluate the appropriateness of the text placement. The point is that the teacher is actively listening and interacting with the children during fluency instruction time, and that kind of active involvement helps maintain classroom order as well as improve children's reading achievement.

As with any of the other components in the framework, the time organization can be flexible. What I mean by this is that the plan does not require block scheduling. It is not necessary to set aside 9:00–11:00 A.M. each day for reading instruction, with each component receiving 30 minutes of uninterrupted time in sequence. School days are more complex than that, and research does not support any particular organization over another. Some teachers like to have two 15-minute fluency periods rather than a single half-hour. Some prefer to use time during the afternoon for this rather than the morning. These are reasonable choices made by reasonable teachers.

Some teachers seek special materials for fluency teaching, usually opting for materials that are heavy on predictability and rhyme. There is no question that poetry can be great fun for fluency time (Shel Silverstein and Jack Prelutsky are especially popular poet choices). However, I recommend caution with regard to such choices and would relegate them to the "we read those occasionally" category. My reasoning is that the research on fluency was not conducted with such materials, and it is not enough that children become fluent with poetry—they must be able to read prose, with its very different rhythms and cadences, as well. A good deal of fluency practice can take place profitably using the same materials used for reading comprehension. There is one problem with this approach, however; the difficulty levels of books used to build comprehension have increased to such an extent that they may be too hard for some children to allow them the best fluency practice (Menton & Hiebert, 1999). Most authorities on reading encourage fluency practice at levels that are instructional (about 95% accuracy on a first reading), and most studies of fluency instruction used materials that were more controlled than some literature-based basals (National Reading

Panel, 2000). However, it is much easier to select appropriate supplementary materials for fluency practice that are nearer to student reading levels when students are working in pairs than when the teacher is doing a whole-class or larger group activity. There may be a benefit to having everyone think about the same ideas in a particular text, but there is no analogous benefit to having everyone practice fluency at exactly the same levels.

## Integrating Instruction

The discussion up to this point makes these aspects of literacy appear to be quite separate. The point of treating them separately in this way is to ensure that each receives adequate and appropriate instructional attention. However, that does not mean that there should be no connections among the parts within teaching. Imagine a morning of instruction in which a teacher has students explore the meanings of a list of words, then has them participate in a guided reading discussion of the meaning of a text, then has them practice fluency through paired reading of another text, and finally has the students writing or revising an essay. The word and text selections and activity choices could be quite good, as could the teacher's implementation of instruction. But relying upon such separate activities is not only unnecessary, it would clearly be inefficient and even confusing.

Why not focus on vocabulary words drawn from the same text that students are reading? This text could be used both for comprehension and fluency, and the students could even write about this text as well. Of course, there is not one singular way to make such combinations. If a text is particularly challenging for students, it might make sense to provide fluency practice first and then have them do the comprehension work (the fluency practice should make the text "easier" by clearing up some of the decoding challenges). Or perhaps it would be best to have the students focus on reading comprehension with a new text, followed by additional oral readings aimed at improving fluency (that should speed up student fluency progress, since they would have already read the text once). Similarly, vocabulary might be emphasized before or after a reading, or both before and after, and use of the vocabulary could be encouraged within the writing experience as well.

The point is that students need substantial work in each of these aspects of literacy, and that means devoting sufficient amounts of time to each with appropriate teacher guidance, scaffolding, and feedback. By focusing such thorough exploration on particular texts (rather than on disparate and disconnected lessons), the teacher increases the chances that students will come away with a deep understanding and facility of each of the texts that are used in reading lessons, and they should be able to do this with reasonable efficiency.

## MONITORING LEARNING

Another requirement in the Chicago Reading Framework—beyond the standards for amount of instruction and content coverage—is that teachers should monitor student learning. Successful teaching depends not only on the use of research-proven instructional techniques but also on teacher awareness of how well the children are doing. Effective teachers pay attention to their children's progress and adjust their efforts accordingly (Shepard, 2000). This is important with word knowledge, comprehension, writing, and fluency, but, again, for this discussion, my examples emphasize fluency monitoring.

Testing can play an obvious role in monitoring student progress, and there are some fine ways to assess whether students can read a text fluently, including Diagnostic Indicators of Basic Early Literacy Skills (Good & Kaminski, 2002), running records (Clay, 1985), and informal reading inventories (Johnson, Kress, & Pikulski, 1987). However, even these informal measures, designed to be administered and readministered, cannot be given often enough to inform instruction as frequently as would be beneficial. By all means, use tests like these early in the year to determine where to start, and give them occasionally throughout the year to check on progress. But between the administrations of these tests, I encourage my teachers to continue to examine their students' fluency development less formally.

One simple way to do this is to maintain written records of students' oral reading performances obtained during teaching. I've always done this on index cards, one per child, but it is now possible to keep such records on a personal digital assistant or similar device if that is easier. However the records are maintained, the teacher listens to each child reading at least once each week (and, yes, you will want to hear some kids more often than that). This means the teacher needs to listen to five or six readers during each fluency period depending on the size of the group, but that isn't too difficult if there are 30–45 minutes per day devoted to fluency. Then the teacher simply makes a note of what the child was reading and how well he or she did.

How do we determine how fluently a child reads? There are really three options. One is to evaluate the accuracy of what a child reads. This means counting (or estimating, since this is an informal look) how many words the child read and how many errors were made. In a second-grade book, 100 words are equivalent to approximately 15 lines of text. I listen to a child read, keeping track of the mistakes. When 15 lines have been completed, I tally up the mistakes and make my calculations. If the youngster made five errors in about 15 lines, that would mean he or she read the text with 95% accuracy. That is good, but it could be better. By monitoring the accuracy of the reading, I can see whether the child is improving.

Another possibility is to consider how fast the child is reading. I'm not talking about speed reading here, just that reading should move along like language. Hasbrouck and Tindal (1992) developed reading speed norms based on their testing of 7,000 children, and these can be useful as well. (Using these norms, I generally shoot for getting my first graders to read at 60 words correct per minute [wcpm] by the end of the school year, my second graders at 90 wcpm, and my third graders at 120 wcpm, with increases of about 10 words per year after that.) I might have a child read for 1 minute and then simply count the number of words read accurately (all the words read in 1 minute minus the errors). Then I record that speed and, again, keep track over several weeks to see whether the child's speed and accuracy are improving. Generally, the research suggests that such data are particularly reliable and valid when the students read for 2 or 3 minutes (Rasinski, 1990; Valencia et al., 2010).

Finally, I can look at how much the reading sounds like language. To assess this, the National Assessment of Educational Progress devised a monitoring rating system in which an oral reading performance is classified based on a 4-point scale or rubric, with 1 being dysfluent and 4 being fluent and expressive (Pinnell et al., 1995). A reading performance is rated a 1 (dysfluent) if it is so choppy that the child is reading word by word. The performance is rated a 2 if the child is reading in two- or three-word phrases but the pauses do not reflect the punctuation or the meaning. The reading is rated a 3 if the child is chunking into two-, three-, or four-word phrases and these reflect the meaning and punctuation (i.e., it is understandable as language). Finally, a reading is rated a 4 if it has the positive pausing characteristics noted for rating of 3 but is more expressive. The teacher can listen to an oral reading performance and rate it using this 4-point scale. The goal is to get children reading at a scale rating of 3 or 4.

By recording this kind of information once or twice per week, a teacher is at a great advantage for adjusting instruction and sharing helpful information with parents (if oral reading were monitored once per week, imagine how much information could be provided to parents on a report card or at conferences). If a child isn't making sufficient progress, this information should lead to some adjustment in instruction: an easier book; the use of an adult volunteer as a reading partner; additional fluency time at home, after school, or during another part of the school day; or greater attention to some aspect of fluency (e.g., building up sight vocabulary).

## SUMMARY

Teachers who have not been teaching fluency, or have not devoted sufficient attention to it, by all means should strive to improve fluency instruction with children. However, fluency instruction works best when it is part of a more complete regimen of reading and writing instruction. Teachers should strive to teach reading and writing for 2–3 hours per day, including instruction in word knowledge (recognition and meaning), fluency, comprehension, and writing. These components should receive roughly equal amounts of instructional attention, and should be taught using research-proven instructional approaches, such as those described by the National Reading Panel (Armbruster, Lehr, & Osborn, 2001). Finally, teachers need to monitor student progress toward the learning goals in fluency and the other components of reading as they teach. By bringing fluency into classroom reading programs in this way, teachers really can raise reading achievement.

## REFERENCES

Armbruster, B. B., Lehr, F., & Osborn, J. (2001). *Put reading first: The research building blocks for teaching children to read.* Jessup, MD: National Institute for Literacy.

Barr, R., & Dreeben, R., with Wiratchai, N. (1983). *How schools work.* Chicago: University of Chicago Press.

Baumann, J. F., Hoffman, J. V., Duffy-Hester, A. M., & Ro, J. M. (2000). The first R yesterday and today: U.S. elementary reading instruction practices reported by teachers and administrators. *Reading Research Quarterly, 35,* 338–377.

Blachowicz, C. L. Z., & Fisher, P. (2000). Vocabulary instruction. In M. L. Kamil, P. Mosenthal, R. Barr, & P. D. Pearson (Eds.), *Handbook of reading research* (Vol. III, pp. 503–524). New York: Longman.

Bond, G. L., & Dykstra, R. (1967). The cooperative research program in first-grade reading instruction. *Reading Research Quarterly, 32,* 345–427.

Chomsky, C. (1975). When you still can't read in third grade: After decoding, what? In S. J. Samuels (Ed.), *What research has to say about reading instruction* (pp. 13–30). Newark, DE: International Reading Association.

Clay, M. M. (1985). *The early detection of reading difficulties* (3rd ed.). Portsmouth, NH: Heinemann.

Coslett, H. B. (2000). Acquired dyslexia. *Seminars in Neurology, 20,* 419–426.

Doyle, W. (1983). Academic work. *Review of Educational Research, 53,* 159–199.

Fielding, L., Kerr, N., & Rosier, P. (2007). *Annual growth, catch-up growth.* Kennewick, WA: New Foundation Press.

Fisher, C. W., & Berliner, D. C. (1985). *Perspectives on instructional time.* New York: Longman.

Fry, M. A., & Lagomarsino, L. (1982). Factors that influence reading: A developmental perspective. *School Psychology Review, 11,* 239–250.

Fuchs, L. S., Fuchs, D., Hosp, M. K., & Jenkins, J. R. (2001). Oral reading fluency as an indicator of reading competence: A theoretical, empirical, and historical analysis. *Scientific Studies of Reading, 5,* 239–256.

Gamse, B. C., Jacob, R. T., Horst, M., Boulay, B., & Unlu, F. (2008). *Reading First impact study final report* (NCEE 2009-4038). Washington, DC: National Center for Education Evaluation and Regional Assistance, Institute of Education Sciences, U.S. Department of Education.

Good, R. H., & Kaminski, R. A. (2002). *DIBELS oral reading fluency passages for first through third grades* (Technical Report No. 10). Eugene: University of Oregon.

Hasbrouck, J. E., & Tindal, G. (1992). Curriculum based fluency norms for grades two through five. *Teaching Exceptional Children, 24,* 41–44.

Johnson, M. S., Kress, R. A., & Pikulski, J. J. (1987). *Informal reading inventories.* Newark, DE: International Reading Association.

Kennedy, B. (2003). Hyperlexia profiles. *Brain and Language, 84,* 204–221.

Menton, S., & Hiebert, E. H. (1999). *Literature anthologies: The task for first-grade readers.* Ann Arbor, MI: Center for the Improvement of Early Reading Achievement.

Meyer, L. A., Linn, R. A., & Hastings, C. N. (1991). Teacher stability from morning to afternoon and from year to year. *American Educational Research Journal, 28,* 825–847.

National Reading Panel. (2000). *Teaching children to read: An evidence-based assessment of the scientific research literature on reading and its implications for reading instruction* (NIH Publication No. 00-4769). Washington, DC: National Institute of Child Health and Human Development.

Perfetti, C. A., Finger, E., & Hogaboam, T. W. (1978). Sources of vocalization latency differences between skilled and less skilled readers. *Journal of Educational Psychology, 70,* 730–739.

Pinnell, G. S., Pikulski, J. J., Wixson, K. K., Campbell, J. R., Gough, P. B., & Beatty, A. S. (1995). *Listening to children read aloud.* Washington, DC: U.S. Department of Education.

Plaut, D. C. (1996). Relearning after damage in connectionist networks: Toward a theory of rehabilitation. *Brain and Language, 52,* 25–82.

Pressley, M., Wharton-McDonald, R., Mistretta-Hapston, J., & Echevarria, M. (1998). Literacy instruction in 10 fourth and fifth grade classrooms in upstate New York. *Scientific Studies of Reading, 2,* 159–194.

Raphael, T. E., & Wonnacott, C. A. (1985). Heightening fourth-grade students' sensitivity to sources of information for answering comprehension questions. *Reading Research Quarterly, 20,* 282–296.

Rasinski, T. V. (1990). Investigating measures of reading fluency. *Educational Research Quarterly, 14,* 37–44.

Roehler, L. R. (1992). Embracing the instructional complexities of reading instruction. In M. Pressley, K. R. Harris, & J. Guthrie (Eds.), *Promoting academic competence and literacy in school* (pp. 427–455). San Diego, CA: Academic Press.

Shanahan, T. (2001). Improving reading education for low-income children. In G. Shiel & U. N. Dhálaigh (Eds.), *Reading matters: A fresh start* (pp. 157–165). Dublin: Reading Association of Ireland/National Reading Initiative.

Shanahan, T. (2002). What research says: The promises and limitations of applying research to reading education. In A. E. Farstrup & S. J. Samuels (Eds.), *What research has to say about reading instruction* (3rd ed., pp. 8–24). Newark, DE: International Reading Association.

Shanahan, T. (2004). *Elements of reading: Fluency.* Austin, TX: Harcourt Supplemental.

Shanahan, T. (2005). Relations among oral language, reading, and writing development. In C. A. MacArthur, S. Graham, & J. Fitzgerald (Eds.), *Handbook of writing research* (pp. 171–184). New York: Guilford Press.

Shanahan, T., & Shanahan, C. (2008). Teaching disciplinary literacy to adolescents: Rethinking content-area literacy. *Harvard Educational Review, 78,* 40–59.

Shavelson, R. J., & Towne, L. (Eds.). (2002). *Scientific research in education.* Washington, DC: National Academy Press.

Shepard, L. (2000). The role of assessment in a learning culture. *Educational Researcher, 29*(7), 4–14.

Stallings, J., & Krasavage, E. M. (1986). Program implementation and student achievement in a four-year Madeline Hunter follow-through project. *Elementary School Journal, 87,* 117–138.

Stanovich, K. E. (1981). Relationship between word decoding speed, general name-retrieval ability, and reading progress in first-grade children. *Journal of Educational Psychology, 73,* 809–815.

U.S. Department of Education, Office of Planning, Evaluation and Policy Development, Policy and Program Studies Service. (2008). *Reading First implementation evaluation final report.* Washington, DC.

Valencia, S. W., Smith, A. T., Reece, A. M., Li, M., Wixson, K. K., & Newman, H. (2010). Oral reading fluency assessment: Issues of construct, criterion, and consequential validity. *Reading Research Quarterly, 45,* 270–291.

Walberg, H. J. (1986). Syntheses of research on teaching. In M. J. Wittrock (Ed.), *Handbook of research on teaching* (3rd ed., pp. 214–230). New York: Macmillan.

Wang, M. C., Haertel, G. D., & Walberg, H. J. (1990). What influences learning?: A content analysis of review literature. *Journal of Educational Research, 84,* 30–43.

Wang, M. C., Haertel, G. D., & Walberg, H. J. (1993). Toward a knowledge base for school learning. *Review of Educational Research, 63,* 249–294.

Young, A., & Bowers, P. G. (1995). Individual difference and text difficulty determinants of reading fluency and expressiveness. *Journal of Experimental Child Psychology, 60,* 428–454.

Zutell, J., & Rasinski, T. (1986). Spelling ability and reading fluency. In J. A. Niles & V. Lalik (Eds.), *35th yearbook of the National Reading Conference* (pp. 109–112). Rochester, NY: National Reading Conference.

# 3

# Reading Expressiveness
*The Neglected Aspect of Reading Fluency*

Paula J. Schwanenflugel
Rebekah George Benjamin

**O**ral reading fluency has shifted in the past decades from a rather neglected reading skill (Allington, 1983; Dowhower, 1991) to a heavily assessed, highly researched facet of overall reading ability. In this chapter, we focus on the topic of reading expressiveness (or reading prosody) because of its inclusion in recent definitions of oral reading fluency. In what follows, we rely on the following definition of reading fluency:

> Fluency combines accuracy, automaticity, and oral reading prosody, which, taken together, facilitate the reader's construction of meaning. It is demonstrated during oral reading through ease of word recognition, appropriate pacing, phrasing, and intonation. It is a factor in both oral and silent reading that can limit or support comprehension (Kuhn, Schwanenflugel, & Meisinger, 2010, p. 240).

Prosody captures the expressiveness of language. It is noted by the rise and falls of pitch, the sense of rhythm and emphasis on certain words and phrases, and the pausing between words and the lengthening of others. It supports linguistic communication and comprehension by enhancing reception of the message and by maintaining key information in working memory (Hirschberg, 2002). In the past 10 years, our understanding of the psycholinguistics of prosody has exploded as psycholinguistics has reduced its reliance on written text to test linguistic theory. However, we have only

35

begun to understand how these more recent developments in prosody theory relate to children's oral reading development. We begin our discussion of the development of reading expressiveness, measured spectrographically (using audio maps of speech), by considering the prosodic features inherent in speech.

The first of these prosodic features is fundamental frequency or, more simply, pitch. Changes in pitch are relative to a speaker's voice range. A child who shows greater range and variability in pitch while reading is perceived as being generally more expressive (Cowie, Douglas-Cowie, & Wichmann, 2002).

Another feature is duration or length. Vowels are typically measured for changes in duration because they take longer to pronounce than consonants. Of interest are phrase-final vowels that may display a feature called phrase-final lengthening. Duration has to be taken in context with the speaker's overall speaking rate. So, faster readers will have shorter phrase-final lengthening and shorter durations of all vowels than slower readers. A child who has been told to read as quickly as he or she can will show less phrase-final lengthening because it is nearly impossible to read both very quickly and with the proper prosody. This is one reason why it is important to include measures of reading, accuracy, speed, *and* prosody when measuring reading fluency.

Stress is a property in speaking that "makes one syllable in a word more prominent than its neighbors" (Himmelmann & Ladd, 2008, p. 248). Stress is perceived as a change in loudness. Stressed syllables tend to be of a higher pitch and longer duration as well as louder. English favors an even distribution of stressed and unstressed syllables, and speakers will add or move stress to keep up a regular stress pattern (e.g., *Toad gave it to the doorman*; Temperly, 2009). In evaluating children's reading prosody, we should look for the stress patterns associated with the language that they speak, while remaining aware that children reading in a language that they do not speak with native-like fluency may not show native-like use of stress.

Pausing is spectrographic silence in oral reading. Slow speakers and readers have more frequent pauses to catch their breath or formulate the message (Goldman Eisler, 1968; Krivokapic, 2007). We should not expect children to pause midsentence simply because it is complex. Nor should we consider a well-placed, midsentence pause in a long, complex sentence an error. However, children do tend to pause before (and sometimes after) words they are having difficulty decoding such that most intrasentential pausing is related to decoding abilities (Miller & Schwanenflugel, 2008).

Prosodic features can engage in *cue trading*, in which one prosodic feature is taken up by another (Beach, 1991). Prosodic changes tend to operate in a correlated fashion (e.g., changes in stress are usually indicated by changes in loudness, duration, and pitch), which has the effect of creating a holistic prosodic impression (Cooper & Paccia-Cooper, 1980).

## WHAT DOES PROSODY RELATE TO LINGUISTICALLY?

Before considering how to evaluate children's reading prosody, we consider what prosody marks linguistically. Different aspects of language affect prosody: discourse and pragmatic information, syntactic information, and lexical information. Our goal here is to provide a description of the various ways in which linguistic information may impact prosody.

### Prosody as an Acoustic Guide to Importance: Discourse and Pragmatics

Most theories of the relationship between discourse features and prosody point to the communicative functions of prosody. Wilson and Wharton (2006) point out that language (and, we assert, particularly written language) is ambiguous. Highlighting certain words or parts of words in any spoken communication allows the listener to better attend to relevant speech by signaling importance. It allows the speaker to disambiguate ambiguous messages by highlighting important terms to ensure that disambiguation happens. It allows the speaker to imply, hint, or generally communicate to the listener a particular intent.

Much about prosody can be interpreted as a way to increase the salience and importance of some words, phrases, or ideas over others. Wilson and Wharton (2006) provide an excellent example that we adapt to illustrate a point:

1. Frog played Toad. He beat him.

Said in typical default prosody, we use our knowledge of parallel structure to assign "he" to the role of "Frog" and "him" to "Toad," and we interpret this second sentence to mean "Frog beat Toad." This interpretation does not feel ambiguous. However, let's say that we use the following prosody instead:

2. Frog played Toad. *HE* beat *HIM*.

In this case, the use of nondefault prosody hints that the usual interpretation may not apply. Essentially, we think, "Okay, why did the speaker stress HE and HIM? Something else must be going on here." We then determine that the statement means the opposite—Toad beat Frog.

This same basic principle is applies to sarcasm and irony:

3. (Frog)—I have one scar, but you just can't see it.
   (Toad)—Really? I got four.
   (Frog)—*WELL, AREN'T YOU SPECIAL!*

If you read this rejoinder aloud with a sarcastic intonation, you probably read it more nasally and slowly, with elongated syllables and pauses (Anolli, Ciceri, & Infantino, 2000; Bryant, 2010; Haiman, 1998). Prosody communicates that the sarcastic statement is different from what has been explicitly stated. Children often miss sarcasm without this specially marked prosody (Capelli, Nakagawa, & Madden, 1990; Whalen & Pexman, 2010), so it is unclear whether even fluent elementary school readers will reflect sarcasm in their oral reading.

Level of information in a discourse hierarchy affects the prosody in which a segment of text is spoken. There are key segments in any discourse that basically set the stage for subsequent text. Adults include longer pauses before and after text segments central in the discourse structure than for text segments representing supportive detail information. These pauses serve as if to bracket the information for the listener (den Ouden, Noordman, & Terken, 2009; Smith, 2004). Quite literally, the pitch for higher segments are higher than those for lower segments (Noordman, Dassen, Swerts, & Terken, 1999). Causally related text segments (important for understanding just about any text) are connected by shorter pauses and faster articulation rates between them. It is unclear whether fluent children will reflect discourse importance in these ways, however.

The introduction of "new" information (i.e., information not believed to be in the listener's current consciousness) in a discourse compared with "given" information (i.e., mentioned or inferable information) shows a similar pattern. Adults place higher pitch or stress on expressions introducing a brand new entity, topic, or paragraph than on entities previously mentioned (Ayers, 1994; Brown, 1983; Sluijter & Terken, 1993). Low pitch indicates that the topical anaphor is in working memory (Wennerstrom, 2001). When shifting topics, speakers slow down and show greater sentence-final lengthening than when they elaborate on them (Smith, 2004). Again, whether developing readers will naturally do this in the process of learning to read fluently is unclear.

That prosody serves to direct listeners to particular information can be seen clearly in the use of contrastive prosody (Carlson, Dickey, Frazier, & Clifton, 2009; Fraundorf, Watson, & Benjamin, 2010; Hirschberg, 2002). Let's look at the following example:

4. Frog looked at the blue and yellow flowers, thinking about which to give Toad. "Here," he said, "have a BLUE one."

In this case, prosody serves to direct the listener (or reader) mentally to the correct antecedent. Children seem to have the capacity to understand the use of contrastive stress by age 5 (Cutler & Swinney, 1987), but whether they will produce contrastive stress in their oral reading is unknown.

There are other prosodic-related mechanisms that are used to create linguistic focus, sending a topic into the foreground or into the background. Among these is the prosody of the it-cleft. Compare the following:

5. It was ON THIS PATH that Toad set out.

6. Toad set out on this path.

Prosody highlighting ON THIS PATH following the it-cleft reinforces that goal. Similarly, direct quotes bring what has been directly quoted into the foreground, whereas indirect quotation moves the same information into the background (Jansen, Gregory, & Brenier, 2001). Contrast the following:

7. Frog said, "There was no one inside."

8. Frog said there was no one inside.

Generally, pitch range is greater for direct than indirect quotes, and the pitch reset following "said" is greater in the directly quoted speech than the indirectly quoted speech. It is unclear whether children bring this knowledge into their oral reading as they learn to read fluently.

Another way in which prosody signals importance is through the use of emotional prosody (Banse & Scherer, 1996; Juslin & Laukka, 2003). Emotional prosody indicates a contrast from unmarked prosody for a given communication and points it out as something that one should pay attention to. Happiness is signaled by fast speech rate, high, rising pitch and variability, and fast voice onsets; and sadness by nearly the opposite. Uncertainty is signaled by a sustained rise in pitch (Hirschberg, 2002). Unfortunately, elementary school children are still in the process of developing an understanding of emotional prosody (Fujiki, Spackman, Brinton, & Illig, 2008; Wells & Peppe, 2003), so whether they express it in their readings when the text suggests the need for it is unknown.

Taken together, it is clear that prosody serves as a guide to the listener (and passage reader) as to what information ought be preserved in working memory for understanding the message and what things have a supportive role. Presumably, as the listener decodes the important information signaled prosodically, the information is maintained in working memory so that it can be linked with incoming information. Long-term memory of the acoustically highlighted discourse is improved as well (Fraundorf et al., 2010). Thus, prosody serves to support comprehension in a very basic way.

That prosodic reading for complex texts among children learning to read has been linked to enhanced comprehension and memory is not a surprise once one understands the functions of prosody in comprehension. Unfortunately, however, we do not know much about children's understanding of these discourse uses of prosody during the period in which they are learning to read.

## Syntax and Sentence Prosody

Prosody at the sentence level is generally assumed to be important for communicating the grammatical structure of a sentence. However, for some researchers, sentence grammar-related prosody exists primarily to avoid ambiguity in communication. This view would hold that, in regular communication, typical syntactically linked cues to sentence structure might be altogether missing or unreliable (Allbritton, McKoon, & Radcliffe, 1996). For others, the underlying syntax of the sentence more or less dictates the prosodic realization of the sentence (Nespor & Vogel, 1986). There is good evidence that adults show a great deal of consistency between each other in terms of reading sentences with similar prosody, even on a cold reading (Koriat, Greenberg, & Kreiner, 2002; Schwanenflugel, Hamilton, Kuhn, Wisenbaker, & Stahl, 2004). There is evidence that appropriate prosodic phrasing leads to better comprehension in adults (Sanderman & Collier, 1997). In what follows, we describe some of the typical sentence-type manifestations of prosody.

Declarative sentences or statements are generally signaled by an initial rising pitch, which then terminates with a falling pitch (called *declination*). As declarative sentences become longer, there is a general flattening out of pitch (Ladd, 1984). Children and adults will display smaller sentence-final declinations despite better fluency as they read complex sentences, but their pitch variability will generally increase to support comprehension (Benjamin & Schwanenflugel, 2010). Within complex sentences, pauses are longer between complex phrases than simple ones (Krivokapic, 2007; Strangert, 1997). These phrasal prosodic boundaries help listeners identify words on either side of the acoustic "edge" (Shukla, Nespor, & Mehler, 2007). In reading, these pauses should occur at grammatical junctures only (Goldman Eisler, 1968; Krivokapic, 2007). Intrasentential pauses tend to be shorter than intersentential ones (Cooper & Paccia-Cooper, 1980). Adult-like handling of phrasing in complex sentences undergoes change throughout childhood (Sadagopan & Smith, 2008). In our work, fluent readers tend to pause more often in grammatically relevant junctures than less fluent readers do (Benjamin & Schwanenflugel, 2010).

Yes–no questions are usually marked by sustained rising pitch. Among these are declarative questions for which this rising pitch is the main distinguishing feature between the statement and question form. Children's understanding of declarative question prosody (e.g., "He wanted to go to school?") is still under development during the period in which they are learning to read (Patel & Grigos, 2006). This rising pitch is not always used for all question types (Miller & Schwanenflugel, 2006). Thus, instructing children to read all question marks with ascending pitch (cf. Hudson, Lane, & Pullen, 2005) would be incorrect. However, more fluent children tend to have more pronounced rising pitch than less fluent children do (Miller & Schwanenflugel, 2006).

Parentheticals, which are sentences that have additional explanatory or commentary information inserted in them somewhere, have their own prosody. In written form, parenthetical information is indicated by parentheses, dashes, or brackets. When spoken, parenthetical information typically exhibits low-level and narrowed pitch ranges, decreased intensity (Grosz & Hirschberg, 1992), as well as an immediate drop in pitch at the onset of the parenthetical (Bodenbender, 2003). Consider the following:

9. Toad went to the movie (honestly, he almost never goes out) and it was totally crowded.

10. Frog said he was being very good (if you can believe it).

Following midsentence parenthetical information, there is sometimes a resetting of the pitch back to the point prior to the interjection and the host sentence goes on as usual, but not always (Dehe, 2009; Kutik, Cooper, & Boyce, 1983). Currently, we know little about how children reflect parentheticals in their oral reading.

Quite possibly, sentence ambiguity is the most studied aspect of sentence prosody. Consider the following sentences:

11. Frog touched (pause) the plate with the flower.

12. Frog touched the plate (pause) with the flower.

As you can see, inserting a pause seems to determine whether "with the flower" modifies the verb phrase "touched" or the noun phrase "the plate." Prosody seems to have immediate effects on parsing decisions in adults while listening (Steinhauer, Alter, & Friederici, 1999). Unfortunately, the speaker has to be aware of the ambiguity in the construction to disambiguate it prosodically for listeners, which they often are not (Snedeker & Trueswell, 2003). For ambiguous sentences, readers, speakers, and listeners rely on a variety of contextual, lexical, and prosodic information to distinguish the underlying sentence structure of temporarily ambiguous sentences (Snedeker & Trueswell, 2004). Children are able to use these sources of information to distinguish between various interpretations of ambiguous sentences, but their ability to use prosody to disambiguate is more fragile than it is for adults (Snedeker & Yuan, 2008).

In sum, as indicated, there are a variety of prosodic sentence patterns that can be noted in children's oral readings. However, we are only beginning to understand how children move from word-by-word reading to fluent reading that reflects most of these patterns.

## Prosody as an Integral Aspect of Processing Words

Stress is an integral feature of the lexical representation of words. Thus, each time we retrieve the meaning of a given word, either reading aloud or silently, we also retrieve its prosodic pattern as we assign phonological characteristics to the word being read (Ashby & Clifton, 2005; Gutiérrez-Palma & Palma-Reyes, 2008). To illustrate, consider this set of noun, verb, and adjective homographs:

13. Frog felt an *increase* in happiness.

14. Toad tried to *increase* Frog's happiness.

15. Frog counted *thirteen* flowers in the garden.

16. Frog saw *thirteen* of them.

Generally, homographic nouns and adjectives are stressed on the first syllable, whereas verbs are stressed on the second, and listeners and readers retrieve this knowledge during lexical processing (Breen & Clifton, 2011). Young children who later struggle in learning to read may have particular difficulty in producing irregularly stressed words (deBree, Wijnen, & Zonneveld, 2006). However, because stress accent is an integral part of retrieving an elaborated lexical representation during the reading process, children who have the particular word form in their vocabularies[1] should be able to read them correctly.

Another of these cues is the information associated with lexical compounding (consider *wishbone, mailbox,* and *blackbird*). Languages vary in the amount of compounding they entail. German and Finnish have a lot of compounding, whereas English has less. Consider the following:

---

[1] A perusal of English words whose grammatical form class is indicated by stress pattern suggests that some words might be more familiar to young children learning to read than others. For example *DIScard, DEtail, PERmit* would seem to be less familiar for children than their counterparts *disCARD, deTAIL,* and *perMIT.*

17. A *blackbird* flew by.

18. A *black bird* was taking a bath by the garden fence.

Compounded stems tend to be shorter and with higher, more level pitch than the same stems presented as part of a phrase, and adult listeners deploy this knowledge receptively to distinguish between the two (Koester, Gunter, Wagner, & Fiederici, 2004). For compound words, the first stem tends to receive greater lexical stress, whereas for the same stem presented as part of a phrase the second stem is elongated (as in "the black bird ... "). Elementary school children should have no difficulty understanding how to construct compound prosody because this prosodic information is part of the lexical entry for compound words (Vogel & Raimy, 2002).

Suffixes play a role in stress placement. Some suffixes do not modify the stress placement on the base word (e.g., *-ness, -ful, -ment,* as in *happiness, wonderful, entertainment*), but others do (e.g., *-ity, -tion, -al* as in *activity, celebration, universal*). Children's understanding of the stress changes required by various suffixes is a predictor of their decoding skills (Jarmulowicz, Hay, Taran, & Ethington, 2008; Jarmulowicz, Taran, & Hay, 2007).

Finally, there are also general prosodic signals that particular words have informational importance. Content words (i.e., nouns, verbs, adjectives, and adverbs) and function words (articles, prepositions, auxiliaries, and pronouns) are distinguishable by their prosodic features. Content words invariably contain at least one stressed syllable, whereas function words tend to be unstressed (Cann, 2001; Selkirk, 1996). Further, content words have more elongated pronunciations than function words do (Bell, Brenier, Gregory, Girand, & Jurafsky, 2009). By enhancing the perceptual salience of content words in this way, prosody ensures that their informational importance to the message gets highlighted. Children who read fluently should demonstrate this differential prosodic salience patterning in their oral reading (Weber, 2006), but this has yet to be shown empirically.

In sum, accessing prosodic form seems to be an integral aspect of word identification and general decoding skill during reading (Whalley & Hansen, 2006; Wood, 2006). Some reading researchers think that there is indeed something special about rhythmic sensitivity (linguistic and otherwise) as a predictor of later word recognition skills during reading (Goswami et al., 2002; Thomson & Goswami, 2008).

## Development of Reading Prosody

Since we begin to understand prosody in spoken language at the very beginnings of language development before literacy is even possible, we know that there must be differences between prosody in language acquisition and reading development. Good reading prosody seems to develop in children along with general reading skills like fluency. Seven-year-olds, for example, who are generally more fluent readers in terms of rate and accuracy, use pausing, pitch, and stress placement differently than poorer readers (Clay & Imlach, 1971). Reading prosody is not totally separate from speech prosody, though, and is likely connected to an awareness of prosodic patterns in language at an early age as phonological awareness may be connected to prosodic sensitivity in spoken language (Suranyi et al., 2009; Goswami et al., 2002). Early on in their reading careers students begin to become more expressive in their reading as they develop skill (Kuhn & Stahl, 2003). We cannot be positive that good prosody enhances other reading outcomes (e.g., fluency and comprehension), but recent work has demonstrated that oral reading prosody differs between readers at various stages of fluency (e.g., Benjamin & Schwanenflugel, 2010).

Dysfluent readers, especially those with reading disabilities, tend to be generally less sensitive to stress features in language (Goswami et al., 2002). Exposure to oral language might be one reason for such differences in young children. Exposure to language during the early years increases a child's vocabulary and predicts both verbal ability and reading achievement in the early elementary years (Walker, Greenwood, Hart, & Carta, 1994). Good stress sensitivity in language may result from exposure to spoken language in the early childhood years (Whalley & Hansen, 2006). Other prosodic features also mark differences between fluent and dysfluent readers: Dysfluent readers are more likely to pause within both sentences and major syntactic phrases, less likely to decrease pitch at the ends of declarative sentences, and less likely to have overall pitch contours matching that of adults (Clay & Imlach, 1971; Schreiber, 1991; Schwanenflugel et al., 2004; Miller & Schwanenflugel, 2006; Benjamin & Schwanenflugel, 2010). These studies also found that readers with good decoding abilities exhibited more appropriate prosody when reading aloud.

Thus, the general development of oral reading prosody may be dependent on decoding skills at the word and text levels. We know that oral reading prosody seems to develop with a child's other reading abilities, and prerequisite skills—like word and text fluency—might allow for greater expressiveness in oral reading. An alternative, but not necessarily conflicting, view is that prosody may function as a linguistic scaffold to assist the reader in chunking text, allowing working memory to process a greater amount of information and short-term memory to store larger quantities of text for comprehension (Frazier, Carlson, & Clifton, 2006).

## Measuring Reading Prosody

Because standards in measuring reading prosody have not yet been set, researchers have used a variety of methods to measure prosodic skills in children. In the following sections, we discuss and evaluate three common methods for measuring prosodic ability: indirect measures, direct measures, and rating scales.

## Indirect Measures

Two basic types of indirect methods have been used to connect prosody with children's reading abilities: stress sensitivity tasks and parsing tasks. Stress sensitivity tasks may involve children listening to sound combinations and indicating where the stressed syllable is. These sound combinations may consist of nonwords or actual words, such as certain compound nouns (e.g., *thirteen*) that have the ability to switch stress positions based on context. Or these tasks may involve modifying stress placement in sentences or word combinations. Some researchers have found that children with reading disabilities, such as dyslexia, are generally less sensitive to prosodic stress than children with normally developing reading abilities (Surányi et al., 2009). This was especially true of English-speaking children when compared to Hungarian children, and this language difference is likely because English is more metrically based than many other languages and stress sensitivity is important for understanding the language. Other researchers have also found that children's performance on these types of rhythm tasks can predict their ability to accurately identify words and can also predict some variance in reading comprehension (Blumstein & Goodglass, 1972; Whalley & Hansen, 2006). These studies demonstrate that much of what is necessary for interpreting spoken English may also be necessary for developing reading skills.

While rhythm tasks look at receptive prosodic awareness, text parsing requires readers to interact with the text and determine where they should place boundaries in a given text. Interpretation can be difficult since the child performs the task while reading silently. Research has indicated that the phrasal knowledge necessary for parsing sentences is linked with more general reading skills like comprehension as well as measures of fluency (Kleiman, Winograd, & Humphrey, 1979; Young & Bowers, 1995). Parsing texts, then, might actually be measuring children's syntactic awareness as well as their ability to comprehend text well enough to segment it into meaningful groups.

## Direct Measures

It is possible to measure a child's oral reading prosody directly, but doing so requires the use of appropriate technology and some level of skill. These direct measures, though, are necessary if precision is the goal, and they are also useful in guiding the development of more user-friendly prosody assessments. There is no standardized way to measure prosody, so researchers have used multiple methods. With limited use of technology, some have created a prosodic *map* based on expert readings of a text (Ravid & Mashraki, 2007). They then scored children's oral readings based on their conformity to the map. This method, though, is very labor intensive, and classroom uses may be limited.

Another direct measurement method is the Tone and Boundary Indices (ToBI) system, which is used largely in linguistics and communication sciences (e.g., Frazier et al., 2006; see also Zervas, Fakotakis, & Kokkinakis, 2008). ToBI focuses on pitch accents within speech as they relate to prosodic phrasing, but it has not been widely used in educational research. The system would likely be too labor intensive for classroom use because ToBI labeling typically takes even experienced labelers 100–200 times the actual recording time (Syrdal, Hirschberg, McGory, & Beckman, 2001).

Varied forms of spectrographic measurements have been used in education-focused studies for analyzing prosody in oral reading (e.g., Benjamin & Schwanenflugel, 2010; Dowhower, 1987; Miller & Schwanenflugel, 2006, 2008; Schwanenflugel et al., 2004). Certain patterns of pause placement and duration, pitch movement, and stress placement within sentences have all been linked with reading skill in children (Benjamin & Schwanenflugel, 2010; Dowhower, 1987; Miller & Schwanenflugel, 2006, 2008; Schwanenflugel et al., 2004). Although this method of measuring prosody is labor intensive, researchers can choose which prosodic features they want to measure and thus use this method with relatively large samples of oral readings. But, again, realistic classroom uses by teachers would seem to be limited.

### Ratings as Measures of Reading Prosody

The most commonly used tool in education studies for measuring prosody is the rating scale. Numerous scales exist, but only a few are consistently found throughout the literature and in classrooms. These include the Allington (1983) scale, various versions of a scale designed by Rasinski and colleagues (Rasinski, 2004; Rasinski, Rikli, & Johnston, 2009; Zutell & Rasinski, 1991), and the National Assessment of Educational Progress (NAEP) scale (Daane, Campbell, Grigg, Goodman, & Oranje, 2005; Pinnell et al., 1995). Each scale differs in scope and format, although all have been developed with the goal of formally incorporating prosody into fluency measures. Such rating scales succeed in adding this third dimension of fluency—in addition to rate and accuracy—that more traditional fluency assessments have not incorporated. These scales were designed to measure fluency as a whole, not simply prosody, so interpreting the ratings can be difficult.

The scales differ in their theoretical foundation as well as their implementation of assessing prosody and fluency as a whole. Although all scales use somewhat subjective descriptions of various fluency skills—as opposed to, for example, asking raters to count exact errors, determine time reading rate, or count prosodic deviations—they differ in what they ask raters to focus on.

The NAEP scale (Pinnell et al., 1995) was developed with the assumption that reading accuracy was a separate construct from fluency, so the creators did not include accuracy in the scale. Because most recent definitions of fluency include accuracy as a component of fluency, this exclusion may be problematic. Children are given scores ranging from 1 to 4 on the scale, and although this simplicity seems to make the scale user friendly, it is unknown how reliably teachers can actually use this rating scale. In the large studies using this scale (Daane et al., 2005; Pinnell et al., 1995), raters were trained for several days prior to rating the oral readings used in the study. Even with significant training, reliability and exact agreement were fairly poor in the initial study (Pinnell et al., 1995). In examining the NAEP scale, it may be somewhat difficult, for example, to distinguish between level 1 and level 2 because both describe poor oral reading. A level 1 reader may sometimes read in phrases, whereas a level 2 reader simply reads in phrases a little more frequently, and both levels indicate that meaningful structure is not being preserved. Finally, the NAEP scale simply does not provide teachers with much information about how children are reading and what can be done to help them improve. It is our belief that assessments should inform instruction, and this rating scale is very limited in its ability to give teachers the information they need to modify instruction for their students.

The Allington scale (Allington, 1983) is similar to the NAEP scale in that it measures fluency along a single dimension (i.e., teachers give children a single score based on the scale). However, the Allington scale has a range of 6 points, and the descriptions at each point are much briefer than those of the NAEP scale. The scale is largely a continuum ranging from "word by word" reading (Allington, 1983, p. 559) to reading with appropriate phrasing, attention to punctuation, emphasis, and imitation of normal speech. Information about the development of the scale is not readily available, and Richard Allington has stated that because scientifically based reading research was not as common in the early 1980s, no psychometric data were available (personal communication, August 25, 2010). However, some researchers have used the scale and obtained their own reliability data (Rasinski, 1985; Young, Bowers, & MacKinnon, 1996), finding that they were able to obtain high interrater reliability coefficients. Overall, the scale seems to be user friendly in its simplicity. Our major concern, however, is that there is very little evidence of the scale's general reliability and validity for use in authentic educational settings. Also, the scale was developed prior to much of the current prosody research available today, research that could and should inform any revisions to the scale for present and future use in classrooms.

While the previous two scales are marked by their simplicity of design, Zutell and Rasinski (1991) published the initial version of a multidimensional scale for assessing fluency—the Multidimensional Fluency Scale (MDFS). Subsequent revisions based on updated definitions of fluency as well as other existing scales (Rasinski, 2004; Rasinski et al., 2009) changed the scale over time, but it remains composed of three to four dimensions, with four rating points along each dimension. The most recent version of the scale (Rasinski et al., 2009) assesses readers on three dimensions: phrasing and expression, accuracy and smoothness, and pacing. This accuracy component is the newest addition to the scale, and appears to fall in line with many definitions of fluency that incorporate accuracy, reading rate, and prosody (e.g., Hudson et al., 2005; Kuhn et al., 2010; National Reading Panel, 2000). Including accuracy in the scale also sets the MDFS apart from others like the NAEP and Allington scales. Another benefit of the scale is that teachers only need to listen to 60 seconds of oral reading when rating students on the scale (Rasinski, 2004). However, to effectively rate students on three or more dimensions, a teacher may have to record students' readings and listen to the recordings more than once. This could present a difficulty for teachers and reading specialists who have limited time for informal fluency assessment. Unfortunately, although several studies have used one of the versions of the MDFS, little interrater reliability evidence is available. A recent large study (Rasinski et al., 2009), however, demonstrated that, with training, raters achieved high interrater agreement when agreement was defined as within 2 points on the 12-point scale (4 points along three dimensions). We believe that more research needs to be done to determine how efficiently and reliably teachers can use this scale, and how likely they are to choose this more complex scale over a simpler scale, such as the NAEP.

## CONCLUSION

Prosody is a complex facet of spoken and written expression. At this point we do not have a great understanding of how much of this knowledge appears in children's oral readings as they gain in reading fluency and overall reading proficiency. We do know that prosody should be a part of the definition and assessment of oral reading fluency (Kuhn et al., 2010). We also know that it has been linked to other aspects of reading fluency as well as reading comprehension in developing readers (Benjamin & Schwanenflugel, 2010; Miller & Schwanenflugel, 2006, 2008). We currently do not know how much children use their prosodic knowledge to assist in their reading comprehension.

On the basis our current understandings of the role of prosody in reading, we believe that teachers should consider including prosody in their fluency instruction and their instructional conversations with students about fluency. We can think of no obvious downside to having teachers model appropriate prosody while reading text to children. Teachers should reasonably ask children to read text with appropriate intonation during oral reading practice. However, the field still needs to gather decisive experimental evidence regarding the causal benefits of a much stronger prosody emphasis in reading instruction relative to other emphases that we might have in reading instruction.

We hope that this chapter has provided you with a sense of the state of our current knowledge regarding the expressiveness aspect of reading fluency. For as much as we know about prosody and the role that it plays in the development of fluency, we still have much to learn.

## REFERENCES

Allington, R. (1983). Fluency: The neglected reading goal. *Reading Teacher, 36*(6), 556–561.

Anolli, L., Ciceri, R., & Infantino, M. G. (2000). Irony as a game of implicitness: Acoustic profiles of ironic communication. *Journal of Psycholinguistic Research, 29*(3), 275–311.

Ashby, J., & Clifton, C. (2005). The prosodic property of lexical stress affects eye movements during silent reading. *Cognition, 96,* 89–100.

Ayers, G. (1994). Discourse functions of pitch range in spontaneous and read speech. *OSU Working Papers in Linguistics, 44,* 1–49.

Banse, R., & Scherer, K. R. (1996). Acoustic profiles in vocabulary emotion expression. *Journal of Personality and Social Psychology, 70,* 614–636.

Beach, C. M. (1991). The interpretation of prosodic patterns at points of syntactic structure ambiguity: Evidence for cue trading relations. *Journal of Memory and Language, 30,* 644–663.

Bell, A., Brenier, J. M., Gregory, M., Girand, C., & Jurafsky, D. (2009). Predictability effects on durations of content and function words in conversational English. *Journal of Memory and Language, 60,* 92–111.

Benjamin, R. G., & Schwanenflugel, P. J. (2010). Text complexity and oral reading prosody in young readers. *Reading Research Quarterly, 45*(4), 388–404.

Blumstein, S., & Goodglass, H. (1972). The perception of stress as a semantic cue in aphasia. *Journal of Speech and Hearing Research, 15*(4), 800–806.

Breen, M., & Clifton, C. (2011). Stress matters: Effects of anticipated lexical stress on silent reading. *Journal of Memory and Language, 64,* 153–170.

Brown, G. (1983). Prosodic structure and the given/new distinction. In A. Culter

& D. R. Ladd (Eds.), *Prosody: Models and measurements* (pp. 67–77). New York: Springer-Verlag.

Bryant, G. A. (2010). Prosodic contrasts in ironic speech. *Discourse Processes, 47,* 545–566.

Cann, R. (2001). Functional versus lexical: A cognitive dichotomy. In R. D. Borsley (Ed.), *The nature and function of syntactic categories* (pp. 37–78). New York: Academic Press.

Capelli, C. A., Nakagawa, N., & Madden, C. M. (1990). How children understand sarcasm: The role of context and intonation. *Child Development, 61,* 1824–1841.

Carlson, K., Dickey, M. W., Frazier, L., & Clifton, C. (2009). Information structure expectations in sentence comprehension. *Quarterly Journal of Experimental Psychology, 62,* 114–139.

Clay, M. M., & Imlach, R. H. (1971). Juncture, pitch, and stress as reading behavior variables. *Journal of Verbal Learning and Verbal Behavior, 10*(2), 133–139.

Cooper, W. E., & Paccia-Cooper, J. (1980). *Syntax and speech.* Cambridge, MA: Harvard University Press.

Cowie, R., Douglas-Cowie, E., & Wichmann, A. (2002). Prosodic characteristics of skilled reading: Fluency and expressiveness in 8–10 year-old readers. *Language and Speech, 45*(1), 47–82.

Cutler, A., & Swinney, D. A. (1987). Prosody and the development of comprehension. *Journal of Child Language, 14*(1), 145–167.

Daane, M. C., Campbell, J. R., Grigg, W. S., Goodman, M. J., & Oranje, A. (2005). *Fourth-grade students reading aloud: NAEP 2002 Special Study of Oral Reading* (NCES 2006-469). Washington, DC: National Center for Education Statistics, Institute of Education Sciences, U.S. Department of Education.

DeBree, E., Wijnen, F., & Zonneveld, W. (2006). Word stress production in 3-year-old children at risk for dyslexia. *Journal of Research in Reading, 29,* 304–317.

Dehe, N. (2009). Clausal parentheticals, intonational phrasing, and prosodic theory. *Journal of Linguistics, 45,* 569–615.

Den Ouden, H., Noordman, L., & Terken, J. (2009). Prosodic realizations of global and local structure on rhetorical relations in read aloud news reports. *Speech Communication, 51,* 116–129.

Dowhower, S. L. (1987). Effects of repeated reading on second-grade transitional readers' fluency and comprehension. *Reading Research Quarterly, 22*(4), 389–406.

Fraundorf, S. H., Watson, D. G., & Benjamin, A. S. (2010). Recognition memory reveals just how contrastive CONTRASTIVE accenting really is. *Journal of Memory and Language, 63*(3), 367–386.

Frazier, L., Carlson, K., & Clifton, C. (2006). Prosodic phrasing is central to language comprehension. *Trends in Cognitive Sciences, 10*(6), 244–249.

Fujiki, M., Spackman, M. P., Brinton, B., & Illig, T. (2008). Ability of children with language impairment to understand emotion conveyed by prosody in a narrative passage. International *Journal of Language and Communication Disorders, 43*(3), 330–345.

Goldman Eisler, F. (1968). *Psycholinguistic. Experiments in spontaneous speech.* New York: Academic Press.

Goswami, U., Thomson, J., Richardson, U., Stainthorp, R., Hughes, D., Rosen, S., et al. (2002). Amplitude envelop onsets and developmental dyslexia: A new hypothesis. *Proceedings of the National Academy of Sciences, 99,* 10911–10916.

Grosz, B. J., & Hirschberg, J. (1992, October). Some intonational characteristics of discourse structure. In *Proceedings: International Conference on Spoken Language Processing* (Vol. 1, pp. 429–432). Banff, Alberta, Canada.

Gutiérrez-Palma, N., & Palma-Reyes, A. (2008). On the use of lexical stress in reading Spanish. *Reading and Writing, 21,* 645–660.

Haiman, J. (1998). *Talk is cheap: Sarcasm, alienation, and the evolution of language.* New York: Oxford University Press.

Himmelmann, N. P., & Ladd, D. R. (2008). Prosodic description: An introduction for field workers. *Language Documentation and Conservation, 2,* 244–274.

Hirschberg, J. (2002). The pragmatics of intonational meaning. In B. Bel & I. Marlien (Eds.), *Proceedings of the Conference Speech Prosody 2002 conference* (pp. 65–68). Aix-en-Provence, France: Laboratoire Parole Langage.

Hudson, R., Lane, H., & Pullen, P. (2005). Reading fluency assessment and instruction: What, why, and how? *Reading Teacher, 58*(8), 702–714.

Jansen, W., Gregory, M. L., & Brenier, J. M. (2001, October). *Prosodic correlates of directly reported speech: Evidence from conversational speech.* Paper presented the ISCA Tutorial and Workshop on Prosody in Speech Recognition and Understanding, Redbank, NJ.

Jarmulowicz, L., Hay, S. E., Taran, V. L., & Ethington, C. A. (2008). Fitting derivational morphophonology into a developmental model of reading. *Reading and Writing, 21,* 275–297.

Jarmulowicz, L., Taran, V. L., & Hay, S. E. (2007). Third graders' metalinguistic skills, reading skills, and stress production in derived English words. *Journal of Speech, Language, and Hearing Research, 50,* 1–13.

Juslin, P. N., & Laukka, P (2003). Communication of emotions in vocal expression and music performance: Different channels, same code? *Psychological Bulletin, 129*(5), 770–814.

Keoster, K., Gunter, T. C., Wagner, S., & Friederici, A. D. (2004). Morphosyntax, prosody, and linking elements: The auditory processing of German nominal compounds. *Journal of Cognitive Neuroscience, 16,* 1647–1668.

Kleiman, G. M., Winograd, P. N., & Humphrey, M. H. (1979). *Prosody and children's parsing of sentences* (Tech. Rep. 123). Urbana: University of Illinois, Center for the Study of Reading.

Koriat, A., Greenberg, S. N., & Kreiner, H. (2002). The extraction of structure during reading: Evidence from reading prosody. *Memory and Cognition, 30,* 270–280.

Krivokapic, J. (2007). Prosodic planning: Effects of phrasal length and complexity on pause duration. *Journal of Phonetics, 35,* 162–179.

Kuhn, M. R., Schwanenflugel, P. J., & Meisinger, E. B. (2010). Aligning theory and assessment of reading fluency: Automaticity, prosody, and definitions of fluency. *Reading Research Quarterly, 45,* 230–251.

Kuhn, M. R., & Stahl, S. A. (2003). Fluency: A review of developmental and remedial practices. *Journal of Educational Psychology, 95*(1), 3–21.

Kutik, E., Cooper, W. E., & Boyce, S. (1983). Declination of fundamental frequency in speakers' production of parenthetical and main clauses. *Journal of the Acoustical Society of America, 73*, 1731–1738.

Miller, J., & Schwanenflugel, P. J. (2006). Prosody of syntactically complex sentences in the oral reading of young children. *Journal of Educational Psychology, 98*, 839–853.

Miller, J., & Schwanenflugel, P. J. (2008). A longitudinal study ofthe development of reading prosody as a dimension of oral reading fluency in early elementary school children. *Reading Research Quarterly, 43*, 336–354.

National Reading Panel. (2000). *Teaching children to read: An evidence-based assessment of the scientific research literature on reading and its implications for reading instruction: Reports of the subgroups* (NIH Publication No. 00–4754). Washington, DC: National Institute of Child Health and Human Development.

Nespor, M., & Vogel, I. (1986). *Prosodic phonology*. Dordrecht, The Netherlands: Foris.

Noordman, L., Dassen, I., Swets, M., & Terken, J. (1999). Prosodic markers of text structure. In K. van Hock, A. Kibrick, & L. Noordman (Eds.), *Discourse studies in cognitive linguistics* (pp. 133–145). Amsterdam: John Benjamins.

Patel, R., & Grigos, M. I. (2006). Acoustic characterization of the question–statement contrast in 4, 7 and 11 year old children. *Speech Communication, 48*, 1308–1318.

Pinnell, G. S., Pikulski, J. J., Wixson, K. K., Campbell, J. R., Gough, P. B., & Beatty, A. S. (1995). *Listening to children read aloud: Data from NAEP's Integrated Reading Performance Record (IRPR) at grade 4* (NCES 95-726). Washington, DC: National Center for Education Statistics, U.S. Department of Education.

Rasinski, T. V. (1985). *A study of factors involved in reader–text interactions that contribute to fluency in reading.* Unpublished doctoral dissertation, Ohio State University.

Rasinski, T. V. (2004). *Assessing reading fluency.* Calverton, MD: Pacific Institute for Research and Evaluation.

Rasinski, T. V., Rikli, A., & Johnston, S. (2009). Reading fluency: More than automaticity? More than a concern for the primary grades? *Literacy Research and Instruction, 48*(4), 350–361.

Ravid, D., & Mashraki, Y. E. (2007). Prosodic reading, reading comprehension and morphological skills in Hebrew-speaking fourth graders. *Journal of Research in Reading, 30*(2), 140–156.

Sadagopan, N., & Smith, A. (2008). Developmental changes in the effects of utterance length and complexity on speech movement variability. *Journal of Speech, Language, and Hearing Research, 51*, 1138–1151.

Sanderman, A. A., & Collier, R. (1997). Prosodic phrasing and comprehension. *Language and Speech, 40*, 391–409.

Schreiber, P. A. (1991). Understanding prosody's role in reading acquisition. *Theory into Practice, 30*, 158–164.

Schwanenflugel, P. J., Hamilton, A. M., Kuhn, M. R., Wisenbaker, J. M., & Stahl, S. A. (2004). Becoming a fluent reader: Reading skill and prosodic features in the oral reading of young readers. *Journal of Educational Psychology, 96*(1), 119–129.

Selkirk, E. (1996). The prosodic structure of function words. In J. L. Morgan & K. Demuth (Eds.), *Signal to syntax: Bootstrapping from speech to grammar in early acquisition* (pp. 187–213). Mahwah, NJ: Erlbaum.

Shulka, M., Nespor, M., & Mehler, J. (2007). An interaction between prosody and statistics in the segmentation of fluent speech. *Cognitive Psychology, 54*, 1–32.

Sluijter, A., & Terken, J. (1993). Beyond sentence prosody: Paragraph intonation in Dutch. *Phonetica, 50*, 180–188.

Smith, C. L. (2004). Topic transitions and durational prosody in reading aloud: Production and modeling. *Speech Communication, 42*, 247–270.

Snedeker, J., & Trueswell, J. (2003). Using prosody to avoid ambiguity: Effects of speaker awareness and referential context. *Journal of Memory and Language, 48*, 103–130.

Snedeker, J., & Trueswell, J. (2004). The developing constraints on parsing decisions: The role of lexical-biases and referential scenes in child and adult sentence processing. *Cognitive Psychology, 49*(3), 238–299.

Snedeker, J., & Yuan, S. (2008). Effects of prosodic and lexical constraints on parsing in young children (and adults). *Journal of Memory and Language, 58*, 574–608.

Steinhauer, K., Alter, K., & Friederici, A. D. (1999) Brain responses indicate immediate use of prosody in natural speech processing. *Nature Neuroscience, 2*, 191–196.

Strangert, E. (1997). Relating prosody to syntax: Boundary signaling in Swedish. In G. Kokkinakis, N. Fakotakis, & E. Dermatas (Eds.), *Proceedings of Eurospeech '97—5th European Conference on Speech Communication and Technology* (Vol. 1, pp. 239–242). Grenoble, France: European Speech Communication Association.

Surányi, Z., Csépe, V., Richardson, U., Thomson, J. M., Honbolygó, F., & Goswami, U. (2009). Sensitivity to rhythmic parameters in dyslexic children: A comparison of Hungarian and English. *Reading and Writing, 22*(1), 41–56.

Syrdal, A. K., Hirschberg, J., McGory, J., & Beckman, M. (2001). Automatic ToBI prediction and alignment to speed manual labeling of prosody. *Speech Communication, 33*(1–2), 135–151.

Temperly, D. (2009). Distributional stress regularity: A corpus study. *Journal of Psycholinguistic Research, 38*, 75–92.

Thomson, J., & Goswami, U. (2008). Rhythmic processing in children with developmental dyslexia: Auditory and motor rhythms link to reading and spelling. *Journal of Physiology, 102*, 120–129.

Vogel, I., & Raimy, E. (2002). The acquisition of compound versus phrasal stress: The role of prosodic constituents. *Journal of Child Language, 29*, 225–250.

Walker, D., Greenwood, C., Hart, B., & Carta, J. (1994). Prediction of school outcomes based on early language production and socioeconomic factors. *Child Development, 65*(2), 606–621.

Weber, R.-M. (2006). Function words in the prosody of fluent reading. *Journal of Research in Reading, 29*(3), 258–269.

Wells, B., & Peppe, S. (2003). Intonation abilities of children,with speech and language impairments. *Journal of Speech, Language, and Hearing Research, 46*(1), 5–20.

Wennerstrom, A. (2001). *The music of everyday speech: Prosody and discourse analysis.* London: Oxford University Press.

Whalen, J. M., & Pexman, P. M. (2010). How do children respond to verbal irony in face-to-face communication? The development of mode adoption across middle childhood. *Discourse Processes, 47,* 363–387.

Whalley, K., & Hansen, J. (2006). The role of prosodic sensitivity in children's reading development. *Journal of Research in Reading, 29*(3), 288–303.

Wilson, D., & Wharton, T. (2006). Relevance and prosody. *Journal of Pragmatics, 38,* 1559–1579.

Wood, C. (2006). Metrical stress sensitivity in young children and its relationship to phonological awareness and reading. *Journal of Research in Reading, 29,* 270–287.

Young, A., & Bowers, P. G. (1995). Individual difference and text difficulty determinants of reading fluency and expressiveness. *Journal of Experimental Child Psychology, 60*(3), 428–454.

Young, A., Bowers, P., & MacKinnon, G. (1996). Effects of prosodic modeling and repeated reading on poor readers' fluency and comprehension. *Applied Psycholinguistics, 17*(1), 59–84.

Zervas, P., Fakotakis, N., & Kokkinakis, G. (2008). Development and evaluation of a prosodic database for Greek speech synthesis and research. *Journal of Quantitative Linguistics, 15*(2), 154–184.

Zutell, J., & Rasinski, T. V. (1991). Training teachers to attend to their students' oral reading fluency. *Theory into Practice, 30*(3), 211–217.

# 4

# The Importance of Adolescent Fluency

David D. Paige

After a slight dip in scores during the first decade of the new century, National Assessment of Educational Progress (NAEP; National Center for Education Statistics, 2009) results for eighth-grade reading achievement increased in 2009 to the identical score reported for 1998! NAEP results distinguish among three levels of performance, where the basic level indicates only partial mastery of the literacy skills necessary to perform at grade level. A score of proficient or better represents command of literacy skills necessary to understand challenging subject matter and is akin to grade-level performance or better. A critical look at the NAEP (National Center for Education Statistics, 2009) results reveals that just 35% of eighth-grade students scored at or above proficient, indicating grade-level or better attainment. This leaves some 65%, almost two-thirds, scoring below proficient, and from this group some 38.5% scored below basic, which accounts for more than one in every three eighth graders. When attention is turned to the nation's 18 largest urban districts, 37% of students scored below basic, 42% at basic, and just 22% at proficient or better (National Center for Education Statistics, 2010).

Clearly, reading achievement at the eighth-grade level suggests that the majority of students will not be able to process adequately more advanced texts in high school thus leading to inadequate preparedness for college and career-readiness that will be part of the Common Core Standards (National Governors Association Center for Best Practices and Council of Chief State School Officers, 2010). A look at the Common Core State Standards reveals that the comprehension of complex tests will be emphasized. Complex texts are those that contain one or more of four qualitative dimensions that make them particularly challenging to students. Appendix B of the standards provides text exemplars of complex texts across grade levels. For example, in complex texts the story structure may be unfamiliar to the reader or the language demands (vocabulary load and sentence structure) might require advanced knowledge. Complex texts may also require specific domains of knowledge in order to be fully understood, or they may require interpretation from multiple levels or perspectives rather than a singular point of view. All of these factors make a text more difficult to understand. Unfortunately, the current level of reading achievement as measured by NAEP (National Center for Education Statistics, 2009) does not suggest that students will encounter such texts with success.

Results from NAEP (National Center for Education Statistics, 2009) are confirmed by other studies suggesting that only one-third of high school graduates are ready for college-level reading (American College Testing, 2010). A recent longitudinal study by Lee (2010) that analyzed results from the NAEP, the Comprehensive Test of Basic Skills, and Terra Nova assessments conducted over the last 28 years found that while reading achievement of fourth graders has increased by about 3 months, achievement at the eighth-grade level has stalled while high school achievement level has actually decreased by 1 year. This evidence strongly suggests that our adolescents are not gaining the skills necessary to achieve at a high level in an environment that is demanding increasingly expanded literacy skills.

One hypothesis to explain this low level of adolescent literacy achievement is that too many students lack fluency with texts. This chapter examines recent research illuminating the importance of reading fluency in the middle and secondary grades. I also discuss the relationships among reading fluency, comprehension, and academic achievement and share new studies that highlight the importance of prosody (reading with expression) and its contribution to reading comprehension. To assist with classroom instruction, I present the strategies of read-alouds and whole-class choral reading and discuss how they can be applied across content areas to build needed fluency (and comprehension) in middle and high school students.

## READING FLUENCY IN RELATION TO ACHIEVEMENT

The relationship between fluency and comprehension of text has been well established (Fuchs, Fuchs, Hosp, & Jenkins, 2001; Jenkins, Fuchs, Espin, van den Broek, & Deno, 2000; Kuhn & Stall, 2003; Pinnell et al., 1995;

Schatschneider et al., 2004; Strecker, Roser, & Martinez, 1998). However, although the fluent reading of text appears to aid comprehension, it does not necessarily cause it. Why is this? Simply identifying that a "relationship" exists between fluency and comprehension does little to explain their codependency, even though teachers and researchers have known for over 100 years that the two are intertwined (Huey, 1968). Rasinski (2000) has pointed out that reading at an adequate pace has a very practical purpose in completing reading in and out of school and plays a role in warding off reader frustration brought on by a languid and labored reading rate, which may result in the reader just giving up. Going beyond these important considerations, what is the essence of the relationship between reading fluency and comprehension? Let's consider a developmental perspective of fluency.

Paris (2005) proposed that many of the subprocesses, or indicators, involved in decoding text are, in fact, constrained skills. In other words, once an individual has achieved proficiency with the skill, there is really little room for additional growth or competency increase. An obvious example of this is letter naming, where the ability to fluently read each of the 26 letters of the alphabet in uppercase and lowercase does not considerably improve once the reader has it mastered. Although not all reading skills are constrained to the same extent, all do require a minimum level of proficiency to enable competent reading. In this regard, Paris and Hamilton (2009) recently proposed that some minimum level of proficiency with various reading subskills—what they refer to as a "threshold" (p. 46)—appears to be critical. Consider again the example of letter knowledge, where almost complete and accurate knowledge is required as a minimum to enable decoding of letter blends and words. Another example is the threshold of approximately 90% decoding accuracy below which a text is considered to be at the "frustration" level for the reader. Accuracy below this minimum threshold means that both reading rate and word accuracy are diminished to the extent that very little comprehension occurs.

A third example is the threshold of oral reading fluency rates at about the 50th percentile. This translates into approximately 150 correct-words-per-minute for an eighth-grade student reading grade-level texts (Hasbrouck & Tindal, 2006). Readers significantly below this threshold level often struggle with both reading fluency and text comprehension. Working toward achieving a minimum threshold with grade-level text is necessary to ensure that readers progress to a developmental level that will result in eventual reading proficiency. At the same time, working to artificially increase fluency beyond adequate rates can be counterproductive to comprehension. With oral reading fluency, conversational rates are just right. Nonetheless, adequate fluency does not ensure comprehension, particularly as readers progress through middle school. This is due to factors beyond fluency such as background knowledge, working memory constraints, vocabulary knowledge, and metacognition.

As one progresses through the acquisition of reading subskills from phonemic awareness and knowledge of the alphabetic principle to application of the knowledge of various letter blends and their constituent sounds, to automatic whole-word and phrase recognition, and finally to fluent reading of connected text with prosody and comprehension, the degree to which these skills are constrained relaxes. Take, for example, the third-grade reader who is fluent with grade-level text and reads with acceptable prosody and comprehension. Automaticity theory (LaBerge & Samuels, 1974; Logan, 1988) suggests that because this reader is fluent with grade-level text, all applicable subskills are also automatic and so have reached their threshold or level of constraint. This means the reader can use much of his or her cognitive resources for comprehension processing. At the same time, fluency with third-grade narrative text does not guarantee that the reader will be fluent several years later, for example, with seventh-grade expository text. The threshold levels for fluency increase as readers progress through the grades. If skills are not continually developed across grades through sufficient experience and practice with a variety of increasingly difficult and varied texts, fluency and comprehension development can stall. Evidence discussed shortly suggests that readers who do not continue to develop threshold levels of fluency as they proceed through school experience insufficient fluency and less than desirable comprehension.

## FLUENCY SKILLS IN STRUGGLING ADOLESCENTS

Considering the NAEP (National Center for Education Statistics, 2009, 2010) results reviewed earlier, the implication is that the literacy issues experienced by U.S. eighth-grade students revolve solely around comprehension. Given what we know about the relationship between oral reading fluency and comprehension, and framing that within the notion of threshold levels (Paris & Hamilton, 2009), it is reasonable to suspect that fluency skills may be inadequate in many adolescent students to fully support comprehension processing. If inadequate fluency skills are, in fact, part of the comprehension issue, this would more fully inform policymakers and educators on the underlying factors that exert downward pressure on NAEP results. An example of such an inquiry to determine the effect of fluency on NAEP results is a study by Pinnell et al. (1995) that found that 44% of fourth-grade students who were assessed as dysfluent with grade-level stories also exhibited poor comprehension on the NAEP assessment. Knowing that practice with increasingly difficult text is necessary to build fluency with advanced text types and structures, it seems logical that if a large proportion of students are dysfluent in the fourth grade, perhaps many of these same students are still disfluent in later grades (Nicholson & Fawcett, 1990; Seidenberg & McClelland, 1989; Snow, Burns, & Griffin, 1998), especially since fluency is not an instructional priority in the intermediate grades and beyond.

To assess the degree to which adolescent students read fluently in middle school, Paige (2011c) tested 227 sixth- and seventh-grade students using the Gray Oral Reading Test–4 (Wiederholt & Bryant, 2001). Their results, graphed in Figure 4.1, show clearly that students who struggle with fluency tend to exhibit poor comprehension and that as fluency skills improve, so does comprehension. Additionally, of the 227 students tested, about two-thirds struggled with both fluency and comprehension. The empirical data suggest that these struggling readers may have yet to approach an adequate threshold level of fluency, and as a result comprehension is negatively affected. Although the reason for these poor fluency outcomes cannot be stated with certainty, the data do suggest a developmental trajectory at the middle school level that will be inadequate to reach acceptable literacy achievement in high school if reading outcomes do not drastically improve.

So what is the level of fluency achievement at the high school level? Do the relationships between fluency and comprehension seen in middle school still exist? To answer these questions, Paige and Magpuri-Lavell (2011) studied the fluency and comprehension skills of 83 ninth-grade students attending a struggling, metropolitan, high-poverty, urban high

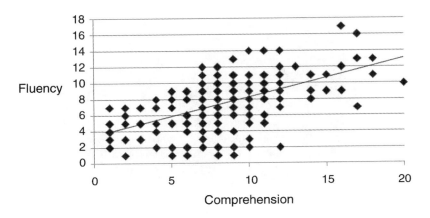

**FIGURE 4.1.** The relationship between fluency and comprehension in middle school students.

school, again using a variety of standardized measures. Results showed that fluency attainment was at the sixth-grade level with comprehension about 1 year below that. Large differences were found between European American and African American students, with the former greatly outperforming the latter but both performing significantly below grade level. To gain additional insight into the oral reading fluency of ninth graders, Paige, Rasinski, and Magpuri-Lavell (2011) measured the prosody of 108 ninth-grade students using the Multidimensional Fluency Scale (Zutell & Rasinski, 1991). Results showed that students were at best semi-prosodic with grade-level narrative text. Additional regression results (Figure 4.2) found that word recognition accuracy predicted 44.1% of total variance in reading comprehension. Prosody predicted an additional 8.8% of the variance in comprehension, suggesting that students who read with expression are better at comprehending what they have read than those who possess poorer prosody. Reading rate was not a significant predictor of comprehension, indicating that reading fast is not what aids comprehension, rather, students who decode accurately and can interpret what they read as evidenced by expressive reading seem to comprehend best.

The significance of both the middle and high school results are twofold. First, achieving grade-level competency with reading fluency is still very important to becoming a competent adolescent reader. Fluency was shown to account for about half of the variance in reading comprehension in both middle and high school struggling readers. This suggests that it cannot be assumed that because students are adolescents they have devel-

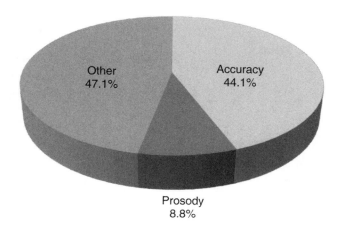

**FIGURE 4.2.** The percentage of variance in word identification accuracy and prosody in ninth-grade reading comprehension.

oped appropriate fluency with grade-level texts. Second, prosody emerges as a significant indicator of oral reading fluency that contributes additional and unique variance to reading comprehension. This has important implications for the development of prosody in readers because it suggests that students with greater prosody comprehend at a higher level.

In their review of the fluency research, Kuhn, Schwanenflugel, and Meisinger (2010) suggest that it is very likely that prosody and comprehension are related. The results of our research suggests that it is. Why might this be?

One reason for the connection between prosody and comprehension may involve working memory. It has been hypothesized that prosody provides the reader with a greater ability to hold an auditory sequence such as a phrase or a sentence in working memory (Frazier, Carlton, & Clifton, 2006; Swets, Desmet, Hambrick, & Ferreira, 2007). This may provide the reader with an advantage in processing textual details beyond that where words are simply encoded one after another with no expression.

A second insight is presented by Erekson (2010), who suggests that prosody enables interpretation of text in two ways. The first is through syntactic prosody, which reflects the effective phrasal interpretation of text such as the correct parsing of words into appropriate phrases and the directing of attention to prosodic markers such as pausing for commas and stopping at periods. Erekson also suggests that a second type of prosody, emphatic prosody, enables improved comprehension. Emphatic prosody encourages text processing beyond that of syntactic or phrasal processing and aids inferential thinking. Erekson explains, for example, that emphatic prosody occurs when a reader is able to apply context to the interpretation of a character's motives and the subsequent voice that is used by the author within the text. This suggests that while the reader already comprehends the text, information gleaned from embedded contextual cues allows for a deeper, more meaningful interpretation. To take this to another level of analysis, consider the work of Vygotsky (1968), who discusses the idea that egocentric speech guides inner thought. Erekson (2010) compares emphatic prosody to Vygotsky's egocentric speech and raises the notion that the former may work to guide the reader during the interpretation of the text and thus provides insight into his or her inner thinking. This layer of cognitive processing, reflected in the reader's interpretation of context and social inference of the story characters, is very much a top-down form of processing.

The evidence presented here suggests that readers who are fluent (word recognition accuary and prosodic reading) with grade-level text gain a comprehension advantage over those who are less fluent. These results indicate that teaching students to read with prosody can potentially pay off with improved comprehension. The points discussed here also lead to the conceptualization that oral reading fluency, when properly defined as including prosody along with the indicators of rate and accuracy, is an interactive process composed of both bottom-up subskill processing and top-down comprehension processing and interpretation of text. Finally, the evidence strongly suggests that an optimal reading rate should simply be a conversational rate; fluency improvement lies in accurate word identification and appropriate prosody. The idea that fluency is reading the text fast with little to no regard for both accuracy and prosody is an incorrect conceptualization of the fluency construct.

## FLUENCY STRATEGIES FOR ADOLESCENTS

What strategies encourage oral reading fluency in adolescent readers by incorporating appropriate reading rate, word identification accuracy, and prosody? Although there are many (see Rasinski, 2010), I discuss two that can be particularly tailored to encourage development of all three indicators of fluent reading. Read-alouds, a familiar strategy in the elementary grades, can be adapted for adolescent readers, and whole-class choral reading has been found to encourage fluent reading with both narrative and expository text.

### Read-Alouds

A popular strategy recommended by authors for adolescent readers is read-alouds (Fisher & Frey, 2008). While read-alouds have been recommended for young readers for some time (Reutzel & Cooter, 2012), evidence suggests that this strategy is beneficial for adolescent readers as well, particularly in terms of developing a positive attitude toward reading (Herrold, Stanchfield, & Serabian, 1989; Ivey & Broaddus, 2001). Read-alouds have also been found to be useful for teaching students effective reading prosody and for building comprehension across content areas (Albright & Ariail, 2005; Irvin, Lunstrum, Lynch-Brown, & Shepard, 1995; Richardson & Gross, 1997).

So how can a read-aloud strategy be implemented with adolescents? What might this strategy look and sound like in a middle or high school classroom? Let's begin by considering how read-alouds can assist students with hearing and developing appropriate prosody, or what I call the rhythm of the words and what Rasinski, Rikli, and Johnston (2009) refer to as "the melodic element in reading" (p. 351). Although text contains prosodic markers such as commas, periods, question marks, and quotations, these are often not completely sufficient for a prosodic reading of the text. To guide and teach students about the nature of prosodic reading, teachers must model multiple readings of various texts that demonstrate to students what prosodic reading—that is, the rhythm of the words—sounds like. In demonstrating the rhythm of the words for students, Trelease (2001) suggests that teachers can make use of a variety of inflections that reflect mood changes and attitudinal stances in story characters, what was discussed earlier as emphatic prosody. Before beginning to model an expressive reading to students, teachers can explain how they determine what type of vocal tone, inflection, or stance to utilize and why it assists in understanding the text. Beck and McKeown (2001) explain that such readings assist students with understanding decontextualized text, that is, written language. Many students may need help with developing prosody because text seldom contains sufficient prosodic markers, forcing readers to make interpretative judgments regarding the intentions of the writer.

Natural questions at this point might center on how to select an appropriate book or passage to read to students and on the length of the reading. Rasinski (2010) offers several suggestions. First, select books or readings that you personally like, because you want to be certain that your enthusiasm for the text comes through in your reading. Second, a read-aloud is a great time to stretch or expand the reading range of your students, so you may want to consider books that students would not normally select for themselves. Finally, the reading you select should provide a connection to what you are teaching in the classroom. A resource to help with choosing a selection by content area is offered by Richardson (2000). The length of the reading can vary widely but generally runs from 10 to 30 minutes (Rasinski, 2010).

After the read-aloud is completed, engaging students in discussion or response to the text to build meaning and understanding becomes important. This can take various forms, ranging from an open class discussion that might be guided by critical open-ended questions from the teacher (Beck & McKeown, 2001) to written response. Discussion might also focus on how the teacher is able to communicate a more enhanced meaning through her or his use of prosody while reading. Other response forms could involve visual sketches or drawings and physical responses such as movement or pantomime (Rasinski, 2010).

## Whole-Class Choral Reading

Whereas much of the reading in the elementary setting is oral in nature (Brenner, Hiebert, & Tompkins, 2009), it is safe to say that silent reading predominates in the middle and high school grades (Hiebert, Wilson, & Trainin, 2010). Research suggests that for students with an adequate ability to decode text, independent reading helps to further develop and enhance not only decoding skills but also vocabulary and comprehension (Cunningham, Perry, Stanovich, & Share, 2002; Share, 1995; Share & Stanovich, 1995). However, for students who lack adequate decoding skills, silent reading may be difficult (Walker, 2008), and as a result, they may not participate in independent reading activities (Fisher, 2004; Reutzel & Cooter, 2012). Students who struggle or are reluctant to read often require closer interaction or collaboration in order to be successful (Guthrie & Wigfield, 2000). One interactive strategy that has been found to be effective in the middle grades is whole-class choral reading (WCCR), where both the teacher and the students read aloud from the same text at the same time (Paige, 2011a, 2011b). WCCR taps into the extrinsic or performance aspect of reading and can be used to create interest in reading on the part of the students.

Paige (2011a) implemented WCCR with sixth-grade students at a middle school in the southeast United States, where approximately 89% of the students were of African American ethnicity and the rest were European American, Hispanic, or Asian. About 43% of students qualified for free- or reduced-priced lunch. WCCR was implemented 5 days a week for 6 weeks. A repeated reading regimen was used where students read the same text each day of the week, with a new text introduced each Monday. Particular attention was paid to the amount of time students spent reading during WCCR. The weekly average time spent reading was 16 minutes. Posttest results showed significant improvement by the WCCR group over the comparison group in the area of phonological decoding and oral reading fluency, with effect sizes of $d = 0.50$ for decoding and $d = 0.64$ for fluency, suggesting large improvements. These results provide support for the notion that students with reasonable decoding knowledge (45th percentile for decoding proficiency) but inadequate fluency (31st percentile) can benefit from monitored reading practice provided by WCCR. It was also found that students generally liked WCCR because it provided them with a means to improve their reading without having to be singled out to read in front of others. This "tent of anonymity" (Paige, 2011a, p. 13) appears to be a feature of WCCR that is important to students and their subsequent success with the strategy, particularly those who struggle the most with fluency.

The implementation of WCCR is very flexible, and it can be used across content areas to increase the time that students actually spend reading text (Paige, 2008). Texts from science, social studies or history, English language arts, and even math can be used to help students gain more time reading, increase familiarity and proficiency with more complicated texts, recognize and decode content vocabulary, and acquire background and subject knowledge. WCCR can benefit both readers who struggle with grade-level reading and are in need of fluency improvement as well as proficient readers, who gain additional practice with grade-level text and the acquisition of background knowledge of the content.

To begin implementation of WCCR, the teacher selects an appropriate text, preferably one that is closely related to the classroom curriculum (see Paige 2011a, 2011b, for a list of implementation steps). With modifications for phrases such as "In Figure 1," "In the chart below," and so on, text can come directly from the textbook. Trade books that are closely aligned with the curriculum are another excellent source and often require fewer modifications. Such books often provide the reader with additional knowledge about the topic while using the same vocabulary. For the middle and secondary grades, the text prepared for WCCR should be about 250 to 300 words long, which equates to roughly a 2- to 2.5-minute reading.

WCCR can be implemented using the method of repeated reading (Rasinski, 1989; Samuels, 1979), where students reread the same text several times in order to increase automaticity with specific words and phrases, resulting in overall fluency with the text. The Wide Reading method (Kuhn et al., 2006), where several different but very similar texts are read throughout the week, is another option that has been shown to be effective in young readers and can also be effective with adolescents. Regardless of the method, the important characteristic of WCCR is that the teacher, by reading the text aloud in unison with the class, is providing monitored support to students through the modeling of correct pronunciation, appropriate reading rate, and prosodic reading.

Once a text has been selected, the teacher should prepare by previewing it for difficult words and phrases. When preparing the text, the teacher can, for example, highlight in boldface the words that are anticipated to be difficult for some students to decode. These words can be reviewed with the class before reading begins. Toward this end, the teacher can, for example, point out each word and have students repeat it after he or she has pronounced it aloud for the class. Sometimes several repetitions of the word may be required so that all students are given an opportunity to recognize the word by sight.

Before the class reads the text together, the teacher can activate prior knowledge about the general theme of the text to aid comprehension. The teacher then models the passage by reading aloud while students follow along with their copy. In doing so, students hear what good reading sounds like, gain a preview of the text and the words they may find difficult, and learn what a prosodic reading of the text should sound like.

After the text has been modeled for the class, the teacher can tell the students that "we will read this passage aloud and with one voice, like a choir," letting the class know that the goal is eventually to read the passage together perfectly, so that all become better readers. At this point, pushback from some students can be expected, because the one thing poor readers do not want to do is read. In this event, the teacher should simply continue implementation of the strategy. The next step is to begin the class reading the passage together, not an easy task because students seldom read a passage aloud in unison. One simple method to get everyone started together is to give a 3-2-1 countdown, after which everyone commences reading. It may take two or three times to get a class started at the same time, but the students will catch on quickly. Once the reading begins, students must follow the teacher's voice, meaning they cannot read ahead of the teacher. The teacher's voice should be thought of as the class metronome that keeps everyone on time and in sync. The text should be read in a conversational manner because this will assist poor readers in maintaining the pace. It may actually be necessary to read the passage at a slightly slower rate than normal so that all can keep up. It is important for the teacher to be standing and to read the passage in a voice that all can hear. During the reading, the teacher should walk about the room to monitor student reading. While leading the reading, it is important for the teacher to listen carefully to the class for misread words, difficult phrases, and student inattention to the prosodic cues in the text. After several readings, student fluency will improve and the teacher can gradually pull back on the vocal volume of reading to allow the class to take the lead. This is an application of the gradual-release-of-responsibility model (Pearson, 1985; Pearson & Gallagher, 1983) in fluency instruction.

By Thursday, students may have mastered the text well enough for the teacher to introduce some variety into the strategy. One method, called antiphonal reading, involves the teacher and students switching reading of sentences. Another action is to split the class into two sections, with each taking turns reading alternating sentences. Echo reading, where the teacher reads a sentence and the students "echo" each sentence until the entire passage has been read, can also be implemented. An idea that captures both student attention and motivation is to audio record the class reading the text on Monday and then again on Friday (Paige, 2006). After recording the text on Monday, play it back for students. After some initial laughing has subsided, a serious teaching opportunity around the characteristics of fluent reading can take place. For instance, ask students how the reading could be improved and guide their thinking to focus on specific elements of reading such as rate, pronunciation, phrasing, and prosody. After listening to the Friday recording, students will notice that they have improved substantially. To help bring this improvement to the full attention of students, it may be helpful to replay the Monday recording immediately followed by the Friday version.

## FINAL THOUGHTS ON ADOLESCENT FLUENCY
## AND COMPLEX TEXTS

This chapter has highlighted the struggle that adolescents encounter with fluent reading and the subsequent comprehension of text. This leads to three vexing questions. First, with proper assessment and instruction around fluency, what percentage of adolescents can potentially become fluent, grade-level readers through high school? Second, what is the potential capacity for schools to increase reading fluency to adequate threshold levels in middle and high school students who arrive with less than proficient fluency? Third, what resources must be leveraged and what systems put in place in order for schools to achieve across-grade fluency in adolescents? These are pressing issues as the approaching implementation and assessment of the Common Core State Standards will require students to be sufficiently fluent to read and understand the complex texts that this curriculum will present. It is only through knowledgeable and dedicated teachers and leaders that the answers to these questions can be found, and the stakes could not be higher.

This brings me to two considerations about the current state of fluency instruction. First, the present level of instructional intensity around fluent reading in the middle and secondary levels appears less than adequate to create fluent readers. If this statement were false, classrooms would be filled with fluent readers, and evidence suggests they are not. Second, developing fluent reading in dysfluent adolescents must extend beyond the doors of primary grade teachers and reading and English/language arts teachers in upper elementary grades and beyond. Herein is where potential hope resides. The majority of adolescents are not disabled readers, because they have acquired fundamental reading skills that can be improved. The problem is that students have not practiced these skills sufficiently to ensure fluent reading with increasingly difficult texts, and declining motivation for reading in adolescence makes them less likely to want to read. Some of these adolescents may have at one time been fluent readers. Unfortunately, instructional and assessment systems as well as curricular emphasis across grades have not sufficiently monitored the continued development of reading skills to ensure attainment of appropriate threshold levels throughout the adolescent grades. This suggests that district and school leaders must work with literacy experts, teacher leaders, and indeed the entire faculty to develop and implement fluency assessment and monitoring systems across the continuum of grades to ensure that each student develops adequate fluency with a variety of increasingly difficult texts. Again, why such a call? A preponderance of data shows that the majority of our students are unable to comprehend grade-level texts. What has been implemented in the past has not been successful for enough students. Indeed, it is time now for the implementation of comprehensive fluency instructional and monitoring systems that all teachers can both "own" and feel responsibility for. Anything less will look like what we have now, which is currently failing too many students.

## REFERENCES

Albright, L. K., & Ariail, M. (2005). Tapping the potential of teacher read-aloud in middle schools. *Journal of Adult and Adolescent Literacy, 48*, 582–591.

American College Testing. (2010). *The condition of college & career readiness 2010.* Retrieved from *www.act.org/research/policymakers/cccr10/pdf/ConditionofCollegeandCareerReadiness2010.pdf.*

Anderman, E. M., & Maehr, M. L. (1994). Motivation and schooling in the middle grades. *Review of Educational Research, 64*, 287–309.

Beck, I. L., & McKeown, M. G. (2001). Text talk: Capturing the benefits of read-aloud experiences for young children. *The Reading Teacher, 55*, 10–20.

Brenner, D., Hiebert, E. H., & Tompkins. R. (2009). How much and what are third graders reading? Reading in core programs. In E. H. Hiebert (Ed.), *Reading more, reading better* (pp. 118–140). New York: Guilford Press.

Cunningham, K. E., Perry, K. E., Stanovich, K. E., & Share, D. L. (2002). Orthographic learning during reading: Examining the role of self-teaching. *Journal of Experimental Child Psychology, 82*(3), 185–199.

Erekson, J. A. (2010). Prosody and interpretation. *Reading Horizons, 50*(2), 80–98.

Fisher, D. (2004). Setting the "opportunity to read" standard: Resuscitating the SSR program in an urban high school. *Journal of Adolescent and Adult Literacy, 48*(2), 138–150.

Fisher, D., & Frey, N. (2008). *Improving adolescent literacy: Content area strategies at work.* Upper Saddle River, NJ: Pearson.

Frazier, L., Carlton, K., & Clifton, C. (2006). Prosodic phrasing is central to language comprehension. *Trends in Cognitive Sciences, 10*(6), 244–249.

Fuchs, L. S., Fuchs, D., Hosp, M. K., & Jenkins, J. R. (2001). Oral reading fluency as an indicator or reading competence: A theoretical, empirical, and historical analysis. *Scientific Studies of Reading, 5*(3), 239–256.

Guthrie, J. T., & Wigfield, A. (2000). Engagement and motivation in reading. In M. L. Kamil, P. B. Mosenthal, P. D. Pearson, & R. Barr (Eds.), *Handbook of reading research* (Vol. III, pp. 403–422). Mahwah, NJ: Erlbaum.

Hasbrouck, J., & Tindal, G. A (2006). Oral reading fluency norms: A valuable assessment tool for reading teachers. *The Reading Teacher, 59*(7), 636–644.

Herrold, W. G., Jr., Stanchfield, J., & Serabian, A. J. (1989). Comparison of the effect of a middle school, literature-based listening program on male and female attitudes toward reading. *Educational Research Quarterly, 13*(4), 43–46.

Hiebert, E. H., Wilson, K. M., & Trainin, G. (2010). Are students really reading in independent reading contexts? An examination of comprehension-based silent reading rate. In E. H. Hiebert & D. R. Reutzel (Eds.), *Revisiting silent reading: New directions for teachers and researchers* (pp. 151–167). Newark, DE: International Reading Association.

Huey, E. B. (1968). *The psychology and pedagogy of reading; with a review of the history of reading and writing and of methods, texts, and hygiene in reading.* Cambridge, MA: MIT Press. (Original work published 1908)

Irvin, J. L., Lunstrum, J. P., Lynch-Brown, C., & Shepard, M. F. (1995). *Enhancing social studies through literacy strategies* (Bulletin, 91). Washington, DC: National Council for the Social Studies.

Ivey, G., & Broaddus, K. (2001). "Just plain reading": A survey of what makes students want to read in middle school classrooms. *Reading Research Quarterly, 36*, 350–377.

Jenkins, J. R., Fuchs, L. S., Espin, C., van den Broek, P., & Deno, S. L. (2000). Accuracy and fluency in list and context reading of skilled and RD groups: Absolute and relative performance. *Learning Disabilities: Research and Practice, 18*(4), 237–245.

Kuhn, M. R., Schwanenflugel, P. J., & Meisinger, E. B. (2010). Aligning theory and assessment of reading fluency: Automaticity, prosody, and definitions of fluency. *Reading Research Quarterly, 45*(2), 230–251.

Kuhn, M. R., Schwanenflugel, P. J., Morris, R. D., Morrow, L. M., Woo, D. G., Meisinger, E. B., et al. (2006). Teaching children to become fluent and automatic readers. *Journal of Literacy Research, 38*(4), 357–387.

Kuhn, M. R., & Stahl, S. A. (2003). Fluency: A review of developmental and remedial practices. *Journal of Educational Psychology, 95*(1), 3–21.

LaBerge, D., & Samuels, S. J. (1974). Toward a theory of automatic information processing in reading. *Cognitive Psychology, 6*, 293–323.

Lee, J. (2010). Tripartite growth trajectories of reading and math achievement: Tracking national academic progress at primary, middle, and high school levels. *American Educational Research Journal, 47*(4), 800–832.

Logan, G. D. (1988). Toward an instance theory of automatization. *Psychological Review, 95*(4), 492–527.

National Center for Education Statistics. (2009). *The nation's report card: Reading 2009* (NCES 2010-458). Washington, DC: Institute of Education Sciences, U.S. Department of Education.

National Center for Education Statistics. (2010). *The nation's report card: Trial urban district assessment reading 2009* (NCES 2010–459). Institute of Education Sciences, Washington, DC: U.S. Department of Education.

National Governors Association Center for Best Practices and Council of Chief State School Officers. (2010). *Common Core State Standards initiative.* Retrieved on March 1, 2011, from *www.corestandards.org/Files/K12ELAStandards. pdf/K12ELA*

Nicholson, R. I., & Fawcett, A. J. (1990). Automaticity: A new framework for dyslexia research? *Cognition, 35*(2), 159–182.

Paige, D. D. (2006). Increasing fluency in disabled middle school readers: Repeated reading utilizing above grade level reading passages. *Reading Horizons, 46*(3), 167–182.

Paige, D. D. (2008). *An evaluation of whole-class choral reading using science text on oral reading fluency in struggling adolescents.* Unpublished doctoral dissertation, University of Memphis.

Paige, D. D. (2011a). 16 minutes of "eyes-on-text" can make a difference: Whole-class choral reading as an adolescent reading strategy. *Reading Horizons, 51*(1), 1–20.

Paige, D. D. (2011b). "That sounded good!": Using whole-class choral reading to improve fluency. *The Reading Teacher, 64*(6), 435–438.

Paige, D. D. (2011c). Engaging struggling adolescent readers through situational interest: A model proposing the relationships among extrinsic motivation, oral reading fluency, comprehension, and academic achievement. *Reading Psychology, 32*(5), 395–425.

Paige, D. D., & Magpuri-Lavell, T. (2011). Unpacking adolescent literacy skills in a high-poverty, urban high school: A study of ninth-grade literacy skills. *Yearbook of the Association of Literacy Educators and Researchers* (Vol. 33).

Paige, D. D., Rasinski, T. V., & Magpuri-Lavell, T. (in press). Is fluent expressive reading important for high school readers? *Journal of Adult and Adolescent Literacy.*

Paris, S. G. (2005). Reinterpreting the development of reading skills. *Reading Research Quarterly, 40*(2), 184–202.

Paris, S. G., & Hamilton, E. E. (2009). The development of children's reading comprehension. In S. E. Israel & G. G. Duffy (Eds.), *Handbook of research on reading comprehension* (pp. 32–53). New York: Routledge.

Pearson, P. D. (1985). Changing the face of reading comprehension instruction. *The Reading Teacher, 38*(8), 724–738.

Pearson, P. D., & Gallagher, M. C. (1983). The instruction of reading comprehension. *Contemporary Educational Psychology, 8*(3), 317–344.

Pinnell, G. S., Pikulski, J. J., Wixon, K. K., Campbell, J. R., Gough, P. B., & Beatty, A. S. (1995). *Listening to children read aloud.* Washington, DC: Office of Educational Research and Improvement, U.S. Department of Education.

Rasinski, T. V. (1989). Fluency for everyone: Incorporating fluency instruction in the classroom. *The Reading Teacher, 42*, 690–693.

Rasinski, T. V. (2000). Speed does matter in reading. *The Reading Teacher, 54*, 146–151.

Rasinski, T. V. (2010). *The fluent reader: Oral and silent reading strategies for building word recognition, fluency, and comprehension* (2nd ed.). New York: Scholastic.

Rasinski, T. V., Rikli, A., & Johnston, S. (2009). Reading fluency: More than automaticity? More than a concern for the primary grades. *Literacy Research and Instruction, 48*(4), 350–361.

Reutzel, D. R., & Cooter, R. B., Jr. (2012). *Teaching children to read: The teacher makes the difference* (6th ed.). Boston, MA: Pearson.

Richardson, J. S. (2000). *Read it aloud! Using literature in the secondary content classroom.* Newark, DE: International Reading Association.

Richardson, J. S., & Gross, E. (1997). A read-aloud for mathematics. *Journal of Adolescent and Adult Literacy, 40*, 492–494.

Samuels, S. J. (1979). The method of repeated readings. *The Reading Teacher, 32,* 403–408.

Schatschneider, C., Buck, J., Torgesen, J. K., Wagner, R. K., Hassler, L., Hecht, S., et al. (2004). *A multivariate study of factors that contribute to individual differences in performance on the Florida Comprehensive Reading Assessment Test* (Technical Report No. 5). Tallahassee: Florida Center for Reading Research.

Seidenberg, M., & McClelland, J. (1989). A distributed, developmental model of word          recognition and naming. *Psychological Review, 96,* 523–568.

Share, D. L. (1995). Phonological recoding and self-teaching: Sine qua non of reading acquisition. *Cognition, 55,* 151–218.

Share, D. L., & Stanovich, K. E. (1995). Cognitive processes in early reading development: Accommodating individual differences into a model of acquisition. *Issues in Education, 1,* 1–57.

Snow, C. E., Burns, M. S., & Griffin, P. (1998). *Preventing reading difficulties in young children.* Washington, DC: National Academy Press.

Strecker, S. K., Roser, N. L., & Martinez, M. G. (1998). Understanding oral reading fluency. In T. Shanahan & F. V. Rodriquez-Brown (Eds.), *47th yearbook of the National Reading Conference* (pp. 295–310). Chicago: National Reading Conference.

Swets, B., Desmet, T., Hambrick, D. Z., & Ferreira, F. (2007). The role of working memory in syntactic ambiguity resolution: A psychometric approach. *Journal of Experimental Psychology, General, 136*(1), 64–81.

Trelease, J. (2001). *The read-aloud handbook* (5th ed.). New York: Penguin.

Vygotsky, L. S. (1968). *Thought and language* (9th ed.) (A. Kozulin Trans.). Cambridge, MA: MIT Press.

Walker, B. J. (2008). *Diagnostic teaching of reading: Techniques for instruction and assessment* (6th ed.). Upper Saddle River, NJ: Pearson/Merrill Prentice Hall.

Wiederholt, J. L., & Bryant, B. R. (2001). *Gray Oral Reading Test* (4th ed.). Austin, TX: PRO-ED.

Zutell, J., & Rasinski, T. V. (1991). Training teachers to attend to their students' oral reading fluency. *Theory into Practice, 30*(3), 211–217.

# 5

# Reading Fluency Revisited
## *Much More Than Fast and Accurate Reading*

Barbara J. Walker
Kouider Mokhtari
Stephan Sargent

In this chapter, we underscore the crucial role of *reading comprehension* as an underlying goal of fluent reading. We argue that, unlike emergent and developing readers, truly fluent readers possess sufficiently well-developed capacities (e.g., able to read words accurately, with appropriate pace, and expression) to read fluently and with comprehension. Although these essential capacities are not synonymous with fluent reading, they play a crucial role in reading ability in that they enable readers to devote the necessary and sufficient attention to the most critical task of reading: comprehending what they read. In support of this argument, we begin by briefly reviewing three different yet complementary views of the complex construct of fluent reading. We then present a set of assessment measures for determining students' reading fluency skills. Finally, we highlight a few instructional strategies aimed at enhancing the reading fluency and comprehension of struggling readers in clinical or classroom settings.

Reading fluency has gained much deserved recognition and attention, especially during the past two decades. Contributing factors to the resurgence of reading fluency include, but are not limited to, (1) calls by prominent researchers for more attention to the role of reading fluency in learning to read (e.g., Allington, 2009); (2) research reports such as "Preventing Reading Difficulties in Young Children" (Snow, Burns, & Griffin, 1998) that emphasize the need for reading fluency to be an important goal for reading assessment and instruction; (3) assessment research reports such as

"Listening to Children Read Aloud" (Pinnell et al., 1995) that show that accurate word-decoding performance among many fourth-grade readers does not necessarily guarantee that students read fluently and with comprehension; (4) commissioned reports such as "Teaching Children to Read: An Evidence-Based Assessment of the Scientific Research Literature on Reading and Its Implications for Reading Instruction" (National Reading Panel, 2000), which identified reading fluency as one of five essential components of effective reading instruction and highlighted effective methods (e.g., repeated reading) for increasing students' word recognition, fluency, and reading comprehension across the grades; and (5) national surveys such as "What's Hot for 2009" (Cassidy & Cassidy, 2009), which reported reading fluency as a "very hot" topic by literacy leaders.

Undoubtedly, these reports have raised the level of awareness of the role of reading fluency in advancing students' reading development among policymakers, literacy researchers, and practitioners. More importantly, they have contributed a great deal to how reading instruction is viewed, assessed, and taught in public schools.

## FLUENCY AND COMPREHENSION

A key reason that reading fluency is viewed as a critical component of reading programs is that it is correlated with reading achievement outcomes, including reading comprehension (Rasinski, 2010). The ability to comprehend what one reads is, in our view, a reasonable expectation for fluent reading. Reading fluency has been associated with reading comprehension in a wide range of correlational and experimental research studies over the past two decades or so. Correlations of reading fluency and comprehension have been reported as high as .81 to .90 between oral reading fluency and reading comprehension. For instance, Pinnell et al. (1995) found that reading fluency was significantly correlated with overall reading proficiency; more fluent readers scored higher on the National Assessment of Educational Progress (NAEP) reading assessment. Fuchs, Fuchs, Hosp, and Jenkins (2001) found a strong association between fluency and comprehension ($r = .91$). Recently, Alt and Samuels (2011) argued that reading fluency assessments must not only assess the characteristics of speed, accuracy, and prosody but also explicitly assess reading comprehension.

## THREE VIEWS OF READING FLUENCY

The increased attention to reading fluency as a critical component of reading instruction has also resulted in greater scrutiny of the construct of "fluent reading," its assessment, and instruction among literacy theorists and researchers. In our review of the literature, we were able to identify at least three schools of thoughts with respect the construct of reading fluency and its role in reading ability. Although these approaches share a general understanding of the basic core components of reading fluency, namely word reading accuracy, reading rate, and expression or prosody, they seem to differ in significant ways with respect to the essential capacities that enable children to read fluently and with comprehension. However, each of these views offers a set of unique ideas, which help present a more complete understanding of fluent reading.

## Developmental View of Reading Fluency

The first view takes a "developmental" approach to reading fluency, its assessment, and instruction. Proponents of this view propose that reading fluency involves the acquisition of basic constituents of reading fluency (Armbruster, Lehr, & Osborn, 2001; Kuhn & Stahl, 2003). During initial reading, one element involves accuracy, including word identification and basic decoding skills, which readers must acquire if they are to mature into fluent readers. Another component is pace, which develops after numerous words can be read accurately and involves quickly connecting word forms and meaning (e.g., Daane, Campbell, Grigg, Goodman, & Oranje, 2005; Hudson, Lane, & Pullen, 2005). Readers in the upper elementary grades and beyond develop broader language skills, which contribute to reading with expression, an essential aspect that integrates fluency and comprehension (Kuhn, Schwanenflugel, & Meisinger, 2010).

An important premise of this view is that children develop fluency alongside comprehension. Children become more fluent as their text understanding increases and become better comprehenders as fluency increases. Rasinski (2004) suggested that "it may be helpful to think of reading fluency as a bridge between the two major components of reading—word decoding and comprehension. At one end of this bridge, fluency connects to accuracy and automaticity in decoding. At the other end, fluency connects to comprehension though prosody, or expressive interpretation" (p. 3). For most developing readers, the acquisition of basic decoding skills progresses in a slow, continuous fashion and often proceeds in successive stages. This view of how children develop into fluent readers has a long history in American reading instruction, and it remains an essential foundation for how reading fluency is viewed, assessed, and taught in schools.

## Linguistic View of Reading Fluency

The second view takes a linguistic approach to the construct of reading fluency. Proponents of this approach (e.g., Chafe, 1988; Chomsky, 1976;

Schreiber, 1980, 1987) place a great deal of emphasis on the role of language capabilities (e.g., awareness of how words are formed and knowledge of how sentences are structured) that appear to be invoked when attempting to read with comprehension. A key aspect of this view is that although accurate and efficient word recognition skills are clearly crucial for reading fluency, they are by no means sufficient when reading for understanding, especially for upper elementary grade readers. The acquisition of reading fluency crucially is said to involve the discovery of the appropriate syntactic structures embedded in the written signals. In order to read with comprehension, the reader must parse the text into syntactically and semantically appropriate units. Support for the involvement of syntactic skills when reading fluently and with comprehension comes from research indicating that some reading comprehension problems develop after third grade, when syntactic complexity of texts used in instruction increases. Syntactic awareness is considered a significant source of reading difficulty and is presumed to account for a significant portion of variance in children's reading comprehension performance. Support for the critical role of syntactic awareness comes from research studies that have shown that upper elementary grade children with comprehension problems have weak syntactic awareness skills (e.g., Mokhtari & Thompson, 2006; Nation & Snowling, 2000; Stothard & Hulme, 1992).

## Automatic Information-Processing View of Reading Fluency

The third view takes an information-processing approach to the construct of fluent reading. Its proponents (e.g., Laberge & Samuels, 1974; Wolfe & Katzir-Cohen, 2001; Samuels, 2004, 2007) emphasize the role of automaticity of basic component skills (i.e., word decoding and accuracy). In fact, initially, fluency was viewed simply as accurate and automatic word identification. Thus, as students gain automaticity, they can devote attention to the task of reading comprehension as an outcome of fluent reading. Recent definitions of automaticity include four properties—speed, effortlessness, autonomy, and lack of conscious awareness (Kuhn et al., 2010)—that contribute to accuracy and automaticity to free up attention so that readers can understand text. Thus, a key aspect of this view is that fluent reading involves the simultaneous orchestration of decoding and comprehension skills. Samuels (2007) noted that definitions of reading fluency that do not include reading comprehension may be endorsing practices and assessments that merely assess the students' ability to "bark at print." However, the ultimate goal is to develop fluent readers who can construct meaning as they read. This view of reading fluency as involving *the simultaneous orchestration of decoding and comprehension processes* has important implications for reading fluency assessment and instruction.

Thus far, we have outlined three views of fluency that seem prevalent in the research literature. In our view, taken together, the three theoretical frameworks provide a more complete view of the rather complex construct of reading fluency. Researchers who have taken a developmental view to reading fluency have taken into account children who are passing through various stages of reading development, which progress from fluent word reading, appropriate pace, and phrasing to expression or prosody. These skills are thought to develop gradually and in broadly defined stages.

Researchers advocating for broader linguistic skills to reading fluency development have taken into account important linguistic skills (e.g., children's ability to develop an awareness of how words are formed and how sentences are constructed). For most of children who struggle to develop effective reading despite good decoding skills, these broader language skills are late emerging during the process of learning to read. Research has shown that weaknesses in these broader skills are significantly associated with difficulties reading and comprehending what one reads.

Proponents of the automaticity or information-processing view of fluent reading have taken into account fluent and mature readers who have fairly well-developed decoding, accuracy, and expression capacities. These proponents believe that efficient fluent readers are able to orchestrate the requisite decoding skills and comprehension *simultaneously*. In other words, as Samuels and colleagues noted, the ultimate and arguably the most important aspect of fluent reading is the readers' ability to perform two quite complex tasks (i.e., identify words and comprehending text) at the same time (Alt & Samuels, 2011). The insights gained from these three theoretical views have important implications for reading fluency assessment and instruction.

## FLUENCY INSTRUCTION

The instructional strategies for developing fluent readers have been inspired by theoretical views of reading fluency. It is important to note that, like the theoretical views, these instructional procedures can serve complex purposes. However, we have organized fluency instruction using the proposed three views of fluency: developmental, linguistic, and automatic processes. It is hoped that these distinctions help clarify why some instructional approaches are used in particular situations.

### Developmental View of Fluency Instruction

In this view, reading fluency is viewed as a component of reading development. Further, fluency is based on critical elements that are learned and used as students progress through literacy development. In fact, Klauda and Guthrie (2008) found support for a multidimensional and developmental view of fluency. Their study indicates that word-level fluency takes front stage during the primary grades and that syntactic-level fluency and passage-level fluency are critical to the intermediate grades. From their research, they suggested that assorted levels such as "word-, syntactic-, and passage-level fluency may be differentially sensitive to alternative interventions" (p. 319).

Initially, there is word-level fluency, where word accuracy and reading words quickly are developed through scaffolding and practice in reading words. To develop word accuracy and an appropriate pace, teachers can use collaborative shared reading or easy books. After acquiring word identification skills, students develop fluency by using appropriate phrasing, where they use sentence structure to predict what words might come next. This is followed by passage-level fluency, where students begin to use expression and prosody. As students consolidate these elements, they naturally construct deeper meaning. Through these tasks, students' literacy develops. Thus, fluency is a critical task related to comprehending text. There are many ways to develop fluency through the stages. Some techniques outlined by levels of reading fluency follow.

## Shared Reading

Used in the primary grades, shared reading is an interactive reading of a predictable book that promotes word identification and reading fluency using teacher modeling and multiple readings. On the first read, the teacher reads a predictable book aloud and then discusses the story meaning with the children. Mesmer (2010) found that when young children read predictable books their reading pace increases. During the second reading, the teacher and students collaboratively read the story while the teacher identifies difficult phrases or sentences. After this reading, the teacher discusses the difficult spots and then models the fluent reading of difficult phrases. In the last reading, the students read the story aloud chorally and the teacher supports them by reading with them if difficulties arise. The fluent reading is always supported by the teacher. The shared reading approach with predictable books is a way to increase fluency in younger students.

## Fluency Development Lesson

A classroom approach that focuses on several aspects of fluency development is the Fluency Development Lesson (FDL) designed by Rasinski, Padak, Linek, and Sturtevant (1994). The FDL approach focuses on improving comprehension rather than on a single element of fluency. However, this approach uses various forms of supported reading to engage students in fluent reading by focusing on performance and word study. The FDL employs short reading passages (a segment from a basal reader or chapter book or a poem) that students reread over a short period of time. In this lesson, the teacher introduces the short passage and reads it several times while students follow. The teacher and the students discuss the meaning and language of the passage. Then they read the passage chorally a couple of times. Next, the teacher divides the students into pairs, where each student practices at least three times while the partner offers encouragement. The students then perform the passage as a choral reading. The teacher and the students select three or four words to add to a word wall and use for word study. Last, the students take the passage home to practice reading for family and friends.

### Responsive Rereading

Formerly known as responsive repeated readings (Walker, Mokhtari, & Sargent, 2006), responsive rereading is a fluency technique designed for older readers who are still struggling with the developmental aspects of reading fluency. Meaning is emphasized throughout, and it moves readers through the developmental levels of fluency in a systematic fashion within one lesson. Readers develop as the text level is increased. The technique uses three readings of a passage where after the first reading the teacher records the miscues on a graph and discusses fluent reading and passage meaning. Before the second and third rereadings, the teacher scaffolds (Chard, Vaughn, & Tyler, 2002; Magno, 2010) and models (Rasinski, Homan, & Biggs, 2009) fluent reading of the passage. After the third rereading, the students and teacher record miscues on the graph again and discuss the strategies to use to develop fluent reading with understanding. The teacher is responsive to how the students read the passage and scaffolds the students' reading through modeling, prompting, strategy conversations, and feedback.

## Linguistic View of Fluency Instruction

In the linguistic view of fluency, teachers select instructional procedures that focus on language aspects of reading. Understanding language use in text such as syntax and passage structure improves the more the students read. Independent reading of many books develops fluency. Additionally, in this view, readers need to parse the text into syntactically and semantically appropriate units. When this occurs, students read smoothly, use appropriate phrasing, and increase expression. Like teachers employing a developmental view, teachers adhering to the linguistic view demonstrate fluent reading processes. However, they focus specifically on how phrases and sentences influence meaning that results in increased reading prosody. They also focus on how reading practice influences knowledge about sentence and passage structure.

## Wide Reading

From a linguistic point of view, Wide Reading that includes high-quality literature at an appropriate level helps students develop an increasing knowledge of sophisticated language structures at the sentence and passage levels. Thus, Wide Reading includes many concepts, among them reading independently, choice silent reading, and reading practice. In fact, a review of research (Kuhn, 2011) on Wide Reading and reading practice revealed that reading multiple similar text results in improved reading fluency. Allington (2009) suggests that reading volume, particularly in easier text, supports both reading fluency and reading achievement. Further, free voluntary reading (Krashen, 2004), where students choose interesting books to read for their own purpose, promotes an increased reading habit. When students choose books to read silently and then have an opportunity to respond to it, they can make improvements in reading fluency (Rasinski, 2010).

## Marking and Modeling Phrase Boundaries

Text segmenting, or marking phrase boundaries (Rasinski, 2010; Dowhower, 1991), is a little used but valuable way to improve reading fluency. It promotes students' "ability to reading in syntactically appropriate and meaningful idea units or phrases" (Nichols, Rupley, & Rasinski, 2009, p. 7). By explicitly marking phrase boundaries, students focus on how phrases in sentences work to promote reading understanding. Thus, by marking phrase boundaries in passages with a slash or vertical line, students' attention is focused on how syntactic structure works. Another way to focus on meaningful phrases is for teachers to model phrasing as they read aloud. Students follow the teachers' model, learning appropriate phrasing. In a review of reading fluency instruction, Chard and his colleagues (2002) recommend modeling reading, including phrasing for students who struggle to read fluently.

## Sentence Combining

Another way to focus on how sentences are constructed to promote fluent reading is sentence combining (Saddler & Graham, 2005). This technique is designed to help students write and understand complex sentences. The teacher shows students how to combine simple sentences to create more complex ones. For example, the teacher might use the following simple sentences: "The dog was white. The dog went to the park. The dog rolled in the mud." Then the teacher shows students how to make the more complex sentence: "The white dog went the park and rolled in the mud." This knowledge of how complex sentences are formed helps students use sentence structure as they read orally. Thus, fluency is improved. In fact, Graham and Hiebert (2010) found that both spelling and sentence combining improved reading fluency.

### Readers Theatre

Readers Theatre is a way to focus on developing prosody so that each student's part is read fluently with expression and prosody. In Readers Theatre, students perform based on a script after practicing reading it multiple times. Several studies have found that Readers Theatre can improve fluency (Rasinski, 2010). In a study of fourth-grade struggling readers participating in an 8-week Readers Theatre intervention, the researchers documented the students' growth in pace and expression (Clark, Morrison, & Wilcox, 2009). In another study using a weekly Readers Theatre instructional format over a school year, students made significant gains in reading fluency (Young & Rasinski, 2009). Yet another study using a similar weekly format found that at the beginning of the program students had difficulty in the area of prosody, or expression. However, by the end of the 6 weeks students read in expressive, rhythmic, and melodic patterns, indicating they had gained an increased understanding of meaningful phrasing and syntax, which aids students in the understanding and interpretation of language (Nichols, Mraz, Caldwell, & Beisley, 2011).

## Automaticity View of Fluency Instruction

Extensive research has shown that methods in which students repeatedly read text improves their ability to read with increasingly accuracy and rate (Kuhn, 2011; Kuhn & Stahl, 2003; Samuels, 2006). If reading rate and accuracy are a concern, as in the automaticity model, a program of unassisted repeated readings or assisted repeated readings is ideal (Samuels, 2006).

### Repeated Readings

In this method, the teacher explains that rereading the text is like practicing a musical instrument or practicing a football play. The rereading helps improve reading and reading fluency. In this procedure, a student reads aloud, while the teacher marks miscues and measures rate. Both reading rate and miscues are charted on a graph to illustrate growth for each reading. Then all students practice reading the passage silently. This is often called "unassisted" repeated reading, because the teacher does not influence the readings. Samuels (2006) suggests that the selection be reread orally no more than four times. In four readings, the benefits of the rereading are realized.

### Paired Reading

Paired repeated reading (Koskinen & Blum, 2009) is another form of repeated readings. Critical to paired repeated reading, however, is providing positive feedback to a partner on the performance aspects of fluency as well as assessing one's own performance using a self-evaluation sheet. The teacher explains how pairs should provide positive feedback for each other on the performance aspects of fluency. Initially, both students read silently to become familiar with the passage. The first student reads the passage three times. After the second and third readings, the partner comments on the improvement the student has shown in word recognition, expression, and phrasing. When both students have read their passages, the students assess their own performance using a self-evaluation sheet. These self-assessments help students realize their progress and success in reading more fluently. In a study with intermediate readers, Koskinen and Blum (1984) compared the outcome of two instructional conditions: paired repeated reading and study activities. They found significant results in favor of the paired repeated reading group in fluency. This group also made fewer semantically inappropriate miscues. Thus, completing self-evaluation sheets and partner evaluation sheets along with paired repeated readings improves fluency and self-assessment.

## ASSESSMENT OF READING FLUENCY

Regardless of the method used, when assisting struggling readers in developing reading fluency, it is important to scaffold student learning and monitor progress. For purposes of this chapter, we have used insights gleaned from the three theoretical views to offer suggestions for assessing and teaching reading fluency to students in various stages of reading development. Specifically, our assessment and instruction strategies take into account developmental aspects of reading fluency (e.g., reading pace, accuracy, and expression), linguistic aspects of reading involving development of broader language skills such as syntax, and information-processing aspects of reading focused on developing students' ability to orchestrate simultaneously decoding and comprehension of text while reading.

## Developmental View of Fluency Assessment

The developmental view maintains that reading fluency involves the gradual acquisition of skills and strategies, which readers accomplish in stages as they mature into fluent readers (e.g., Kuhn & Stahl, 2003; Nichols et al., 2009). Such skills may include reading pace, accuracy, phrasing, and expression. The use of instruments such as the Multidimensional Fluency Scale (Rasinski, 2004) to measure these basic skills appears to be in line with this developmental view of fluency.

### Multidimensional Fluency Scale

When using this scale, each student reads a passage of text orally, and the instructor evaluates the reading based on the multiple dimensions of this scale: phrasing, smoothness, and pace (see Table 5.1). First, phrasing is assessed. The teacher rates whether a student's reading is well phrased and mostly in clauses/sentence units or whether reading is monotonic with little sense of phrase boundaries. Also, the teacher notes smoothness of reading. As the child reads, the teacher considers whether reading is generally smooth or if there are frequent extended pauses, sound-outs, and repetitions. Finally, the teacher rates the student's pace and expression of reading. The teacher observes whether reading is consistently conversational or if it is slow and laborious.

Individually, these scales provide a tremendous amount of diagnostic data for each student. In addition, teachers can use combined scores for an overall examination and tracking of reading fluency. Zutell and Rasinski (1991) assert that teachers can use this measure and feel confident in its validity and reliability, with reported coefficients as high as .99.

## Linguistic View of Fluency Assessment

The linguistic view emphasizes the role of language competencies that students use when attempting to read and construct meaning from text, especially for those in the upper elementary grades. This view posits that the discovery of the appropriate syntactic structures embedded in the written signals is crucial to development of fluency. Klauda and Guthrie (2008) found that knowledge of syntax is strongly correlated with reading comprehension. This underlying aspect of reading ability, although critically important, has not been accounted for in assessments of fluency. While there are no standard assessments of syntactic knowledge or awareness, we believe that procedures such as the cloze or the maze can be used to make inferences about students' ability to use syntactic information when reading to make sense of text.

**TABLE 5.1. Multidimensional Fluency Scale**

Phrasing

1. Monotonic with little sense of phrase boundaries, frequent word-by-word reading.
2. Frequent two- and three-word phrases, giving the impression of choppy reading; improper stress and intonation that fail to mark ends of sentences and clauses.
3. Mixture of run-ons, midsentence pauses for breath, and possibly some choppiness; reasonable stress/intonation.
4. Generally well phrased, mostly in clause and sentence units, with adequate attention to expression.

Smoothness

1. Frequent extended pauses, hesitations, false starts, sound-outs, repetitions, and/or multiple attempts.
2. Several "rough spots" in text where extended pauses, hesitations, etc., are more frequent and disruptive.
3. Occasional breaks in smoothness caused by difficulties with specific words and/or structures.
4. Generally smooth with some breaks, but word and structure difficulties are resolved quickly, usually through self-correction.

Pace

1. Slow and laborious.
2. Moderately slow.
3. Uneven mixture of fast and slow reading.
4. Consistently conversational.

Expression and Volume

1. Reads with little expression or enthusiasm in voice; little effort to make text sound like natural language; tends to read in a quiet voice.
2. Some expression; begins to use voice to make text sound like natural language in some areas of the text, but not others; focus remains largely on saying the words; still reads in a quiet voice.
3. Sounds like natural language throughout the better part of the passage; occasionally slips into not reading with expression; voice volume is generally appropriate throughout the text.
4. Reads with good expression and enthusiasm throughout the text; sounds like natural language; is able to vary expression and volume to match his/her interpretation of the passage.

*Note.* Based on Zutell and Rasinski (1991).


## Cloze Procedure

Using a text of 200–400 words, the teacher deletes targeted words (often every fifth, seventh, or ninth word), replacing them with a blank. The student reads the passage, filling in the blanks. This form of assessment is useful to reveal how the student is able to use knowledge of syntax to make sense of text (Walker, 2012). Closely related is the maze procedure (Guthrie, Seifert, Burnham, & Caplan, 1974). In this modification of the cloze procedure, students choose from one of three answers provided in each blank instead of having to generate an answer independently. Both provide useful insights as to how the student is able to utilize syntax.

A related method of assessing an important aspect of reading fluency (namely expression or prosody) uses rating scales (Kuhn et al., 2010). In 1985, the Commission on Reading published *Becoming a Nation of Readers,* stating that current standardized tests should be supplemented with periodic observations of reading fluency. Since then, various scales and assessment instruments have been devised to measure reading fluency. The NAEP added a measure of reading fluency to its fourth-grade assessment of reading in 1992. The NAEP assessment of reading used a four-tier fluency scale that combines the performance attributes of phrasing (based on syntax) and expression (based on features of prosody). The pupils read a passage orally that was recorded and later the reading was rated based on a predetermined scale (see Table 5.2).

Using this rating scale, a teacher can decide if students need to improve expression or phrasing. Kuhn and her colleagues (2010) suggest "it is possible that the construction of a good prosodic reading (compared with an inappropriate rendering) might improve comprehension" (p. 236).

## Automaticity View of Fluency Assessment

The third view of reading fluency emphasizes the role of automaticity of basic component skills such as word recognition and accuracy. Once students master these skills, they may devote increased attention to the task of comprehension. Comprehending text is certainly expected of fluent readers. The following assessments measure these basic components as well as how students construct meaning from the text.

### Rate and Accuracy Assessment

Kuhn and her colleagues (2010) suggest that automatic word recognition remains an integral part of fluency and plays a prominent role in how children construct meaning from text. When measuring only rate and accuracy, it is suggested to use a curriculum-based measurement (CBM) of oral reading fluency. The CBM assessment is based on the number of words read aloud correctly in 1 minute from passages randomly selected from a textbook currently used in the school curriculum, thus focusing on the performance attributes of accuracy and rate of reading. Reading aloud from curriculum materials demonstrates the "strongest relation with socially important, widely used criterion measures of reading" (Fuchs & Deno, 1992, p. 233). The CBM assessment method has been found to have adequate reliability and validity as a measure of reading fluency.

Other persuasive arguments exist for the use of 1-minute timed readings. Reading researchers generally agree that "scores from the oral passage

**TABLE 5.2. NAEP Oral Reading Fluency Scale**

Level 4

Reads primarily in larger, meaningful phrase groups. Although some regressions, repetitions, and deviations from text may be present, those do not appear to detract from the overall structure of the story. Preservation of the author's syntax is consistent. Some or most of the story is read with expressive interpretation.

Level 3

Reads primarily in three- or four-word phrase groups. Some smaller groupings may be present. However, the majority of phrasing seems appropriate and preserves the syntax of the author. Little or no expressive interpretation is present.

Level 2

Reads primarily in two-word phrases with some three- or four-word groupings. Some word-by-word reading may be present. Word groupings may seem awkward and unrelated to larger context of sentence or passage.

Level 1

Reads primarily word-by-word. Occasional two-word or three-word phrases may occur, but these are infrequent and/or they do not preserve meaningful syntax.

*Note.* From Pinnell et al. (1995).

reading test appear to be a feasible and psychometrically useful method for assessing reading ability" (Fuchs, Fuchs, & Maxwell, 1988, p. 27; Kuhn, 2004; Fuchs, 2004). Moreover, correlations between CBM measures of oral fluency and tests of reading comprehension are quite high (Fuchs & Deno, 1992). Finally, results of 1-minute timed readings also correlate highly with standardized tests of reading achievement (Fuchs et al., 2001; Stage & Jacobsen, 2001). Many educators perceive rate and accuracy as the goals of reading and consequently measure these alone when assessing. Recent tests (often mandated) used nationally have brought rate and accuracy into many American classrooms, identifying how many words children can read in 1 minute at their level of chronological placement.

While rate and accuracy are worthwhile goals, a recent study found that an assessment that includes prosody and comprehension provides a richer understanding of fluency and is a stronger predictor of reading comprehension (Valencia et al., 2010). Thus, when assessing reading fluency, it is important to ensure that readers are reading with comprehension. Recent research indicates that teachers should help ensure that readers "are not focusing on rate at the expense of meaning" (Kuhn et al., 2010, p. 45). Samuels (2002) concurs, noting that "the final and the most important property of fluency reading is the ability to perform two difficult tasks simultaneously ... the ability to identify words and comprehend text at the same time" (p. 167). Thus, other aspects of fluency (e.g., rate, accuracy) should not be the only features measured, especially at the exclusion of exploring how students are able to construct meaning from the text. To assess comprehension as an important piece of reading fluency, Samuels (2002) suggests that the teacher select two passages on topics not familiar to the student. These passages (at the student's estimated reading level) should be between one-half and two pages and of approximately equal length. One passage is used to measure reading comprehension and the other listening comprehension. The teacher reads the passage for listening comprehension aloud and asks questions afterward. The student reads the other passage orally for reading comprehension and then retells everything he or she can remember from the story (oral retelling). This assessment provides valuable information about both oral reading and comprehension (Samuels, 2002). Clearly, the construct of fluent reading is a complex set of skills that are meaningfully intertwined with reading comprehension performance. As such, it requires a rich set of assessments that can and should lead to better reading instruction.

## SUMMARY

Reading fluently with comprehension is a critical aspect of the reading process. In fact, the goal of all reading instruction is to improve comprehension while reading. This important outcome of reading requires that readers have sufficiently well-developed word-level skills (e.g., reading words accurately and at an appropriate rate), broader language skills (e.g., awareness of lexical and syntactic structures), and passage understanding (awareness of text structures and meaning structures). In this chapter, we have outlined three views of fluency: developmental, linguistic, and automaticity. The developmental view focuses on how students cultivate fluency through the grades while the linguistic view focuses on how language works, including phrasing and intonation. The automaticity view focuses on the role of automaticity of basic component skills (i.e., word decoding and accuracy) and how students can instinctively associate what words look like with what they mean. Following this explanation, we have presented instructional procedures that promote fluency. We have further aligned each with a theoretical view. Several assessment strategies are available to help literacy professionals determine student needs and monitor their progress in increasing fluent reading with comprehension.

## REFERENCES

Allington, R. (2009). If they don't read much: 30 years later. In E. H. Hiebert (Ed.), *Reading more, reading better* (pp. 30–54). New York: Guilford Press.

Alt, J. S., & Samuels, J. S. (2011). Reading fluency: What is it and how should it be measured? In A. McGill-Franzen & R. Allington (Eds.), *Handbook of reading disability research* (pp. 173–182). New York: Taylor & Francis.

Anderson, R. C., Hiebert, E. H., Scott, J. A., Wilkinson, I. A. G., & Commission on Reading. (1985). *Becoming a nation of readers: The report of the Commission on Reading.* Champaign, IL: Center for the Study of Reading.

Armbruster, B. B., Lehr, F., & Osborn, J. (2001). *Put reading first: The research building blocks for teaching children to read: Kindergarten through grade 3.* Washington, DC: National Institute for Literacy.

Cassidy, J., & Cassidy, D. (2009). What's hot for 2009. *Reading Today, 26*(4), 1, 8.

Chafe, W. (1988). Punctuation and the prosody of written language. *Written Communication, 5,* 396–426.

Chard, D. J., Vaughn, S., & Tyler, B. J. (2002). A synthesis of research on effective interventions for building reading fluency with elementary students with learning disabilities. *Journal of Learning Disabilities, 35*(5), 386–407.

Chomsky, C. (1976). After decoding: What? *Language Arts, 53*(3), 288–296, 314.

Clark, R., Morrison, T. G., & Wilcox, B. (2009). Readers' Theater: A process of developing fourth-graders' reading fluency. *Reading Psychology, 30,* 359–385.

Daane, M., Campbell, J., Grigg, W., Goodman, M., & Oranje, A. (2005). *Fourth-grade students reading aloud: NAEP 2002 special study of oral reading* (NCES 2006-469). Washington, DC: U.S. Government Printing Office.

Dowhower, S. L. (1991). Speaking of prosody: Fluency's unattended bedfellow. *Theory into Practice, 30,* 165–175.

Fuchs, L., Fuchs, D., & Maxwell, L., (1988). The validity of informal reading comprehension measures. *Remedial and Special Education, 9*(2), 20–28.

Fuchs, L., & Deno, S. L. (1992). Effects of curriculum within curriculum based measurement. *Exceptional Children, 58*(3), 232–242.

Fuchs, L., Fuchs, D., Hosp, M., & Jenkins, J. (2001). Oral reading fluency as an indicator of reading competence: A theoretical, empirical, and historical analysis. *Scientific Studies of Reading, 5,* 239–256.

Fuchs, L. S. (2004). The past, present, and future of curriculum-based measurement research. *School Psychology Review, 33*(2), 188–192.

Graham, S., & Hebert, M. (2010). *Writing to read: Evidence for how writing can improve reading.* New York: Carnegie Corporation of New York.

Guthrie, J. T., Seifert, M., Burnham, N. A., & Caplan, R. T. (1974). The maze technique to assess and monitor reading comprehension. *The Reading Teacher, 28*(2), 161–168.

Hudson, R. F., Lane, H. B., & Pullen, P. C. (2005). Reading fluency assessment and instruction: What, how, and why. *The Reading Teacher, 58*(8), 702–714.

Klauda, S. L., & Guthrie, J. T. (2008). Relationships of three components of reading fluency to reading comprehension. *Journal of Educational Psychology, 100,* 310–321.

Koskinen, P. S., & Blum, I. H. (1984). Repeated oral reading and the acquisition of fluency. In J. A. Niles & L. A. Harris (Eds.), *Changing perspectives on research in reading/language processing and instruction: 33rd yearbook of the National Reading Conference* (pp. 183–187). Rochester, NY: National Reading Conference.

Koskinen, P. S., & Blum, I. H. (2009). Paired repeated reading: A classroom strategy for developing fluent reading. In T. Rasinski (Ed.), *Essentials of reading fluency.* Newark, DE: International Reading Association.

Krashen, S. (2004). *The power of reading: Insights from the research.* Portsmouth, NH: Heinemann.

Kuhn, M. (2004). Helping students become accurate, expressive readers: Fluency instruction for small groups. *The Reading Teacher, 58*(4), 338–344.

Kuhn, M. (2011). Fluency: A review of developmental and remedial practices. In R. L. Allington & A. McGill-Franzen (Eds.), *Handbook of reading disability research* (pp. 307–314). New York: Taylor & Francis.

Kuhn, M., Schwanenflugel, P., & Meisinger, E. (2010). Aligning theory and assessment of reading fluency: Automaticity, prosody, and definitions of fluency. *Reading Research Quarterly, 45*(2), 230–251.

Kuhn, M. R., & Stahl, S. A. (2003). Fluency: A review of developmental and remedial practices. *Journal of Educational Psychology, 95,* 3–21.

LaBerge, D., & Samuels, S. (1974). Toward a theory of automatic information processing in reading. *Cognitive Psychology, 6,* 293–323.

Magno, C. (2010). The effect of scaffolding on children's reading speed, reading anxiety, and reading proficiency. *TESOL Journal, 3,* 92–98.

Mesmer, H. A. (2010). Textual scaffolds for developing fluency in beginning readers: Accuracy and reading rate in qualitatively leveled and decodable text. *Literacy Research and Instruction, 49,* 20–39.

Mokhtari, K., & Thompson, B. (2006). How problems of reading fluency and comprehension are related to difficulties in syntactic awareness skill among fifth graders. *Reading Reasearch and Instruction, 46,* 73–94.

Nation, K., & Snowling, M. J. (2000). Factors influencing syntactic awareness skills in normal readers and poor comprehenders. *Applied Psycholinguistics, 21,* 229–241.

National Reading Panel. (2000). *Teaching children to read: An evidence-based assessment of the scientific research literature on reading and its implications for reading instruction.* Washington, DC: National Institute of Child Health and Human Development.

Nichols, W. D., Mraz, M., Caldwell, S., & Beisley, R. (2011). Increasing students' oral reading fluency through Readers Theatre. In B. Walker & C. Dybdhal (Eds.), *Powerful instruction: Helping struggling readers in K–6 classrooms.* Norwood, MA: Christopher-Gordon.

Nichols, W. D., Rupley, W., & Rasinski, T. (2009). Fluency in learning to read for meaning: Going beyond repeated reading. *Literacy Research and Instruction, 48,* 1–13.

Pinnell, G. S., Pikulski, J. J., Wixon, K. K., Campbell, J. R., Gough, P. B., & Beatty, A. S. (1995). *Listening to children read aloud* (Report No. 23-FR-04). Washington, DC: National Center for Education Statistics.

Rasinski, T. V. (2004). *Assessing reading fluency.* Honolulu: Pacific Resources for Education and Learning.

Rasinski, T. W. (2010). The art and science of teaching reading fluency In D. Lapp, & D. Fisher (Eds.), *Handbook of research on teaching the English language arts* (3rd ed., pp. 286–337). New York: Routledge.

Rasinski, T., Homan, S., & Biggs, M. (2009). Teaching reading fluency to struggling readers: Method, materials, and evidence. *Reading & Writing Quarterly: Overcoming Learning Difficulties, 25,* 192–204.

Rasinski, T. V., Padak, N. D., Linek, W. L., & Sturtevant, E. (1994). Effects of fluency development on urban second-grade readers. *Journal of Educational Research, 87*(3), 158–165.

Rasinski, T., Riki, A., & Johnston, S. (2009). Reading fluency: More than automaticity? More than a concern for the primary grades? *Literacy Research and Instruction, 48*(4), 350–361.

Saddler, B., & Graham, S. (2005). The effects of peer-assisted sentence combining instruction on the writing performance of more and less skilled young writers. *Journal of Educational Psychology, 97,* 43–54.

Samuels, S. J. (2002). Reading fluency: Its development and assessment. In S. Samuels & A. E. Farstrup (Eds.), *What research has to say about reading instruction* (pp. 166–183). Newark, DE: International Reading Association.

Samuels, S. J. (2004). Toward a theory of automatic information processing in reading, revisited. In R. B. Ruddell & N. J. Unrau (Eds.), *Theoretical models and processes of reading* (pp. 1127–1148). Newark, DE: International Reading Association.

Samuels, S. J. (2006). Toward a model of reading fluency. In S. Samuels & A. E. Farstrup (Eds.), *What research has to say about fluency instruction* (3rd ed., pp. 24–46). Newark, DE: International Reading Association.

Samuels, S. J. (2007). The DIBELS tests: Is speed of barking at print what we mean by reading fluency? *Reading Research Quarterly, 42*(4), 563–566.

Schreiber, P. A. (1980). On the acquisition of reading fluency. *Journal of Reading Behavior, 12,* 177–186.

Schreiber, P. A. (1987). Prosody and structure in children's syntactic processing. In R. Horowitz & S. J. Samuels (Eds.), *Comprehending oral and written language* (pp. 243?270). New York: Academic Press.

Shinn, M. R. (Ed.). (1989). *Curriculum-based measurement: Assessing special children.* New York: Guilford Press.

Snow, C. E., Burns, M. S., & Griffin, P. (1998). *Preventing reading difficulties in young children.* Washington, DC: National Academy Press.

Stage, S. A., & Jacobsen, M. D. (2001). Predicting student success on a state-mandated performance-based assessment using oral reading fluency. *School Psychology Review, 30*(3), 407–420.

Valencia, S. W., Smith, A. T., Reese, A. M., Li, M., Wixson, K., & Newman, H. (2010). Oral reading fluency assessment: Issues of construct, criterion, and consequential validity. *Reading Research Quarterly, 45*(3), 270–291.

Walker, B. J. (2012). *Diagnostic teaching of reading: Techniques for instruction and assessment* (7th ed.). Upper Saddle River: NJ: Pearson/Prentice Hall.

Walker, B. J., Mokhtari, K., & Sargent, S. (2006). Reading fluency: more than fast and accurate reading. In T. Rasinski, C. Blachowicz, & K. Lems (Eds.), *Fluency instruction: Research-based best practices* (pp. 86–105). New York: Guilford Press.

Wolf, M., & Katzir-Cohen, T. (2001). Reading fluency and its intervention. *Scientific Studies of Reading, 5,* 211–239.

Young, C., & Rasinski, T. (2009). Implementing readers theatre as an approach to classroom fluency instruction. *The Reading Teacher, 63,* 4–13.

Zutell, J., & Rasinski, T. V. (1991). Training teachers to attend to their students' oral reading fluency. *Theory into Practice, 30*(3), 211–217.

# 6

# Fluency

## The Link between Decoding and Comprehension for Struggling Readers

David J. Chard
John J. Pikulski
Sarah H. McDonagh

**F**luency is receiving substantial attention currently from both researchers and practitioners. In part, this attention was stimulated over a decade ago by a Report of the National Reading Panel (2000), which identified fluency as one of only five critical components of reading: phonemic awareness, phonics, vocabulary, fluency and comprehension. Despite the increased focus on fluency, for struggling readers, fluency as a measure of rate and accuracy has definitely received greater attention. However, its reciprocal relationship to comprehension is frequently ignored as a focus for remedial instruction.

## DEFINING READING FLUENCY

Fluency has sometimes been viewed as essentially an oral reading phenomenon (Rasinski & Hoffman, 2003). However, because most readers spend a relatively small amount of time engaged in oral reading compared with silent reading, a definition of fluency needs to encompass more than oral reading. The International Reading Association's *The Literacy Dictionary: The Vocabulary of Reading and Writing* defines fluency as "freedom from word identification problems that might hinder comprehension" (Harris &

Hodges, 1995, p. 85). This definition expands our understanding of reading fluency to include comprehension. Samuels (2002), a pioneer in research and theory in reading fluency, cites this expanded definition as a major force in elevating the importance of fluency in the field of reading. The National Assessment of Educational Progress established that there is a significant and positive relationship between oral reading fluency and reading comprehension (Pinnell et al., 1995). However, this relationship is fairly complex. Alt and Samuels (2011) suggest that the field has misunderstood the definition of fluency, interpreting it to mean the simultaneous application of reading speed and comprehension. Strecker, Roser, and Martinez (1998), in their review of fluency research, note: "The issue of whether fluency is an outgrowth or a contributor to comprehension is unresolved. There is empirical evidence to support both positions" (p. 300). However they conclude: "Fluency has been shown to have a 'reciprocal relationship' with comprehension, with each fostering the other" (p. 306).

A comprehensive definition, then, would relate the centrality of fluency to reading comprehension and its established dimensions. Previously, we proposed the following synthesis of definitions:

> Reading fluency refers to efficient, effective word recognition skills that permit a reader to construct the meaning of text. Fluency is manifested in accurate, rapid, expressive oral reading and is applied during, and makes possible, silent reading comprehension. (Pikulski & Chard, 2005, p. 510)

We believe that the issue of a definition is not trivial but rather is central to making important decisions about the teaching and assessment of fluency for struggling readers. For example, Alt and Samuels (2011) have suggested that the misunderstanding of the relationship between fluency and comprehension has led to invalid measures of fluency that are actually just measures of speed (Alt & Samuels, 2011). Rather than a surface view of reading fluency that might lead to practices of telling students to read faster, our definition suggests a deep construct view of fluency. A deep construct view considers fluency broadly as part of a developmental process of building oral language and decoding skills that form a bridge to reading comprehension for readers, resulting in a reciprocal, causal relationship with reading comprehension. More specifically, we contend that this deep construct view considers four dimensions of fluency: oral reading accuracy, oral reading rate, quality of oral reading, and reading comprehension. It becomes necessary to think about fluency as part of a child's earliest experiences with print and with the phonology that becomes associated with that print. In this view, efficient decoding is consistently related to comprehension. In the next section, we describe several theories related to reading fluency and their contribution to our understanding of how fluency develops.

## HISTORICAL DEVELOPMENT
## OF THE CONSTRUCT OF READING FLUENCY

An early discussion of the construct of reading fluency is found in Edmund Huey's (1908/1968) classic publication, however, most discussions of fluency trace their modern theoretical foundations to the 1974 seminal article by LaBerge and Samuels. LaBerge and Samuels argued that human beings can attend to only one thing at a time. However, we are able to do more than one thing at a time if we alternate our attention between two or more activities or if one of the activities is so well learned that it can be performed automatically. Reading successfully is a complex interaction of language, sensory perception, memory, and motivation. To illustrate the role of fluency, it helps to characterize this multifaceted process as including *at least* two activities: (1) word identification or decoding and (2) comprehension, or the construction of the meaning of text. In order for reading to proceed effectively, the reader cannot focus attention on both word identification and comprehension. Understanding an author's message involves making inferences, responding critically, and so on, and it *always* requires attention. The nonfluent reader can alternate attention between the two processes; however, this makes reading a laborious, often punishing process. If attention is drained by decoding words, little or no capacity is available for the attention-demanding process of comprehending. Therefore, automaticity of decoding—a critical component of fluency—is essential for high levels of reading achievement.

Perfetti (1985) applied the LaBerge and Samuels argument to an information-processing approach to understanding the importance of efficient lower level processes in fluent, connected text reading. His "verbal efficiency theory" highlights the importance of lower level lexical skills in reading and explains the impact of processing information at multiple levels of reading comprehension. He suggests that lower level processes (e.g., word identification) must reach a minimum performance level before higher level processes can be performed simultaneously during reading. When lower level processes are performed inefficiently, higher order processes will attempt to compensate. Breznitz's (2006) research supports the verbal efficiency theory by demonstrating that slow processing speed can become habitual and may result in slower comprehension. When a reader is forced to read more quickly, his or her overall reading performance may benefit. Perfetti's theory assumes that resource demands can be reduced through learning and practice, and efficiency may be enhanced through careful allocation of attention resources.

In contrast, Logan's (1988) memory-based theory of fluency—the instance theory of automatization—suggests that automaticity and fluency are based on memory retrieval. Three key assumptions of Logan's memory-based theory include (1) obligatory encoding, (2) obligatory retrieval, and (3) instance representation (Logan, 1997). "Obligatory encoding" refers to focusing attention on a stimulus (e.g., a word) and storing details of that stimulus in memory. "Obligatory retrieval" suggests that merely attending to a stimulus is sufficient to retrieve previous exposures or similar stimuli from memory. "Instance representation" refers to the coding and storage of each memory trace of experiences with a stimulus in memory. Each memory trace is coded and stored separately regardless of prior experience with the stimulus. Logan (1988) contends that information recall is automatic when it relies on retrieval of stored instances from memory. "Stored instances" refer to the theoretical memory traces laid down in the brain each time a task is executed. As the number of trials on a task increases, the strength of the number of memory traces or instances also increases.

In his further refinement of the theory, Logan (1997) suggests that automaticity develops as a consequence of the "power law," which states that the reaction time to a stimulus decreases as a result of practice and repetition. The level of automaticity developed is dependent on the amount of practice, the level of consistency in the task environment, and the number of relevant instances of the task recorded in memory. As the reader's knowledge base expands and becomes accurate, performance becomes reliant on memory retrieval rather than problem solving (Logan, 1997). Based on Logan's theory, as students read words, they lay down traces for each word. If the word is read frequently enough, the cumulative practice with that word results in an increased likelihood that the word will be recognized upon further exposures and that the speed with which it will be recognized will increase. Although we are attracted to the obvious notion that frequent practice with words will speed subsequent access to those words, we believe Logan's theory alone does little to help guide fluency instruction for struggling readers.

Stanovich (1986) also contributed to the contemporary focus on reading fluency. He demonstrated a clear relationship between fluency and the amount of reading in which a reader engages. Readers who achieve some fluency are likely to be readers who read more extensively than those who lack fluency, because the latter find reading difficult. Stanovich points out that as a result of reading more extensively, readers grow in all the skills that contribute to fluency and in fluency itself. Nonfluent readers who avoid reading fall further and further behind.

As we mentioned earlier, the report of the National Reading Panel (2000) significantly elevated the level of attention to fluency. The Panel's review largely reflected the position that "fluency develops from reading practice" (p. 3-1). Therefore, they devoted much of their review to analyzing the research support that exists for two major approaches to providing students with reading practice: "First, procedures that emphasize repeated oral reading practice or guided repeated oral reading practice; and second, all formal efforts to increase the amounts of independent or recreational reading that students engage in" (p. 3-5). Basically, the panel concluded that there is substantial evidence to support the use of the repeated reading procedures. However, they raised questions about the evidence supporting independent Wide Reading for promoting fluency: "There seems little reason to reject the idea that lots of silent reading would provide students with valuable practice that would enhance fluency and, ultimately, comprehension ... it could be that if you read more, you will become a better reader; however, it also seems possible that better readers simply choose to read more" (p. 3-21). In essence, they concluded that although there is very strong correlational support for independent reading contributing to fluency, there is no convincing experimental research to show that increasing independent reading will increase fluency or reading achievement.

The prior discussion of fluency and related research is certainly not a comprehensive review. Many important research findings are omitted. For more comprehensive discussions of fluency, readers are encouraged to consult reviews such as those by Chard, Ketterlin-Geller, Baker, Doabler, and Apichatabutra (2009), the National Reading Panel (2000), Rasinski, Reutzel, Chard, and Linan-Thompson (2011), Reutzel (1996), Strecker et al. (1998), and the entire summer 1991 (Volume 30, no. 3) issue of the journal *Theory into Practice*.

Although each of these reviews is clearly instructive, the position we take here is one that addresses the need of systematic, long-term, explicit fluency instruction along with careful monitoring and assessment for struggling readers. Rather than focusing solely on how to improve fluency when it is not developing as expected, it would seem helpful to examine the elements of early literacy that contribute to fluency. For this purpose, we turn to yet another theory that attempts to explain the relation of word-reading development to reading fluency.

## EHRI'S STAGES OF READING DEVELOPMENT AND FLUENCY

Ehri (1995, 1998, 2005) has developed a carefully researched, elegant theory of the stages through which readers systematically progress in order to achieve fluency. Her theory is in line with a "deep" developmental construct of fluency. We review her theory because it brings coherence to much of the research on fluency and it offers a framework for instruction designed to promote and improve fluency. Ehri distinguished five stages of reading development.

Readers at the *prealphabetic stage* have no appreciation of the alphabetic principle—the idea that in alphabetic languages like English there is a systematic relationship between the limited number of sounds and the graphic forms (letters) of the language. At the pre-alphabetic stage, children attempt to translate the unfamiliar visual forms of print into familiar oral language through visual clues in the print. Children might remember the word *monkey* by associating the descending shape of the last letter with a monkey's tail. Obviously this is not a productive approach and quickly leads to confusion since *my, pony,* and many other words would also be read as *monkey*. It would also not be productive in an alphabetic language (e.g., English, Spanish) to pursue an instructional approach that emphasizes word shape rather than a more generalizable approach to word recognition.

At the *partial alphabetic stage*, readers have learned that letters and sounds are related. However, they are not able to deal with the full complexity of the sounds in words and are unable to make complete use of the letter–sound relationships. Therefore, children focus on the most salient parts of a word and consequently use initial and, later, final letters as the clues to a printed word's pronunciation. If readers at this stage learn that the letter sequence *g-e-t* is *get*, they may focus just on the *g* and the sound it represents to identify the word. However, using this strategy of focusing on the first letter, the letter sequences *give, go,* and *gorilla* might also be identified as *get*. Although children at this stage of development will make errors in identifying words, they can make progress toward becoming fluent because they have developed the insight that the letters of a word are clues to the sounds of the word.

As children become more familiar with letters and sounds, they move into the *fully alphabetic stage*. Now, even though they may never have seen the word *bug* in print before, if they know the sounds commonly associated with the letters *b-u-g*, they can think about the sounds for each of the letters and blend them together to arrive at the pronunciation of the word. As a result of encountering the printed word *bug* several times, as few as four according to a widely cited study (Reitsma, 1983), children come to accurately and instantly identify the word *bug* without attending to the individual letters, sounds, or letter–sound associations. Ehri (1998) describes skilled reading in the following way: "Most of the words are known by sight. Sight reading is a fast-acting process. The term *sight* indicates that sight of the word activates that word in memory including information about its spelling, pronunciation, typical role in sentences, and meaning" (pp. 11–12). This instant, accurate, and automatic access *to all these dimensions* of a printed word is the needed *fluency* that will allow readers to focus their attention on comprehension rather than on decoding. It is important to note that Ehri's theory and research incorporates Logan's power law but goes further to indicate that it is the careful processing of print in the fully alphabetic stage that leads to this rapid, instant recogni tion. Partial alphabetic readers store incomplete representations of words and, therefore, confuse similar words such as *were, where, wire,* and *wore.* However, once the word form is fully processed, with repeated encounters of the word, it is recognized instantly.

Readers who recognize whole words instantly have reached the *consolidated alphabetic stage.* They also develop another valuable, attention-saving decoding skill. In addition to storing words as units, repeated encounters with words allow a reader to store letter patterns across different words. A multiletter unit *-ent* will be stored as a unit as a result of reading the words *went, sent,* and *bent.* Upon encountering the word *dent* for the first time, a consolidated alphabetic reader would need to connect only two units, *d* and *-ent,* rather than the four units that the fully alphabetic reader would need to combine. Although this approach to reading a word is faster than blending the individual phonemes, it is not as fast and efficient as sight recognition of the word. Readers who have reached the consolidated stage of reading development are in a good position to progress toward increasingly efficient fluency; however, in addition to these advanced word identification skills, they also need to increase their language vocabulary development in order to reach advanced levels of fluent reading.

The final *automatic stage* is characterized by instant recognition of words and the ability to apply advanced decoding strategies with competence and automaticity. Readers in the automatic stage unconsciously apply multiple strategies to decode and confirm unfamiliar words, resulting in accurate, fluent reading (Ehri & McCormick, 1998). This stage is characteristic of mature readers.

The previous research focuses singularly on the readers' development. However, fluency and fluency difficulties are influenced not only by learner factors but by other factors as well. In the following section, we review these other factors that contribute to fluency difficulties and discuss how to use this information when working to improve fluency for struggling readers.

## FACTORS CONTRIBUTING TO FLUENCY DIFFICULTIES FOR STRUGGLING READERS

To best understand an instructional program based on a deep construct of fluency for struggling readers, it is helpful to understand the etiology of individual differences in reading fluency. Torgesen, Rashotte, and Alexander (2001) identified the following five factors that impact a child's ability to read fluently:

1. The proportion of words in text that are recognized as orthographic.
2. Variations in the speed with which sight words are processed.

3. Speed of processes that are used to identify novel words.
4. Use of context to increase word identification.
5. Speed with which word meanings are identified.

We next describe each factor within the context of our definition of fluency, highlighting the reciprocal relationship between fluency and comprehension.

The ability to read words as orthographic chunks or units increases speed of word recognition. This speed in word recognition enables readers to focus on constructing meaning from text. Torgesen, Rashotte, et al. (2001) found that the ability to identify words by sight is the variable most strongly related to connected text reading rate in students with and without reading disabilities.

Individuals vary in the speed with which sight words are processed based on the number and quality of exposures to the word (Ehri, 1997; Logan, 1988) or on differences in processing speed (Breznitz, 2006; Wolf, Bowers, & Biddle, 2000). If words are not effectively assimilated into a child's sight word repertoire, speed of word identification will be reduced as the child attempts to decode the word. Bower and Wolf (cited in Levy, 2001) hypothesize that slow processing speed is related to slow letter processing. Difficulties with word identification, peripheral processing, and letter processing result in inhibited processing of larger orthographic units and dysfluent reading. Breznitz (2006) notes that "reading requires a high degree of synchronization in terms of speed and location of the incoming information" and that individuals with dyslexia reflect a less than optimal synchronization (p. 126). These findings support a focus on a deeper construct of fluency that points to providing instruction that encompasses a broader range of reading skills and behaviors to support reading comprehension.

Speed of processing novel words is reduced when words are not recognized as orthographic chunks (i.e., spelling patterns) or morphemes. Reading novel words requires conscious analysis, including phonetic decoding, recognition by analogy to known words, and guessing from the context or meaning of the passage (Torgesen, Rashotte, et al., 2001). If processing at the subskill level is not automatic and requires conscious analysis, reading comprehension will be compromised. Additionally, it appears problematic to allow readers to focus only on the subskill level because it may result in habitually slow reading (Breznitz, 2006).

Evidence indicates that while fluent readers do not rely on passage context for word identification, struggling readers and beginning readers do (Ben Dror, Pollatsek, & Scarpati, cited in Torgesen, Rashotte, et al., 2001; Pring & Snowling, cited in Torgesen, Rashotte, et al., 2001). Although the role of context for beginning and poor readers in reading fluency is unclear, Torgesen, Rashotte, et al. (2001) suggest that combining the use of vocabulary and background knowledge with passage context during reading may be a contributing factor in accurate, fluent word recognition. Struggling readers with limited vocabulary and background knowledge may be less able to construct meaning from a passage, resulting in slow, effortful reading. This assertion is supported by the theories of fluency development proposed by Ehri (1997), LaBerge and Samuels (1974), and Perfetti (1985) and further supports the adoption of a deeper construct of fluency.

Torgesen, Rashotte, et al. (2001) posit that the ability to rapidly identify the meaning of words while reading connected text has the potential to affect oral reading fluency. If students are able to accurately decode and identify the meaning of a word while reading connected text, speed can be maintained and comprehension can occur. If students are unable to recognize the meaning of a word rapidly and must actively reflect on word meanings while reading, both fluency and comprehension will decline. There is evidence that differences in the ability to recognize the meaning of words (vocabulary growth) result in differences in developing sight word vocabularies in favor of students who understand the meaning of words (Cunningham & Stanovich, 1998; Torgesen, Alexander, et al., 2001).

Each of the five factors that Torgesen, Rashotte, et al. (2001) identified as contributing to fluency difficulties for struggling readers provide additional support for a deeper construct of fluency. It is evident from an analysis of these factors that the development of fluency for struggling readers should encompass instruction in multiple skills, including phonemic awareness, decoding, vocabulary, oral language, and connected text reading. Instruction across multiple skills has the potential to positively impact both independent text-reading fluency and comprehension and should be considered when planning and providing instruction to struggling readers.

## AN INSTRUCTIONAL PROGRAM FOR STRUGGLING READERS BASED ON A DEEP CONSTRUCT OF FLUENCY

Our perception is that until recently some, though certainly not all, educators took a rather simplistic approach to developing fluency that is summed up in the phrase: "Read, read, read." The expectation was that if students read more, they would achieve fluency. However, research and theory suggest that at least some students will need expert instruction and teacher guidance in order to progress efficiently through the stages of reading development. We propose an eight-step program for developing fluency. Some of the steps, such as building the graphophonic foundation for fluency or high-frequency vocabulary, are usually accomplished in a relatively short period of time (e.g., often 1–2 years), while others, such as building oral language skills, are unending. Our goal in this chapter is to outline the rationale and the breadth of instruction needed for developing a deep construct of fluency with struggling readers. We give some references that offer suggestions for instructional strategies and materials, but space limitations preclude treating each of these areas in depth. The eight-step program for struggling readers should include explicit and systematic instruction that:

1. Builds the graphophonic foundations for fluency, including phonological awareness, letter familiarity, and phonics.
2. Builds and extends vocabulary and oral language skills.
3. Provides expert instruction and practice in the recognition of high-frequency vocabulary.
4. Teaches common word parts and spelling patterns.
5. Teaches, models, and provides practice in the application of a decoding strategy.
6. Uses appropriate texts to coach strategic behaviors and to build reading speed.
7. Uses repeated reading procedures as an intervention approach for struggling readers.
8. Monitors fluency development through appropriate assessment procedures.

## BUILDING THE GRAPHOPHONIC FOUNDATIONS FOR FLUENCY

Ehri lists three prerequisite "graphophonic" capabilities as foundations for fluency: (1) letter familiarity, (2) phonemic awareness, and (3) knowledge of how graphemes typically represent phonemes in words.

Strickland and Schickendanz (2009) offer practical, research-based approaches to developing graphophonic skills, including letter familiarity, in emergent readers. Instruction in the area of phonological awareness has been addressed widely (e.g., Adams, Foorman, Lundberg, & Beeler, 1998; Blachman, Ball, Black, & Tangel, 2000; O'Connor, Notari-Syverson, & Vadasy, 2007).

The importance of the three graphophonic factors is fully documented in numerous research reports (e.g., Adams, 1990; National Reading Panel, 2000). In order to move from the pre-alphabetic stage to the partial and fully alphabetic stages, students need to grasp the alphabetic principle and to apply efficiently information about the relationship between the letters and sounds (phonics) to recognize words. This clearly requires a high level of familiarity with letter forms as well as the ability to segment and blend the smallest units of spoken language—phonemes.

Building these foundations for struggling readers requires systematic progression from simpler to more complex tasks. For example, for phonemic awareness, instruction should progress on a continuum from simple tasks such as rhyming to more complex tasks such as blending and segmenting. Alphabetic principle instruction should begin with simple skills such as letter–sound identification and progress to more advanced skills such as reading multisyllabic words and more complex sentences. Phonemic awareness and alphabetic principle instruction should occur in concert. Activities to build the graphophonic foundations for fluency that can be implemented alongside a commercially produced core reading program include poetry reading that focuses on target sounds and words, matching pictures to word types, and manipulating letter tiles to spell words using known letter–sounds.

## ORAL LANGUAGE FOUNDATIONS FOR FLUENCY

In addition to the graphophonic skills, Ehri's (1995, 1998, 2005) theory requires a foundation in language skills so that students are familiar with the meanings of words and phrases as well as with their syntactical or grammatical function. These language skills provide a gateway for fluent reading whereby students read with appropriate speed, accuracy, and prosody, with each contributing to and an outcome of comprehension (Kuhn, 2011).

We know that the relationship between reading comprehension and vocabulary knowledge is strong and unequivocal (Kame'enui & Baumann, 2012; Stanovich, 1986). However, developing the oral language and vocabulary skills of children is one of the greatest challenges facing us as educators, particularly for those children who are learning English as a second language or who spend their preschool years in language-restricted environments. Many excellent resources exist for meeting this challenge. Recent examples include texts by Beck, McKeown, and Kucan (2002) and Blachowicz and Fisher (2009) as well as Nagy's (1988) highly regarded International Reading Association publication.

Ehri (1995, 1998, 2005) shows that progress in reading beyond the beginning stages is dependent on oral language development, pointing out that reading words, particularly reading them fluently, is dependent on familiarity with them in their oral form. If the syntactic and meaning aspects of the word are to be activated, they must be part of what the reader knows through oral language development. In order for the word recognition process as proposed in Ehri's theory to be complete, it must connect with meaning that has been developed as another aspect of language development. Consider the following words: *zigzags* and *onychophagia*. Mature readers have no trouble rapidly decoding the first word, even though it is one of the least frequent words in *printed* English. However, it takes mature readers much longer to arrive at a pronunciation of the second word because it not only appears infrequently in print but is also very infrequently used in speech and, therefore, is not likely to be a word in their mental lexicon. Unless a printed word can connect with both the phonological memory for the word and the syntactical and meaning aspects of the word, it cannot be fluently decoded or read. It seems unfortunate that many surface discussions of fluency fail to make the point that fluency is dependent on readers' vocabulary as well as decoding skills.

To facilitate oral language and vocabulary growth for struggling readers, explicit and systematic instruction is required. Instructional approaches might include preteaching unfamiliar high-utility vocabulary and vocabulary essential to the meaning of a passage using a picture, synonym, or concise definition prior to read-alouds. Instruction can occur in whole class or small groups. Vocabulary instruction in small groups should be heterogeneous to enable students with more limited vocabularies to dialogue with those with rich vocabularies. Opportunities for additional practice and review of taught words can be provided using strategies such as word walls, where high-frequency vocabulary is posted and practiced; semantic mapping; use of questioning to promote deep processing; and relating new vocabulary to meaningful experience.

Not only do oral language and vocabulary growth enable the reading of passages with appropriate speed and accuracy for all readers, but readers' oral language and vocabulary growth may also be related to their reading prosody. Rasinski et al. (2011) define prosody as "an area of phonology that focuses on the rhythmical and tonal features of speech that are layered upon individual phonological segments and include stress, pitch and duration" (p. 292). In lay terms, reading with prosody refers to reading aloud in a manner that replicates spoken language. Reading with attention to stress, pitch, and duration may play a direct role in the ability to read fluently and to comprehend passage meaning. Research has revealed strong correlations between informal ratings of prosody and silent reading comprehension in elementary and secondary school students (Daane, Campbell, Grigg, Goodman, & Oranje, 2005; Pinnell et al., 1995). Kuhn (2011) proposes an interactive relationship between prosody and comprehension whereby each contributes to and is an outcome of children's understanding of the text. However, research has yet to ascertain the relationship between prosody and overall reading ability and, if this relationship does exist, the extent to which prosody directly impacts reading fluency and overall reading achievement (Rasinski et al., 2011).

## TEACHING HIGH-FREQUENCY VOCABULARY

High-frequency words are those words that appear over and over again in our language, words such as *the, of, and, at,* and *to.* Instant recognition of high-frequency words plays an important role in developing fluency for struggling readers (Torgesen & Hudson, 2006). In order to effectively teach high-frequency words to struggling readers, instruction should address both a broad range of high-frequency words that individuals can recognize on sight and the efficiency with which these words are recognized (Torgesen, Rashotte, et al., 2001; Cramer & Rosenfield, 2008).

One approach to building fluent recognition of high-frequency vocabulary, exceedingly popular with primary grade teachers, is the use of word walls (Cunningham, 2000). A second approach is to prepare a 5 × 5 grid in which students practice high-frequency words to the level of fluency by placing one new word and four review words randomly in each row. Students are provided an untimed practice, and then do a timed recall of the words, working towards a desired criterion rate (e.g., 1 word per second). Cunningham also offers a variety of other methods for teaching high-frequency words, as do Bear, Invernizzi, Templeton, and Johnston (1996).

Ehri's (1995, 1998, 2005) theory and research also offer important, practical teaching suggestions. High-frequency words have often been seen as a serious challenge because many of them do not lend themselves to straightforward application of decoding skills; they are, in the jargon of reading instruction, phonically irregular—words such as *the*, *of*, *was*, and *have*. Teaching high-frequency words can be difficult. This difficulty may very well be a contributor to the periodic abandonment of phonics approaches and the rise of whole-word approaches to teaching beginning reading skills, with accompanying emphasis on drill using flash cards to force children to read the words as a whole. Ehri's work suggests that they also contain many letter–sound regularities and that these regularities are the best mnemonics for developing accurate, instant recognition. For example, while the word *have* does not follow the generalization about the effect of a final *e* on a preceding vowel sound, the *h*, *v*, and *e* all behave as they should, and the *a* does represent a sound that it often represents. Ehri suggests that we should point out the regular elements of "irregular" words in order to help children gain instant recognition of them. This is a practice rarely mentioned by "experts" or used by teachers, but it might play a very important role in avoiding difficulty with such words and thus promoting the development of fluency.

## RECOGNIZING WORD PARTS AND SPELLING PATTERNS

Word parts and spelling patterns are combinations of letters such as *at*, *ell*, *ick*, *op* that are found as units in many words that appear in beginning reading texts. Like Ehri (1997, 1998, 2005), Samuels (1999, 2002) maintains that the size of the unit that is recognized during reading varies between beginning and experienced readers. Beginning readers rely on cues at the single letter–sound level and integrate the use of word parts, spelling patterns, and word reading as they become more capable. Proficient readers are able to identify word parts, spelling patterns, and whole words as units automatically. Differences in strategy use between beginning and proficient readers suggest a differential reliance on word parts and spelling patterns, which depends on the individual stage of reading development.

Consistent with this view, Menon and Hiebert (2011) suggest that struggling readers experience difficulty developing proficiency identifying single letter–sounds (phonemes), and that instruction in larger grain-size units, such as word parts and spelling patterns, appears to hold additional benefit to working at the individual phoneme level. Furthermore, exposure to these larger grain sizes in connected texts would provide students additional opportunities to develop automaticity with word parts and spelling patterns while reading connected text. This view is supported by Kuhn (2011) in her observation that isolated decoding instruction and word work fail to generalize to the reading of connected text.

Here again, Cunningham (2000) and Bear et al. (1996) are among the many resources that offer practical teaching suggestions, including a list of the most common word parts found in beginning reading materials. Lovett et al. (2000) provide additional validated instructional approaches to teaching word parts.

Introducing students to multiple-letter units clearly moves students from the fully alphabetic to the consolidated alphabetic stage. However, Ehri's (1997, 1998, 2005) research and theory offer an important instructional generalization: Students should first be introduced to and made cognizant of the individual letters and sounds that constitute the rime (a fully alphabetic approach) in order to better recall and identify the unit that they constitute. In addition, Torgesen, Wagner, Rashotte, Alexander, and Conway (1997) offer further caution. They assert that isolated instruction in word parts and spelling patterns alone is not sufficient to develop reading fluency for struggling readers. Word parts and spelling patterns will only enable children to reach satisfactory levels of oral reading fluency if they are routinely used and practiced in reading connected text and if the amount of connected text reading is sufficient to maintain growth.

## TEACHING A DECODING STRATEGY

There are several major ways in which words can be recognized or identified in print: instantly as units; through recognition of and blending of phonic elements; through the context in which they appear, including language/sentence context and picture clues; and by checking the phonetic re-spellings in a dictionary or glossary. Ehri's theory (1997, 1998, 2005) is clear: The best way to recognize words is through instant recognition that drains no attention. All other approaches require attention. However, when a word is not instantly recognized, it is useful for readers to be strategic. Struggling readers frequently experience difficulty in being strategic during reading.

In kindergarten and the beginning of first grade, emphasis is on moving young readers from the partial to the fully alphabetic stages of reading, with particularly careful attention to the graphophonic characteristics of the word. By mid-first grade, the goal is to move students increasingly into the consolidated alphabetic stage. The italicized portion of the strategy is recommended as young readers and struggling readers become familiar with word parts.

1. Look at the letters from left to right.
2. As you look at the letters, think about the sounds for the letters.
3. Blend the sounds together *and look for word parts you know* to read the word.
4. Ask yourself: Is this a word I know? Does it make sense in what I am reading?
5. If it doesn't make sense, try other strategies (e.g., pronouncing the word another way, reading on).

Readers who are at the partial and fully alphabetic stages will need to look carefully at the word they are trying to identify and think about the sounds the letters are likely to represent and then use the skill of phoneme blending to try to arrive at the correct decoding or pronunciation of the word. Because some words are not completely phonically regular, students should then be encouraged to ask themselves whether their use of phonics results in the identification of a word that makes sense—that it is a word they have heard before and that it fits the context of what they are reading. As children begin to move from the fully alphabetic to the consolidated alphabetic stage of development, in addition to using phonic elements, they should also be encouraged to look for word parts (chunks) and spelling patterns that they know, such as phonograms. The order of phonics and word parts *followed by* use of context appears to be by far the best order.

Use of context as the primary approach to identifying words has serious limitations. First, if the context is highly predictive of a word, it is likely that students will not pay attention to the graphic information of the word. Careful processing of the printed form is what eventually enables a reader to recognize that word instantly. This is a major limitation of the predictable texts that use very heavy, artificial context to allow word identification. Second, context rarely leads to the correct identification of a specific word. Ehri's review of research suggests that the words in a text that carry the most meaning can be correctly identified by context only about 10% of the time. However, context and the other approaches to decoding words do play an important role in decoding—that of confirming the identification of words. As Ehri puts it:

> As each sight word is fixated, its meaning and pronunciation are triggered in memory quickly and automatically. However, the other word reading processes do not lie dormant; their contribution is not to identify words in text but to *confirm* the identity already determined. Knowledge of the graphophonic system confirms that the word's pronunciation fits the spelling on the page. Knowledge of syntax confirms that the word fits into the structure of the sentence. Word knowledge and text memory confirm that the word's meaning is consistent with the text's meaning up to that point. (1998, p. 11; emphasis added)

## USING APPROPRIATE TEXTS TO PROMOTE FLUENCY

In order to progress in their fluency, students need to engage in the practice and application of their growing word identification skills to appropriate texts. Appropriate texts are particularly critical for students who have difficulty with word identification skills. Guided reading has once again emerged as a useful way to match students and texts. Resources such as those based on the work of Fountas and Pinnell (1996) offer guidance in selecting texts and providing appropriate instruction with those texts.

Menon and Hiebert (2011) suggest that text selection plays a significant role in remediating fluency difficulties, specifically the consideration of text difficulty and orthographic features of texts for students with learning disabilities. In the remediation of fluency difficulties, instructional texts in which a child reads accurately appear to produce the greatest outcomes, rather than texts that produce frustration. Furthermore, Menon and Hiebert assert that students with reading difficulties attributed to a phonological deficit may develop word attack skills most effectively by reading highly decodable texts, while students with a rate deficit may benefit more from an approach designed to address automaticity and fluency. Students identified with both phonological and rate deficits may benefit from reading texts that embed both approaches. Hiebert and Fischer (2002) proposes that texts be designed and selected using the text elements by task (TExT) model, whereby struggling readers read passages in which the cognitive load is reduced, that contain more repetitions of fewer words, more linguistic patterns such as frequency within the English language, and consistent vowel patterns. Instructional materials currently used in American classrooms are not constructed in a systematic way in their repetition of core words or linguistic elements to support struggling readers. These findings suggest that the features of the texts being used to promote fluency should be carefully considered.

## USING REPEATED READING PROCEDURES

As noted earlier in this chapter, the 2000 Report of the National Reading Panel was unequivocal in its support of repeated reading procedures. The references describe a range of procedures in sufficient detail to allow teachers to use them with students who need extra support in developing fluency. These procedures include repeated reading (Samuels, 1979), neurological impress (Heckelman, 1969), radio reading (Greene, 1979), paired reading (Topping, 1987), and "a variety of similar techniques" (p. 3-1). A review of these approaches suggests substantial differences in the procedures used and the amount of teacher guidance offered (Chard, Vaughn, & Tyler, 2002; Kuhn & Stahl, 2000). However, all appear to have merit. Features of effective procedures for struggling readers invlude (1) brief daily practice, (2) repeated oral reading of passages, (3) overlap of shared words across passages, (4) consistency in text context, (5) controlled text difficulty, (6) provision of corrective feedback, (7) teacher-modeled text reading, (8) audiotaped modeled reading, (9) repeated reading with a partner, (10) cross-age tutoring with a partner, and (11) specified performance criterion levels of fluency (Chard et al., 2002; Kuhn & Stahl, 2000; National Reading Panel, 2000).

Although the efficacy of repeated reading in developing reading fluency for children with learning disabilities is well documented (Chard et al., 2002; Kuhn & Stahl, 2003; Yang, 2006), there has been some question as to whether the evidence base used in support of its merits is robust in its representation of repeated reading as a suitable intervention for students at risk for and experiencing learning disabilities (Chard et al., 2009; Menon & Hiebert, 2011). Menon and Hiebert (2011) suggest an alternative hypothesis that "repeated reading increases the total amount of text read and that increases to print exposure [may] alone contribute to fluency development" (p. 63). This is supported by the findings of Kuhn and others (Kuhn & Stahl, 2004; Kuhn et al., 2006; Kuhn, 2011), who suggest that wide reading was as effective as repeated reading in increasing reading fluency and more effective in increasing reading comprehension where little or no attention is paid to the linguistic content of texts. Contemporary research suggests that a range of instructional approaches may contribute to increases in reading accuracy, speed, comprehension, and prosody (Kuhn, 2011; Rasinski et al., 2011).

Four principles for supporting reading fluency in students with reading disabilities have demonstrated efficacy with all students (Rasinski, 2003; Kuhn, 2011): (1) modeling fluent reading; (2) provision of practice in a range of text types, including narrative, expository, poetry, and speeches; (3) provision of support during reading; and (4) appropriate phrasing.

Recent research suggests that strategies such as repeated reading, wide reading (Kuhn, 2009), and partner reading incorporating a comprehension component (Kuhn, 2011) are effective for increasing oral reading fluency.

## ASSESSMENT OF FLUENCY FOR STRUGGLING READERS

As noted at the beginning of this chapter, fluency has been referred to as the "neglected aspect" of reading. The assessment of fluency, in particular, appears to have received very limited attention. There are few research studies that have investigated how fluency should be assessed or what criteria should be applied to determine whether or not fluency has been achieved. Readers are encouraged to review Deno (1985), Fuchs, Fuchs, Hamlett, Walz, and Germann (1993), Hasbrouck and Tindal (1992), and Shinn, Good, Tilly, Knutson, and Collins (1992) for examples of work done in the area of fluency assessment.

The National Reading Panel (2000) concludes: "A number of informal procedures can be used in the classroom to assess fluency: informal reading inventories, miscue analysis, pausing indices, and reading speed calculations. All these assessment procedures require oral reading of text, and all can provide an adequate index of fluency" (p. 3-9). Although few experimental studies have been conducted using these informal procedures, it may very well have been that the panel's recognizing the very practical need for classroom assessment led them to endorse procedures that may not have the strong research support they more typically require in other parts of the report.

Alt and Samuels (2001) contrast definitions and suggest that the field has misunderstood the definition of fluency and that it means the simultaneous application of reading speed and comprehension. They argue that this has led to invalid measures of fluency that are actually only measures of speed (e.g., curriculum-based measurement [CBM] and Diagnostic Indicators of Basic Early Literacy Skills [DIBELS]).

> Because misuse of the tool [CBM] has led to the misperception that the development of efficient word recognition skills leads to improved comprehension (Calfee & Piontkowski, 1981), CBM has been widely used around the country to determine if a student is a fluent reader. In fact, McGlinchey and Hixon (2004) assessed the correlation between CBM and standardized reading scores and found supporting evidence for concurrent validity. However,

Cramer and Rosenfield (2008) found no correlations between reading speed and reading fluency. What's more, Pressley, Hilden, and Shankland (2005) not only found no correlation, but found reading speed to be a poor predictor of reading fluency. (Alt & Samuels, 2011, p. 178)

To meet calls for assessment of fluency in concert with assessment of comprehension and prosody, there are many published informal inventories that can be practically used to periodically assess the four dimensions of fluency that are necessary for a full, deep, developmental construct of fluency: oral reading accuracy, oral reading rate, quality of oral reading, and reading comprehension. Teachers who want to assess selective aspects of fluency can use guidelines that have been suggested for assessing oral reading rate and accuracy (e.g., Hasbrouck & Tindal, 1992; Rasinski, 2003). Likewise, procedures have been established for assessing the quality of oral reading using standardized rubrics that go beyond rate and accuracy, such as that based upon NAEP data (Pinnell et al., 1995).

A more comprehensive review of the research related to fluency assessment is beyond the scope of this chapter. However, we recommend that teachers take measures of fluency beginning in the middle of first grade. At second grade and beyond, assessments should occur at least at the beginning, middle, and end of a school year to gauge progress in this important area and to check periodically throughout the year any students who are making doubtful progress.

## CONCLUSIONS

Although the construct of fluency may have been neglected in the past, it is receiving much deserved attention presently. A very strong research and theoretical base indicates that while fluency in and of itself is not sufficient to ensure high levels of reading achievement, fluency is absolutely necessary for that achievement because fluency depends upon and typically reflects comprehension. If a reader has not developed fluency, the process of decoding words drains his or her focus, and insufficient attention is available for constructing the meaning of texts.

Fluency builds on a foundation of oral language skills, phonemic awareness, familiarity with letter forms, and efficient decoding skills. Ehri's description of the stages of word recognition explains how readers come to recognize words by sight through careful processing of print.

Substantial research has also been conducted on how best to develop fluency for students who do not yet have it. Although there is a dearth of experimental research studies on developing fluency through increasing the amount of independent reading, there is substantial correlational evidence showing a clear relationship between the amount students read, their reading fluency, and their reading comprehension. However, students who are struggling with reading are not in a position to engage in Wide Reading, and they may need more guidance and support in order to develop fluency. Research shows that a variety of procedures based on repeated readings can help struggling readers to improve their fluency.

While more research is needed on the issues of adequate rates of fluency at various grade levels and for judging the quality of oral reading, there is agreement that the comprehensive assessment of fluency must include measures of oral reading accuracy, rate, and quality. There is also growing agreement that these dimensions of fluency must be assessed within the context of reading comprehension. Fluency with accompanying high levels of reading comprehension is of ultimate advantage to readers. By defining fluency as a deep construct, we seek to articulate carefully the features of reading development and their role in the reciprocal relationship between fluency and comprehension. Moreover, a deeper construct of fluency provides a clearer focus for systematic intervention, remediation, and assessment for struggling readers.

## REFERENCES

Adams, M. J. (1990). *Beginning to read: Thinking and learning about print.* Cambridge, MA: MIT Press.

Adams, M. J., Foorman, B. R., Lundberg, I., & Beeler, T. (1998). *Phonemic awareness in young children.* Baltimore, MD: Brookes.

Alt, S. J., & Samuels, S. J. (2011). Reading fluency: What is it and how should it be measured? In A. McGill-Franzen & R. L. Allington (Eds.). *Handbook of reading disability research* (pp. 173–181). New York: Routledge.

Bear, D. R., Invernizzi, M., Templeton, S., & Johnston, F. (1996). *Words their way.* Columbus, OH: Merrill.

Beck, I. L., McKeown, M. G., & Kucan, L. (2002). *Bringing words to life.* New York: Guilford Press.

Blachman, B. A., Ball, E. W., Black, R., & Tangel, D. M. (2000). *Road to the code: A phonological awareness program for young children.* Baltimore, MD: Brookes.

Blachowicz, C., & Fisher, P. J. (2009). *Teaching vocabulary in all classrooms* (4th ed.). Columbus, OH: Merrill.

Breznitz, Z. (2006). *Reading fluency: Synchronization of processes.* Mahway, NJ: Erlbaum.

Calfee, R. C., & Piontkowski, D. C. (1981). The reading diary: acquisition of decoding. *Reading Research Quarterly, 6,* 346–373.

Chard, D. J., Ketterlin-Geller, L. R., Baker, S. K., Doabler, C., & Apichatabutra, C. (2009). Repeated reading interventions for students with learning disabilities: Status of the evidence. *Exceptional Children, 75,* 263–281.

Chard, D. J., Vaughn, S., & Tyler, B. J. (2002). A synthesis of research on effective interventions for building fluency with elementary students with learning disabilities. *Journal of Learning Disabilities, 35*, 386–406.

Cramer, K., & Rosenfield, S. (2008). Effect of degree of challenge on reading performance. *Reading and Writing Quarterly, 24*(1), 119–137.

Cunningham, A. E., & Stanovich, K. E. (1998, Spring/Summer). What reading does for the mind. *American Educator,* 8–15.

Cunningham, P. M. (2000). *Phonics they use.* New York: Longman.

Deno, S. (1985). Curriculum based measurement: An emerging alternative. *Exceptional Children, 52*, 219–232.

Ehri, L. C. (1995). Stages of development in learning to read words by sight. *Journal of Research in Reading, 18*, 116–125.

Ehri, L. C. (1997). Sight word learning in normal readers and dyslexics. In B. Blachman (Ed.), *Foundations of reading acquisition and dyslexia* (pp. 163–189). Mahwah, NJ: Erlbaum.

Ehri, L. C. (1998). Grapheme–phoneme knowledge is essential for learning to read words in English. In J. L. Metsala & L. C. Ehri (Eds.), *Word recognition in beginning literacy* (pp. 3–40). Mahwah, NJ: Erlbaum.

Ehri, L. C. (2005). Learning to read words; Theory, findings, and issues. *Scientific Studies of Reading, 9*(2), 167–188.

Ehri, L. C., & McCormick, S. (1998). Phases of word learning: Implications for instruction with delayed and disabled readers. *Reading and Writing Quarterly, 14*(2), 135–163.

Fountas, I. C., & Pinnell, G. S. (1996). *Guided reading: Good first teaching for all children.* Portsmouth, NH: Heinemann.

Fuchs, L. S., Fuchs, D., Hamlett, C. L., Walz, L., & Germann, G. (1993). Formative evaluation of academic progress: How much growth can we expect? *School Psychology Review, 22*, 27–48.

Greene, F. P. (1979). Radio reading. In C. Pennock (Ed.), *Reading comprehension at four linguistic levels* (pp. 104–107). Newark, DE: International Reading Association.

Harris, T. L., & Hodges, R. E. (1995). *The literacy dictionary: The vocabulary of reading and writing.* Newark, DE: International Reading Association.

Hasbrouck, J. E., & Tindal, G. (1992). Curriculum based fluency norms for grades two through five. *Teaching Exceptional Children, 24*, 41–44.

Heckelman, R. G. (1969). A neurological-impress method of remedial-reading instruction. *Academic Therapy, 4*, 277–282.

Hiebert, E. H., & Fisher, C. W. (2002). *Text matters in developing fluent reading.* Unpublished manuscript.

Huey, E. B. (1968). *The psychology and pedagogy of reading; With a review of the history of reading and writing and of methods, texts, and hygiene in reading.* Cambridge, MA: MIT Press. (Originally work published 1908)

Kame'enui, E. J., & Baumann, J. F. (Eds.). (2012). *Vocabulary instruction: Research to practice* (2nd ed.). New York: Guilford Press.

Kuhn, M. R. (2011). Interventions to enhance fluency and rate of reading. In A. McGill-Franzen & R. L. Allington (Eds.), *Handbook of reading disability research* (pp. 307–314). New York: Routledge.

Kuhn, M. R., Schwanenflugel, P. J., Morris, R. D., Morrow, L. M., Woo, D., Meisinger, B., et al (2006). Teaching children to become fluent and automatic readers. *Journal of Literacy Research, 38,* 357–387.

Kuhn, M. R., & Stahl, S. A. (2000). *Fluency: A review of developmental and remedial practices.* Ann Arbor, MI: Center for the Improvement of Early Reading Achievement.

Kuhn, M. R., & Stahl, S. A. (2003). Fluency: A review of developmental and remedial strategies. *Journal of Educational Psychology, 95*(1), 3–21.

LaBerge, D., & Samuels, S. J. (1974). Towards a theory of automatic information processing in reading. *Cognitive Psychology, 6,* 293–323.

Levy, B. A. (2001). Moving the bottom: Improving reading fluency. In M. Wolf (Ed.), *Dyslexia, fluency, and the brain* (pp. 307–331). Timonium, MD: York Press.

Logan, G. D. (1988). Toward an instance theory of automatization. *Psychological Review, 95*(4), 492–527.

Logan, G. D. (1997). Automaticity and reading: Perspectives from the instance theory of automatization. *Reading and Writing Quarterly, 13*(2), 123–146.

Lovett, M., Borden, S. L., Lacerenza, L., Frijters, J. C., Steinbach, K. A., & DePalma, M. (2000). Components of effective remediation for developmental reading disabilities: Combining phonological and strategy based instruction to improve outcomes. *Journal of Educational Psychology, 92*(2), 263–283.

McGlinchey, M. T., & Hixon, M. D. (2004). Using curriculum-based measurement to predict performance on state assessments in reading. *School Psychology Review, 33,* 192–203.

Menon, A., & Hiebert, E. H. (2011). Instructional texts and the fluency of learning disabled readers. In A. McGill-Franzen & R. L. Allington (Eds.), *Handbook of reading disability research* (pp. 57–67). New York: Routledge.

Nagy, W. E. (1988). *Teaching vocabulary to improve reading comprehension.* Newark, DE: International Reading Association.

National Reading Panel. (2000). *Teaching children to read: An evidence-based assessment of the scientific research literature on reading and its implications for reading instruction* (NIH Publication No. 00-4769). Washington, DC: National Institute of Child Health and Human Development.

O'Connor, R. E., Notari-Syverson, A., & Vadasy, P. F. (2007). *Ladders to Literacy: A kindergarten activity book* (2nd ed.). Baltimore, MD: Brookes.

Perfetti, C. A. (1985). *Reading ability.* New York: Oxford University Press.

Pikulski, J. J., & Chard, D. J. (2005). Fluency: Bridge between decoding and reading comprehension. *The Reading Teacher, 58,* 510–519.

Pinnell, G. S., Pikulski, J. J., Wixson, K. K., Campbell, J. R., Gough, P. B., & Beatty, A. S. (1995). *Listening to children read aloud.* Washington, DC: Office of Educational Research and Improvement, U.S. Department of Education.

Pressley, M., Hilden, K., & Shankland, R. (2005). *An evaluation of end-of-grade 3 Dynamic Indicators of Basic Early Literacy Skills (DIBELs): Speed reading without comprehension, predicting little.* East Lansing, MI: Literacy Achievement Research Center.

Rasinski, T. V. (2003). *The fluent reader: Oral reading strategies for building word recognition, fluency, and comprehension.* New York: Scholastic.

Rasinski, T. V., & Hoffman, J. V. (2003). Oral reading in the school literacy program. *Reading Research Quarterly, 38,* 510–522.

Rasinski, T. V., Reutzel, D. R., Chard, D., & Linan-Thompson, S. (2011). Reading fluency. In M. L. Kamil, P. D. Pearson, E. B. Moje, & P. P. Afflerbach (Eds.), *Handbook of reading research* (Vol. IV, pp. 286–319). New York: Taylor & Francis.

Reitsma, P. (1983). Printed word learning in beginning readers. *Journal of Experimental Child Psychology, 75,* 321–339.

Reutzel, D. R. (1996). Developing at-risk readers' oral reading fluency. In L. Putnam (Ed.), *How to become a better reader: Strategies for assessment and intervention* (pp. 241–254). Englewood Cliffs, NJ: Merrill.

Samuels, S. J. (1979). The method of repeated readings. *The Reading Teacher, 32,* 403–408.

Samuels, S. J. (1999). Developing reading fluency in learning disabled students. In R. J. Sternberg & L. Spear Swerling (Eds.), *Perspectives on learning disabilities: Biological, cognitive, contextual* (pp. 176–189). Boulder, CO: Westview Press.

Samuels, S. J. (2002). Reading fluency: Its development and assessment. In A. E. Farstrup & S. J. Samuels (Eds.), *What research has to say about reading instruction* (3rd ed., pp. 166–183). Newark, DE: International Reading Association.

Shinn, M. R., Good, R. H., Tilly, D., Knutson, N., & Collins, V. (1992). Curriculum based measurement of oral reading fluency: A confirmatory analysis of its relation to reading. *School Psychology Review, 21*(3), 459–479.

Stanovich, K. E. (1986). Matthew effects in reading: Some consequences in individual differences in the acquisition of literacy. *Reading Research Quarterly, 21,* 360–407.

Strecker, S. K., Roser, N. L., & Martinez, M. G. (1998). Understanding oral reading fluency. In T. Shanahan & F. V. Rodriguez-Brown (Eds.), *47th yearbook of the National Reading Conference* (pp. 295–310). Chicago, IL: National Reading Conference.

Strickland, D. S., & Schickendanz, J. (2009). *Learning about print in preschool: Working with letters, words and links with phonemic awareness* (2nd ed.). Newark, DE: International Reading Association.

Topping, K. (1987). Paired reading: A powerful technique for parent use. *The Reading Teacher, 40,* 608–614.

Torgesen, J. K., Alexander, A. W., Wagner, R. K., Rashotte, C. A., Voeller, K., Conway, T., et al.. (2001). Intensive remedial instruction for children with severe reading disabilities: Immediate and long-term outcomes from two instructional approaches. *Journal of Learning Disabilities, 34*(1), 33–58, 78.

Torgesen, J. K., & Hudson, R. F. (2006). Reading fluency: Critical issues for struggling readers. In S. J. Samuels & A. E. Farstrup (Eds.), *What research has to say about fluency instruction* (pp. 130–158). Newark, DE: International Reading Association.

Torgesen, J. K., Rashotte, C. A., & Alexander, A. W. (2001). Principles of fluency instruction in reading: Relationships with established empirical outcomes. In

M. Wolf (Ed.), *Dyslexia, fluency, and the brain* (pp. 307–331). Timonium, MD: York Press.

Torgesen, J. K., Wagner, R. K., Rashotte, C. A., Alexander, A. W., & Conway, T. (1997). Preventive and remedial interventions for children with severe reading disabilities. *Learning Disabilities, 8*(1), 51–62.

Wolf, M., Bowers, P. G., & Biddle, K. (2000). Naming speed processes, timing, and reading: A conceptual review. *Journal of Learning Disabilities, 33*(4), 387–407.

Yang, J. (2006). *A meta-analysis of the effects of interventions to increase reading fluency among elementary school students.* Unpublished doctoral dissertation, Vanderbilt University, Nashville, TN.

# 7

# "Hey Teacher, When You Say 'Fluency,' What Do You Mean?"

## Developing Fluency in Elementary Classrooms

D. Ray Reutzel

> Fluent reading, like the thread of life itself ..., is intrinsically elegant in both form and cadence.... We certainly know it when we see it, and we are quick to celebrate it, along with the trajectory of success it portends.
>
> —KAME'NEUI AND SIMMONS (2001)

It was a crisp, bright fall morning at Paragon (pseudonym) Elementary School in a diverse inner-city school district in the Rocky Mountain region of the United States. Over a 6-year period, the teachers in this school had received copious amounts of professional development as a part of their involvement with a Federal *Reading First* grant competitively awarded to high-poverty, low-performing school districts. After several years of learning, applying, and refining, the teachers felt relatively confident about their ability to provide systematic, explicit, and effective fluency instruction and practice after overcoming a singular focus on "getting kids to read fast and accurate." This is the story of their struggles and successes.

These teachers had tried for several months to move beyond merely focusing on helping children to read 1-minute short samples of grade-level text faster and faster to meet established performance benchmarks. They were involved in establishing classroom instructional routines that provided varied reading fluency instruction and reading practice based upon students' individual needs as identified through screening and progress monitoring assessment. On this particular day, a literacy professor who worked as the state-appointed technical assistant (the author of this chapter), a school-based reading coach, and the district Reading First coordinator had been asked to observe two teachers' reading fluency instruction block—Mrs. Enrico, a third-grade teacher, and Ms. Parker, a fourth-grade teacher.

We began our observations in Mrs. Enrico's third-grade classroom. The children were seated on the floor around a screen where Mrs. Enrico was displaying, using a document camera and computer projector, an information book titled *American Symbols: The Statue of Liberty* (Sorenson, 2003). She informed the children that she was going to model fluent oral reading of this third-grade-level information text. She read the text aloud, evidencing appropriate pauses, expression, and a conversational reading rate. Upon completion, she asked the children to indicate whether they felt she had read the text fluently by giving her thumbs-up or thumbs-down. Most of the children gave their teacher a thumbs-up. Two, however, gave her oral reading a thumbs-down and when questioned by Mrs. Enrico, they replied, "You didn't sound right when you read it. You sounded funny." Mrs. Enrico aked, "What didn't sound right?" The two students responded that there were some words in the text they didn't understand very well. Mrs. Enrico then identified three French words in the text, repeated them, and asked whether they were the problem, and the two students nodded their heads. "I guess I should have explained that these words were French and should have told you their meanings before I read this passage," commented Mrs. Enrico. She then took a minute to say these words again, explaining the meanings of the words and phrases, and asked the children to say these words orally as she pointed to them on the screen. Next, Mrs. Enrico invited the children to read the text with her in choral unison. She reminded them to use "phrasing and expression as signaled by the punctuation" as they read while she pointed to the words on the projected page. Each punctuation mark had been covered with a small piece of highlighter tape so that the students' would pay particular attention to them as they read. The team of observers came away reflecting on how this lesson had moved beyond the typical focus of instruction seen months before, when teachers were pushing students to read faster without attention to expression, phrasing, or understanding. We could see that the professional development we had given with a focus on developing fluency was beginning to take hold in this classroom.

Next, we walked across the school building to Ms. Parker's fourth-grade classroom to observe her fluency lesson. Students' desks were arranged in a U shape facing the whiteboard and computer screen, where she had displayed a PowerPoint presentation of the book *Rock: A Remarkable Resource* (Rubin, 2005). Ms. Parker had also prepared a poster displaying the elements of fluent oral reading: accuracy, rate, expression, and comprehension. Before reading the text aloud, Ms. Parker discussed each of the elements of fluent reading with the group. She instructed the children to listen carefully as she read aloud and to be prepared to comment on her reading of this science text relative to three of the elements of fluent reading—accuracy, rate, and expression.

Ms. Parker read the text aloud, surprising her students by modeling hesitant, mostly accurate reading with a few inaccuracies dispersed throughout the reading and in a monotone voice. The children giggled as she modeled this partially accurate, poorly phrased, and expressionless reading. When her reading concluded, children's hands shot into the air. "I know what you did wrong," one round-faced, brown-eyed little girl blurted out. "You sounded like you were a machine, sort of like a robot reading aloud; you didn't have expression." Ms. Parker encouraged more observations and evaluations of her reading from the children, and then replied, "Oh, so you think you could do better, do you?" They all responded in a choral "Yes!" "Okay," she said, "I want you to pair up with a partner and practice reading pages 2–7 of this text together. I will distribute a book for each pair to read together. At first, one of you is to be the listener and the other one is to be the reader. The reader is to practice reading the text out loud until the listener says it is a good example of fluent reading. Then you are to exchange the roles of reader and listener. When you are finished, I will select several readers to come up and read these pages aloud to the whole class using the document camera and the computer projector. We will then give feedback to each reader using our fluency poster on the wall. Any questions?" She pauses. "Okay, then start working. We have about 20 minutes."

During the practice time, Ms. Parker moved among the pairs, listening and providing feedback. All the children were very much engaged. At the end of practice time, Ms. Parker invited three children to read one to two pages aloud and receive feedback from their peers. As we exited the classroom, we expressed even greater satisfaction with this reading fluency lesson.

That same day, we met after school with both these teachers as well as the other teachers in grades 2–4. We complimented Mrs. Enrico and Ms. Parker on the strong points of their lessons, such as their efforts to (1) model, (2) explicitly teach the elements of fluency, (3) provide guided practice, and (4) offer constructive and informative feedback. Next, we asked all the teachers to discuss in small groups any concerns they still had about providing fluency practice and instruction. Several teachers asked how they could foster students' ability to self-monitor their fluent reading of texts and to know how to "fix up" their fluency across a range of text difficulty levels and text types. Other teachers wondered whether their time was well allocated between instruction and practice. They wanted a better sense of the daily fluency instruction routine, in which students received explicit instruction and systematic practice for developing fluency and the ability to self-monitor and self-adjust oral reading processes to produce fluent oral renditions of texts. To accomplish this aim, we undertook an in-depth study of current and past research and professional literature on fluency in weekly after-school group meetings to continue to refine and improve the reading fluency instruction and practice offered in this school.

## UNDERSTANDING READING FLUENCY:
## "YOU CAN'T TEACH WHAT YOU DON'T KNOW"

As we began our study of fluency, we found that there wasn't a single, agreed-upon definition of fluency in the literature. For example, Samuels (1979) defined a "lack of fluency" as being characterized by a slow, halting pace; frequent mistakes; poor phrasing; and inadequate expression. Harris and Hodges (1995) defined fluency as "the clear, easy, written or spoken expression of ideas" (p. 85). And according to the National Reading Panel, "Fluent readers can read text with 1) speed, 2) accuracy, and 3) proper expression" (p. 3-1). In a more recent discussion of fluency, Samuels (2007) argued quite convincingly that fluent reading "is the simultaneity of decoding and comprehension that is the essential characteristic of reading fluency. Secondary characteristics of fluency such as speed, accuracy, and expression are indicators, but not the essential characteristics. For example, I can read Spanish orally with accuracy and speed, but I am unable to understand what I have read. Am I fluent in Spanish? No! Nor does the ability to read nonsense jabberwocky with expression capture the essential characteristic of fluency" (p. 564).

Our continuing study of reading fluency also led us to reconsider the place and importance of oral versus silent reading, levels of text difficulty, text genres, and varying forms of reading fluency practices found in the elementary classroom (Hiebert & Reutzel, 2010). The history of oral and silent reading, much like the field of reading generally, has been characterized by the swinging of the pendulum of fashion. Prior to and during the early part of the 20th century, oral reading ability and performance were highly valued as a cultural asset (Rasinski, 2010; Smith, 2002). However, with the advance of research early in that century, it was demonstrated that reading silently seemed to hold an advantage for readers in terms of both reading rate and comprehension (Huey, 1908). Moreover, the utility and superiority of silent reading seemed apparent, since most adult readers engaged almost exclusively in silent reading compared with oral reading (Rasinski, 2010; Rasinski, Reutzel, Chard, & Linan-Thompson, 2010).

This along with the rise of round robin or "barbershop" reading practices in elementary classrooms, which led to the ritualistic routine of having one student read aloud while others passively listened until it was their turn, culminated in the general elevation of silent reading practice over oral reading practice in schools (Eldredge, Reutzel, & Hollingsworth, 1996). More recently, based on the analyses and findings of the National Reading Panel (2000) regarding effective fluency practice, oral reading practice has once again been prioritized over silent reading practice, at least in the earliest stages of reading development. The National Reading Panel's (2000) meta-analysis of fluency studies showed that fluency practice is most effective when the reading practice is oral versus silent; when it involves repeated readings of a text (more than twice); and when students receive guidance or feedback from teachers, parents, volunteers, and peers.

When the National Reading Panel (2000) concluded that research evidence was insufficient to endorse independent silent reading as evidence-based practice, many school administrators and classroom teachers began to shy away from providing students time for practice independent reading. With teachers being held accountable for students' meeting benchmarks, standards, and growth targets, educational practices that do not have substantial empirical evidence of effectiveness are increasingly marginalized.

In addition, literacy scholars have recently criticized practice conditions associated with independent silent reading (Kelley & Clausen-Grace, 2006; Reutzel, Fawson, & Smith, 2008; Stahl, 2004). Concerns regarding independent silent reading include (1) student self-selection of reading materials, (2) student engagement and time on task, (3) accountability of students, and (4) interactions around text (Hiebert & Reutzel, 2010; Stahl, 2004). Sending students off to read on their own without teacher guidance, interaction, instruction, monitoring, or accountability has not been shown to promote effective independent reading practice in schools (Hiebert & Reutzel, 2010). As a consequence, classroom teachers would do well to resist the seductive practice of allowing students to go off on their own to silently and independently "model" reading. Although the intuitive appeal for oral or silent independent reading practice is strong, evidence calls into question the typically accepted practice conditions implemented in many classrooms. However, when independent silent reading practice is accompanied by active teacher instruction, guidance, interaction, and monitoring, along with classroom structure of the environment and procedures, students' reading development and engagement flourish. When students are left to the independent silent reading practices of yesteryear, where everyone "does their own thing" without teacher intervention, interaction, structure, monitoring and accountability, current evidence is anything but convincing that such conditions produce either able or motivated readers.

Recent evidence suggests that for kindergarten and first-grade readers oral repeated reading is most effective (National Reading Panel, 2000; Wright, Sherman, & Jones, 2010). However, as students develop automaticity with text decoding in the second grade, oral Wide Reading becomes more effective than repeated reading (Stahl, 2004; Kuhn, 2005). Once students evidence automaticity in orally reading a wide variety of text genres and types, it is time for teachers to help them convert their fluent oral reading into fluent silent reading (Hiebert, 2006; Hiebert & Reutzel, 2010; Reutzel, Jones, & Neuman, 2010; Reutzel, Jones, Fawson, & Smith, 2008).

As we continued our study of reading fluency, we found that there exists some continuing confusion around the idea of automaticity in reading as it relates to the development of fluency in elementary-age children. "Automaticity" is a term coined by reading theorists LaBerge and Samuels (1974) to indicate that the ability to decode words has become so well developed that little cognitive attention is needed or used to decode words, and thus the bulk of processing attention can be directed to other functions, such as comprehending text meaning. We have found that some authors in the professional literature (Blevins, 2001; Wolf & Katzir-Cohen, 2001) advocate timed practice on word patterns and high-frequency word list drills. Although such practice may be useful in developing automatic decoding of words, it leaves unaddressed matters of phrasing and expression, which are essential to the development of fluency. In fairness, none of these authors recommend developing fluency from timed word list drills alone, but there are classrooms in which such word list drills occupy an inordinate amount of time and significance because fluency is only measured as a function of word-reading accuracy and speed, which constitutes decoding automaticity but not reading fluency.

We found also a number of authors and researchers who have, through a variety of processes, developed guidelines for appropriate reading rates by grade level. For example, Hasbrouck and Tindal (1992, 2005) and Howe and Shinn (2001) provide listings of 1-minute reading rate norms that span grades 1–8. Most of these reading rate norms adjust for accuracy using a metric called words correct per minute (wcpm). We also noted that fluency rate norms seem to begin with midyear first-grade readers, which implies that a focus on reading fluency development in first-grade classrooms ought to be delayed until initial decoding processes have been well taught and students are approaching proficiency or automaticity with word-level decoding. Recent research on reading rate norms suggests that first-grade readers ought to be able to read about 53 wcpm by the end of first grade (Hasbrouck & Tindal, 2005). In our discussions, we questioned whether 1-minute reading rate norms would hold up if the text difficulty, type, genre, or even amount of time (e.g., 3 minutes or 10 minutes of reading) was varied.

We found little information about how expression and intonation affect fluency (Dowhower, 1991; Rasinski et al., 2011). What we did discover, however, is that the effect of fluency on comprehension versus the effect of comprehension on fluency is still largely poorly understood (Rasinski et al., 2011). We also found that most measures of oral reading expression make use of scales (Zutell & Rasinski, 1991) in which teachers make judgments about the prosodic features of oral reading rather than relying on more exact measures similar to those used by speech–language pathologists.

We also found that fluency, much like reading comprehension, needs to be developed across text types and levels of text difficulty. The RAND Reading Study Group (2002) described how the reader, the text, the task, and the context all work together in unique ways to affect reading comprehension performance. This also seems to be true with respect to fluency development (National Reading Panel, 2000). Just because a student can read narrative or poetic texts fluently does not necessarily imply a concurrent ability to read information or expository texts with similar facility. We found from our study of fluency research that when levels of text difficulty increase, most students' reading rates decrease. Researchers are, at present, unclear about which levels of text to use for fluency practice and instruction (Stahl & Heubach, 2006). In their review of fluency developmental and remedial practices, Kuhn and Stahl (2000) recommended the use of instructional-level text for fluency instruction and practice. More recently, however, Stahl and Heubach (2006) indicated that the level of text used for fluency practice should be directly related to the amount of support students have to help them read the text. The act of students' going off alone and reading provides little support, and thus the text used for fluency practice should be no higher than independent-level reading. Compare this with one-to-one reading, which provides high levels of support. In this situation, students can practice reading fluency using frustration-level text. What is not known at present is how much "frustration" students can tolerate and yet still gain effective reading fluency practice (Hiebert & Reutzel, 2010). Taken together, these findings suggest that reading fluency is not a perfectible process, at least not in the early elementary school years.

Finally, we determined from our studies that, although fluency practice and instruction are essential components of high-quality reading instruction in the elementary years (Stahl, 2004), too much of a good thing can be a bad thing! In their short-term study, Anderson, Wilkinson, and Mason (1991) found that too much attention and time spent on developing word-level decoding automaticity within a reading lesson detracted from students' ability to comprehend the text. In its later review of fluency instruction, the National Reading Panel (2000) found that fluency lessons ranging in length between 15 and 30 minutes showed promising effects on students' fluency development for the time allocated.

Although in the past decade fluency instruction and practice have assumed a position of central prominence in the discourse on effective classroom literacy instruction, many classroom teachers remain somewhat bewildered about how to teach and practice fluency effectively in the classroom with children of differing reading levels. On the one hand, we believe that a bright future awaits fluency research, instruction, and classroom practice. We, like many of our colleagues, realize that Allington was correct in 1983, and that fluency instruction must no longer be a neglected goal of reading instruction. On the other hand, to relegate fluency practice and instruction to the oral repeated reading of 1-minute text samples does not bode well for the future of fluency development in classrooms. The development of reading fluency requires careful instruction, practice, and systematic transition from oral repeated reading to wide reading to silent reading as students acquire greater word-decoding automaticity and reading fluency, including expression and comprehension. This means that fluency instruction and practice in classrooms will need to be differentiated to meet the developmental needs of the student ranging in reading abilities found in today's classrooms (Hiebert & Reutzel, 2010; Reutzel & Cooter, 2012).

## METAFLUENCY INSTRUCTION:
## A MISSING PIECE OF EFFECTIVE FLUENCY INSTRUCTION

Hoffman (2003) rightfully points out that the "interface between fluency and comprehension is quite tight" (p. 5). High-quality fluency instruction, similar to high-quality reading comprehension instruction, is largely permeated with understanding and constructing meaning. An instructional focus on developing only the observable performances of reading fluency—accuracy, rate, and expression—is insufficient to produce the desired outcomes in fluent oral renditions.

Because fluency and comprehension are so tightly connected, many aspects of high-quality reading comprehension instruction also pertain to providing high-quality fluency instruction. For example, comprehension monitoring is a critical part of self-regulation of the comprehension process, helping students to increase their understanding and independence as a reader. It is not enough for students to be taught comprehension strategies or processes; they must also become aware of when reading processes are going along as they should (Pressley, 2002). The same can be said of fluency development. For children to become self-regulating, fluent readers, they must become aware of what fluency is, whether or not it is going along as it should, and what can be done about it if it is not. To begin this process, children must learn what fluency is—not just how it sounds. They must understand the elements and concepts associated with fluency and the language necessary for talking and thinking about fluency, and become aware of what fluency should sound like in oral reading.

To further drive home this important point, Hoffman (2003) asserts, "Work to develop the meta-language of fluency with your students, which includes concepts of expression, word stress, and phrasing. It will serve you well in explicit instruction" (p. 6). Students need to know that fluency is an important goal of reading instruction. They need to know what fluency is, and they need to have the language, so that teachers and students can talk specifically about fluency as a concept and as a performance to be examined and developed. They must develop an awareness of fluency in order to monitor it, fix it, and improve it. Students must own the concepts, elements, and language; have an awareness of and the ability to apply fix-up strategies; and understand the varying purposes of fluency in order to self-regulate and improve it. We must not only facilitate reading fluency practice but also cultivate a deeper appreciation among students of the importance of fluency as a personal goal of reading improvement. Equally important, we need to develop students' understanding of what we mean when we say that reading is fluent and that they can fix up their fluency when they perceive it isn't going along as it should.

## What Is Meant by "Metafluency"?

Because comprehension and fluency processes are so integrally intertwined, we reviewed research that explored the concept of metacomprehension or metacognitive monitoring (Good, Simmons, & Kame'enui, 2001; Pinnell et al., 1995; Rasinski, 2010). Vygotsky (1962) described the acquisition of knowledge as having two distinct phases: (1) automatic, unconscious acquisition processes followed by (2) gradual increases in active, conscious control over the acquisition of knowledge. According to Brown (1980), metacognition is "the deliberate conscious control of one's own cognitive actions" (p. 453). Readers who are in tune with their own cognitive processes are aware of what they need to know as well as how and when to actively intervene to ensure that the acquisition of knowledge is proceeding as it should.

From Brown's (1980) review of comprehension-monitoring research, we reasoned that because comprehension monitoring, or metacomprehension, is fundamental to the improvement of comprehension, so then is fluency monitoring, or "metafluency," fundamental to the improvement of fluency. Explicitly teaching children the metalanguage of fluency (e.g., accuracy, rate, or speed; reader's purpose; text difficulty; and expression, phrasing, smoothness, stress, pitch, and volume) is important in developing their ability to think and talk about fluency as an object that they can consciously monitor and control. Along with explicitly teaching the concepts and language associated with fluency, we believe that teachers need to build into children's emerging reading strategy repertoire a propensity to monitor the status of their own reading fluency. Children also need to know how to take steps to "fix up" ineffective or inefficient fluency behaviors.

To further our understanding of this concept of *metafluency,* we naturally looked to high-quality comprehension instruction as a frame of reference. We found that high-quality comprehension instruction is characterized by explicit explanations, modeling, descriptions, and demonstrations, followed by guided practice, both in groups and individually, that gradually transfers the responsibility for comprehension strategy use from the teacher to the students. We reasoned that high-quality fluency instruction would likely look once again very similar to high-quality comprehension instruction. It is from these studies and our own discussions of fluency and comprehension-monitoring research that we coined the term "metafluency."

In coining this term, we created and refined a fluency instructional framework supported by the findings of the scientific reading research that extend fluency instruction further into the somewhat less well-understood domain of developing children's metafluency ability—the knowledge and the language to talk about what fluency is; the propensity or inclination to self-monitor one's own fluency; and learning how to take conscious, strategically selected steps to increase one's own reading fluency. After completing our study of the literature on reading fluency, we began to construct an instructional routine for providing evidence-based, effective reading fluency instruction and practice in elementary classrooms.

## AN EVIDENCE-BASED FLUENCY INSTRUCTION ROUTINE: HELPING ALL CHILDREN BECOME FLUENT READERS

The evidence-based fluency instruction routine (EFIR) was designed to provide optimally effective fluency instruction for elementary-age children. The fluency and comprehension instructional research previously reviewed suggested that children need:

- Explicit, systematic explanation and instruction about the elements of reading fluency.
- Rich and varied modeling and demonstrations of fluent reading.
- Guided oral reading practice with appropriately challenging and varied texts on a regular basis.
- Guided repeated rereading or multiple rereadings of the same text.
- Assessment and self-monitoring of oral reading fluency progress.
- Information on how to fix-up faltering reading fluency.
- Genuine audiences and opportunities for oral reading performance.

Using the guidelines from the National Reading Panel (2000), we also determined that daily fluency instruction for 15–30 minutes should be an essential part of the daily reading instructional routine or schedule. An occasional flirtation with fluency instruction would not provide the systematic instruction and regular practice necessary to achieve fluency for many children.

## The EFIR Daily Routine

The EFIR daily routine is organized around three major time periods. The first time period is intended for developing students' metafluency or understanding of the concepts of expression, word stress, phrasing, and so on through teacher explanation, modeling, demonstrations, description, and definition of the elements of fluent oral reading. About 5–7 minutes of the EFIR is allocated to developing students' metafluency. Many teachers have constructed excellent instruction charts—displayed in their classrooms—based on the teaching of metafluency, as found in Figure 7.1.

The second period of the EFIR—with a time allocation of 20 minutes—is designed to provide children with guided group and individual repeated oral reading using a variety of practice formats and approaches. The third

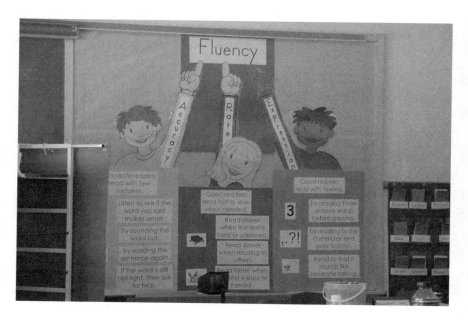

**FIGURE 7.1.** Instructional display for teaching metafluency and fix ups. Photo taken by D. Ray Reutzel, 2007. 2nd Grade, Gramercy Elementary School, Ogden City School District, Ogden, Utah.

and final time period of the EFIR is for assessment and monitoring and takes about 2–3 minutes. The daily routine of the EFIR is summarized in Figure 7.2.

## EFIR Daily Lesson Framework

A daily lesson framework was developed as a part of the overall design of the EFIR. It was designed to maintain a rapid pace, moving the lesson along from high teacher input and responsibility to high student activity and responsibility. The design of the lesson was based on the comprehension instructional model of *gradual release of responsibility* (Pearson & Gallagher, 1983). How this model works in practice is described later in this chapter.

### Explicit Explanation

The EFIR begins with an explicit explanation, description, or definition of the importance of reading fluency and the elements, terms, and *metalanguage* of fluent oral reading as defined in the research and professional literature: (1) accuracy, (2) rate, and (3) expression. For example, the teachers in this project developed a classroom poster where the elements of fluency are defined and described in "kid-friendly" language, as shown in Figure 7.1. This poster is displayed and referred to frequently as teachers explicitly, intentionally, and systematically teach and model for children the concepts, terms, and elements associated with fluent oral reading. The underlying thinking behind the explicit explanation part of the EFIR is that children need to clearly understand what oral reading fluency is in order to produce, monitor, or increase it, either with guidance or independently. Text from a

---

*I. Teacher explanation and modeling of the elements and nature of fluent oral reading*

5–7 Minutes

*II. Guided group or individual repeated oral reading practice*

20 Minutes

*III. Group and/or individual assessment and progress monitoring*

2–3 Minutes

**Total Daily Scheduled Time: 30 Minutes**

---

**FIGURE 7.2.** The evidence-based fluency instruction routine (EFIR) daily routine.

typical classroom poster used in the explicit explanation part of the EFIR is shown in Figure 7.3.

## Teacher Monitoring and Clarification

Of course, explicit explanation, description, or definition of the elements associated with fluent oral reading is insufficient to make the point with most young readers. They need to see and hear models of what one means by these terms. The next part of the EFIR involves teacher modeling, think-alouds, and demonstration of the elements associated with fluent oral reading. Teachers select one of the essential elements of fluent oral reading fluency for a daily focus (i.e., accuracy). For example, the teacher might select the focus of accuracy when reading the poem "You Need to Have an Iron Rear" by Jack Prelutsky (1984, p. 15) for this lesson.

> You need to have an iron rear
> To sit upon a cactus,
> Or otherwise, at least a year
> Of very painful practice.

After reading this poem aloud and with accuracy to the children, the teacher reminds them that accurate oral reading is *reading what is on the page*. Next, to pique the attention of some less than attentive learners, the teacher tells the students that she will perform an inaccurate oral reading of the same poem. Their job is to follow along as she reads and catch her reading inaccurately or not reading what is on the page. For example, the teacher might read the poem as follows:

> You need to *wear* an iron *tear*
> To *look* upon a cactus,
> Or otherwise, at least a *spear*
> Of very painful practice.

---

Becoming a fluent oral reader is an important part of becoming a good reader. In order to become a fluent oral reader, you need to ...

1. Read accurately, or read what is on the page.
2. Vary the speed of reading according to your purpose(s) and how difficult the text is for you to read.
3. Read with appropriate volume, expression, phrasing, and smoothness.
4. Remember the important ideas from your reading.

---

**FIGURE 7.3.** Classroom poster of essential elements of fluent oral reading.

After an inaccurate oral reading of this poem, the teacher invites the children, usually amid snickering and giggles, to comment on the accuracy of the "inaccurate" modeling of oral reading. We have often noticed greater discussion and attention among students after nonmodeling of the focus fluency element, in this case the inaccurate reading, than after accurate renditions. When we ask children why this was the case, they indicate that the miscues tended to reveal the characteristics of fluent reading more obviously than did examples of fluent oral reading. As a result, children become very active in attempting to "detect" the teacher's inaccuracies or other fluency element flaws during an announced "nonmodeling" of the fluency element under focus.

### Group-Guided Repeated Reading Practice and Monitoring

After explaining, defining, describing, modeling, demonstrating, and discussing a focus oral reading fluency element, the teacher involves the whole class in guided, repeated oral readings of the text, poem, or story that had been previously modeled. During this part of the EFIR, the teacher uses various types of choral reading, such as echoic, unison, antiphonal, mumble, line-a-child, and so on. For those who are unfamiliar with these choral reading variations, we recommend Opitz and Rasinski's (2008) *Good-Bye Round Robin* or Rasinski's (2010) *The Fluent Reader*. After the first reading of the text as a group, the teacher stops and asks children to assess their oral reading fluency using an informal fluency-monitoring rubric that highlights the elements of fluent oral reading that the teacher has previously explicitly explained and modeled. This informal oral reading fluency-monitoring rubric makes use of a simple dichotomous rating scale of "yes" or "no" or for the younger children a display of smiling or frowning faces (see Figure 7.4). The teachers can produce this rubric in a variety of sizes. One version of the oral reading fluency-monitoring rubric is enlarged and laminated as a classroom poster. With lamination of the rubric poster, the teacher can use water-based or dry-erase markers to mark the oral reading fluency items and then easily erase these marks for later reuse of the poster.

The teacher begins by using a think-aloud process to show *how* she rated the group's oral reading fluency on each of the three elements of oral reading fluency. She also explains *why* she gave the ratings she did on each item. After modeling this process a few times, the teacher *shares and gradually releases* the fluency-monitoring process to the children through three phases. In the first phase of the release of responsibility for fluency monitoring, the teacher shares the task of monitoring fluency by asking the children to rate their oral reading fluency on each element displayed in the rubric first, and explaining why she thought the children gave the rating they did. Of course, children correct the teacher if she does not give the right reasons!

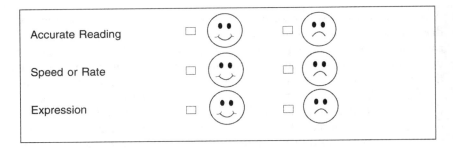

**FIGURE 7.4.** Informal oral reading fluency-monitoring rubric.

In phase two of the release, the teacher continues sharing the responsibility for completing the task of rating the group's oral reading fluency by rating each oral reading fluency item and then asking the children to explain why she might have rated the group's oral reading fluency as she did. Finally, the teacher fully releases the task of rating the group's oral reading fluency by asking the children to both rate and explain the ratings on the informal fluency assessment poster.

Children are also taught how to fix up specific fluency problems through teacher explanation, modeling, and group or individual practice. The teacher explains specific types of fluency problems and "fix-up" steps for each type of fluency problem displayed in a classroom poster. The teacher models specific fluency problems and then how to use the poster to get ideas about how to fix up fluency. Children are then encouraged to use these fix-up strategies with other classmates and by themselves during group and individual oral reading practice each day. Fix-up strategies are presented in Figure 7.5.

### Individual-Guided Oral or Silent Repeated or Wide Reading Practice

Next in the EFIR comes guided individual or partner practice depending upon students' level of fluency development. First-grade or struggling students who have not yet achieved automatic decoding ability at the basic level—single-syllable word decoding—and do not know high-frequency sight words need to continue practicing for fluency by repeatedly reading a single text aloud, three to five times, and receiving feedback from someone, be it a teacher, parent, volunteer, or peer. Second-grade or struggling students who have achieved the ability to automatically decode single- and multiple-syllable words and recognize high-frequency sight words can practice for fluency by reading aloud widely a new or unfamiliar text each day with feedback. Unlike classroom practices such as independent read-

*Accuracy*

1. Slow your reading speed down.
2. Look carefully at the words and the letters in the words you didn't read on the page.
3. Think about whether you know this word or parts of this word. Try saying the word or word parts.
4. Make the sound of each letter from left to right and blend the sounds together quickly to say the word.
5. Listen carefully to see whether the word you said makes sense.
6. Try rereading the sentence again.
7. If the word still doesn't make sense, then ask someone to help you.

*Rate*

1. Adjust your reading speed to go slower when the text is difficult or unfamiliar.
2. Adjust your reading speed to go faster when the text is easy or familiar.

*Expression*

1. Try to read three or more words together before pausing, stopping, or taking a breath.
2. Take a big breath and try to read to the comma or end punctuation, without stopping for another breath.
3. Read so that you sound like "someone talking."

**FIGURE 7.5.** Fluency fix-up strategies for major fluency elements.

ing, where children may or may not be reading and receive no guidance or feedback, or round robin reading, where only one child at a time gets to read a part of the text aloud only once and receive feedback, teachers use paired-reading approaches, such as buddy, peer, or dyad reading, to optimize each student's practice time and the oral reading feedback each student receives.

Pairs of readers are either same-age peers or older peers from another age- or grade-level classroom. Each pair of children alternates roles of reader and listener. As pairs practice, they are reminded to consult the fluency-monitoring scoring rubric poster as well as the fix-up poster for ways to offer feedback to their peers during individual oral reading practice (see Figure 7.4). After each oral reading by the reader, the listener provides feedback using the same fluency-monitoring rubric printed on a small, wallet-size card. Guided, oral repeated reading practice with feedback is one of the methods that produced the largest effect sizes and student gains for early fluency development in the studies analyzed by the National Reading Panel (2000). On the other hand, if students can read orally and widely with fluency and are achieving fluency benchmarks in the third grade, recent research offers several evidence-based approaches for transitioning students from guided oral to scaffolded silent reading (Hiebert & Reutzel, 2010; Reutzel, Jones, et al., 2008).

### Reading Performance

Once children, especially beginners, sense their emerging fluency, they want to demonstrate it for others. To provide an alternative approach and purpose for fluency practice, teachers in our project arranged for children to perform their practiced oral reading for an audience of either parents or other students in the school building. When preparing an oral reading performance, teachers use one of three well-known oral reading instructional approaches: (1) Readers Theatre, (2) radio reading, or (3) read around (Opitz & Rasinski, 2008). Each of these oral reading performance approaches is used for specific text types. For children who want to share a favorite poem read-aloud with the group, we use the read around process, where each student, in turn, identifies and rehearses a passage, poem, or story text to share (Tompkins, 1998). For performing information texts, we use radio readings, as described by Greene (1979), Rasinski (2010), and Searfoss (1975). The idea for radio readings is to perform a text well enough that the listener can picture the events. Information texts are divided into four parts for a group of readers. Then each reader practices his or her part of the information book, with feedback from a peer. Students then read their part of the book, in turn, as if they are broadcasting a news flash on the radio. For practicing and performing stories or plays, teachers turn to Readers Theatre, scripts for which are readily available on the Internet. Two of our favorite websites are *www.readingsa-z.com/books/scripts.php* and *www.readers-theatre.com.*

In addition to these more formal opportunities to perform oral readings for other audiences, teachers also provide a daily closing session where children can share their oral readings with their classmates using a practice called "reading corners." In reading corners, four children are selected on a daily basis to (1) give a book, text, poem, or story talk in which they tell the other children briefly about the text they have been reading and (2) orally read a selected passage or paragraph from their selected text to a small group of class members, usually six to eight peers. Peers listen to each text talk and select which of the reading corner texts they would most like to hear. We have found that the reading corners approach also encourages children to learn the art of book selling or promotion, and helps to develop their fluent oral reading performance skills. This part of the EFIR is brief, usually about 5 minutes or less.

Although the explanation of the EFIR offered here is lengthy and detailed, the actual flow of the EFIR each day is briskly paced and, as we indicated earlier, lasts for only 30 minutes. In fact, keeping the pace brisk and varying the text type and difficulty level keep the routine from becoming boring and repetitive.

As expected, the fluency achieved using just one type of task or text is insufficient, and children require instruction and practice with a variety of reading fluency tasks, text types, and levels of challenge. Because many of our teachers were familiar with and used leveled readers for providing guided reading, as in Fountas and Pinnell (1996), we relied heavily upon A–Z book levels to help us provide texts of appropriate levels of challenge. However, more recently, we have begun to use Lexile leveling instead of A–Z (see *www.lexile.com*). We also felt that at each grade level children should practice oral and silent reading fluency with a variety of text types, including stories, poems, journal entries, jokes, articles, and information books. In grades 2–6 we found that we needed to provide new, fresh, or novel short, high-interest texts for group oral reading fluency practice nearly every day. In grades K–1, multiple days of oral reading fluency practice with the same texts were often needed to move the oral reading of a text to fluency.

## Fluency Instruction Scope and Sequence

As we worked together to develop the EFIR, we also found that teachers wanted and needed guidance on a scope and sequence of fluency-related skills, tasks, and texts. To meet this need, we developed and used the scope and sequence of fluency concepts, skills, and so on, in Figure 7.6 in our project classrooms.

## ASSESSING FLUENCY AND METAFLUENCY GROWTH

According to the definition of the National Reading Panel (2000), "fluent readers" can read text with speed, accuracy, and proper expression. To this definition, we add the element of comprehension as in Samuels (2007). With this more comprehensive definition in mind, we determined that adequate assessment of fluency would involve periodic sampling of children's reading rate, decoding accuracy, expression, and comprehension. The EFIR fluency assessment model is shown in Figure 7.7. In this model, we use the average of three 1-minute reading samples to examine students' decoding accuracy and reading rate. To assess expressive reading, we used Zutell and Rasinski's (1991) Multidimensional Fluency Scale. By using these simple assessments, a comprehensive assessment of reading fluency can be acquired within roughly 1.5 minutes of teacher time per student, or about 4.5 minutes per day.

*Fluency Concepts*
- ☐ Accuracy: (1) reading accurately, and (2) reading inaccurately.
- ☐ Rate: (1) Reading too fast, (2) reading too slow, and (3) reading at "just the right rate" for the text or task.
- ☐ Phrasing: (1) Reading with appropriate phrasing, (2) reading with two or three word phrasing, and (3) word-by-word reading.
- ☐ Expression: (1) Reading with appropriate pitch, stress, and intonation and (2) reading in a monotone style.

*Fluency Texts*
- ☐ Poetry
- ☐ Song lyrics
- ☐ Stories
- ☐ Plays
- ☐ Jokes, riddles, and comics
- ☐ Information books
- ☐ Newspapers
- ☐ Magazines
- ☐ Directions or instructions

*Student Fluency Tasks*
- ☐ Word part and word recognition drills
- ☐ Oral reading practice - group and individual
- ☐ Monitoring and fix-up
- ☐ Performance
- ☐ Assessment

**FIGURE 7.6.** Fluency instruction scope and sequence chart.

We determined that children's fluency would be sampled at least three times annually using the average score taken from three 1-minute reading samples (Rasinski, 2010). This is accomplished by giving every child in the class three preselected grade-level passages to read aloud. To save time during the instructional day, the teacher asks three students to go to a fluency recording station to read the passage. Each student records his or her own audio file on an MP3 recorder. They push record, state their name, and turn on a 1-minute egg timer. When the timer sounds, they are to stop reading and turn off the recorder. Next, use the MP3 player to record their name and retell what they can remember from their reading. They repeat this procedure with two more passages. The teacher listens to three students reading three passages each evening, or about 20 minutes of audio files per day, until all students have recorded their passages. This requires about 180 total minutes of recorded passages in a class of 25 students. The

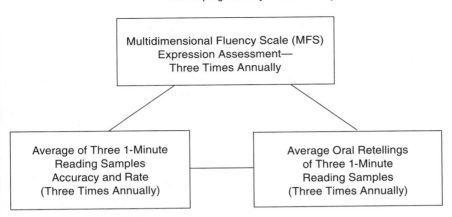

**FIGURE 7.7.** Evidence-based fluency instruction routine (EFIR) assessment model.

teacher marks errors on a copy of the orally read passages and records the total number of words read correctly and the number of errors. Using the criteria of Howe and Shinn (2001), reading accuracy of 95% accuracy or higher is judged as adequate. For students who struggle, more frequent progress monitoring of fluency may be necessary, perhaps as often as every 2 weeks. For these students, using a rate and accuracy chart as shown in Figure 7.8 can be motivating as it illustrates their fluency progress over time (Reutzel & Cooter, 2011).

When using a rate and accuracy tracking chart as in Figure 7.8, children are taught that fluency progress is being made when the reading rate line is going up and the error line is going down. Along with this measurement of fluency, teachers also ask children to record an oral retelling of the passage to rate for comprehension assessment purposes. This very simple, yet comprehensive, ongoing measurement of fluency and comprehension informs teachers, parents, and each child on a regular basis about the student's reading development.

## FUTURE DIRECTIONS IN FLUENCY RESEARCH

If students are going to be able to read fluently at grade level, teachers and students must give increased and sustained attention to the development of oral and silent reading fluency.

Many issues associated with developing reading fluency remain unsettled. We list a few here that are of major importance:

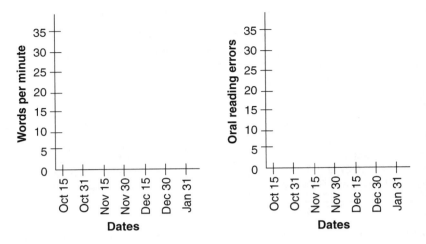

**FIGURE 7.8.** Rate and accuracy tracking chart. From Reutzel and Cooter, *Strategies for Reading Assessment and Instruction: Helping Every Child Succeed, 4th Edition,* © 2011, p. 215. Reprinted by permission of Pearson Education, Inc., Upper Saddle River, NJ.

- Is reading prosody affected by reading accuracy, rate, or comprehension or vice versa?
- Does fluency precede comprehension, or is reading fluency a consequence of comprehension? Or do the two occur simultaneously?
- How do English language learners develop reading fluency in English (August & Shanahan, 2006; Fitzgerald, 2008)?
- How many new words should be introduced in new texts as students develop their reading fluency in more difficult texts?
- Which levels of text difficulty are optimal for independent practice compared with group or individual practice with and without feedback?
- Which types of texts lend themselves most appropriately to fluency development?
- What is the motivational value (both positive and negative) of repeated readings and reading performance?
- When and how should teachers help students transfer their oral reading fluency to silent reading?
- When is fluency most influenced by students' decoding abilities compared with their vocabulary and comprehension abilities?
- What is fluency's long-term effect on reading comprehension and reading achievement?
- How much of the variance in reading achievement is due to the

uniqueness of the fluency instruction compared with simply spending greater amounts of time in engaged reading?

- Is there an optimal proportion of time allocated to instruction fluency instruction compared with practice?
- Are current reading fluency assessment tools and procedures acting to inhibit necessary attention to reading comprehension and engagement in classrooms?
- Can readers sustain 1-minute reading rates over longer time periods when reading longer texts?
- At what point does inaccurate reading interfere with reading comprehension?
- Are current fluency assessment tools of sufficient quality to allow educators to make informed judgments about which instructional interventions are best for inaccurate or slow readers?

Answers to these questions and others await the work of future research studies and investigation. For now, we believe the elements of effective fluency instruction are becoming more widely understood. How to package the multiple elements of effective fluency instruction and practice to obtain the optimal benefit for all children also awaits the incremental but steady march of future research progress.

## REFERENCES

Allington, R. L. (1983). Fluency: The neglected goal of reading. *The Reading Teacher, 36,* 556–561.

Anderson, R. C., Wilkinson, I. A. G., & Mason, J. M. (1991). A microanalysis of the small-group, guided reading lesson: Effects of an emphasis on global story meaning. *Reading Research Quarterly, 26,* 417–441.

August, D., & Shanahan, T. (2006). *Developing literacy in second language learners: Report of the National Literacy Panrl on language-minority children and youth.* Mahwah, NJ: Erlbaum.

Blevins, W. (2001). *Building fluency: Lessons and strategies for reading success.* New York: Scholastic.

Brown, A. L. (1980). Meta-cognitive development and reading. In R. J. Spiro, B. C. Bruce, & W. F. Brewer (Eds.), *Theoretical issues in reading comprehension: Perspectives from cognitive psychology, linguistics, artificial intelligence, and education* (pp. 453–481). Hillsdale, NJ: Erlbaum.

Dowhower, S. L. (1991). Speaking of prosody: Fluency's unattended bedfellow. *Theory Into Practice, 30*(3), 158–164.

Eldredge, J. L., Reutzel, D. R., & Hollingsworth, P. M. (1996). Comparing the effectiveness of two oral reading practices: Round-robin reading and the shared book experience. *Journal of Literacy Research, 28*(2), 201–225

Fitzgerald, J., Amendum, S. J., & Guthrie, K. M. (2008). Young Latino students' English-reading growth in all-English classrooms. *Journal of Literacy Research, 40,* 59–94.

Fountas, I. C., & Pinnell, G. S. (1996). *Guided reading instruction: Good first teaching for all children.* Portsmouth, NH: Heinemann.

Good, R. H., Simmons, D. C., & Kame'enui, E. J. (2001). The importance and decision-making utility of a continuum of fluency-based indicators of foundational reading skills for third-grade high-stakes outcomes. *Scientific Studies in Reading, 5*(3), 257–288.

Greene, F. (1979). Radio reading. In C. Pennock (Ed.), *Reading comprehension at four linguistic levels* (pp. 104–107). Newark, DE: International Reading Association.

Harris, T. L., & Hodges, R. E. (Eds.). (1995). *The literacy dictionary: The vocabulary of reading and writing.* Newark, DE: International Reading Association.

Hasbrouck, J. E., & Tindal, G. (1992). Curriculum-based oral reading fluency norms for students in grades 2 through 5. *Teaching Exceptional Children, 24,* 41–44.

Hasbrouck, J. E., & Tindal, G. (2005). *Oral reading fluency norms, grades 1–8.* Retrieved September 15, 2011, from *www.jhasbrouck.com*

Hiebert, E. H. (2006). Becoming fluent: Repeated reading with scaffolded texts. In S. J. Samuels & A. E. Farstrup (Eds.), *What research has to say about fluency instruction* (pp. 204–226). Newark, DE: International Reading Association.

Hiebert, E. H., & Reutzel, D. R. (Eds.). (2010). *Revisiting silent reading: New directions for teachers and researchers.* Newark, DE: International Reading Association.

Hoffman, J. V. (2003). Foreword. In T. V. Rasinski (Ed.), *The fluent reader: Oral reading strategies for building word recognition, fluency, and comprehension* (pp. 5–6). New York: Scholastic.

Howe, K. B., & Shinn, M. M. (2001). *Standard reading assessment passages (RAPS) for use in general outcome measurements: A manual describing development and technical features.* Eden Prarie, MN: Edformations.

Huey, E. B. (1908). *The psychology and pedagogy of reading.* New York: Macmillan.

Kame'neui, E. J., & Simmons, D. C. (2001). The DNA of reading fluency. *Scientific Studies of Reading, 5*(3), 203–210.

Kelley, M., & Clausen-Grace, N. (2006). R5: The sustained silent reading makeover that transformed readers. *The Reading Teacher, 60*(2), 148–156.

Kuhn, M. R. (2005). A comparative study of small group fluency instruction. *Reading Psychology, 26*(2), 127–146.

Kuhn, M. R., & Stahl, S. A. (2000). Fluency: A review of developmental and remedial practices (Center for the Improvement of Early Reading Achievement Report No. 2-008). Ann Arbor: University of Michigan.

LaBerge, D., & Samuels, S. J. (1974). Toward a theory of automatic information processing in reading. *Cognitive Psychology, 6,* 293–323.

National Reading Panel. (2000). *Teaching children to read: An evidence-based assessment of the scientific research literature on reading and its implications for reading instructions* (NIH Publication No. 00-4769). Washington, DC: National Institute of Child Health and Human Development.

Opitz, M. F., & Rasinski, T. V. (2008). *Good-bye round robin: 25 effective oral reading strategies* (2nd ed.). Portsmouth, NH: Heinemann.

Pearson, P. D., & Gallagher, M. C. (1983). The instruction of reading comprehension. *Contemporary Educational Psychology, 8*(3), 317–344.

Pinnell, G. S., Pikulski, J. J., Wixson, K. K., Campbell, J. R., Gough, P. B., & Beatty, A. S. (1995). *Listening to children read aloud: Oral fluency.* Washington, DC: National Center for Educational Statistics, U.S. Department of Education.

Prelutsky, J. (1984). You need to have an iron rear. In *The new kid on the block* (p. 15). New York: Greenwillow Books.

Pressley, M. (2002). Improving comprehension instruction: A path for the future. In C. Collins-Block, L. B. Gambrell, & M. Pressley (Eds.), *Improving comprehension instruction: Rethinking research, theory, and classroom practice* (pp. 385–399). San Francisco: Jossey-Bass.

RAND Reading Study Group. (2002). *Reading for understanding: Toward an R&D program in reading comprehension.* Santa Monica, CA: Science and Technology Policy Institute, RAND Education.

Rasinski, T. V. (2010). *The fluent reader: Oral and silent reading strategies for building fluency, word recognition, and comprehension* (2nd ed.). New York: Scholastic.

Rasinski, T. V., Reutzel, D. R., Chard, D., & Linan-Thompson, S. (2011). Reading fluency. In M. L. Kamil, P. D. Pearson, E. B. Moje, & P. P. Afflerbach (Eds.), *Handbook of reading research* (Vol. IV, pp. 286–319). New York: Routledge.

Reutzel, D. R., & Cooter, R. B., Jr. (2011). *Strategies for reading assessment and instruction: Helping every child succeed* (4th ed.). Boston: Allyn & Bacon.

Reutzel, D. R., & Cooter, R. B., Jr. (2012). *Teaching children to read: The teacher makes the difference* (6th ed.). Boston: Pearson/Allyn & Bacon.

Reutzel, D. R., Fawson, P. C., & Smith, J. A. (2008). Reconsidering silent sustained reading: An exploratory study of scaffolded silent reading (ScSR). *Journal of Educational Research, 102*(1), 37–50.

Reutzel, D. R., Jones, C. D., Fawson, P. C., & Smith, J. A. (2008). Scaffolded silent reading (ScSR): An alternative to guided oral repeated reading that works! *The Reading Teacher, 62*(3), 194–207.

Reutzel, D. R., Jones, C. D., & Newman, T. H. (2010). Scaffolded silent reading: Improving the conditions of silent reading practice in classrooms. In E. H. Hiebert & D. R. Reutzel (Eds.), *Revisiting silent reading: New directions for teachers and researchers* (pp. 129–150). Newark, DE: International Reading Association.

Rubin, A. A. (2005). *Rock: A remarkable resource.* New York: Sundance/Newbridge.

Samuels, S. J. (1979). The method of repeated readings. *The Reading Teacher, 32*(4), 403–408.

Samuels, S. J. (2007). The DIBELS tests: Is speed of barking at print what we mean by fluency? *Reading Research Quarterly, 42*(4), 563–566.

Searfoss, L. W. (1975). Radio reading. *The Reading Teacher, 29,* 295–296.

Smith, N. B. (2002). *American reading instruction.* Newark, DE: International Reading Association.

Sorenson, L. (2003). *American symbols: The Statue of Liberty.* Northborough, MA: Newbridge.

Stahl, S. (2004). What do we know about fluency? In P. McCardle & V. Chhabra (Eds.), *The voice of evidence in reading research* (pp. 187–211). Baltimore, MD: Brookes.

Stahl, S. A., & Heubach, K. (2006). Fluency-oriented reading instruction. In K. A. Dougherty Stahl & M. C. McKenna (Eds.), *Reading research at work: Foundations of effective practice* (pp. 177–204). New York: Guilford Press.

Tompkins, G. E. (1998). *Fifty reading strategies step by step.* Upper Saddle River, NJ: Merrill/Prentice-Hall.

Vygotsky, L. S. (1962). *Thought and language.* Cambridge, MA: MIT Press.

Wolf, M., & Katzir-Cohen, T. (2001). Reading fluency and its intervention. *Scientific Studies in Reading, 5*(3), 211–238.

Wright, G., Sherman, R., & Jones, T.B. (2010). Developmental considerations in transferring oral reading skills to silent reading. In E. H. Hiebert & D. R. Reutzel (Eds.), *Revisiting silent reading: New directions for teachers and researchers* (pp. 57–66). Newark, DE: International Reading Association.

Zutell, J., & Rasinski, T. V. (1991). Training teachers to attend to their students' oral reading fluency. *Theory into Practice, 30,* 211–217.

# PART II

# BEST PROGRAMS, BEST PRACTICES

# 8

## Battling on Two Fronts
### Creating Effective Oral Reading Instruction

Melanie R. Kuhn
Gwynne E. Ash
Megan Gregory

**W**hen we wrote our chapter for the first edition of this book, we focused on the extensive use of round robin reading in the classroom (along with its equivalents of popcorn, popsicle, and combat reading). We also discussed ways to eliminate round robin reading from the curriculum as well as ways of replacing it with effective forms of oral reading instruction (Ash & Kuhn, 2006). Unfortunately, several years later, we find ourselves having to do battle on a second front since the notion that fluent reading is rapid reading has taken hold in many elementary classrooms in the United States (Applegate, Applegate, & Modla, 2009). This notion has been driven, to a large extent, by assessments that focus on words correct per minute (wcpm) as proxies for students' broader reading development (Kuhn, Schwanenflugel, & Meisinger, 2010; Samuels, 2007). Given these changes, in this chapter we address not only the issue of round robin reading but also the perceived need for increasing learners' reading rate. We also reconsider the importance of fluency in closing the achievement gap (Stanovich, 1980) and present effective instructional alternatives that can be readily integrated into the classroom. However, we begin with a brief discussion of fluency's role in the reading process.

## WHAT IS FLUENCY AND WHY IS IT IMPORTANT?

To understand the importance of fluency in the reading process, it is essential to understand the roles of both automaticity and prosody in the comprehension of text.

### Automaticity, Prosody, and Comprehension

In order to be fluent, readers not only need to identify words accurately, they must also recognize the vast majority of them effortlessly or automatically. This is important because individuals have a limited amount of attention available for reading (e.g., Samuels, 2004); as a result, any attention expended on word recognition is attention unavailable for comprehension. In order for readers to concentrate on the meaning of the text rather than on determining the words, they need to automatize their word recognition, a process that occurs as readers repeatedly encounter words in print.

However, while automaticity has a central role in fluency, it also involves prosody, or those elements of language, such as intonation, stress, tempo, and appropriate phrasing, that make up expressive reading (e.g., Dowhower, 1991; Schreiber, 1991). When these elements are applied to oral reading, they not only allow reading to take on the qualities of speech, they also contribute to shades of meaning and a richer understanding of what is written. As such, prosody is likely to contribute to learner engagement with text, adding nuance to the reading and helping to bring it to life. Further, recent research indicates that prosody contributes to comprehension beyond that made by automatic word recognition (Benjamin & Schwanenflugel, 2010).

### Re-Creating Balance: Phrasing, Pacing, and Intonation in Assessment

Given that both prosody and automaticity are central components of reading fluency, it may seem odd that the dominant assessment tools focus so heavily on automaticity through their reliance on reading rate. This is because tools such as the Dynamic Indicators of Basic Early Literacy Skills (Good & Kaminski, 2002), AIMSweb (Shinn & Shinn, 2002), and other forms of curriculum-based measures (Deno, 1985) view reading rate and accuracy to be effective proxies for general reading ability. In other words, these assessments consider the use of wcpm as a valid way to measure students' reading growth. If students' wcpm meets certain criteria, then they are deemed to be making appropriate progress; if not, then they are considered to be at risk and in need of intervention (e.g., Kuhn et al., 2010).

However, when wcpm is considered to be the primary, or exclusive, measure of fluency, there is a privileging of rate and accuracy at the expense of prosodic elements of reading, such as phrasing and appropriate expression. And if the goal is to get students to read quickly, with a minimum number of errors, it is unsurprising that instruction begins to reflect this goal as well. Further, because many of these assessments are considered to be high-stakes measures, the pressure to create instruction that increases the number of words read quickly and accurately can become even more intense (Paris, 2005, 2008).

Unfortunately, an overemphasis on rate can actually impede rather than enhance comprehension. For example, such instruction can shift learners' focus away from, or actually interfere with, the construction of meaning (e.g., Samuels, 2007). In fact, recent research indicated that while reading rates have increased significantly, there has not been a corresponding increase in comprehension (Valencia et al., 2010). It is possible that this reflects a relationship between rate *and* prosody, that it is not simply an increase in speed but also an incorporation of appropriate pacing and phrasing that allows for the construction of meaning. Further, the pace of reading often varies (Hudson, Pullen, Lane, & Torgeson, 2009; Kuhn et al., 2010). We find that our own reading rate changes depending not only on the difficulty of the material we are reading (we often read more slowly when we are working on a more complex text) but also on the situation (we are more likely to read a novel for entertainment at a quicker rate than, for example, a journal article we want to use in our instruction, even if they are at equivalent levels of difficulty). As such, it seems important that learners become flexible readers rather than simply fast readers.

Although there are issues surrounding prosody scales (e.g., Hudson et al.,, 2009 ; Torgesen & Hudson, 2006), such as a lack of precision, their use balances out some of the problems that occur when only measures of rate and accuracy are used. Further, because all the elements of fluency relate not only to each other but to comprehension as well (Daane, Campbell, Grigg, Goodman, & Oranje, 2005), the use of measures that reflect accuracy, automaticity, *and* prosody seem to provide a more nuanced understanding of students' reading development.

## HOW ROUND ROBIN READING FAILS TO DEVELOP FLUENCY

The second concern we address in this chapter is one that goes back much further than the past decade or so (e.g., Rasinski & Hoffman, 2003), that of round robin reading. Despite a broad recognition that the procedure and its equivalents of popcorn, popsicle, and combat reading are ineffective reading strategies (Ash & Kuhn, 2006), they are still in use in a number of classrooms. When teachers who used the procedures were asked why they did so, there was a clear sense that this was an effective means of reading development. Among the reasons teachers cited were the beliefs that the procedures were seen as helpful in evaluating students' reading development, improving their reading fluency, allowing students access to difficult text and better ensuring their comprehension of reading material, and engaging the students in their reading while improving their self-confidence, listening skills, word identification, and vocabulary knowledge.

Unfortunately, we argue that although the reasons just outlined appear to lend credence to the approaches, upon deeper examination, it becomes readily apparent that this is not the case. For instance, in his studies of disfluent readers in the primary grades, Allington (1977, 1980) found that the turn-taking aspect of round robin reading meant that these students got very little practice in actual reading. Stanovich (1986) also argued that one result of limited access to connected text is increased difficulties in the literacy development of struggling readers, which, in turn, increases the gap in achievement between fluent and disfluent readers. Further, Allington (1980) found that the interruptive nature of turn taking provided poor models of skilled reading for students by presenting disfluent oral reading examples. Such interruptions further prevent students from developing their proficiency in word decoding since peers or the teachers often provide struggling readers with the words before they can decode them independently. Developing such independence in decoding is considered crucial to reading development because it is intricately linked to automaticity, a key component of fluent reading (LaBerge & Samuels, 1974; Stanovich, 1980).

Additionally, round robin reading has been demonstrated to be damaging to students' social and emotional growth (Opitz & Rasinski, 1998). In her case study of middle school readers, Ivey (1999) found that the practice of round robin reading caused great stress for the students who were not reading on grade level (as well as boredom for those who were). One student felt embarrassed to read aloud without practice. Another student who appeared to enjoy round robin reading, often volunteering to read, later confessed, "I raise my hand [to read] 'cause I want to read and get it done with 'cause the slow people read, and it takes them forever to get it done, what we have to read" (p. 186). And while emotional and social damage is problematic enough, students' embarrassment and anxiety when connected to reading seems to work against their development of positive identities as readers.

However, unless teachers are presented with valid alternatives, it will be difficult to replace either round robin reading (or popcorn, popsicle, or combat reading) or the focus on speed as a means of ensuring students' success on high-stakes tests. It is hoped that we, along with the other authors of this text, can begin to provide just such a range of effective approaches that can be used in their stead.

## PRACTICES FOR IMPROVING STUDENTS' FLUENCY, COMPREHENSION, AND MOTIVATION

Although many practices in this book focus on improving students' fluency and comprehension, we focus here on two complementary fluency approaches, two comprehension strategies, and two practices for improving motivation and engagement. We feel adamantly that fluency is best developed through the reading of connected text. When students are provided with sufficient opportunity to practice real reading with appropriate support or scaffolding, learners often develop adequate rate, along with the aspects of pacing that prevent their reading from sounding like a race (Kuhn et al., 2010). Similarly, by embedding such instruction into a variety of instructional situations, it will be possible to stretch students' access to challenging texts, thereby meeting many of the goals identified by teachers in the previous section.

### Fluency-Oriented Reading Instruction

Fluency-Oriented Reading Instruction (FORI) is designed for the shared reading component of a literacy curriculum, but could be modified for small-group instruction and even used for tutoring one or two struggling readers. FORI (Stahl & Heubach, 2005) is based on a weekly format that incorporates echo, choral, and partner reading into a systematic lesson plan. The original intervention took place with second graders who were reading below grade level, and was developed in response to a mandate that teachers use only grade-level texts for their literacy instruction. It was created in the hopes that it was possible to provide teachers with a means of making such texts more accessible. Although the procedure is quite straightforward, it has been shown to be successful with students who are having trouble working with grade-level material. (See Figure 8.1.)

Although the FORI procedure was originally used with selections from basal readers or literature anthologies, it can be used with any text that is part of the literacy curriculum, including trade books. However, it is essential that the selection be somewhat challenging for the learners and that each student have his or her own copy of whatever material is being read. In many classrooms, it is the case that there is particular story or expository piece that is a required part of the weekly literacy curriculum. As a result, there may be a corresponding sense of accountability attached to these selections. In practice, this can mean a need to dedicate a greater proportion of class time to their instruction. The FORI procedure allows for the development of meaningful lessons around such selections. At the same time, the approach provides room for integrating additional reading materials—and instructional approaches—into the literacy curriculum. In

When pairing up students for partner activities, the conventional wisdom has been to match the most gifted reader with the one who needs the most help, the next most gifted reader with the student who needs the next most help, and so on, until the two middle readers are matched with each other. Unfortunately, this method is not the most useful one for matching students who can support each others' reading. Often the more proficient reader takes over, doing all of the reading and depriving the reader who needs support the practice she or he might need to become a better reader. Likewise, the reader who needs support cannot support the gifted reader in his or her needs.

To create pairs, list students in descending order from the most proficient reader to the reader who needs most support. In a class of 24, for example, this would mean that the most proficient reader was #1 and the one who needs the most support is #24. Divide the class list in half, with numbers 1–12 on one list and numbers 13–24 on another. Align the two lists so that #1 is lined up with #13, #2 with #14, #3 with #15, and so on, until #12 is matched with #24.

With students matched in this way, in each pair there will be a student who is capable of supporting the student with greater needs, but there will not be such a great difference between their proficiencies. The student with greater needs will still be able to be an active partner, and she or he will also be able to support the more proficient reader.

**FIGURE 8.1.** Choosing partners for peer-supported activities.

fact, FORI should not be viewed as the only literacy instruction; instead, it is important that multiple types of literacy learning, including a range of whole-class, small-group, and individual reading approaches, opportunities to write, and a focus on word study, be part of a balanced curriculum.

In terms of specifics, FORI involves the teaching of a single, challenging text over a 5-day period (see Figure 8.2). The first day begins with the introduction of the week's selection. This can start with the type of activities that would typically be used for prereading instruction, such as highlighting important vocabulary, building background knowledge, or previewing the text. However, rather than having students attempt to read the text themselves on the first day, the teacher should read the selection to the learners while they follow along in their own copies. This allows students to concentrate on comprehending the text while providing them with the pronunciation of any unknown words. Upon completing the first reading of the text, there should be a discussion of the material; this further reinforces the notion that text comprehension is the primary goal. The second day involves an echo reading of the text; this approach can be made even more effective by integrating comprehension questions at natural stopping points throughout the selection (Stahl, 2008).

The third day's lesson is the shortest of the week, consisting of a simple choral reading of the material with the students. Depending upon the

| Monday (Day 1) | Tuesday (Day 2) | Wednesday (Day 3) | Thursday (Day 4) | Friday (Day 5) |
|---|---|---|---|---|
| • Teacher introduces selection to class using prereading activities. <br> • Teacher reads the selection to class while class follows along. <br> • Teacher and class discuss selection to develop text comprehension. | • Teacher and students echo read selection. <br> • Comprehension should be developed through various strategies such as teacher and student questioning, visualization, etc. | • Teacher and students choral read selection. <br> • Additional comprehension activities can be undertaken, but the primary focus of day 3 is choral reading of the text. | • Students partner-read selection. <br> • Additional comprehension activities can be undertaken, but the primary focus of day 4 is partner reading of the text. | • Students complete postreading extension activities. <br> • Activities may include writing in response to story, discussion of character motivations, summarization, etc. |

**FIGURE 8.2.** Fluency-Oriented Reading Instruction weekly routine.

amount of time that can be allocated to shared reading on this day, it might be possible to integrate a second choral reading of the material into the lesson. The fourth day involves asking students to partner-read alternating pages of the text. By day 4, the students should be fairly comfortable with the text, having encountered it at least three times previously. Additionally, the support that partners provide one another should allow them to read the text successfully. Further, if there is time after completing their first reading, the partners should be asked to reread the selection again; for this second reading, they would read the pages opposite those they read initially. The last day of the FORI lesson plan consists of simply implementing the type of postreading extension activities that usually accompany a text; for example, students might summarize a selection, complete graphic organizers of the material, or write in response to the reading.

The FORI program provides students with modeling, support or assistance, a focus on appropriate phrasing, and, perhaps most importantly, ample opportunities to read substantial amounts of connected text. Although some teachers find the format to be a bit tedious, the vast majority of students actually enjoy the predictability and consistent routine (Kuhn et al., 2006). What is critical, however, is that the material being used is long enough for students to read for an extended period of time (between 20 and 40 minutes per day) and that the texts are sufficiently challenging (e.g., grade-level texts if the majority of students in a class or group are reading below grade level or above-grade-level texts if the majority are reading at grade level). When these conditions are in place, FORI has been shown to help students make significant gains in terms of their reading ability.

## Wide FORI

Despite the benefits we found for FORI, when compared with a Wide Reading alternative that used less repetition (Wide FORI), the Wide Reading approach proved to be equally, if not more, effective at improving students' reading ability. Although the Wide FORI method is similar to the original FORI in many ways, three texts, rather than one, are read over the course of a week (see Figure 8.3). This allows learners to encounter many words in multiple contexts and has the potential to expose students to a broader range of concepts as well. This method relates to Logan's (1997) notion that breadth as well as depth are central to the development of automaticity. As with the FORI approach, the primary text for the Wide FORI lessons is

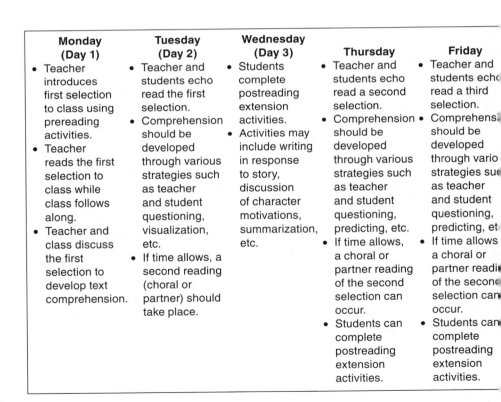

| Monday (Day 1) | Tuesday (Day 2) | Wednesday (Day 3) | Thursday | Friday |
|---|---|---|---|---|
| • Teacher introduces first selection to class using prereading activities.<br>• Teacher reads the first selection to class while class follows along.<br>• Teacher and class discuss the first selection to develop text comprehension. | • Teacher and students echo read the first selection.<br>• Comprehension should be developed through various strategies such as teacher and student questioning, visualization, etc.<br>• If time allows, a second reading (choral or partner) should take place. | • Students complete postreading extension activities.<br>• Activities may include writing in response to story, discussion of character motivations, summarization, etc. | • Teacher and students echo read a second selection.<br>• Comprehension should be developed through various strategies such as teacher and student questioning, predicting, etc.<br>• If time allows, a choral or partner reading of the second selection can occur.<br>• Students can complete postreading extension activities. | • Teacher and students echo read a third selection.<br>• Comprehens should be developed through vario strategies su as teacher and student questioning, predicting, et<br>• If time allows a choral or partner readi of the secon selection can occur.<br>• Students can complete postreading extension activities. |

**FIGURE 8.3.** Fluency-Oriented Reading Instruction weekly routine.

usually the basal or literature anthology selection that is required as part of many literacy curricula; however, any shared reading text can be used.

Critically, because the approach involves three texts over the course of a week, the amount of time spent on the first selection is, by necessity, reduced. As a result, only 3 days should be spent on this text, as opposed to the 5 days allocated in the original FORI method. The first day involves prereading activities to introduce the text, reading the selection to the class as students follow along, and a discussion of the reading. On the second day an echo reading of the text should take place, followed by a choral or partner reading if time allows. The third day centers around the implementation of whatever extension activities are appropriate for the material (see days 1, 2, and 5 of the FORI approach, respectively, for a more detailed plan of these days' lessons). The remaining lessons incorporate the reading of the second and third texts on days 4 and 5, respectively. These texts should be echo read, and the reading followed by a discussion of the selections with the learners. Further, if time allows, the students should undertake a second reading of the material; whether this reading consists of echo, choral, or partner reading will depend on students' comfort with the material, difficulty of the text, and amount of time available. Again, it is essential that the texts be substantive enough to ensure that students are spending between 20 and 40 minutes each day actually engaged in reading. Although it may seem difficult to find enough texts for class sets, instructors might consider literature anthologies from previous years, texts from guided reading groups and classroom and school libraries that can make a full set, articles from magazines subscribed to by the school or individual classrooms (like *National Geographic for Kids*), content area text or trade books, or material downloaded and copied from trustworthy computer sites (such as NASA, which has a plethora of reading materials designed to be appropriate for a range of reading levels).

## PRACTICES FOR IMPROVING STUDENTS' COMPREHENSION

In the cooperative groups implemented in jigsaw (Aronson, Blaney, Sikes, Stephan, & Snapp, 1978; Aronson, Blaney, Stephan, Rosenfield, & Sikes, 1977) and reciprocal teaching plus (Ash, 2002), students are responsible for their own learning; however, they also have the opportunity to construct meaning socially with their peers. As with teacher-led guided reading, instructional organizations for structuring small-group work with text allow students the opportunity to mimic what good readers do. These practices frame reading with activities that mirror what good readers do while they read and allow students to practice strategy use in a supportive environment.

## Jigsaw

Jigsaw (e.g., Aronson et al., 1977, 1978; Gunter, Estes, & Schwab, 1995) is an adaptation of a basic strategy to increase student interdependence. First, students are assigned to one of several heterogeneously grouped study teams with a text or text segment to read and a set of questions or goals to discuss. All the students in this group become "experts" on that particular text. These experts are responsible for teaching the content of their area to other students, who read and become experts on other sections of text. Once the study groups have answered their questions or met their goals, each member of the study team "jigsaws," or joins representatives from each other's team to form a jigsaw group. Each member of the new group teaches the piece in which he or she has developed expertise from his or her study team. The teacher then evaluates the students' knowledge of all of the information either individually or according to jigsaw groups.

## Reciprocal Teaching Plus

Reciprocal teaching plus (Ash, 2002) was developed based on reciprocal teaching (Palincsar & Brown, 1984), a strategy that focuses students on four aspects of their reading: making and revising predictions, asking questions, clarifying difficult points and vocabulary, and summarizing the material. In the beginning, the teacher models reciprocal teaching with the students, demonstrating how to use the four parts of the strategy and eventually moving students toward using the strategy in peer-led small groups or pairs. In these small groups or pairs, students read predetermined sections of text silently, stopping at designated stopping points and taking turns leading a discussion that includes questioning, summarizing, clarifying, and predicting.

The reciprocal teaching plus adaptation takes this very effective strategy and incorporates critical literacy perspectives. In addition to the four elements, students address a fifth element: the critical evaluation of a text, identifying the author's perspective and analyzing what points of view are left out of the current text. Prompts that teachers can use to help students with the fifth element—analyzing the perspective of the author and text—include:

- Whose story is being told? What is the author's point of view or perspective?
- Is the author taking one side or another? Does the author tell the reader that he or she is doing this?
- Whose story is not being told? Why might that be?
- What might another point of view or perspective be?

Reciprocal teaching plus models how students can read literally, inferentially, and critically, with guidance and feedback from their peers and their teacher.

## PRACTICES FOR IMPROVING
## STUDENTS' MOTIVATION/ENGAGEMENT

Research suggests that students are more motivated to complete their reading if they are given a specific purpose or task to complete through their reading. The two activities presented here—problematic perspectives and SPAWN—ask students to gather, evaluate, and apply knowledge from their reading to creative discussion and writing tasks.

### Problematic Perspectives

In problematic perspectives (Vacca & Vacca, 2005), a teacher designs a hypothetical scenario related to the content in the reading assignment. For example, a teacher getting ready to have students read a text on the Revolutionary War in the United States might ask the students to consider the following scenario:

> You are a 14-year-old son of a prosperous Tory farming family, living in a rural part of the Massachusetts Bay Colony in 1774. You know that in Boston, and in other parts of the colonies, there have been men who have protested recent taxing acts of the English government. Your family, as Tories, is loyal to King George III, and your family (mostly your father) finds these protests to be traitorous. Yet you have friends whose families believe that England has violated their rights, taxing them in this way and preventing them from having power to decide on tax laws that affect them, their products, and their profits. You also believe that it is unfair for England to prevent people from making a living due to the high taxes they have levied ("levied" means to impose) to pay for the French and Indian War. At dinner, your father tells you that you must not spend time with friends who are not Tories. To spend time with your friends, you must defend their beliefs, even though you are unsure of your own beliefs yourself and even though you know that your father greatly disapproves of your friends' beliefs. What would you say to your father? Why? Can you imagine a similar situation happening in the United States today? What might it be based on?

Before asking the students to read, the teacher presents the scenario, allows the students to discuss the problem, asks the students questions that might help them think about the scenario in different ways, and seeks possible solutions from the students. Then the teacher asks the students to read the text, thinking about the scenario and how their possible solutions might be affected by the information they read. Following their reading, students are asked to reconsider the scenario and again share possible solutions.

## SPAWN

SPAWN (Special Powers, Problem Solving, Alternative Viewpoints, What If, Next) (Martin, Martin, & O'Brien, 1984) is a series of writing assignments that ask students to consider the content that they are about to read from multiple perspectives and to creatively apply their knowledge to their writing or discussion tasks. For example, before reading a section of *Holes* (Sachar, 1998), the teacher shares the following assignments:

- *S (Special Powers)*—You have been granted special powers. You are able to read minds, and you discover the purpose for having the boys dig the holes. Who would you tell? Why? How would telling someone affect the story and its outcome?
- *P (Problem Solving)*—When Stanley had the sunflower seeds, he chose to take responsibility for their theft and, even though he did not steal them, to hold his place in the pecking order of the boys of Tent D. How could you have handled the problem differently?
- *A (Alternative Viewpoints)*—Pretend you are Mr. Pendanski (Mom). How do you view the boys of Tent D in particular and the boys of Camp Green Lake in general? How do you view Mr. Sir and the Warden? What do you think the purpose of your job is? What do you think the Warden thinks that the purpose of your job is?
- *W (What If)*—What if the Warden had punished Stanley, instead of punishing Mr. Sir, for the theft of the sunflower seeds? How might the story have been different?
- *N (Next)*—You are a "camper" at Camp Green Lake. You see Zero walk away; then later, Stanley also runs away. What might you do next?

After using these prompts to set students' purpose for reading, the teacher has them read the selected section silently. After reading the section, students are placed in heterogeneous small groups and are asked to discuss some of the assignments in their group and to write individual responses to others.

We hope we have convincingly argued that these approaches better meet students' needs, from building fluency to helping developing their comprehension, than engaging in either a focus on speed or the use of round robin reading and its variants. We believe that there are a number of strategies here, and throughout the book, that can be used to develop more engaging and effective literacy instruction. However, we also suggest closely observing students' responses to the methods being currently used and the proposed approaches for a week or so and comparing them. Then ask students how both types of activities make them feel. We are confident that the students' responses will speak for themselves.

## REFERENCES

Allington, R. L. (1977). If they don't read much, how are they ever going to get good? *Journal of Reading, 21*, 57–61.

Allington, R. L. (1980). Teacher interruption behaviors during primary grade oral reading. *Journal of Educational Psychology, 72*, 371–377.

Applegate, M. D., Applegate, A. J., & Modla, V. B. (2009). "She's my best reader; she just can't comprehend": Studying the relationship between fluency and comprehension. *The Reading Teacher, 62*, 512-521.

Aronson, E., Blaney, N., Sikes, J., Stephan, G., & Snapp, M. (1978). *The jigsaw classroom*. Beverly Hills, CA: Sage.

Aronson, E., Blaney, N. T., Stephan, C., Rosenfield, R., & Sikes, J. (1977). Interdependence in the classroom: A field study. *Journal of Educational Psychology, 69*, 121-128.

Ash, G. E. (2002, March). Teaching readers who struggle: A pragmatic middle school framework. *Reading Online*, available at *www.readingonline.org/articles/art_index.asp?HREF=ash/index.html*.

Ash, G. E., & Kuhn, M. R. (2006). Meaningful oral and silent reading in the elementary and middle school classroom: Breaking the round robin reading addiction. In T. Rasinski, C. Blachowicz, & K. Lems (Eds.), *Fluency instruction: Research-based best practices* (pp. 155–172). New York: Guilford Press.

Benjamin, R. G., & Schwanenflugel, P. J. (2010). Text complexity and oral reading prosody in young readers. *Reading Research Quarterly, 45*, 388–404.

Daane, M. C., Campbell, J. R., Grigg, W. S., Goodman, M.J., & Oranje, A. (2005). *Fourth-grade students reading aloud: NAEP 2002 special study of oral reading. The nation's report card* (NCES 2006-469). Washington, DC: U.S. Department of Education, Institute of Education Sciences.

Deno, S. L. (1985). Curriculum-based measurement: The emerging alternative. *Exceptional Children, 52*(3), 219–232.

Dowhower, S. L. (1991). Speaking of prosody: Fluency's unattended bedfellow. *Theory into Practice, 30*(3), 165–175.

Good, R. H., III, & Kaminski, R. A. (2002). *Dynamic Indicators of Basic Early Literacy Skills* (6th ed.). Eugene, OR: Institute for the Development of Educational Achievement. Retrieved November 30, 2009, from *dibels.uoregon.edu*

Gunter, M., Estes, T., & Schwab, J. (1995). *Instruction: A models approach*. Needham Heights, MA: Allyn & Bacon.

Hudson, R. F., Pullen, P. C., Lane, H. B., & Torgesen, J. K. (2009). The complex nature of reading fluency: A multidimensional view. *Reading and Writing Quarterly, 25*(1), 4–32.

Ivey, G. (1999). A multicase study in the middle school: Complexities among young adolescent readers. *Reading Research Quarterly, 34,* 172–192.

Kuhn, M. R., Schwanenflugel, P. J., & Meisinger, E. B. (2010). Aligning theory and assessment of reading fluency: Automaticity, prosody, and definitions of fluency. Invited review of the literature. *Reading Research Quarterly, 45,* 232–253.

Kuhn, M. R., Schwanenflugel, P. J., Morris, R. D., Morrow, L. M., Woo, D., Meisinger, B., et al. (2006). Teaching children to become fluent and automatic readers. *Journal of Literacy Research, 38,* 357–387.

LaBerge, D., & Samuels, S. J. (1974). Toward a theory of automatic information processing in reading. *Cognitive Psychology, 6,* 293–323.

Logan, G. D. (1997). Automaticity and reading: Perspectives from the instance theory of automatization. *Reading and Writing Quarterly, 13,* 123–146.

Martin, C. E., Martin, M. A., & O'Brien, D. G. (1984). Spawning ideas for writing in the content areas. *Reading World, 11,* 11–15.

Opitz, M. F., & Rasinski, T. V. (1998). *Good-bye round robin.* Portsmouth, NH: Heinemann.

Palincsar, A. S., & Brown, A. L., (1984). Reciprocal teaching of comprehension-fostering and comprehension-monitoring activities. *Cognition and Instruction, 2,* 117–175.

Paris, S. G. (2005). Reinterpreting the development of reading skills. *Reading Research Quarterly, 40*(2), 184–202.

Paris, S. G. (2008, December). *Constrained skills—so what?* Oscar Causey address presented at the annual meeting of the National Reading Conference, Orlando, FL.

Rasinski, T. V., & Hoffman, J. V. (2003). Oral reading in the school curriculum. *Reading Research Quarterly, 38,* 510–522.

Sachar, L. (1998). *Holes.* New York: Scholastic.

Samuels, S. J. (2004). Toward a theory of automatic information processing in reading, revisited. In R. B. Ruddell & N. J. Unrau (Eds.), *Theoretical models and processes* (pp. 1127–1148). Newark, DE: International Reading Association.

Samuels, S. J. (2007). The DIBELS tests: Is speed of barking at print what we mean by reading fluency? *Reading Research Quarterly, 42*(4), 563–566.

Schreiber, P. A. (1991). Understanding prosody's role in reading acquisition. *Theory into Practice, 30*(3), 158–164.

Shinn, M. R., & Shinn, M. M. (2002). *AIMSweb training workbook: Administration and scoring of reading maze for use in general outcome measurement.* Eden Prairie, MN: Edformation.

Stahl, K. A. D. (2008). Creating opportunities for comprehension within fluency-oriented reading. In M. R. Kuhn & P. J. Schwanenflugel (Eds.), *Fluency in the classroom* (pp. 55–74). New York: Guilford Press.

Stahl, S. A., & Heubach, K. (2005). Fluency-oriented reading instruction. *Journal of Literacy Research, 37,* 25–60.

Stanovich, K. E. (1980). Toward an interactive-compensatory model of individual differences in the development of reading fluency. *Reading Research Quarterly, 16,* 32–71.

Stanovich, K. E. (1986). Matthew effects in reading: Some consequences of individual differences in the acquisition of literacy. *Reading Research Quarterly, 21,* 360–407.

Torgesen, J. K., & Hudson, R. F. (2006). Reading fluency: Critical issues for struggling readers. In S. J. Samuels & A. E. Farstrup (Eds.), *What research has to say about fluency instruction* (pp. 130–158). Newark, DE: International Reading Association.

Vacca, R., & Vacca, J. (2005). *Content area reading* (8th ed.). Boston: Allyn & Bacon.

Valencia, S. W., Smith, A. T., Reece, A. M., Li, M., Wixson, K. K., & Newman, H. (2010). Oral reading fluency assessment: Issues of construct, criterion, and consequential validity. *Reading Research Quarterly, 45,* 270–291.

# 9

# "Jonathon Is 11 but Reads Like a Struggling 7-Year-Old"

*Providing Assistance for Struggling Readers with Audio-Assisted Reading Programs*

Meryl-Lynn Pluck

"Ben can't read even the simplest of books, and he'll be turning 9 next
 month."

"Jeremy decodes at a very slow pace, with no fluency at all."

"Katie can decode at a reasonable level, but her comprehension is very
 poor."

"Daniel is a very reluctant reader—he cannot read well and won't
 practice."

"Jason is 10 and refuses to read the books at his instructional reading
 level of 6 years."

Comments like these, substantiated by objective data, were typical of those
written on the 85 referrals for reading assistance that flooded my desk
when I was Resource Teacher of Reading (RTR) in Nelson, New Zealand.
These 85 referrals were from 19 schools serviced by one RTR, and there
were probably hundreds of other, equally needy students whose teachers
hadn't bothered submitting referrals that they knew would get no further
than my desk. What was I to do? Realistically, I could provide assistance
to 10–12 students a year at most, if I ran myself ragged visiting students
in their schools, tutoring them individually for half an hour four times a

week. Half of these students would be discontinued after a year; then they needed ongoing monitoring to ensure that they continued to make gains in their reading.

I was no mathematician, but it was obvious to me that I would never clear the backlog of current and future referrals in my lifetime. Also, decisions about who should be included on the roll when a space became available were extremely difficult to make. Would the best choice be a younger student who didn't have a lot of ground to cover to catch up or an older student for whom this might be a last chance to receive specialized assistance? Also, with so many students awaiting assistance, how long could individual assistance be justified for those on the roll? Should I risk discontinuing students early if they had almost caught up with their peers but could so easily drop back without support?

It became apparent that I needed a program that would meet the needs of not only students waiting for assistance but also the many struggling readers who hadn't been referred for help. The program should also help the RTR to prioritize students who needed intensive individual instruction, and support those students who had recently been discontinued from the RTR roll but still needed support and practice. This program would need to reach readers at a "rainbow" of levels and their teachers as well.

## PROGRAM DESIGN

Considering the economic and staffing realities, it was apparent that I needed to set up an intervention that could be implemented easily, effectively, and economically by teachers and paraprofessionals in the schools. Being Reading Recovery trained and, as a postgraduate student at Auckland University, further educated by Professor Marie Clay in the theory and practice of teaching older struggling readers, I had firm ideas about what would characterize an effective intervention. An effective intervention would need to:

- Be capable of lifting, maintaining, and continuing to improve students' reading skills, including comprehension.
- Be supportive and nonthreatening for students who were afraid of failing.
- Be enjoyable for students who were turned off by reading.
- Result in improved attitudes toward reading.
- Provide a good model for students to aspire to and emulate.
- Engage students in lots of reading (Stanovich, 1992).
- Feature texts that were not only leveled so that students could experience success with them at their instructional reading levels but

also of high interest for students whose interest levels exceeded their reading levels.

- Incorporate repeated reading (Samuels, 1979).
- Require students to demonstrate their reading to a tutor conversant with the techniques of praising, pausing, and prompting (McNaughton, Glynn, & Robinson, 1985).
- Encourage independence and allow students to make decisions and take control.

I had read about the success Chomsky (1976) and Carbo (1978) experienced with struggling readers using audio-assisted reading programs, and it became apparent to me that a form of tape-assisted reading could be tailored to incorporate the features I believed would make an effective intervention for the struggling readers in my district. Furthermore, I believed that schools could implement such a program easily; that it would be cost-effective, because paraprofessionals could work with small groups of students; and that students would enjoy it.

Getting this program off the ground involved many hours of seeking permission from publishers and authors to tape-record their stories, fundraising for equipment, book leveling, tape-recording and copying, writing initial guidelines, and sorting and organizing equipment, staff, work spaces, and students. Fifteen schools in my district took up the challenge to make a difference for their struggling readers, and 43 of the 85 students referred for assistance and more than 100 of their peers joined the program (Pluck, 1995) and became Rainbow Readers. The first pilot study would be used both to measure and to refine the process; it would be an example of formative research.

## RAINBOW READING PILOT STUDY (PLUCK, 1995)

### Participants

Eighty-five students, between 6.5 and 13.0 years of age, had been referred to the RTR for assistance with their reading and writing. Their instructional reading levels ranged from 5 years to over 13 years. Some students had been in Reading Recovery programs for 6-year-olds, and all were students for whom teachers had the most concern and difficulty in providing programs, because they had the most significant difficulties in reading in their schools.

Forty-nine students were considered to have needs that could be met by the Rainbow Reading program. Their reading levels were below their chronological ages, yet they could read at or above the 6.5- to 7-year level. This group was reduced in number to 43, because six students moved away from the district during the year and follow-up data were unavailable. The 43 Rainbow Reading students ranged in age from 7.8 to 12.8 years (average 10.1 years) at initial testing in February 1993. Their reading levels at this time ranged between 6.5–7 years and 10–11 years, with an average level of 8–8.5 years.

## Measures

In February 1993, the 85 students who had been referred to the RTR for assistance with their reading were assessed using unseen graded text or Informal Prose Inventory passages (New Zealand Department of Education Reading Advisory Service, 1984) to establish their current instructional reading levels. An instructional reading level was defined as the highest level a student could read after a minimal, standard orientation, with 90% accuracy or more. Comprehension was also checked but for the purposes of this study was not used as a criterion for establishing reading level. For the 43 Rainbow Reading program students, this assessment was repeated in August and again in December by independent testers in schools and yet again the following February. Students' instructional reading levels at initial assessment in February were their starting levels on the Rainbow Reading program, which for most began in March. If students were initially assessed as having an instructional reading level of 6.5–7 years, they started at the 7- to 7.5-year level, which was at the time the easiest level in the Rainbow Reading program.

## Materials

With the help of generous donations, the following equipment was purchased by the RTR service and loaned to students: personal cassette players with headphones, battery chargers, rechargeable batteries, taped stories, book bags, and handbooks.

Stories used were chosen from issues of the *New Zealand School Journal* (these are published each year, so no date is given), which is distributed free of charge to all schools. Selections included 130 short (200–600 words), high-interest stories and articles. Permission to record stories was obtained from the publisher and from authors. Stories were graded at six different levels of difficulty (7–12 years) according to the publishers' recommendations based on the Elley noun frequency method (Elley & Croft, 1989). Stories were identified in the order of the colors in a rainbow, which resulted in the Rainbow Reading program name. Stories were tape-recorded by trained readers, who read fluently at specified rates and slowly enough for students to follow along.

## The Instructional Setting and Tutors

Groups of between four and six students were withdrawn from their classrooms to work with teachers or paraprofessionals employed by the schools. Handbooks and minimal training (45 minutes) were provided for tutors. Rainbow Reading practice can take place within students' classrooms, but all the tutors in this study preferred to withdraw students to practice outside the classroom. The places of practice varied markedly, from libraries, staff rooms, spare classrooms, or offices to book storage rooms. In all cases, it was emphasized that Rainbow Reading practice was in addition to the regular classroom reading program.

## Liaison and Monitoring

To ensure fidelity of treatment, liaison visits by the author, the RTR, initially took place every 2 weeks and were later reduced to just once every 3 weeks. During liaison visits, tapes were exchanged, students' and teachers' records in the students' handbooks were checked, and progress, promotion, and any concerns were discussed.

## Instructional Process

The instructional process was also standardized so that the treatment could be examined. Each school and tutor followed the same process and agreed that:

- Schools would operate the program for half an hour per group, five times a week, until students' instructional reading levels matched their chronological ages.
- Students would be assessed to determine their instructional reading level, the optimal starting level of the program.
- Students would read instructional-level material and receive an orientation to the book.
- Students would practice reading the book while listening to the audiotape until they believed they could read the book well without the tape.
- Students would read the book independently to confirm whether they needed more practice with or without the book or whether they were ready to conference with their teacher.
- During the conference, the teacher would listen to the student read and check for accuracy, comprehension, and prosody (pace, smoothness, and expression). If the student read easily with 95%-plus accuracy, good understanding, and prosody, the process would begin again with a new book.

- A record of practice would be kept in the student's handbook, where the student would enter the book titles and the number of practices that were needed before he or she could read the books easily. After each conference, the teacher would write a brief positive note about what he or she observed and recommendations for future practice.
- Students would be assessed for readiness to move on to a new level when they could read an unseen book at their current level easily, with good understanding and prosody. Alternatively, they could demonstrate readiness to practice with books at the next level if they could read unseen books at that level with instructional accuracy.

## Results

Forty-three students spent between 9 and 32 weeks (average 27.5 weeks) in the Rainbow Reading program. Time spent varied depending on, for example, the school or class timetable, availability of tutor time and space, student interest, or discontinuation because skills level had reached the point where continued participation was no longer considered necessary.

Students made gains of, on average, 2.2 years and up to 4 years in their reading level. At retesting, in February 1994, 23 of the 43 students could read at levels equivalent to or higher than their chronological ages. These particular students averaged 28.2 weeks on the program. Before students began practicing on the Rainbow Reading program, they were, on average, reading 1.7 years below their chronological ages, ranging between 0.5 and 3.5 years behind what is considered to be average for their ages. Twelve months later, after an average of 27.5 weeks on the program and after a 6-week holiday break, students had improved their reading to the extent that they were reading, on average, just 0.5 years below their chronological ages.

The four students initially assessed as having instructional reading levels of 6.5–7 years all made significant progress, ranging from 1.75 to 2.75 years in reading level. The majority of students made the most progress in the first 18 weeks of the program between March and August, improving, on average, by only 0.17 years between August and December. Most students continued to improve their reading level over the holiday break, making average gains of 0.4 years between December and February.

## CONFIRMATORY STUDIES

Since the initiation of the program in Nelson, more than 80% of New Zealand's schools have begun to use Rainbow Reading, and a number of action research and other studies have been carried out. Two that are reported here are of special interest because the participants were older students, typically with more delay, a longer history of struggle, and corresponding poor attitudes about learning to read. Some were also learning English as a second language.

## Tape-Assisted Repeated Reading for a Group of Low-Progress Readers in a Secondary School

Langford (2001) chose Rainbow Reading as the intervention for her class of 15 low-progress readers (many of whom spoke English as a second language), at levels ranging from years 8–10 (12- to 14-year-olds), in an Auckland secondary school. A paraprofessional facilitated the program, providing students with a half-hour of reading practice daily for 8 weeks. Analyses of test results revealed that students made, on average, 1.2 years progress in reading level and comprehension, along with an average gain of 9.7 months in word recognition skills. Five of the students made 2 years progress in reading. The overwhelming response of the students to the program was positive. The researcher concluded, "It is a very worthwhile intervention to recommend for secondary schools that need assistance in meeting the needs of their low-progress readers" (p. 21).

## Is Tape-Assisted Reading an Effective Support Program?

Harlow (2001) and Piper (2009) introduced Rainbow Reading to year 8 (12- and 13-year-old) students in their schools following the instructional protocol. Harlow's 24 students made average gains of 1.9 years in reading level (range: 1–3 years) in just 15 weeks on the program, as tested using the PROBE Reading Assessment (Parkin, Parkin, & Pool, 1999). The average increase in Rainbow Reading levels (a level is equivalent to 12 months' progress in reading) was 3.6 years (range: 3–5 years). Piper's twelve 11- and 12-year-old students, all English language learners, made highly significant gains—of 2.5 years on average—in just 10 weeks. Harlow reported that the program

> Provides a good model by a good reader, it focuses on what reading is all about (understanding the author's intent), it reinforces and extends the child's existing language patterns, it allows for the much needed extra practice without pressure from others, it shifts the focus away from getting all the words right and the child has control over their learning environment. (p. 10)

Furthermore, students enjoyed the program, rarely had to be reminded to practice, asked to take the books home to read to their parents, and were generally very positive.

## Using Audiotaped Read-Along Stories with Low-Progress Readers

In 2001, an action research study was commissioned to determine the effect of the Reading Rainbow program on students' reading, writing, and related skills (Nalder & Elley, 2004). The research was designed to investigate whether, and how much, the Rainbow Reading program would assist slow-progress students of several age groups across a range of schools. The sample comprised 30 students in eight elementary schools in suburban Auckland, the largest city in New Zealand. Students, who were, on average, 2 years behind in reading, were tutored with the Rainbow Reading tape-assisted program for 18 weeks.

The schools represented a wide range of socioeconomic levels, from below average to high, and included many different ethnic and language groups. At the outset of the study, the mean age of participants was 9 years 6 months, with a range from 7 years 2 months to 12 years 2 months. The students for whom English was a second language came from a variety of countries, including Samoa ($n = 4$), South Korea ($n = 3$), Tonga ($n = 2$), and several East European countries. Most had lived in New Zealand between 1 and 3 years, and most spoke their first language at home. Particular research questions were addressed:

1. How much progress in reading ability does a selected group of 30 low-progress readers make when students follow the tape-assisted Rainbow Reading program for a period of 4 months?
2. Do the benefits of such a program spread to writing, spelling, and oral language skills?
3. Do second-language (L2) learners benefit as much as first-language (L1) users?

The selected students were required to participate in the Rainbow Reading program at least four times each week over a period of two school terms (20 weeks reduced to 18 weeks, with 2 weeks spent pre- and posttesting). Three students ended their treatment before the end of the two-term period, after 8, 11, and 12 weeks of participation, respectively, because they had made enough progress to manage without further assistance. Four students continued the program for 4–6 weeks beyond the two-term period because they needed more time to be able to work at their current class level.

Even when a maturation factor was allowed for, results showed significant gains in reading age levels, word recognition, reading accuracy, comprehension, writing fluency, spelling, and oral language, with L2 students showing strong gains. Because the intervention took place over a period of 4 months, it was judged important to allow for this time lapse in evaluating the results. Such an adjustment had not been common in earlier studies, because most delayed readers make little progress at all in an intervention of only 2 or 3 months. Hence, for each test with age norms, the actual pretest scores were increased by 2 months, which represents half the duration of the project. The assumption is made that these students, who progressed at less than half the normal rate since starting school, might have been expected to make no more than 2 months progress in the 4 months of the intervention. No such adjustment was made for the writing and oral language tests because they had no age norms.

## Reading Age Levels

All but two of the students made good progress up the Rainbow Reading level scale during the intervention. A sign test showed a significant difference ($z = 4.65$, $n = 29$, $p < .01$). Fourteen students were able to read text at a level more than 2 years higher than where they started, and 12 more moved up by 1.8 years. With the aid of the audiotapes and guided practice, these 26 students, who had made so little progress before, had caught up, on average, more than two grade levels and were thus able to read books at their expected grade level.

## Word Recognition

Using the Burt Word Reading Test (New Zealand Council for Educational Research, 1981), 24 of 29 students (83%) showed greater progress than expected, and seven of them gained more than 12 months in the 4-month intervention. The researchers used a rank test of paired observations to test for significance and found a $z$ score of 4.20 ($n = 28$; $p < .01$). On the skill of recognizing words in isolation, students showed significant improvement during the intervention. Six of the L2 students demonstrated noticeable gains of more than 12 months on this skill, while only one of the L1 students did so.

## Reading Accuracy

On the Neale Accuracy Test (Neale, 1999), 21 of the 28 students (75%) showed greater progress than expected ($z = 3.66$, $n = 28$, $p < .01$), and three of them made gains of 12 months or more. Their ability to read text aloud without error clearly improved during the intervention. Once again, the L2 students showed greater gains. In fact, the student profiles for word recognition and accuracy in reading text aloud were very similar. The gain scores rose and fell together.

## Reading Comprehension

On the Neale Comprehension Test (Neale, 1999), 17 students (of 28) exceeded expectation, which was only just enough to show a marginally significant gain on a one-tailed test ($z = 2.05$, $n = 28$, $p < .05$). It seems that the ability to comprehend unfamiliar text while reading aloud is given a boost by a 4-month tape-assisted reading intervention, but the gain is less impressive than that for the other skills.

## Spelling

On the Peters Spelling Test (Peters, 1970), 18 of 25 students (72%) exceeded expectation, indicating that there were positive effects on spelling ability during the intervention ($z = 3.11$, $n = 25$, $p < .01$). Six students achieved gains of more than 1 year. (The number of participants was reduced to 25 on this test because of absences.)

## Writing

Although there were no norms in the writing test to allow for a maturation factor during the 4-month intervention as there were for the previously mentioned assessments, it was clear that most students made large gains in the volume of their writing. Overall, 25 of 29 students (86%) showed gains in volume, and 21 students increased their score by more than the standard deviation (16.0). The rank test for paired observations produced a significant $z$ value of 4.44 ($n = 29$, $p < .01$).

## Oral Language

On the Van Hees Oral Language Pretest (Van Hees, 1999), three students had a perfect score, so with three absentees, the sample was reduced to 23. Of these students, 18 (78%) showed improvement, and 13 improved by more than the pretest standard deviation of the whole group. The sign test was used to check significance because there were many tied ranks, and the resulting $z$ value was 3.84 ($n = 23$, $p < .01$).

## English Language Learners

The researchers concluded that there is little room for doubt that English language learners benefited from the tape-assisted reading program. The L2 students actually showed more consistent gains than the L1 students. The L1 students showed clear improvements on 71% of the comparisons made between their respective pre- and posttest scores, while the L2 students showed gains on 85%. The main difference was found in the Neale Comprehension Test, where L1 students showed gains on 47% of the comparisons, while L2 students showed gains on 85%. On all tests, L2 students improved as much or more than L1 students. The rate of improvement for L2 students was more than twice the L1 rate in the case of reading comprehension and spelling, and almost as great in word recognition and reading accuracy (1.90 and 1.86 times the L1 gains, respectively).

## The Highest and Lowest Achievers

When scores were compared across the measures, it was discovered that five students stood out because they showed very few gains. These students failed to show improvement on 51% of the test comparisons, and these same students made minimal progress in the Rainbow Reading program also. Three moved up by less than 1 year, whereas the typical gain was more than 2 years. Analysis of the research records showed that two of these students had fewer sessions than most, and another student was described as "low ability."

By contrast, 10 students stood out because they made impressive gains on most tests. For instance, in a period of only 4 months an L2 (South Korean) student improved more than 4 years on the Rainbow Reading levels, more than 2 years in spelling, and more than 12 months in both word recognition and accuracy. The Rainbow Reading program was clearly of great benefit to him. The nine other "rapid recoverers" showed consistent gains in nearly every case, with several jumps of more than 2 years. Again, the improvement of the L2 students is apparent.

Teachers and students spoke positively about the program, and most students claimed to enjoy reading after the intervention. Further analysis showed that the students who read the most books during the intervention improved the most. The researchers noted that, in many cases, the program was not always administered as intended. For example, teachers had committed to implementing the program for a half-hour four times a week, but there were many distractions in that period. Thus, students had an average of 50.45 sessions, which is 22 fewer than the number prescribed. Under ideal conditions, the researchers reported, the level of impact might well have been greater. Nevertheless, the results were very pleasing. For students making regular progress, which these students were not, if we expect 1 month of gain for 1 month of instruction, we would predict these students to make 4 months progress in their reading. These students, however, made, on average, gains of 26 months, or more than six times the expectation. The researchers concluded that there is a definite place for a tape-assisted reading program in helping low-progress students to improve their reading and language abilities.

## GLOBAL INTEREST

With the introduction of a website, news about the success of the program spread around the world. For example, through distributors, Rainbow Reading sells extensively in the United Kingdom, Australia, South Africa, Singapore, Hong Kong, and Sweden. In English-speaking countries, it is used successfully to help struggling readers and English language learners. Elsewhere it is used to support students learning English as a foreign language. A different version of the resources (called New Heights) using the same proven formula has hence been developed for American students, and it has been well received and widely used. Rainbow Reading, as well as being international, is multilingual, with a version in Maori; the language of New Zealand's indigenous people.

## FURTHER DEVELOPMENTS

Innovation, it is clear, is never a finite business. The world changes, and ongoing research contributes to our knowledge and understanding, which influence how we, as educators, choose to teach and what we, as publishers, choose to publish to support teachers. Feedback from customers promotes new thinking. Technology changes, and we have had to make the move from audiotapes to CDs and now MP3 files.

The research on effective techniques for fostering fluency has encouraged me to develop new resources. After my first perusal of Tim Rasinski's book *The Fluent Reader* (2003), I congratulated myself, because it seemed that our audio-assisted reading programs incorporated the key features of good fluency-building programs emerging around the world:

- Text at an appropriate level of difficulty.
- Repeated readings when students practice, with and without the audio support.
- Modeled reading by the voice on the audio support.
- Supported reading with the audio component.
- Opportunities for students to respond to what they've read, with optional text-related activities.
- Performance demonstration when students read to their teacher.

Indeed, Rasinski (2003) refers to our program as being "synergistic" (p. 123) because it incorporates so many successful features and strategies for achieving fluency. However, I was still searching for a technique to address the question most frequently asked of me by educators: "How do you get students, particularly the older ones, to engage in the repeated readings we know they need?" My answer usually involves factors relating to the nature of the books, such as having the books be of high interest and written in such a manner (often with a surprise ending) that students want to read them again and again. A special series (ToXic) was hence published (with audio support, of course) to address the interests of reluctant boys with subjects involving body gunk, killer creatures, and vile vultures. Yet another special series (Selections) was developed (again with audio support) to address the needs and interests of struggling teenage and adult readers with very low reading abilities.

Other suggestions for encouraging repeated readings are dependent on convincing the students that such practice is worthwhile or necessary:

- Explaining to students that repeated readings are a requirement of the program that is proven to help them to become better readers.
- Comparing repeated reading to the practice students do in other areas of their life in which they want to achieve well, such as sports or music practice.
- Ensuring that when students demonstrate their reading to their teacher, it needs to be easy, fluent, and well understood before they are given permission to move on to another book. In other words, "If you're bored with the book you're reading, read it well, and you won't have to read it any more!"

When I attended the Fluency Institute of the International Reading Association in Orlando, Florida, in 2003, and learned more about Readers Theatre, it became apparent to me that this technique would encourage students to engage happily and willingly in repeated readings: They need to be fluent if they are going to perform for an audience of their peers. No student I've ever encountered wants to be perceived publicly as a stumbling reader. Repeated readings would definitely be needed to achieve the level of fluency required for performing for an audience or making a recording. And how much more powerful the scripts would be if they were multi-leveled, so students of mixed ability could practice alongside each other, and if the scripts were accompanied by specially prepared audio support for modeling and support.

It was, hence, my mission since attending the Fluency Institute to trial test and subsequently publish Speak Out Readers Theatre scripts and write the guidelines for teachers and students. The scripts were indeed well received, and as well as enjoying the practice, it is clear that students' fluency is also much improved, and both the presenters and the audience really look forward to performance days. The next step is publishing a digitized version of the scripts with synchronized text highlighting with audio support so students can practice individually with the computer or in a group with scripts projected onto a whiteboard.

Throughout the development and publishing of resources to improve students' reading fluency, I have been acutely aware that reading comprehension is, for most students (and their teachers), the largest hurdle. A program (Comprehension Strategies Instruction [CSI]) that supports teachers to teach comprehension strategies was hence developed in partnership with Neale Pitches. CSI employs a model of gradual release, from teacher modeling to cooperative learning (think–pair–share) and independent reflection. In CSI students in grade 3 and beyond learn to apply several reading strategies to content from language arts, math, science, and social studies. The program comprises interactive, whiteboard-enabled digital short texts for use in shared/modeled reading, audio-assisted hard-copy texts for practice and applying skills learned in cooperative learning, and an independent reflection journal for each student. Chapter books in both hard copy and digitized format support and enable students to apply comprehension strategies when reading longer texts.

From the schools using Rainbow Reading, New Heights, Speak Out Readers Theatre, and CSI, the comments I'm now more likely to receive from teachers are as follows:

> "Ben is 11. He has no trouble with his reading since making over 4 years progress in 2 years on the Rainbow Reading program."
> "Jeremy loves books since he's been practicing on the New Heights reading program. He now reads with good pace and excellent expression."
> "Katie's been working on comprehension strategies instruction, and her comprehension is much improved."
> "Daniel is a no longer a reluctant reader. The ToXic series has helped him to become a much better reader, and he's now a bit of a bookworm."
> "Jason is now 12. He has made fantastic progress in his reading, happily practicing with the Speak Out Readers Theatre and reading parts well at his instructional reading level."

And last, one of my favorites:

> "Jonathon is now 12 and, thanks to Rainbow Reading, reads fluently at an age-appropriate level."

## REFERENCES

Carbo, M. (1978). Teaching reading with talking books. *Reading Teacher, 32*(3), 267–273.

Chomsky, C. (1976). After decoding, what? *Language Arts, 53*(3), 288–296.

Elley, W. B., & Croft, A. C. (1989). *Assessing the difficulty of reading materials: The noun frequency method*. Wellington: New Zealand Council for Educational Research.

Harlow, S. (2001). *Is tape assisted reading an effective support program?* Unpublished manuscript.

Langford, J. (2001, July). "Tape assisted repeated reading" for a group of low progress readers in a secondary school. *Reading Today for Tomorrow*, pp. 14–21. Retrieved from *www.rainbowreading.co.nz/assets/files/cms/langford.pdf*.

McNaughton, S., Glynn, T., & Robinson, V. (1985). *Pause, prompt and praise: Effective tutoring for remedial reading*. Birmingham, UK: Positive Products.

Nalder, S., & Elley, W. (2004). Interesting results from Rainbow Reading research, 2001–2003. *Reading Forum NZ, 19*(1).

Neale, M. (1999). *Neale analysis of reading ability*. Melbourne: Australian Council for Educational Research.

New Zealand Council for Educational Research. (1981). *Burt Word Reading Test*. Wellington, NZ: Author.

New Zealand Department of Education Reading Advisory Service. (1984). *Informal Prose Inventory*. Wellington, NZ: Author.

Parkin, C., Parkin, C., & Pool, B. (1999). *PROBE Reading Assessment*. Whangarei, New Zealand: Triune.

Peters, M. L. (1970). *Success in spelling*. Cambridge, UK: Cambridge Institute of Education.

Piper, M. (2009). *Rainbow Reading study—St. Therese school*. Unpublished manuscript. Retrieved September 26, 2011, from *www.rainbowreading.co.nz/assets/files/cms/eslsttherese.pdf*.

Pluck, M. J. (1995). *Rainbow Reading programme: Using taped stories: The Nelson Project* [*Reading Forum, NZ*, Term 1]. Auckland: New Zealand Reading Association. Retrieved September 26, 2011, from *www.rainbowreading. co.nz/assets/files/cms/nelsonproject.pdf*.

Rasinski, T. V. (2003). *The fluent reader: Oral reading strategies for building word recognition, fluency, and comprehension*. New York: Scholastic.

Samuels, S. J. (1979). The method of repeated readings. *Reading Teacher, 32*, 403–408.

Stanovich, K. (1992). Differences in reading acquisition: Causes and consequences [*Reading Forum NZ*, Term 3]. Auckland: New Zealand Reading Association.

Van Hees, J. (1999). *Diagnostic and literacy assessment in English*. Auckland: Kohia Teachers' Center.

## CONTACT INFORMATION
## ABOUT COMMERCIALLY PRODUCED MATERIALS

*CSI (Comprehension Strategies Instruction)*. South Pacific Press Ltd, Box 19088, Wellington, 6149, New Zealand. Distributed in the United States by Pacific Learning, P.O. Box 2723, Huntington Beach, CA 92647-0723.

*New Heights*. Learning Media Limited, Box 3293, Wellington 6001, New Zealand. Distributed in the United States by Brightpoint Literacy (*www.brightpointliteracy.com/browse/New-Heights/24*).

*New Zealand School Journals.* Learning Media Limited, Box 3293, Wellington 6001, New Zealand.

*PROBE (Prose Reading Observation, Behaviour and Evaluation of Comprehension).* (1999). Informal Reading Inventory. Triune Publications, Box 10023, Te Mai, Whangarei, New Zealand.

*Rainbow Reading Program.* Rainbow Reading Program, Ltd., P.O. Box 561, Nelson, New Zealand.

*ToXic.* Rainbow Reading Program, Ltd., P.O. Box 561, Nelson, New Zealand.

*Selections.* Rainbow Reading Program, Ltd., P.O. Box 561, Nelson, New Zealand.

*Speak Out Readers Theater,* South Pacific Press Ltd, Box 19088, Wellington, 6149, New Zealand. Distributed in the United States by Pacific Learning, P.O. Box 2723, Huntington Beach, CA 92647-0723.

# 10

## The Fluency Development Lesson
### A Model of Authentic and Effective Fluency Instruction

Belinda Zimmerman
Timothy Rasinski

*Dear Dr. Rasinski:*

*I have been totally depressed lately. My grandson, Ricardo, just completed first grade and the teacher indicated that he is reading below grade level—especially with his fluency. He is one of the lowest readers in his class. On the plus side, his vocabulary is excellent as is his comprehension.*

*His parents read to him every night as I do when he is with us all day on Wednesdays. And my wife, Jane, and I have also helped him with lessons when he is at our house.*

*I tried to get him into the reading program at KSU that his first-grade teacher recommended, but [a clinic director] said they were already filled. However, she said Ricardo would be first on the list if someone dropped out.*

*I found the wonderful list of books to read that you posted on-line. What a fantastic resource! So I am checking out several of these and working my way through them, having Ricardo read each book several times.*

*If you have any suggestions or know of a good program I could purchase, let me know. He loves catching and examining insects and enjoys catching different kinds of fish. (Last year he caught by himself a 5.5-pound bass in the backyard lake at our house.)*

*But I feel at a loss in terms of how I can best help him. Can you give me some suggestions?*

*Sincerely,*
*Raymond Shearing*

*Dear Mr. Shearing,*

*I can sympathize with your concerns. It is frustrating to watch a child struggle with learning to read. It's even more painful when that child is someone you love and care about. You're on the right track looking for material that can engage Ricardo in reading about things he is interested in. You're also on the right track by asking him to read them several times. At our clinic, we work with students to help them learn to be more fluent using an instructional approach called the Fluency Development Lesson (FDL). I'll send you some information about the FDL as soon as I can. Until then, congratulate Ricardo on his big bass and don't give up hope. Kids like Ricardo can and do learn to read and to read well.*

*Sincerely,*
*Dr. Timothy Rasinski*

What we love about this (real with pseudonym) e-mail we shared is how clearly the writer articulates his sense of concern and frustration for his struggling grandson. We also appreciate the ways in which Ricardo's parents have worked to set the stage for him to learn to read and the ways his grandparents have pitched in to assist. However, no matter how helpful parents and grandparents are, they are not reading professionals and lack the tools and experience that reading professionals utilize to assist children who struggle to learn to read. In this chapter, we share one of those tools that we call the Fluency Development Lesson (FDL).

## RESEARCH ON FLUENCY

Fluency is a developmental process that bridges word identification and reading comprehension (Pikulski, 2006). When readers read fluently, they read effortlessly. To read fluently, readers must be able to decode the words on the printed page accurately and automatically with appropriate prosody or expression. As fluency increases, so does readers' ability to derive meaning from the text and to appreciate the subtleties contained within a passage.

Word recognition automaticity is one of two major components of fluency. It refers to the ability to read (decode) words not only accurately but also automatically. Automatic word decoding allow readers to be so natural and effortless in their decoding that they can focus their limited amount of cognitive resources on making meaning, the more important part of reading, rather than word decoding. Fluency also involves the ability to read orally in such a way that the reading sounds like meaningful spoken language. Reading with appropriate expression allows readers to elaborate on the meaning of the passage through reading speed, volume, tone, emphasis, inflection, and pausing. With fluency, readers develop the ability to decode and comprehend at the same time in order to produce meaningful, expressive reading. As Rasinski (2006) notes, in order to achieve fluency, readers need to be able to

> read the words on the printed page accurately, effortlessly, or automatically so that readers can preserve their limited cognitive resources for the more important task in reading—comprehension—and with appropriate prosody or expression so as to give meaning to the words that is implied through emphasis, phrasing, and intonation. (p. 3)

When students are unable to gain automatic and accurate decoding skills, they not only struggle with reading comprehension but also fall behind their peers in academic achievement, and attaining successful progress becomes increasingly difficult (Dudley, 2005). Once students with reading difficulties enter middle and high school, the motivation to read and reread tends to decline. These students avoid tasks that require reading and often experience greater frustration, anxiety, and disappointment, resulting in less patience for participation in reading activities (Rasinski, 2010).

Fluency matters for both oral and silent reading. Once students gain proficiency in decoding and word identification and can read basic books, silent reading develops, and students begin to use in-the-head thinking processes to access the meaning in texts (Clay, 2005). Research has shown that readers who read orally with good fluency also read silently with good comprehension; and readers whose oral reading is marked by poor fluency tend to be readers who struggle with silent reading comprehension (Daane, Campbell, Grigg, Goodman, & Oranje, 2005; Pinnell et al., 1995).

The goal of silent reading according to Topping (2006) is the "extraction of maximum meaning at maximum speed in a relatively continuous flow" (p. 173) so that readers are cognitively freed up to deal with higher level thought processes. Silent reading is needed for students to succeed in school and perform well on tests that require strong silent fluency capabilities. Interestingly, silent reading fluency is often emphasized the least, yet is expected and tested the most (Gregg, 2010).

Fluency might well be considered a goal in and of itself. However, Topping (2006) asserts that the value of fluency is in what it enables. Reading fluency has been characterized as "multidimensional" (Rasinski, 2004) because it makes possible several things:

- Accuracy in word decoding: Fluent readers no longer use their limited attentional resources to sound out words. They are able to word solve with minimal effort.
- Automatic word recognition of words embedded in connected text: Automaticity is achieved when readers make a cognitive shift from *conscious*, accurate decoding to *automatic* accurate decoding (Samuels, 2002; Stanovich, 1991). At this stage, words are recognized on sight with immediate accuracy.
- Comprehension: Perhaps most importantly, fluency enables comprehension, which is the premier goal of reading. When readers have automaticity and accuracy under control, they can capitalize on this reserved brain energy to make sense of the text.

Another important consideration in proficient reading and fluency development is the amount of time spent reading. In fact, Gambrell (1984) found that primary grade students read connected text in school for less than 9 minutes a day and, even more troubling, struggling readers spent only 1 or 2 minutes per day reading. Paul (1996) found that the average amount of time devoted to reading for all grade levels in U.S. schools is a mere 7.1 minutes per day. Given these findings as well as the research supporting fluency development (Kuhn & Stahl, 2003; National Reading Panel, 2000; Rasinski & Hoffman, 2003), there clearly exists a great need to increase the amount of time students spend practicing reading connected text in classrooms.

Thus, reading fluency is an essential goal when it comes to discussing developing proficient readers. This is because fluency allows readers to focus on content, which is the foremost intent of reading instruction. Simply put, the comprehension levels of fluent readers are increased because readers are freed up to focus on the deeper meanings and nuances of the text rather than expending excessive cognitive energy on decoding and word solving. Kuhn and her colleagues (2006) report that "fluency is seen as a factor in the reader's ability to understand and enjoy text" (p. 359). Therefore, when reading is uninhibited by the taxing processes involved with word identification, students can place more emphasis on reading to learn and reading for enjoyment and recreation. Conversely, in the absence of fluency, readers tend to associate reading with difficult, tedious work. This may lead to feelings of reading resistance, avoidance, anxiety, or at the least a sense of apathy as readers become disconnected from finding meaningful purpose in their reading (Bintz, 1993; Lenters, 2006; Zbornik, 2001). Instructional practices that provide students with routines that increase the amount of reading while meaningfully engaging students in the process hold promise for offsetting struggling students' negative perceptions toward more favorable, enthusiastic attitudes toward reading.

## THE FLUENCY DEVELOPMENT LESSON

The FDL is an instructional model that may be differentiated to meet the needs of all learners, yet it originated as a framework for fluency intervention. The FDL was developed by Rasinski, Padak, Linek, and Sturtevant (1994) as a supplement to the regular reading program to assist students experiencing difficulties in fluency and in learning to read. It incorporates essential elements of effective fluency instruction—model fluency reading, assisted reading, repeated reading, and word study—into a synergistic instructional routine. The goal of the FDL is to provide instruction and practice in fluency in a focused routine that incorporates principles of effective fluency instruction in such a way that the various elements interact with one another in order to produce an instructional effect that is greater than the sum of the elements themselves (Padak & Rasinski, 2008; Rasinski, 2010).

The FDL model was designed for primary children, but has been found to work well with elementary and middle school students too. Depending on the age and the level of reading proficiency, the teacher selects and makes multiple copies of brief passages (two per student) of 50–150 words. However, with emerging readers or those with extremely limited English language proficiency, it is appropriate to choose texts with fewer words. Ideal texts are those that lend themselves to oral interpretive reading and that contain a strong voice. Among these text types or genres are poetry, song lyrics, monologues (including letters, journals, and diaries), dialogues, and scripts. Such texts are meant to be rehearsed and eventually performed orally with fluency. When students rehearse texts that are engaging and meant to be performed for an audience, fluency instruction becomes authentic and motivating. A growing body of research has demonstrated that when students engage in the rehearsal and performance of such materials, fluency and overall reading performance improve (Griffith & Rasinski, 2004; Martinez, Roser, & Strecker, 1998/1999; Young & Rasinski, 2009). Oral support reading, word study, and at-home practice are also features of the intervention. A day and time is reserved each week for the students to perform the text.

In a yearlong implementation of the FDL in urban second-grade classrooms where students were generally struggling readers, regular and consistent use of the FDL yielded positive learning outcomes. Substantial achievement in both reading fluency and overall reading progress was made compared with student progress from the previous year and compared with students not engaged in the FDL (Rasinski et al., 1994). Perhaps the greatest evidence of the effectiveness of the FDL lies in its instructional longevity. Rasinski (2010) reports that teachers continued to practice the FDL with their students well beyond the completion of the study.

An outline of a daily FDL plan (Zimmerman & Rasinski, 2011) is presented next:

1. The teacher or a more capable reader expressively reads a short text aloud to the students.
2. Distribution of copies of the text to the students with a second prosodic reading. Students follow along as the text reading is modeled for them.
3. Discussion of the passage with attention to developing comprehension, vocabulary, and quality of the oral reading by the teacher or other reader.
4. Multiple choral readings of the passage by students.
5. Multiple paired oral reading practice of the passage by students.
6. Student performance of the passage with attention to word recognition, accuracy and expression.
7. Addition of interesting and/or difficult words chosen by students and the teacher to the word wall, with discussion.
8. A brief word study activity from the words chosen from the passage (and other words chosen from previous days). This can include word sorts, word games, focusing attention on word families, and so on.
9. Creation of individually student-written and shared response to the text.
10. Students perform the passage for an audience of peers or others.
11. Students put one copy of the passage into a poetry folder for later reading in school. The second copy is sent home for further practice at home with parents and other family members.

## WEEKLY IMPLEMENTATION OF THE FDL

The FDL can also be adapted as a multiple-day routine. Specific instructions for classroom implementation over the course of a week are provided next (adapted from Zimmerman & Rasinski, 2011):

MONDAY

1. The teacher reads and rereads the text to the class, modeling his or her best fluent, phrased, and expressive reading. The job of the students is to relax and enjoy the teacher's lively and engaging performance.
2. The teacher discusses with the class the meaning of the text as well as the quality of his or her reading.
3. The teacher distributes copies of the text to each student.
4. The teacher reads the text again aloud to the students. The students are directed to follow along silently with their own copies or with the copy that has been displayed. Students are encouraged to relax and enjoy.
5. To achieve reading fluency, multiple opportunities to practice are necessary. Thus, the entire class reads the text chorally several times. The teacher creates variety by having students read the passage or portions of it in groups. For example, the teacher might say, "All those whose favorite sport is football, please stand and read" or "All those with summer birthdays, please stand and read." The teacher may also ask the class to reread the poem in a variety of prosodic voices: their deepest or highest voices, loud or soft voices, and happy or sad voices.

TUESDAY

6. The class reads and rereads the text again chorally. The teacher may request variations on choral reading.
7. The class divides into pairs. Each pair finds a quiet spot, and one student practices reading the text to a partner three times. The partner's job is to follow along in the text, provide help when needed, and give positive feedback to the reader. After the first three readings, the roles are switched. If possible, one partner should be at least a slightly stronger reader. The partners should be taught to use positive feedback when they see improvement in the other's reading and/or effort.

WEDNESDAY

8. The class reads and rereads the poem again chorally. The teacher may request variations on choral reading.
9. The teacher has children meet with partners again. The students identify three to five words from the text that they find interesting, fun to say, or challenging, and the words are written on a word

wall (chart) as well as entered into students' individual word journals or word banks. The teacher may also select words for study. Over time, the collection of words on the word wall and in the word journals or banks grows.

10. Student partners or small groups engage in word card activities for word practice, such as word games, word sorts, building sentences, arranging the word cards in alphabetical order, and so forth. This helps the students to build word recognition, automaticity, and understanding.

## THURSDAY

11. The class reads and rereads the text again chorally.
12. The teacher allows the children 5–10 minutes to prepare for poetry performances that will take place the following day. The children may present individually, in partners, or in small groups. The students enjoy having choice in how and with whom to present.

## THURSDAY OR FRIDAY

13. The teacher asks for volunteers to perform the text. Individuals, pairs, and groups of up to four perform the reading for the class. The teacher makes arrangements for students to perform the text for the school principal, secretary, other classes, and so on. The performing students are lavished with praise and applause! Performance day is a real celebration of the students' developing fluency and facility with reading.
14. Students take a copy of the text home and read it to their parents/ caregivers over the weekend. Parents are asked to listen to their child read as many times as they would like and to praise their child's efforts.

## EFFECTIVENESS OF THE FDL IN ACTION

A reading program is only so good to the extent that it improves students' reading performance. Does the FDL actually help students become more fluent readers? In a recent implementation of the FDL in the Kent State University Summer Reading Clinic, we assessed its effectiveness with 35 students at risk in reading who had just completed grades 1, 2, and 3 and were identified by their classroom teachers as significantly behind in their reading development.

The Kent State University Summer Reading Clinic provides reading intervention for struggling readers over a period of 5 weeks, and comprises 18 instructional sessions, each lasting 85 minutes. One intervention teacher (a graduate student at the university working on a master's degree in reading specialization) works with two or three students during this period. The FDL was implemented with students on a daily basis. It is considered the core instructional activity in the clinic. In addition to the FDL, students also engaged in sustained silent reading, choral reading and singing, word games, and camp-like activities that involved reading and writing.

For this study, we collected pre- and posttest data in order to determine student fluency gains. The 35 students were assessed in reading fluency using gains in reading rate (words correct per minute on grade-level reading materials), perhaps the most frequently administered assessment of fluency currently used (Rasinski, 2004). Results of students' gains in fluency are reported in Table 10.1. *t*-tests indicate that students made significant progress (*p* < .001) from pretest to posttest on fluency.

Students at all three grades demonstrated significant gains in reading fluency over the course of the reading clinic. In order to determine whether the students' gains in fluency were meeting or exceeding established norms for gains in fluency, we compared the students' fluency gains with the normal expected reading fluency gains by grade level based on fluency norms reported by Hasbrouck and Tindal (2006) and adapted by Read Naturally (2011), a popular fluency instruction program.

All students in the reading clinic began the program reading at fluency rates that were substantially below the end-of-year 50th percentile norms for their respective grade levels. Yet at every grade level students who received FDL instruction made 5-week gains in reading fluency that were substantially greater (50 to over 100%) than the normal expected gains suggested by Hasbrouck and Tindal (2006; Read Naturally, 2011). It should be noted that although the gains we report were achieved over 5 weeks of instruction, students only received instruction during 18 days

**TABLE 10.1. Mean Student Gain in Reading Fluency on Grade-Level Passages Using the FDL over 5 Weeks of Instruction**

| Student grade level | Pretest | Posttest | Mean gain in reading fluency (wcpm) over 5 weeks | Normal expected gain in reading fluency (wcpm) over 5 weeks[a] |
|---|---|---|---|---|
| 1 | 35 | 49 | + 14 | +9.5 |
| 2 | 61 | 73 | + 12 | +6.0 |
| 3 | 69 | 82 | + 13 | +5.5 |

*Note.* wcpm, words correct per minute.
[a]Hasbrouck and Tindal (2008).

of those 5 weeks, not the 25 days one would normally expect. Moreover, although fluency was measured in terms of reading rate, not once during the entire reading clinic were students asked or even encouraged to read fast or to practice reading to improve their reading rate. Nevertheless, students' demonstrated gains in fluency at all grade levels reported were remarkable. Although not a primary focus of the present study, our analyses also demonstrated that students manifested commensurate gains in reading comprehension.

## DISCUSSION

Using the FDL in classroom or clinical instruction has the potential to provide positive outcomes for student reading fluency (and ultimately in overall reading achievement). First, the FDL advances learning by providing students with increased time spent reading connected text. As Gambrell (1984) suggests, simply by increasing the amount of time spent reading connected text, substantial benefits for struggling readers can accrue.

Second, the FDL provides teachers with a simple, flexible, time-efficient, and effective instructional routine utilizing authentic texts for improving reading fluency using the proven methods of model fluent reading, assisted reading, repeated reading, and word study in a synergistic manner. Improvements in word recognition automaticity (as in this study) as well as in word recognition accuracy and comprehension (as in previous studies) have been found as a result of implementing the FDL on a regular and consistent basis.

Importantly, the feedback students receive from the teacher, classmates, and others for whom they perform is critical in assisting them to understand how improved reading skills benefit their learning and in developing students' confidence in their own reading. The positive and formative feedback from others helps motivate students to improve their reading. As students take in and consider the feedback that relevant others provide to them, they become better able to evaluate their own reading, and self-correction grows. As Kuhn et al. (2006) suggest, confidence and motivation are enhanced as students begin to see themselves in a new light—as assured and poised readers.

The use of authentic, connected, and meaningful texts is also an important component of the FDL. In the FDL, the iterative readings of authentic texts followed by eventual performance for an audience cultivates a focus not on increased speed but on reading for meaning and a meaningful oral interpretation of the passage. It is this authentic sense-making that is the ultimate goal of the FDL. In this way, students not only develop an ability to read with great automaticity, as measured by reading at a faster pace, but also are better able to comprehend what they read.

Significantly, our data suggest that students retain and transfer the learning they gain from the FDL to other new reading episodes. Furthermore, because best practice with the FDL suggests that texts should vary from day to day or week to week and that discussion and activities should focus on the meaning of the passage, student attention is directed to understanding what the words mean within the larger context of the text.

As a result of the focus on understanding that connected text is purposeful text, students are directed to think more broadly about the written word. Hence, students who are taught using the FDL shift their attention from "sounding words out" to asking themselves what the words signify or indicate for the progression of meaning in the text. As such, students approach the reading task with comprehension in mind and mentally refer back to meaning as the goal of their reading. In short, based on the results of the present and previous studies, the regular use of the FDL suggests student learning gains in the following academic and motivational areas:

- Increased word recognition automaticity as measured in words correct per minute.
- Increased word recognition accuracy as measured by percentage of words correct on grade-level and instructional-level materials.
- Increased comprehension as measured by retelling, summarization, and instructional discussion.
- Increased confidence in and motivation for reading as measured by observation of engagement and number of stories or books read.

## CONCLUSION

Clearly, we believe the FDL shows great promise for regular classroom and clinical intervention instruction as teachers work to engage struggling readers with authentic texts for reading. As we assured the concerned grandfather whose e-mail began this chapter, struggling readers can and do learn to read when exposed to authentic iterative text in ways that scaffold reading for them. As students become aware of their progress, they gain confidence that they, too, can become fluent readers. As teachers see their progress, they gain confidence that the instruction they are providing for students truly models that of data-driven best practice. The result is happier and more confident learners, more effective teachers, and more fully engaged and comprehensive reading classrooms where expressive and meaningful reading is shared and celebrated.

## REFERENCES

Bintz, W. P. (1993). Resistant readers in secondary education: Some insights and implications. *Journal of Reading, 36*, 604–615.

Clay, M. M. (2005). *Literacy lessons designed for individuals: Part 2 teaching procedures.* Portsmouth, NH: Heinemann.

Daane, M. C., Campbell, J. R., Grigg, W. S., Goodman, M. J., & Oranje, A. (2005). *Fourth-grade students reading aloud: NAEP 2002 special study of oral reading.* Washington, DC: U. S. Department of Education, Institute of Education Sciences.

Dudley, A. M. (2005). Rethinking reading fluency for struggling adolescent readers. Retrieved August 18, 2011, from *www.ccbd.net/documents/bb/spring2005pp16–22.pdf.*

Gambrell, L. B. (1984). How much time do children spend reading during teacher-directed reading instruction? In J. A. Niles & L. A. Harris (Eds.), *Changing perspectives on research in reading/language processing and instruction: Thirty-third yearbook of the National Reading Conference* (pp. 193–198). Rochester, NY: National Reading Conference.

Gregg, F. N. (2010). *Why do we stress silent reading fluency?* Retrieved September 2, 2010, from *kelareadingsystem. com/silent.aspx.*

Griffith, L. W., & Rasinski, T. V. (2004). A focus on fluency: How one teacher incorporated fluency with her reading curriculum. *The Reading Teacher, 58,* 126–137.

Hasbrouck, J., & Tindal, G. A. (2006). Oral reading fluency norms: A valuable assessment tool for reading teachers. *The Reading Teacher, 59*(7), 636–644.

Kuhn, M. R., Schwanenflugel, P. J., Morris, R. D., Morrow, L. M., Woo, D. G., Meisinger, E. B., et al. (2006). Teaching children to become fluent readers and automatic readers. *Journal of Literacy Research, 38,* 357–387.

Kuhn, M. R., & Stahl, S. A. (2003). Fluency: A review of developmental and remedial practices. *Journal of Educational Psychology, 95,* 3–21.

Lenters, K. (2006). Resistance, struggle, and the adolescent reader. *Journal of Adolescent & Adult Literacy, 50*(2), 136–146.

Martinez, M., Roser, N. L., & Strecker, S. (December 1998/January 1999). "I never thought I could be a star": A Readers Theatre ticket to fluency. *The Reading Teacher, 52,* 326–334.

National Reading Panel. (2000). *Teaching children to read: An evidence-based assessment of the scientific research literature on reading and its implications for reading instruction* (NIH Publication No. 00-4769). Washington, DC: National Institute of Child Health and Human Development.

Padak, N. D., & Rasinski, T. V. (2008). *Evidence-based instruction in reading: A professional development guide to fluency.* Boston: Pearson.

Paul, T. (1996). *Patterns of reading practice.* Madison, WI: Institute for Academic Excellence.

Pikulski, J. J. (2006). Fluency: A developmental and language perspective. In S. J. Samuels & A. E. Farstrup (Eds.), *What research has to say about fluency instruction* (pp. 70–93). Newark, DE: International Reading Association.

Pinnell, G. S., Pikulski, J. J., Wixson, K. K., Campbell, J. R., Gough, P. B., &

Beatty, A. S. (1995). *Listening to children read aloud*. Washington, DC: U.S. Department of Education, Office of Educational Research and Improvement.

Rasinski, T. V. (2004). *Assessing reading fluency*. Honolulu: Pacific Resources for Education and Learning. Retrieved September 2, 2010, from *www.prel.org/products/re_/assessing-fluency.htm*.

Rasinski, T. V. (2006). *Reading fluency for adolescents: Should we care?* Retrieved May 12, 2011, from *www.ohiorc. org/adlit/inperspective/issue/2006–09/Article/feature.aspx*.

Rasinski, T. V. (2010). *The fluent reader: Oral and silent reading strategies for building fluency, word recognition and comprehension* (2nd ed.). New York: Scholastic.

Rasinski, T. V., & Hoffman, J. V. (2003). Oral reading in the school literacy curriculum. *Reading Research Quarterly, 38*, 510–522.

Rasinski, T. V., Padak, N., Linek, W., & Sturtevant, E. (1994). The effects of fluency development instruction on urban second grade readers. *Journal of Educational Research, 87*, 158–164.

Read Naturally. (2011). *Hasbrouck-Tindal table of oral fluency norms*. Retrieved June 21, 2011, from *www.readnaturally.com/howto/orftable.htm*.

Samuels, S. J. (2002). Reading fluency: Its development and assessment. In A. E. Farstrup & S. J. Samuels (Eds.), *What research has to say about reading instruction* (3rd ed., pp. 166–183). Newark, DE: International Reading Association.

Stanovich, K. E. (1991). Word recognition: Changing perspectives. In R. Barr, M. L. Kamil, P. Mosenthal, & P. D. Pearson (Eds.), *Handbook of reading research* (Vol. II, pp. 418–452). New York: Longman.

Topping, K. J. (2006). Paired reading: Impact of a tutoring method on reading accuracy, comprehension, and fluency. In T. Rasinski, C. Blachowicz, & K. Lems (Eds.), *Fluency instruction: Research-based best practices* (pp. 173–191). New York: Guilford Press.

Young, C., & Rasinski, T. (2009, September). Implementing Readers Theatre as an approach to classroom fluency instruction. *The Reading Teacher, 64*(1), 4–13.

Zbornik, J. (2001). *Reading anxiety manifests itself emotionally, intellectually*. Lakewood, OH: LRP Publications.

Zimmerman, B. S., & Rasinski, T. V. (2011). *Fluency development processes: Implications for practice*. Manuscript submitted for publication.

# 11

## Paired Reading

*Impact of a Tutoring Method on Reading
Accuracy, Comprehension, and Fluency*

Keith J. Topping

### WHAT IS FLUENCY?

Fluency is not an entity, "benchmarkable" competence, or static condition. Fluency is an adaptive, context-dependent process. Even expert readers will show dysfluency when confronted with a text on an unfamiliar topic that provides challenge greatly beyond their independent reading level, however high that level might be. Fluency is of little value in itself—its value lies in what it enables: the allocation of the reader's attention to comprehension.

For silent reading, I define fluency as "the extraction of maximum meaning at maximum speed in a relatively continuous flow, leaving spare simultaneous processing capacity for other higher order processes." This definition assumes the text is at an appropriate level of difficulty for the reader.

For reading out loud, the task (and therefore the definition) is more demanding, since among the higher order processes the reader must have an awareness of audience needs and the capability to manage the prosodic demands for expressiveness (e.g., varying phrasing, stress, intonation, pitch, rhythm, loudness, pauses).

Already two definitions of fluency have been implied, and it becomes more complex. Simple assumptions can prove misleading. For example, just reading faster might result in reduced accuracy. Fast reading, even if still accurately decoded, might not automatically result in good comprehension. A number of factors interact with each other in the area of fluency. An attempt is made to map these factors in the model of fluency presented next. All of this has implications for how we might effectively intervene to enhance fluency and how we might usefully measure it.

This chapter thus asserts a fluid definition of fluency conceptualized within an information-processing or "resource-allocation" model, while mapping the many varieties of fluency and the consequently varied implications for intervention and measurement. Socioemotional factors are given equal prominence with cognitive aspects.

## THE DEEP PROCESSING FLUENCY MODEL

The deep processing fluency (DPF) model presented here (Figure 11.1) groups relevant factors into four sectors, arranged sequentially:

- Predisposing factors
- Surface fluency factors
- Strategic fluency factors
- Deep fluency factors

This suggests further definitional complexity—three different kinds of fluency! These progress toward fluency as both input and output in the "deep processing" of reading. Additionally, even the apparent linearity of the model is beguiling, since there are feedback loops, including from "end" to "beginning." Actually, the model is recursive. However, its components are explored in a stepwise manner.

Predisposing factors facilitating the development of fluency ("entry skills" if you prefer) include:

- *Management of text difficulty.* (Fluency is not likely to be developed on material that is much too hard or easy. Have teachers leveled books and taught students readability self-checking strategies?)
- *Time exposed; time on task; time engaged.* (Simply allocating silent reading time is not enough. Have teachers ensured that time is allocated for reading to ensure exposure to text *and* that that time is spent on task, *and* that that time is spent actually engaged with the task?)
- *Vocabulary (listening or reading).* (Have teachers, parents, and peers engaged students in increasingly complex dialogue and had them listen to stories to develop their receptive vocabulary and facilitate decoding when these words are encountered in print?)

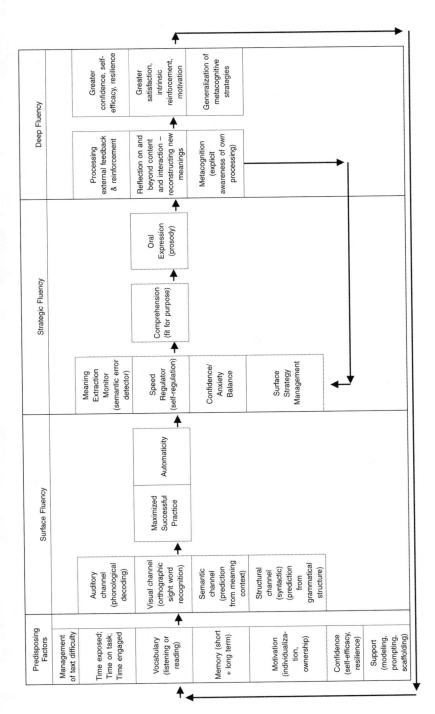

**FIGURE 11.1.** The Deep Processing Fluency (DPF) model.

- *Memory (short and long term).* (Both visual and verbal short- and long-term memory are needed. Teachers can help develop memory, but should avoid abstract games that might have no effects generalized to reading.)
- *Motivation (individualization, ownership).* (Have teachers considered individual student reading preferences, offered balanced access to fiction and nonfiction to tap existing motivation, respected multiple and gendered literacies and home cultures, and sought to bridge discontinuity among home, community, and school interests and competences rather than promote only "schooled" literacy experiences?)
- *Confidence (self-efficacy, resilience).* (Have teachers created a classroom ethos free of fear of failure, shame at error, and obsession with "the right answer," where strategic risk taking is seen as normal? But beware abstract self-esteem-building exercises that might not generalize to reading. And remember that too much confidence is almost as unhelpful as too little—students benefit from high but realistic expectations.)
- *Support (modeling, prompting, scaffolding).* (Have teachers made available a variety of supports for students attacking texts above their current independent readability level—involving assistants, volunteers, or peers in modeling fluent reading, prompting while reading, and other forms of scaffolding, such as audiotapes?)

Even if a highly energetic teacher were able to provide all these, different students will always have different profiles of strengths and weaknesses across these factors. With luck and good management, they will make the best of what they have available as they seek to develop fluency.

In developing "surface fluency," different students will also have different profiles of strengths and weaknesses in the four major channels for extracting meaning:

- Auditory channel (phonological decoding).
- Visual channel (orthographic sight word recognition).
- Semantic channel (prediction from meaning context).
- Structural (syntactic) channel (prediction from grammatical structure).

Stanovich (1984) described this as an "interactive–compensatory" model. Of course, some written languages and some specific texts or parts of texts are intrinsically more accessible through particular channels (e.g., Finnish through the auditory channel, Mandarin through the visual channel). Unfortunately, for our students, English is a complex mongrel language, requiring some capability in all channels.

Nonetheless, given reasonable availability of predisposing factors and reasonable competence in most if not all of the channels, students who have substantial practice reading will, over time, develop automaticity in extracting meaning. It will become less effortful, require less concentration, use up fewer mental resources—until, of course, the difficulty of the book increases and the student has to start trying hard all over again. Some students prefer to avoid this never-ending struggle for self-improvement, and might at the age of 7 decide that they can read ("fluently") and coast along reading at that level for the rest of their lives. In fact, it is not "practice that makes perfect" but rather *successful* practice *at an appropriate level of difficulty* that yields wider automaticity. Consequently, teachers need to monitor not only volume of student practice in and out of school, but also its quality, its challenge level in relation to student proficiency, and the successfulness of that practice in leading to high-quality comprehension.

Some revealing comments from students about their real reading strategies during sustained silent reading were recorded by Griffith and Rasinski (2004, p. 134):

> "I only read the third paragraph of each page. My teacher was always at her desk grading papers, so it didn't really matter."
>
> "I started at the top, skipped a hunk, and then read the bottom."
>
> "I lifted up the book in front of my face and looked for the 'fancy' words."
>
> "I looked at the pictures and then told the story by the pictures."
>
> "I wanted to read as fast as my friend, so I watched her as she read. I only read the bottom line of each page and turned the page when she did. But she made 100% on her Accelerated Reader quiz and I only made 20%."

Notwithstanding these difficulties and evasions, many students do achieve a reasonable degree of surface fluency, albeit in some cases almost accidentally. That is, given a book at their independent readability level, they can read it reasonably accurately, at a reasonable speed, and with reasonable continuity (this can be construed as a definition of surface fluency). Some, unfortunately, see this as the end of the road. In fact, this automaticity gives them spare processing capacity, which can be deployed to move on to the next stage of fluency development—strategic fluency.

However, moving on requires more focused strategy on the part of the readers. Some try to apply their strongest surface fluency channel to all words, on a "one size fits all" basis. Given the nature of the English language, this is only likely to be effective and efficient a quarter of the time. Some readers apply their strongest surface fluency channel to all words first, then quickly revert to their second strongest if that proves ineffective, and so on. Some apply any channel that comes to mind, hoping for the best from random chance. However, the most capable readers tend to analyze the nature of the problem word and choose a channel they judge most likely to maximize success for that word. Such surface strategy management does not necessarily operate at an explicit level; it might have developed inductively or intuitively and been automatized without ever having been made explicit, much as how to ride a bicycle is rarely made explicit. It is typically done at considerable speed.

Furthermore, moving on also requires awareness that greater speed might result in reduced accuracy and greater accuracy might result in reduced speed. It requires a balancing act between a notional meaning extraction monitor (semantic error detector) and a speed regulator in the child's brain, the balance suited to the purpose of the reading task in hand. The spare processing capacity available has to be able to handle two competing processes at the same time—and to do so at some speed. (Perhaps boys tend to be weaker readers because they can't multitask?) The well-known U-shaped relationship between anxiety and performance is also relevant here. If the student regards the book as easy, anxiety will be low and confidence high, and the speed regulator will be dominant: The student will read fast but possibly not accurately, even though the book is easy. If the student regards the book as hard, anxiety will be high and confidence low, the meaning monitor will be dominant: The student will read accurately but very slowly. Of course, if speed becomes very slow, the interaction with memory becomes important. By the time the last word in the sentence has been decoded, the student has forgotten the beginning, let alone why on earth he or she wanted to read it in the first place.

If the student manages this balancing act with reasonable success, good comprehension will result. Remember (from Figure 11.1) that there are no guarantees that *surface* fluency will lead to good comprehension—only that it will lead to rapid and accurate decoding, which might be little more than "barking at print." In strategic fluency, however, good comprehension is almost inevitable. Of course, there are interesting questions about what exactly "good comprehension" is. Does it mean extracting every last drop of meaning the author put in there? Was the author aware of all the meaning that might be in there? And can any text mean exactly the same to all readers? How "good" comprehension has to be might vary according to the purposes and intentions of the reader, which might change as he or she is reading the text.

Leaving such complexities aside for the moment, we now behold a generally strategically fluent silent reader who is a "good comprehender." The final step within strategic fluency requires even more spare processing capacity—moving to fluent oral reading with expression (prosody). As noted, this requires all of the foregoing and, in addition, the reader must have an awareness of audience needs and the capability to manage the prosodic demands for expressiveness in response to audience needs and text complexities (e.g., varying phrasing, stress, intonation, pitch, rhythm, loud-ness, speed, pauses).

Having mastered all of this to a greater or lesser extent, our strategic readers have good reason to feel pleased, but the next stage of deep fluency beckons, and this requires even more spare processing capacity—the ulti-mate goal in the DPF model. At this stage, readers not only have excellent comprehension of text content, but have spare capacity to go beyond it in personal reflection on content, reconstructing new meanings. They are also able to process and reflect upon external feedback and reinforcement, such as audience responses to a read-aloud. Perhaps most importantly, they have spare capacity to begin to develop metacognition (explicit awareness of the nature of their own processing, most and least effective strategies in spe-cific contexts, and their relative strengths and weakness). This has connec-tions to the Reutzel concept of "metafluency" (see Chapter 7, this volume). Such explicit awareness is a prerequisite for more effective self-regulation of deeply fluent reading, and the deep processing model (Figure 11.1) shows a feedback loop back into surface strategy management.

From these developments stem powerful socioemotional effects, not the least of them greater confidence, self-efficacy, and resilience as a reader (and perhaps as a learner in general). The reader feels greater satisfaction as well as the intrinsic reinforcement and motivation that are associated with learner autonomy. Additionally, the metacognitive awareness gained in the area of reading might generalize spontaneously or deliberately to other sub-jects or other aspects of the student's life.

Given that this definition of fluency is complex, there are many dif-ficulties with measuring fluency in a reliable and valid way. This is all very well, the practitioner might think, but what am I supposed to *do* about it? Let us move to a relatively simple intervention to promote fluency.

## PAIRED READING (DUOLOG READING)

A method specifically designed for peer-assisted learning (also widely used by parents, classroom assistants, and volunteer tutors) is "paired reading" (PR). It features many of the desirable components in the model of fluency (Figure 11.1). Unfortunately, over the years this name for this structured and well-evaluated method has sometimes been applied by other workers to vaguely similar or quite dissimilar practices that have not been evaluated. Consequently, the structured and evaluated method was renamed "duolog reading" in an attempt to establish a greater distinction (this name was chosen by 100 teachers in Texas). In this chapter, however, I continue to refer to it by its original name.

The PR method for peer or parent tutoring is a form of supported oral reading that enables students to access and comprehend texts somewhat above their independent readability level, within a framework of predictable and nonintrusive error correction. This structured support used with high-motivation texts offers dysfluent readers a flow experience, which is likely to impact their reading style and socioemotional aspects of the reading process.

## What Is PR?

PR is a straightforward and generally enjoyable way for more able readers to help less able readers develop better reading skills (i.e., a form of cross-ability tutoring). The method is adaptable to any reading material, and tutees select texts that are of intrinsic interest to them but a little above their independent readability level (otherwise the support of PR is pointless). This might include newspapers, magazines, community literature, or texts in electronic environments. Of course, the texts must be within the independent readability level of the tutor, but a relatively modest differential in reading ability is recommended if the hope is to improve the reading of the tutor as well as the tutee. The pair might use the "five-finger test" of readability:

1. Open a page at random.
2. Spread 5 fingers on one hand.
3. Place fingertips on the page at random.
4. Child attempts to read the five words.
5. Repeat on another four pages.

If the tutee has struggled on several words but not more than five, the book is about right in terms of difficulty. If the tutor has struggled on more than one or two (peculiar) words, the book is too hard for the tutor. This is not perfectly scientific, it but gives the pair a ritual to remind them to think about readability. Additionally, if the tutee has a fanatical interest in one topic that is not shared by the tutor, negotiation is needed.

Encouragement to read "little but often" is usual. Pairs commit themselves to read at least three times per week for at least 10 minutes per session for at least 6 weeks. This minimum frequency is needed in order to develop automaticity with the technique and give it a fair test. At the end of 6 weeks, pairs consider whether they wish to continue with greater or lesser frequency or even at all or perhaps to vary partners or some aspect of the method.

The technique has two main aspects. Initially, tutor and tutee read out loud simultaneously in close synchrony. This is termed "reading together."

The tutor adjusts his or her reading speed to the tutee's pace. The tutee must read all the words out loud correctly. Errors are corrected merely by the tutor again giving a perfect example of how to read the error word and ensuring that the tutee repeats it correctly, and then the pair continues reading.

The second aspect is "reading alone" or independent reading. When the tutee feels confident enough to read a section of text unsupported, he or she signals—by a knock, nudge, or other nonverbal sign—for the tutor to be silent. The tutor praises the tutee for taking this initiative and subsequently praises the tutee very regularly, especially for mastering very difficult words or spontaneously self-correcting.

Any word not read correctly within a pause of 4 seconds is treated as an error; the tutee is not left to struggle. When the tutee makes an error when reading alone, the tutor corrects this as before (by modeling and ensuring perfect repetition) and then joins back in reading simultaneously. (However, tutors often have difficulty learning to give the tutee this time to self-correct, without which they will never learn to self-correct.) Throughout there is a great deal of emphasis on praising the tutee for correct reading and pausing from time to time to discuss the meaning of the text. Figure 11.2 illustrates the flow of the aspects of the technique of "paired reading" (PR).

Initially, much reading is usually done simultaneously, but as the tutee improves and makes more appropriate choices of reading materials, more and more independent reading occurs (until the tutee becomes more ambitious and chooses harder books, of course). Any tendency to rush on the part of the pupil is usually resolved by consistent use of the correction procedure (although sometimes a shorter pause is needed initially) and/or visually "pacing" the reading, with the reader pointing to each word as it is to be pronounced (usually only on harder texts with smaller print and closer spacing).

Young readers sometimes assume that they are expected to read more and more alone as they get better at reading. In fact, this is only true if they stick to books of the same difficulty. It is much more advantageous if, as they improve, they tackle harder and harder books and, therefore, still need a good deal of support from reading together. Some readers regard silent reading as the "grown-up" way of reading and might be resistant to reading together, especially if the point of it is not made clear to them and they do not use it to attack texts beyond their independent readability level.

PR can do a lot of good, but equally important is that it seems to do little harm and to be widely ideologically acceptable. PR works in parallel with a school reading curriculum based on look-and-say, phonics, language experience, pictograms, precision teaching, direct instruction,

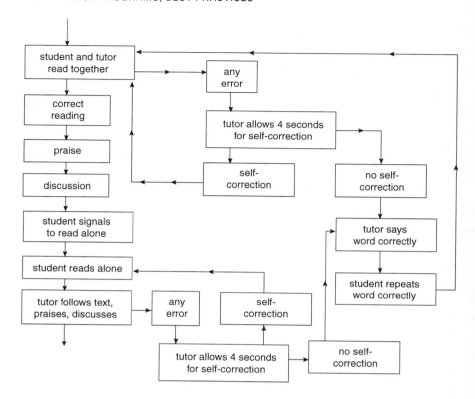

**FIGURE 11.2.** Paired reading.

or any other kind of approach. Those who wish to read more about the theoretical underpinnings of PR and its connections with the wider literature on how children learn to read should consult Topping and Lindsay (1992c).

It will now be clear that "paired reading" is a specific name for a specific technique. It is *not* any old thing that two people feel like doing together with a book. Unfortunately, the name has become too widely misused. You will often meet people who say "Oh yes, we do that paired reading." When you actually *look* at what they are doing, you often find that it is nothing like the specific method we have just described.

Further details of the method can be found in the sources listed at the end of this chapter in the Resources section, including specimen leaflets for peer and parent tutors, checklists for monitoring implementation integrity, and so on. Topping (2001) gives detailed organizational advice for planning and operating a good-quality implementation.

## What Are the Advantages of PR?

1. Children are encouraged to pursue their own interests in reading material. They have more enthusiasm from reading about their own favorite things, and so try harder. PR gives them as much support as they need to read whatever book they choose.

2. Children are more in control of what's going on: Instead of having reading crammed into them, students make decisions themselves in the light of their own purposes (e.g., about choice of books, going onto reading alone, going on longer in the session).

3. There is no failure: It is impossible not to get a word right within 4 seconds.

4. PR is very flexible: The child determines how much support is necessary, which can vary, depending on myriad factors such as current level of interest, mood, degree of tiredness, confidence, difficulty of the books and so on.

5. The child gets lots of praise: It's much nicer to be told when you're doing well instead of just being moaned at when you go wrong.

6. There's lots of emphasis of understanding—getting the meaning out of the words—and that's what reading is all about. It's no use being able to read the words out loud mechanically without following the meaning.

7. PR gives continuity: It eliminates stopping and starting to "break up" hard words, which often causes children to forget the beginning of the sentence by the time they get to the end. With PR it is easier for children to make sensible guesses at new words based on the meaning of the surrounding words.

8. During reading together, a child can learn by example to read with expression and the right pacing (e.g., by copying how the tutor pauses at punctuation or gives emphasis to certain words).

9. Children are given a perfect example of how to pronounce difficult words, instead of being left to work it out themselves and then perhaps thinking their own half-right efforts are actually 100% correct.

10. When doing PR, children get a bit of their own peaceful, private attention from their helper, which they might not otherwise have had. There is some evidence that just giving children more attention can actually improve their reading.

11. PR increases the amount of sheer reading practice children get. Because children are supported through books, they get through them faster. The number of books read in a week increases, the number of words

children look at in a week increases, and more words stick in their memory.

12. PR gives tutors a clear, straightforward, and enjoyable way of helping tutee, so no one gets confused, worried, or bad-tempered about reading.

In short, PR addresses many components of the process model of fluency (Figure 11.1). Additionally, an extended version of the technique (paired reading and thinking) provides a specific methodology to bridge students into strategic fluency and deep fluency (see Resources section).

## Does PR Work?

PR is a well-evaluated method, the focus of a great many studies over the years. The U.K. government included it their review of the effectiveness of literacy interventions (Brooks, 2007) and recommended it as part of the national literacy strategy. Importantly, it has been shown to work both in carefully controlled research studies and in naturalistic large-scale field trials. It has been used as an intervention for students with reading delay and also as a broad-spectrum mainstream method deployed inclusively for all students. Gains in reading comprehension as well as reading accuracy are very commonly reported. The PR research literature has been reviewed by Topping and Lindsay (1992a) and Topping (1995, 2001).

Studies reported in the literature include 19 control or comparison group studies. Control group studies are generally considered by researchers to yield better quality data capable of supporting firmer conclusions. Overall, the mean accuracy gain was 2.5 times larger for the experimental group than for the control group. For comprehension, experimental gain was 2.1 times larger than control gain. Where effect sizes were calculable for parent-tutored projects, the mean accuracy effect size was 1.6 for accuracy and 1.4 for comprehension. For peer-tutored projects, the overall effect size for reading accuracy was 2.2 and for reading comprehension 1.6 (but with great variability), including results from peer tutors and tutees. These effect sizes are large when compared with those cited in other meta-analytic reports. Fifteen studies compared PR with some other intervention technique. Overall, PR gains averaged 1.5 times the alternative intervention gains.

Topping (1995) reported large-scale field study data from one school district, with a substantial majority of schools voluntarily participating (i.e., no selection of "cooperative" or "enthusiastic" schools). In 37 comparison or control group projects (580 students participant, and 446 comparison control children), scores in both accuracy and comprehension for participant children were statistically significantly greater than for controls. The overall effect size for reading accuracy was 0.9 and for comprehension 0.8, less than that reported on average in the literature (as might have been expected) but nevertheless substantial (although reduced by high control group variance). Twenty-three projects featured baseline measures (total $n = 374$), using each student as his or her own control over time. Overall, gains in the intervention phase in reading accuracy were twice as large as gains in the baseline period. Follow-up data were gathered in 17 projects over short periods (typically 4 months) and longer periods (typically 12 months). PR students continued to show accelerated rates of gain over the follow-up period, although not as sharply as during the intensive phase of the intervention (some of these students would have continued with PR, some not). There was no evidence of "washout" of experimental gains over time. It is considered unrealistic to expect acceleration at well above normal rates to continue indefinitely. Gains in reading accuracy were similar for parent-tutored, same-age peer-tutored, and cross-age peer-tutored participants. Pre–post gains of peer tutors were greater than for peer tutees in reading accuracy, but the difference was not statistically significant. There was a tendency for participants of lower socioeconomic status to make larger gains in reading accuracy.

Data from 10 peer tutor projects were reported in Topping (1987), the follow-up data in Topping (1992b), the socioeconomic data in Topping and Lindsay (1992b), data on the effectiveness of PR in ethnic minority homes in Topping (1992a), subjective feedback from a great many participants in Topping and Whiteley (1990), and the effect of gender differences in peer PR in Topping and Whiteley (1993). Research on the use of PR with adults of limited literacy was reported in Scoble, Topping, and Wigglesworth (1988).

A large-scale randomized controlled trial (RCT) of PR peer tutoring in 80 Scotland schools with 9- to 12-year-olds was reported by Topping, Thurston, McGavock, and Conlin (2012). On long-term evaluation, cross-age PR was significantly better than regular teaching, but same-age PR was not. However, on short-term evaluation, PR tutors and tutees did significantly better than control students in both years, and cross-age PR and same-age PR were similarly effective. Low socioeconomic students, students with lower reading ability, girls, and students who tutored or were tutored in both reading and math did significantly better. Technical aspects of correction were good and tutor miscorrection was very low. Interest in the book and book discussion were also frequent. However, other important behaviors in the process of PR were rarely seen. Thus, implementation was somewhat variable.

PR studies have emanated from a number of other countries, including Brazil (Cupolillo, Silva, Socorro, & Topping, 1997; Murad & Topping,

2000). Research in the United Kingdom has developed into paired reading and thinking (PRT). McKinstery and Topping (2003) found PRT very effective in high school settings, and Topping and Bryce (2004) found that PRT added value in thinking skills for tutees in elementary school when compared with standard PR.

## What about PR and Fluency?

Given the difficulties of finding a measure of fluency that is more than superficial (mentioned previously), directly researching the impact of PR on fluency in a way in keeping with the model of fluency (Figure 11.1) is a tough assignment. However, there have been some studies (often small scale) that have explored the impact of PR on fluency, reading style, self-correction rates, and reader confidence with both elementary and high school students. The main findings are summarized here, but more details of these studies are found in Topping (1995).

Considering both parent tutor and peer tutor research, eight studies in the literature found reduced error rates in paired readers and no cases of error rate increase. In seven studies, paired readers showed decreases in rate of refusal to attempt to read a word, and two studies found an increase. Seven studies found an increase in use of context, one found no difference, and no studies found a decrease. Regarding the rate or speed of reading, four studies showed an increase and none demonstrated a decrease. Four studies showed an increase in self-correction rate and none had a decrease. In three studies, the use of phonics increased, and in no case was there a decrease. Although not all these differences reached statistical significance (unsurprising in small-scale studies) and only a few studies used either non-participant control or alternative-treatment comparison groups, strong, consistent trends emerge from all these studies considered together.

In the RCT study (Topping et al., 2011), class gain in reading test score was plotted against the mean number of mistakes per minute. Results demonstrated an optimum rate for mistakes—about one mistake every two minutes. When book discussion was plotted against reading test score gain, there were greater gains when the pair stopped reading to talk about the book once every 5 to 7 minutes (not more frequently, although less made little difference).

If children "learn to read by reading," one factor in the effectiveness of PR (or any supplemental tutoring intervention) might be the influence of extra reading practice alone. Thus, other things being equal, more time spent doing PR should be associated with greater gains in reading skill. Some workers have explored this relationship. However, only small correlation coefficients between reading accuracy/comprehension and time spent reading during a PR project have been found, so PR does not work merely by increasing time spent on reading. In the RCT study, significant pre–post gains in self-esteem (improved beliefs about personal reading competence) were seen in both same-age and cross-age pairings, for tutees and tutors, but not for controls. In addition, the scores of cross-age tutors showed further gains in self-worth, indicating that working with younger tutees provided extra benefits (Topping et al., 2011). Whether improved self-esteem has a causative role or is a result of improved reading skill is still open to question.

The general pattern is of PR resulting in greater fluency, fewer refusals (greater confidence), greater use of context, and a greater likelihood of self-correction as well as fewer errors (greater accuracy) and better phonic skills. One mistake every 2 minutes and book discussion every 5 to 7 minutes seem optimal. There is some evidence that PR might work by developing self-esteem rather than through more mechanical means. There are implications here for all stages of the DPF model (Figure 11.1).

## SUMMARY AND CONCLUSION

Fluency is an adaptive, context-dependent process. With a text of an appropriate level of difficulty for the reader, it involves the extraction of maximum meaning at maximum speed in a relatively continuous flow, leaving spare simultaneous processing capacity for other higher order processes. An information-processing or resource allocation model of fluency is proposed, which groups relevant factors into four sectors: predisposing factors, surface fluency, strategic fluency, and deep fluency.

The specific structured method for peer, parent, or volunteer tutoring known as paired reading or duolog reading was described and its advantages outlined. PR is a well-evaluated method, has been the focus of a great many studies over the years, and is included in governmental evidence-based recommendations. Research has included many positive control and follow-up studies. Effect sizes from studies in the literature are very large, and those from unselected schools in districtwide field trials still substantial. Pre–post reading gains were evident for both peer tutees and peer tutors. Weaker readers and those of lower socioeconomic status tended to gain more.

PR does not work just by increasing time engaged with reading, and its role in the development of self-esteem seems to be important. PR has been found to result in greater fluency, fewer refusals (greater confidence), greater use of context, and a greater likelihood of self-correction as well as fewer errors (greater accuracy) and better phonic skills. There are implications here for all stages of the fluency model. PR has also now been broadened into PRT, extending higher order reading skills (Topping, 2001).

# REFERENCES

Brooks, G. (2007). *What works for children with literacy difficulties? The effectiveness of intervention schemes* (3rd ed.). London: Department for Education and Skills. Retrieved February 1, 2011, from *www.education.gov.uk/publications//standard/publicationDetail/Page1/RR380*.

Cupolillo, M., Silva, R. S., Socorro, S., & Topping, K. J. (1997). Paired reading with Brazilian first-year school failures. *Educational Psychology in Practice, 13*(2), 96–100.

Griffith, L. W., & Rasinski, T. V. (2004). A focus on fluency: How one teacher incorporated fluency with her reading curriculum. *The Reading Teacher, 58*(2), 126–137.

McKinstery, J., & Topping, K. J. (2003). Cross-age peer tutoring of thinking skills in the high school. *Educational Psychology in Practice, 19*, 199–217.

Murad, C. R., & Topping, K. J. (2000). Parents as reading tutors for first graders in Brazil. *School Psychology International, 21*(2), 152–171.

Scoble, J., Topping, K. J., & Wigglesworth, C. (1988). Training family and friends as adult literacy tutors. *Journal of Reading, 31*, 410–417.

Stanovich, K. E. (1984). The interactive-compensatory model of reading: A confluence of developmental, experimental, and education psychology. *Remedial and Special Education, 5*(3), 11–19.

Topping, K. J. (1987). Peer tutored paired reading: Outcome data from ten projects. *Educational Psychology, 7*, 133–145.

Topping, K. J. (1992a). The effectiveness of paired reading in ethnic minority homes. *Multicultural Teaching, 10*(2), 19–23.

Topping, K. J. (1992b). Short- and long-term follow-up of parental involvement in reading projects. *British Educational Research Journal, 18*, 369–379.

Topping, K. J. (1995). *Paired reading, spelling and writing: The handbook for teachers and parents.* London: Cassell.

Topping, K. J. (2001). *Thinking reading writing: A practical guide to paired learning with peers, parents and volunteers.* New York: Continuum International.

Topping, K. J., & Bryce, A. (2004). Cross-age peer tutoring of reading and thinking: Influence on thinking skills. *Educational Psychology, 24*, 595–621.

Topping, K. J., & Lindsay, G. A. (1992a). Paired reading: A review of the literature. *Research Papers in Education, 7*, 199–246.

Topping, K. J., & Lindsay, G. A. (1992b). Parental involvement in reading: The influence of socio-economic status and supportive home visiting. *Children and Society, 5*, 306–316.

Topping, K. J., & Lindsay, G. A. (1992c). The structure and development of the paired reading technique. *Journal of Research in Reading, 15*, 120–136.

Topping, K. J., Miller, D., Thurston, A., McGavock, K., & Conlin, N. (2011). Peer tutoring in reading in Scotland: Thinking big. *Literacy, 45*(1), 3–9.

Topping, K. J., Thurston, A., McGavock, K., & Conlin, N. (2012). Outcomes and process in reading tutoring. *Educational Research.*

Topping, K. J., & Whiteley, M. (1990). Participant evaluation of parent-tutored and peer-tutored projects in reading. *Educational Research, 32*(1), 14–32.

Topping, K. J., & Whiteley, M. (1993). Sex differences in the effectiveness of peer tutoring. *School Psychology International, 14*(1), 57–67.

## RESOURCES

U.K. Department of Education "What Works?" series: Brooks, G. (2007). *What works for children with literacy difficulties? The effectiveness of intervention schemes* (3rd ed.). London: Department for Education and Skills. Retrieved February 1, 2011, from *www.education.gov.uk/publications/eOrderingDownload/pri_lit_what_works0068807.pdf*.

The Thinking, Reading, Writing website (*www.dundee.ac.uk/eswce/research/projects/trw* and *www.dundee.ac.uk/eswce/research/projects/trwresources*) has many free resources for PR and other methods associated with the book *Thinking Reading Writing: A Practical Guide to Paired Learning with Peers, Parents And Volunteers* (Topping, 2001). The web resources include the Topping (1995) review of outcome research on PR.

The Read On project website (*www.dundee.ac.uk/eswce/research/projects/readon*) includes many free practical resources, an online teacher's manual, data on evaluation, and links to online text for Paired Reading and Thinking (*www.dundee.ac.uk/eswce/research/projects/readon/onlinetext*) and video (below).

A video on peer tutoring in paired reading and paired thinking (Topping & Hogan, 1999) is also available (*www.dundee.ac.uk/eswce/research/projects/readon/resourcesforteachers*). The International Reading Association distributes a PR video pack made by the North Alberta Reading Specialist Council in consultation with the author (*www.reading.org*), which includes work with adults with reading difficulty. Renaissance Learning distributes a video pack in the United States that focuses on peer tutoring in schools (*www.renlearn.com*), but look for the "new" name "duolog reading."

Topping, K. J. (2001). *Tutoring by peers, family and volunteers*. Geneva: International Bureau of Education, United Nations Educational, Scientific and Cultural Organisation. (Also in translation in Chinese, Spanish, Catalan, Polish, and Portuguese). Available at *www.ibe.unesco.org/International/Publications/EducationalPractices/prachome.htm*.

Topping, K. J. (1989). Lectura conjunta: Una poderosa técnica al servicio de los padres. *Comunicación, Lenguaje y Educaci?n, 3–4*, 143–151. Spanish translation of Topping, K. J. [1987]. Paired reading: A powerful technique for parent use. *The Reading Teacher, 40*, 608–614.

Topping, K. J. (2001). *Peer assisted learning: A practical guide for teachers*. Cambridge, MA: Brookline Books. Available at *www.dundee.ac.uk/eswce/people/kjtopping/publications/plearning.htm*.

# 12

## "Everybody Reads"

*Fluency as a Focus for Staff Development*

Camille L. Z. Blachowicz
Mary Kay Moskal
Jennifer R. Massarelli
Connie M. Obrochta
Ellen Fogelberg
Peter Fisher

**E**vanston/Skokie School District 65 is a leafy, lakefront suburb north of Chicago, with a richly diverse population reflected both in the teachers and students in its schools. Education is critical to this university town, and the gap between high- and low-achieving students receives a lot of attention. Looking at the district benchmark assessments, it appeared that fluency of reading was one factor that differentiated achieving students from those who were lagging behind. Taking counteraction, the district reading coordinator sought support from the Reading Center at National Louis University where fluency instruction was a regular emphasis in its reading improvement programs and in the training of reading specialists. Together, the district and the college embarked on a collaborative investigation to see whether instruction for fluency could improve student performance. Along the way, the process of developing this program resulted in a staff development program and volunteer program that is continuing beyond the scope of the initial project.

The project, called Everybody Reads, was funded by the Illinois State Board of Education. It had three goals:

1. To develop classroom-tested models for building reading fluency in grades K–3.
2. To design a tutoring model for fluency to be delivered by volunteer tutors.
3. To increase the impact of the process by not only training teachers and tutors but also developing a cadre of teacher leaders who could direct the project after the grant period ended.

In this chapter, we describe the ways in which fluency instruction had a threefold outcome for the district: It improved the fluency of the elementary students in the project, provided an excellent focus for the development of an effective volunteer tutoring program, and provided a point of departure for teacher staff development that led teacher inquiry far beyond this single instructional issue.

## WHY WAS *FLUENCY* THE TARGET FOR STUDENTS?

The ability to read fluently (at a good rate, with good accuracy and proper intonation and phrasing) is highly correlated with many measures of reading competence (Kuhn, Schwanenflugel, & Meisinger, 2010; Miller & Schwanenflugel, 2008). For the reader, fluency requires good decoding skills, the strategies to orchestrate these in reading real text, and comprehension to monitor what is being read to make sure it sounds like language.

For the teacher, listening to students read and charting their development in fluency is also a way to measure the effect of instruction and to provide input for further instructional planning. Unlike most standardized measures, which only show large changes in behavior, fluency measurement is sensitive to small increments of improvement (Shinn, 1989). Unlike standardized measures, the practice involved in the reading of a fluency measurement passage can also help students' reading. Not only is fluency a good *measure* of reading performance, but working toward fluency is also a good *treatment* for reading difficulties. Having students do a lot of reading at an appropriate level, with a teacher, tutor, or peer supporting them and helping them self-monitor, is a good way for students to practice their way to competence (Moskal & Blachowicz, 2006; Rasinski, 2010, 2011).

## WHY IS FLUENCY A GOOD FOCUS FOR STAFF DEVELOPMENT?

With respect to staff development, fluency work also embeds several issues that are critical to classroom instruction and deal with the real empirical questions of teachers. Teachers who are concerned with their students' fluency need to ask and answer several questions that have ramifications far beyond the realm of fluency instruction:

"How do I know what my class can handle?"
"What materials do I need so that everybody can read?"
"How do I build activities into the day so that every student reads every day at an appropriate level?"
"How do I measure and show growth?"

These rich questions grow out of investigations of fluency but have much further-reaching effects on classroom instruction.

## WHAT WAS THE WORKING MODEL FOR THE STAFF DEVELOPMENT COMPONENT?

Two primary teachers from each of Evanston's 12 public schools and one from a participating private school worked for 2 years, after school and during the summer, to design the project, which was supported administratively by the district Director of Reading. University faculty led monthly meetings and worked with three master teacher–facilitators. More than 300 students were involved in the project, with four targeted students from each classroom also receiving extra individual help.

Teachers came together to ask questions about fluency and to receive resources, articles and books, videos, and ideas from the facilitators. After each meeting, teachers tried strategies, read articles, and then brought back new ideas to the group. Each teacher who volunteered received either a stipend or district credit for pay scale advancement. Participants needed to commit to trying out strategies and reporting back to the group and their principals. They decided on the goal of developing a set of classroom activities that would not add another layer of curriculum to the day but rather would "put a fluency spin" on all the instruction typically done (Rasinski, 2010, 2011). This fluency spin would increase the incidence of the following instructional activities:

- More modeling of fluent reading.
- More support during reading in the roles of teacher, tutor, or partner.
- More repeated reading practice in various forms.
- More emphasis of good phrasing and expression in reading.
- More careful matching of students and texts.

As an example, a teacher using poetry would be sure to read aloud the poem under study several times or have students hear a recorded version of the poem, so they would have good first models. The teacher and the students would do choral reading or support reading, with the teacher phasing out his or her reading as the students gained in confidence. After the readings of the poem, the teacher might conduct a mini-lesson on punctuation and phrasing, often having students draw pause marks or stop signs as reminders to stop and underline phrases where the words went together. Then they would read to each other, in partner sets or with take-home poems, for further practice. The materials were now easy for the students to read independently, and this provided an easy way for students to share their new skills with family members.

Teachers worked during the year to develop a handbook of teacher resources (favorites were Opitz, Rasinski, & Bird, 1998, and Stahl & Kuhn, 2002) and sample videos. The teachers, along with district and university staff, created transparencies, handouts, and PowerPoint presentations to match the issues that teachers decided were important and could be shared with other teachers in school mini-workshops. The handbooks were organized around these topics, which reflected the inquiry questions pursued over the course of the year:

1. "What is fluency, and why is it important?"
2. "How do I assess and observe my students and make a fluency snapshot of my whole class?"
3. "How do I match students with materials?"
4. "What are some methods for increasing fluency in the classroom?"
5. "What is an individual tutorial model for increasing fluency?"

A teacher can't do fluency work without knowing students' reading levels and what materials match their needs. For assessment, teachers decided to use the Classroom Fluency Snapshot (Blachowicz, Sullivan, & Cieply, 2001) to provide a quick overview of each classroom in the fall, winter, and spring as a "thermometer" of progress (see Figure 12.1). Once it was clear that there was a range of reading levels in each class, the teachers asked for sessions on material leveling and then organized their own work sessions on leveling. They developed ways to store and share materials in schools and created a video on organizing materials as a resource for others. So the seemingly simple concept of fluency led to a significant amount of teacher inquiry and sharing.

## WHY IS FLUENCY A GOOD "HOOK" FOR A VOLUNTEER PROGRAM?

Not only the district staff development initiatives but also the school volunteer program benefited from the stimulus of investigating fluency. Schools

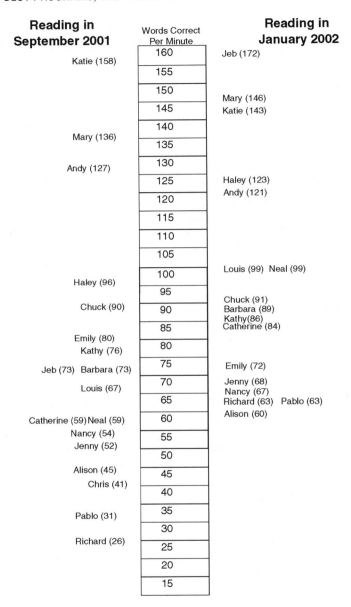

**FIGURE 12.1.** Classroom Fluency Snapshot—second grade. In January, these second graders read the first few pages of the grade 2 text *Commander Toad and the Planet of the Grapes* by Jane Yolen. Shading indicates typical oral reading rates for second graders as indicated in Barr, Blachowicz, Bates, Katz, and Kaufman (2007, p. 29).

and classrooms are often encouraged to make use of reading volunteers, but the suggestion is often more complicated than it seems (Blachowicz, 1999). Tutors must be trained so that what they teach is appropriate to the students with whom they are working. They need to understand the task and to be able to see progress. Furthermore, many tutors have a limited amount of time to donate to their tutoring, sometimes only once a week, so continuity for the students must be built into programs. Finally, the tutoring must not take too much attention away from the teacher, or the value becomes questionable. Given all these concerns, fluency work is a "natural" for tutoring, because fluency is a simple concept to explain and one that is salient to most nonprofessionals. They know when a student "sounds good." Also, methods for building fluency can be routinized, so that a simple model can be developed and used by several tutors who may work on different days with the same child.

The first step in the Everybody Reads tutoring component, which began in year 2 of the project, was adapting the teachers' model for individual instruction in order to make a tutor handbook. The model used was a modified repeated reading format (see Figure 12.2). The teacher would select an appropriate book, one that was familiar or on an appropriate level for the student to be tutored, and put it in the tutor handbook. After an introduction and any modeling necessary, the tutor would have the student read the book two or three times and record rate and accuracy. After each reading, the pair also evaluated the reading and completed a record sheet (see Figure 12.3). At the end of the session, the tutor and child made a graph showing reading rate and miscue rate over several readings for the student to take home (see Figure 12.4).

Each classroom had a volunteer notebook in place, with which contained the following:

- The child's current book.
- Blank record sheets.
- A pocket pouch with colored pencils, ruler, and stopwatch or digital watch.
- A book list with the books listed by level, with the number of words indicated for a quick calculation of words correct per minute.
- A section for performance records for each child.
- A communication section for written notes between tutors and teacher.

Using this notebook, if one volunteer worked with a student on Monday, the next volunteer could pick up at the appropriate point on Wednesday, and each could see the other's notes and comments and responses from the teacher. Each student had at least two individual volunteer sessions per week, with each session averaging 15–20 minutes.

1. Select a book or passage of approximately 100–150 words at instructional level. Count the number of words, record on a Post-It, and place it at the end of the passage.

2. Ask the student to read the passage orally. Time how many seconds it takes from start to finish, noting the error(s) as the child reads.

3. Have a calculator available to calculate the reading rate:
   (use the record sheet if you have one)
   
   # of words in the passage – # of miscues = # of words read correctly
   
   # of words read correctly × 60 divided by # of seconds = number of words read correctly in 1 minute (wcpm)!

If the number of errors is more than 15 (or 85%), an easier text should be chosen.

4. Review the errors with the student and ask him or her to read again. Time the reading. Calculate the errors and rate. Praise any improvement and discuss goals.

5. One more time, review the errors with the student and ask for one last reading. Time the reading. Calculate the errors and rate. Praise improvement and discuss goals. Remember that increased rate is not the goal for everyone. Some students need more attention to phrasing and intonation. You may wish to not calculate rate for some students.

6. Chart the rate and errors from all three readings. Display the impressive results.

7. You may want to continue this process for several days until a predetermined rate has been achieved. Be sure to chart each improvement.

*Typical oral reading rates*

| | |
|---|---|
| First grade | 30–70 words per minute |
| Second grade | 60–90 |
| Third grade | 80–110 |
| Fourth grade | 95–120 |
| Fifth grade | 110–140 |
| Sixth grade | 110–150 |

**FIGURE 12.2.** Time repeated reading procedure.

The volunteers had a first training session using the visuals and handouts prepared by the team. They were mentored during the year by the teacher and the volunteer supervisor, and were also invited to two to three more meetings for learning and debriefing. The volunteer supervisor was a parent/volunteer who was also enrolled in a graduate program in reading.

Child's Name _____ Date _____

Book Title _____

Start Page _____ End Page _____ Number of Words _____

Recorder _____

........................................................................................................

**First Reading**

Number of Seconds _____ Number of Miscues _____

____ words − ____ miscues = ____ correct words − ____ seconds × 60 = ____ wcpm

(e.g., 100 words − 5 miscues = 95 correct words − 120 seconds × 60 = 48 words

correct per minute)

|                              | Always |   |   | Rarely |   |
|------------------------------|--------|---|---|--------|---|
| Correct use of punctuation   | 5      | 4 | 3 | 2      | 1 |
| Read with expression         | 5      | 4 | 3 | 2      | 1 |

........................................................................................................

**Second Reading**

Number of Seconds _____ Number of Miscues _____

____ words − ____ miscues = ____ correct words − ____ seconds × 60 = ____ wcpm

|                              | Always |   |   | Rarely |   |
|------------------------------|--------|---|---|--------|---|
| Correct use of punctuation   | 5      | 4 | 3 | 2      | 1 |
| Read with expression         | 5      | 4 | 3 | 2      | 1 |

........................................................................................................

**Third Reading**

Number of Seconds _____ Number of Miscues _____

____ words − ____ miscues = ____ correct words − ____ seconds × 60 = ____ wcpm

|                              | Always |   |   | Rarely |   |
|------------------------------|--------|---|---|--------|---|
| Correct use of punctuation   | 5      | 4 | 3 | 2      | 1 |
| Read with expression         | 5      | 4 | 3 | 2      | 1 |

........................................................................................................

**FIGURE 12.3.** Fluency record sheet.

Over the course of the year, lead volunteers emerged. These community members who had special interest in the project added to and refined the volunteer handbook and strategies, a process that is ongoing.

## WHAT WERE THE RESULTS?

### Student Growth in Fluency in the Classroom

The primary goal had, of course, been the improvement of student fluency. Second grade was the target grade for this project, because this is when students must move beyond the initial stages of decoding to develop some fluency to make the next leap in reading improvement. Three sec-

| wcpm | Miscues | | | Child's Name | Yolanda | |
|---|---|---|---|---|---|---|
| | | | | Book | This is the Bear | |
| | | | | Date | 1/27/06 | |
| 100 | 20 | | | | | |
| 90 | 18 | | | | | |
| 80 | 16 | | | | | |
| 70 | 14 | | | | | |
| 60 | 12 | | | | | |
| 50 | 10 | | | | | |
| 40 | 8 | | | | | |
| 30 | 6 | | | | | |
| 20 | 4 | | | | | |
| 10 | 2 | | | | | |
| 0 | 0 | | | | | |
| | Reading | | 1 | 2 | 3 | 4 |

wcpm    ─────────────

Miscues    ■■■■■■■■■■■■■■

**FIGURE 12.4.** Sample fluency graph.

ond-grade classrooms participating in the project were compared with contrasting classrooms from the same grade and school that did not participate; an analysis of covariance that controlled for pretest level was used to examine the fluency gains in words correct per minute. The gains in the project classrooms were statistically superior to those of their matched grade-level and school contrast classrooms ($F = 2.472$, $p < .038$) (see Figure 12.5).

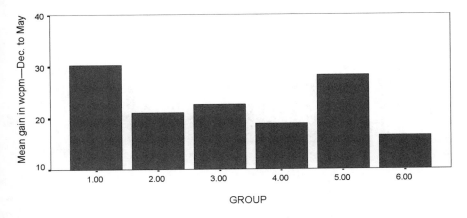

**FIGURE 12.5.** Second-grade fluency gains by class. Experimental: 1, 3, 5; contrast: 2, 4, 6.

## Individual Improvement

There was also a statistically significant effect for those students receiving the volunteer fluency training. Figure 12.6 shows gains in fluency when the students who received the individual volunteer tutoring were compared, in matched pairs, with students with the same pretest benchmark scores. *T*-tests showed that tutored students experienced significantly greater gains in fluency over the course of the 6-month trial than students in the control group ($t = -2.86$, $p < .010$). It is interesting to note that the effect seemed to be greatest for the most disfluent students. In all but two pairs, all students were also "gap" students, who represented ethnic minorities of the district whose cumulative performance was continually lower than nonminority students. This provided lots of impetus for teachers to help gap students catch up in their reading through extra reading practice and instruction.

## Teacher Growth

All 25 participating teachers completed a postprogram evaluation on their learning, using a 5-point Likert scale and anecdotal comments. The mean response scores were the following:

| | |
|---|---|
| Increased my knowledge and expertise | 5.0 |
| Provided new techniques and strategies | 4.9 |
| I intend to continue using these strategies after the project | 4.8 |
| Encouraged me to undertake further professional development | 4.8 |

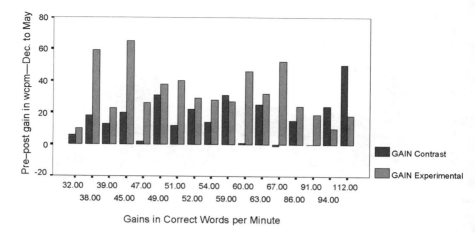

**FIGURE 12.6.** Second-grade fluency gains—comparison of matched pairs. Data of students in the Fluency Project are presented as the right-hand bar of each pair.

With respect to whether the program could be extended further, in the anecdotal comments section, 17 of the 25 teachers said they had used the new assessment strategies to share information with parents during conferences. All of the teachers reported sharing materials and strategies with others in their school.

As a further test of the commitment of teachers to supporting and spreading the project, participating teachers volunteered to offer an in-district course on fluency using the created materials. Seventy-three new district teachers signed up for the course, which was then offered at four different school sites in the district. This continued in year 4 of the project, 2 years after university and state support ended. The local press and media shared the project with the community in print and video, and the Illinois State Board of Education offered a complete set of project materials available on its website. Teachers also presented the project at local and state reading councils and were invited to other schools and districts to disseminate the model.

## Volunteers

Volunteers surveyed were uniformly positive about the program and had many fine ideas for extension and refinement. Seventy percent of the volunteers committed to another year. The second year support for the project continued to climb; the number of volunteers grew from 42 to 57, with more coming forward every day. Four volunteers enrolled in programs to become certified teachers or reading specialists. The district hired the volunteer coordinator from the project, and one volunteer offered to assist her. With the growth of the project, the role of the volunteer coordinator expanded, serving, in addition, as the point of contact for the many other districts that sought support in implementing the model in their own schools.

## A FINAL WORD

Like Topsy, Everybody Reads is a project that "just growed." It demonstrated how a simple concept such as fluency development can inspire deep and meaningful inquiry by classroom teachers and volunteers, who then take charge of the direction and development of further investigation. Project teachers became models for other teachers in their building, and ways of improving literacy instruction schoolwide were addressed. Teachers saw the benefit to their students, and subsequently schools have become involved in other long-term professional development. Additionally, the project served as a model of how to use parent volunteers successfully. Too often we have seen volunteers stop coming to schools because they feel they do not make a difference. In this case the difference in the students and the benefits of volunteers' work were obvious. As one volunteer who is also a district parent said:

> "This has gotten a lot of us really excited about what *we* can do to help our children, and it helped me understand one thing the teachers are doing to make our children better readers. With the charting process, we can *see* the growth in the children, and so can they and their teachers. We all get excited. It's motivating for all of us and makes us feel successful and want to do more. We're the 'Everybody Reads' Team!"

## REFERENCES

Barr, R., Blachowicz, C. L. Z., Bates, A., Katz, C., & Kaufman, B. (2007). *Reading diagnosis for teachers: An instructional approach* (5th ed.). Boston: Allyn & Bacon.

Blachowicz, C. L. Z. (1999, May). *Preparing reading specialists for their roles.* Paper presented at the 44th annual convention of the International Reading Association, San Diego, CA.

Blachowicz, C. L. Z., Sullivan, D., & Cieply, C. (2001). Fluency snapshots: A quick screening tool for your classroom. *Reading Psychology, 22*(2), 83–94.

Kuhn, M. R., Schwanenflugel, P. J., & Meisinger, E. B. (2010). Review of the research: Aligning theory and assessment of reading fluency: Automaticity, prosody, and definitions of fluency. *Reading Research Quarterly, 45,* 230–251.

Miller, J., & Schwanenflugel, P. J. (2008). A longitudinal study of the development of reading prosody as a dimension of oral reading fluency in early elementary school children. *Reading Research Quarterly, 43,* 336–354.

Moskal, M. K., & Blachowicz, C. (2006). *Partnering for fluency.* New York: Guilford Press.

Opitz, M., Rasinski, T., & Bird, L. (1998). *Good-bye round robin: Twenty-five effective oral reading strategies.* Portsmouth, NH: Heinemann.

Rasinski, T. (2010). *The fluent reader: Oral and silent reading strategies for building fluency, word recognition and comprehension* (2nd ed.). New York: Scholastic.

Rasinski, T. (2011). The art and science of teaching reading fluency. In D. Lapp & D. Fisher (Eds.), *Handbook of research on teaching the English language arts* (3rd ed., pp. 238–246). New York: Taylor & Francis.

Shinn, M. R. (1989). *Curriculum-based measurement: Assessing special children.* New York: Guilford Press.

Stahl, S. A., & Kuhn, M. R. (2002). Making it sound like language: Developing fluency. *The Reading Teacher, 55*(6), 582–584.

# 13

# Hijacking Fluency and Instructionally Informative Assessments

Danielle V. Dennis
Kathryn L. Solic
Richard L. Allington

**A**t some point over the past decade or so, the definition of "fluency" has changed to become widely viewed as a measure of rate and accuracy (Dowhower, 1991; Nathan & Stanovich, 1991; Rasinski & Hoffman, 2003). Overlooking the role of prosodic features in oral reading fluency has led to an onslaught of standardized assessments of fluency such as Diagnostic Indicators of Basic Early Literacy Skills (DIBELS) and Test of Word Reading Efficiency. These assessments are being used in classrooms across the country to determine the reading rates of students, but they are ignoring phrasing and intonation, and they are ignoring fluency. Thus, "word recognition automaticity" may be a better term to describe what these standardized assessments are actually measuring. Nathan and Stanovich (1991) suggest this shift is a result of the work of cognitive psychologists who study reading. Matching this assertion with the historical interpretation of reading research presented by Alexander and Fox (2004), who propose that 1976 to 1985 encompassed the "Era of Information Processing," perhaps we can begin to determine a precise time period for the exchange of definitions as well as the influx of standardized assessments. This would also account for the role played by the LaBerge–Samuels (1974) model of automatic information processing in reading, which suggests that we have a limited capacity for storing information. When we read, the goal is to use minimal attention for decoding words—to be automatic—so maximum attention may be used for comprehension of text.

Despite efforts to popularize curriculum-based measures (Deno, 1985), which are designed to use oral reading of passages from classroom texts to provide teachers with fluency data to monitor growth in reading, the newer decontextualized standardized assessments seem more commonly used today even though they provide more generalized data. What does this mean for students in today's classrooms? If assessment drives instruction, and results of decontextualized assessments of automaticity are used to determine achievement levels, then is it fair to assume that instruction is also becoming more generalized and less in tune with what individual students need?

In this chapter we discuss several key points relating to the re/conceptualization of fluency. Though we ask the following questions, their purpose is to provoke thought and further research into the concept of fluency rather than definitive answers.

- What does a more comprehensive definition of fluency bring to the table?
- Do standardized measures of reading fluency provide teachers with enough information to make sound instructional decisions?
- What is the role of prosody in reading fluency?
- Is assessing fluency as a curriculum-based measurement important?
- Volume or frequency? Selecting interventions that work in training readers to be fluent.

## WHAT DOES A MORE COMPREHENSIVE DEFINITION OF FLUENCY BRING TO THE TABLE?

The most widely used definition of fluency is that represented by the automatic information processing in reading presented by LaBerge and Samuels (1974). While Samuels (1987, 1994, 2007) considers prosody a component of automaticity, prosodic features are rarely acknowledged in work citing the LaBerge–Samuels model. Automaticity is an important feature of skilled reading, however, we agree with Kuhn and Stahl (2003) that fluency includes accuracy, automaticity, and prosody as separate elements. Each of these factors works in conjunction with the others. Thus, without possessing *all* of these skills, a reader does not display fluency. Because fluency is not meant to be the end goal in reading (Allington, 1983), it must be recognized as the bridge between decoding and comprehension. However, many schools are treating fluency as an end it itself—a race to read the most words in the shortest amount of time (Allington, 2009; Rasinski, 2004). In order to create meaningful fluency instruction, this view of fluency as automaticity alone must become more comprehensive: It must include accuracy and prosody as well. In other words, simply using one component of fluency—or even two—to determine what makes a reader "good" detracts from fluency and from curricular decision making as a whole.

For example, accuracy is one component of reading fluency. Many readers are able to decode accurately, but the process they use is extremely slow and demands capacity, which leads to the breakdown of comprehension (Nathan & Stanovich, 1991; Samuels, 1979, 2007). However, readers who are both accurate and automatic have increased information-processing capacity available while reading, allowing more attentional capacity to be allocated to comprehension. Furthermore, readers who are capable of incorporating prosodic features in an oral reading of text are able to comprehend the meaning of the text, as evidenced through their correct placement of phrasing, pitch, stress, and tone.

Importantly, by providing a definition of fluency that includes all three factors, teachers may rethink their instructional methods for increasing fluency.

Currently, in some schools, teachers concerned about standardized automaticity assessment are having their students read timed word lists or decontextualized passages. In these types of exercise, after practicing the text, students are then asked to reread it orally. Typically, teachers time the student and count the errors made during the reading of the text. Zutell and Rasinski (1991) suggest that these practices develop students into readers who are less aware of the meaning of text, because their sole concern is to increase the rate at which they read. Is this the goal of their teachers? We think not. However, a misunderstanding of the definition of fluency, or a lack of knowledge regarding all components related to it, may lead teachers (and students) to believe that by increasing automaticity they are working to enhance the comprehension capabilities of their students. By embracing a more comprehensive definition of fluency, researchers may focus on methods for training and encouraging teachers (and students) to attend to prosodic factors in oral reading fluency.

## DO STANDARDIZED MEASURES OF READING FLUENCY PROVIDE TEACHERS WITH ENOUGH INFORMATION TO MAKE SOUND INSTRUCTIONAL DECISIONS?

Fuchs, Fuchs, and Deno (1982) consider standardized assessments reliable and robust when comparing the performance of individual students with that of a group of students. However, they suggest standardized assessments are not valid measures for designing instruction or placing students in special programs. This is due to the limited content validity of standardized assessments. Caldwell (2002) contends it is dangerous to compare the reading rates of different students because of the variability inherent in rate measures. Variability can occur for many reasons, including interest, familiarity with a passage or subject, text structure, or the purpose of the reader. Instead, Caldwell suggests that teachers assess student reading fluency through informal interactions and by using their own judgment to gain insight into development. Similarly, Rasinski (1999) proposes that there is not a "right" reading rate for students. Instead, prediction equations were developed, which provided a method for estimating target reading rates at varying levels of development. This allows teachers to gauge growth of their students' reading rate over time using contextualized readings. These suggestions, however, are not congruent with the nature of standardized assessments of fluency.

DIBELS, for example, is standardized in an attempt to identify students who are reading below grade level and are considered at risk (Hintze, Ryan, & Stoner, 2003). Hintze and colleagues cite DIBELS as an effective measurement for determining individual progress as well as "grade level feedback toward validated instructional objectives." The four subtests of DIBELS include Letter Naming Fluency, Initial Sound Fluency, Phonemic Segmentation Fluency, and Passage Reading. Results from these subtests would suggest that struggling readers are lacking skills in one or more of the areas. Thus, instruction is linked to the teaching of isolated skills, including phonemic awareness and word recognition—something Allington (1983) cautioned against. Other researchers also warn of such practices, arguing there is no evidence suggesting that this type of instruction improves fluency or comprehension (Ivey & Baker, 2004; Samuels, 2007; Schwanenflugel, Hamilton, Melanie, Wisenbaker, & Stahl, 2004).

We believe the evidence indicates that young children become better readers by reading, and that early literacy skills are best taught in the context of reading connected text (Dahl & Freppon, 1995; Sacks & Mergendoller, 1997). A decontextualized instructional focus on exact word recognition may lead students further from literacy, as their motivation becomes correct word calling rather than making sense of what they read (Allington, 1983; Samuels, 2007; Zutell & Rasinski, 1991). Despite the claims that DIBELS is a reliable measure of reading fluency, our data tell a different story.

## Our DIBELS Story

In Florida, as well as many other states, DIBELS was a mandated assessment in schools receiving funding under the federal Reading First program.

(It is noteworthy that in 2009 the U.S. Department of Education defunded their program, and Florida has since eliminated DIBELS testing as a state requirement.) We present DIBELS data from two third-grade classrooms in a Florida Reading First school. The data were from the third DIBELS assessment in the spring of the year. Our purpose in compiling the data was to determine how well the readability of the passages correlated with students' performance. Elliott and Tollefson (2001) argue that results from DIBELS assessments are both reliable and valid, and should be used more frequently by teachers to determine appropriate skills to teach individual students. Our results indicate something quite different.

The question we asked was, how well did the students' ($n$ = 39) DIBELS scores correlate across the three passages they read in the spring assessment. These standardized passages were presented by the publisher as being of equivalent difficulty (using readability analyses). We found that individual student scores varied substantially from passage to passage. Several sets of student scores are presented next (the scores represent the number of words in each passage the child read correctly in the standard 1-minute period).

| | Passage | | | |
| | 1 | 2 | 3 | Variability in wcpm |
|---|---|---|---|---|
| S4 | 118 | 81 | 71 | 47 |
| S13 | 66 | 38 | 46 | 28 |
| S14 | 92 | 60 | 69 | 32 |
| S25 | 90 | 73 | 54 | 36 |
| S30 | 94 | 79 | 45 | 49 |
| S31 | 165 | 128 | 109 | 56 |
| S32 | 97 | 64 | 69 | 33 |
| S34 | 80 | 66 | 47 | 33 |
| S35 | 74 | 44 | 35 | 39 |
| S38 | 81 | 52 | 58 | 29 |

Remember that these passages are supposedly of equivalent difficulty. Nonetheless, as shown, significant variability in reading automaticity is evident in these data from 25% of participants.

There were students who exhibited little variability, but these were typically the slowest readers, a result also reported by Flurkey (1998) in his analysis of reading rates of good and poor readers. For example:

| | | | | |
|-----|----|----|----|----|
| S8 | 48 | 37 | 41 | 11 |
| S9 | 30 | 28 | 25 | 5 |
| S17 | 26 | 13 | 21 | 13 |
| S27 | 34 | 31 | 25 | 9 |
| S33 | 36 | 32 | 36 | 4 |

These children seem not to have developed automaticity of word recognition, at least when reading these passages, which were difficult for them. But the DIBELS passages were not the texts these children were reading everyday, and so it remains unclear where their teachers might begin with an instructional plan. Generalized findings of nonautomatic and perhaps inaccurate reading of standard passages may reliably indicate that these children are struggling with reading acquisition, but the performances offer little useful information that a teacher might use in planning next week's lessons.

We also calculated the correlation between passage difficulty (of the three passages that each student read) and DIBELS performance as another way to examine the consistency of reading rate and accuracy from passage to passage. Overall, the student performances on DIBELS fell in one of three ranges. For one group ($n$ = 11) of students the correlation of performances across the three passages was below .25. For another group ($n$ = 16) the correlation was between .26 and .50. The final group ($n$ = 12) had correlation coefficients above .50. A low correlation coefficient means that students' performance on passages of purported equivalent difficulty varied greatly.

These low correlation coefficients indicate both that passage difficulty on DIBELS is unreliable and that fluency rating for students is inconsistent at best. All of this suggests that Caldwell's (2002) concern about variability needs serious consideration and clouds interpretation of the data. Passages obviously vary, even those that the test publisher suggests are of equivalent difficulty.

So how might such data be useful for instructional planning? This is difficult to say. The consistently slow readers are obviously in big trouble, but it seems likely that would be obvious without DIBELS testing or any other sort of standardized testing. But the most useful information one might gather from children reading aloud would be unavailable from a standardized test. What we might learn from a curriculum-based measure, something like a running record (Johnston, 2000) of oral reading of classroom texts, is whether the child is reading with sufficient accuracy that the text is at an appropriate level of difficulty for that child. We could also use a fluency rubric (Zutell & Rasinski, 1991; Rasinski, 2004) to evaluate whether the child can read the classroom text with prosody, which would suggest both automaticity and the roots of understanding. None of this is available from the standardized tests. But it is standardized tests of automaticity that are now widely used.

## WHAT IS THE ROLE OF PROSODY IN READING FLUENCY?

Researchers agree that fluent readers follow a certain trajectory in their development of prosodic features (Dowhower, 1991; Schreiber, 1991; Schwanenflugel et al., 2004). Although the three components of fluency—accuracy, automaticity, and prosody—are equally important, readers first exhibit accurate reading, then reading with automaticity, and finally use of prosodic features. The question of prosody as it is related to comprehension is that of the chicken and the egg. There is limited research suggesting comprehension is obtained once a reader is able to utilize appropriate suprasegmental cues. However, Schwanenflugel et al. (2004) suggest that prosody is a result of reading with comprehension. Does prosody then become the end goal in reading? Is it important for readers to use such intonation, pitch, and stress in order to be considered a proficient reader?

Furthermore, in the information-processing model, attention, or pattern recognition, involves the question of how we recognize environmental stimuli as exemplars of concepts already in memory (Leahey & Harris, 2001). In order for information to move from the sensory memory to the working memory, pattern recognition must be activated. One example of pattern recognition is speech perception—more specifically, phonemes and suprasegmental cues. Comprehension, however, occurs further along in the information-processing model, when information is encoded from the working memory to long-term memory. According to the information-processing model then, suprasegmental cues would be necessary prior to the comprehension of text.

Obviously, more research must be conducted to determine the precise role prosody plays in reading fluency. Our assertion, however, is that prosody's role—whether the chicken or the egg—is a necessary component to oral reading fluency, and must be a goal of reading instruction and a feature of fluency assessment.

There are problems with including prosody in classroom assessments of fluency. The first is the type of measurements used. Rubrics have been devised, that allow teachers to rate students on prosodic features (Caldwell, 2002; Pinnell et al., 1995; Zutell & Rasinski, 1991; Rasinski, 2004). However, research on the use of rubrics to assess reading fluency has been limited at best (Dowhower, 1991; Schreiber, 1991; Schwanenflugel et al., 2004). There is evidence that teachers can use rubrics to provide reliable information about reading and writing development (Koretz, Stecher, Klein, & McCaffrey, 1994). However, we feel that lack of training in fluency assessment and instruction, as well as the focus on currently popular standardized assessments, limits the use of such rubrics in today's classrooms.

Educators, however, must recognize that prosody has a role in reading fluency. Caldwell (2002) suggests that teachers utilize a fluency rubric during classroom silent reading time to measure student reading fluency. This is a time when teachers can sit next to individual students and have them read aloud quietly from a selected text. Often the books being read during this period are the most appropriate for fluency assessment. This is due to the fact that during silent reading students generally choose books at their independent level, which allows for a more accurate assessment of all components of fluency, including prosody. We can induce word-by-word reading in almost any subject by providing students with difficult text. It is, then, critical that fluency data are collected from texts that students can read accurately. In other words, we should not be surprised that a first grader fails to exhibit fluency if given a junior novel, such as a Harry Potter book (e.g., Rowling, 1998). Likewise, a struggling fifth-grade reader might also be unable to read a junior novel with fluency but might demonstrate fluency when reading an early chapter book, such as one from the Junie B. Jones series (Park, 1992).

It is when a student exhibits accurate but dysfluent reading in independent-level texts that it is time to provide appropriate instruction. Schreiber (1991) maintains that instruction in fluency is often ignored because it is assumed that once students are able to decode automatically they will recognize the syntactic cues and demonstrate prosodic features while reading orally. In making such an assumption, teachers overlook one of the three components of fluency and, we contend, leave out a key factor of reading instruction. However, this may be rectified through the use of teacher modeling of fluent reading, paired reading by students (Caldwell, 2002), and the use of audio-recorded books.

## IS ASSESSING FLUENCY AS A
## CURRICULUM-BASED MEASURE IMPORTANT?

Although Elliott and Tollefson (2001) suggest "the DIBELS measure represents many of the best features of alternative assessments," we believe measuring fluency in context leads to a more accurate oral reading fluency level. In fact, Fuchs, Fuchs, and Compton (2004) caution practitioners against the use of measures of nonsense word fluency—expressly DIBELS—in favor of the curriculum-based word identification fluency measure. Words in the context of stories or informational texts are typically read more accurately and at a faster rate than the same words presented in lists. Passage reading, then, provides a more accurate rendering of a student's oral reading fluency (Jenkins, Fuchs, van den Broeck, Espin, & Deno, 2003).

Deno (1985) defines curriculum-based measurement (CBM) as a repeated measure of performance being drawn from one curriculum. The CBM is both valid and reliable (Deno, 1992). Fuchs et al. (2004) provide teachers with information that allows them to gauge reading fluency growth over time. Because the readings are drawn from classroom texts, they tend to be of comparable difficulty, and repeated administrations of the CBM depict students' short- and long-term growth (Markell & Deno, 1997). Unlike standardized assessments, CBMs are successful because they provide classroom-based results related to an individual student. Teachers can use CBM fluency data to make judgments about placement in appropriate text levels as well as fluency development.

It is important to note that, although school psychologists or trained measurement specialists typically administer standardized assessments (Hintze et al., 2003), classroom teachers are better served when they administer CBM themselves. This affords teachers the opportunity to be involved in the assessment process, which allows for insight into individual students' performance that is not provided by the percentile rankings or grade equivalency scores that come from standardized tests. Teacher training in the proper use of CBM is vital, because assessments that are conducted correctly provide teachers with valuable information for making curricular decisions (Fuchs, Deno, & Mirkin, 1984). The goal for the use of CBM is for teachers to develop a database for each student to determine how effective the individual instructional plan is for that student (Deno, 1992).

## VOLUME OR FREQUENCY?

In order for students to become more fluent readers, they must have ample time to practice reading both in and outside of school (Allington, 1977, 1983, 2009). If we want our struggling readers to become fluent, we must provide them with text that they can read accurately (Allington, 2002). When students are given texts that they can read with accuracy and automaticity, they are provided with opportunities to practice using prosody.

What interventions are successful for increasing oral reading fluency? Perhaps the most widely known method for developing reading fluency is repeated readings (Allington, 1983; Kuhn & Stahl, 2000; Samuels, 1979). Samuels (1979, 1987, 1994) describes repeated readings as a process in which students read and reread a passage until they can do so with accuracy and fluency. Kuhn and Stahl (2000) reviewed more than 100 studies of fluency training of various sorts. Using a vote-counting method, the authors found that fluency training is typically effective, although it was unclear whether this is a result of specific instructional features or simply greater volume of reading. They also found that assisted approaches seem to have an advantage over unassisted approaches, and repetitive approaches do not seem to have a clear advantage over nonrepetitive approaches. Finally, they argue that effective fluency instruction moves beyond a focus on improving automatic word recognition to include a focus on rhythm and expression or prosodic features of language.

The National Reading Panel (2000) found that repeated reading worked better for improving word-reading accuracy on the target passages than for improving fluency. Rashotte and Torgeson (1985) compared repeated reading with simply allowing students to read independently for a comparable period of time. There were no differences in outcomes between the repeated and extended reading interventions, with both producing improved fluency.

Unfortunately, few studies have contrasted fluency interventions with extended independent reading interventions. However, Kuhn (2005a, 2005b) and colleagues (2006) conducted several studies comparing extended reading (increased time spent reading) and repeated reading (reading the same material multiple times). Their findings all point to extended reading being more powerful in fostering not just fluency but accuracy and vocabulary development. Repeated reading works better than no treatment, but just a little repeated reading with lots of extended reading of independent-level texts seems the best route for fostering fluency. Unfortunately, extended reading practice has few proponents supporting it as a tool to help struggling readers become not just more fluent readers but better readers.

## SUMMARY

Current standardized assessments and instructional programs seem to focus more on reading automaticity than reading fluency. We believe there must be a shift back to a focus on reading fluency if we expect to impact positively students' reading abilities. Definitions of oral reading fluency must include three components: accuracy, automaticity, and prosody. Without focus on and instruction in each of these elements, students will simply be word callers without the capability to transfer to reading comprehension.

With the increased popularity of standardized tests of reading automaticity, we worry that instruction for individual students is becoming more generalized. As evidenced in "Our DIBELS Story," administrators and teachers should not rely on claims made by publishers regarding the reliability and validity of data from standardized measures of reading automaticity. With an abundance of standardized assessments set to measure isolated aspects of literacy, we fear that instruction and assessment are becoming too compartmentalized.

Placing each facet of literacy into a separate "box," teachers and students are inundated with multiple programs that "are proven to teach" each individual skill. However, there is little evidence of overall improvement in reading from these programs. This is a dangerous aspect of standardized testing and standardized programmatic decision making. Why would students see reading as one connected and integrated process when instruction separates all the elements of reading?

We must arm our teachers with expert training on the components of reading fluency as well as how those components are linked to other elements of reading, such as comprehension. With this training, teachers will be able to make informed decisions regarding instruction and will have the capability of assessing students using their own judgment rather than that of a test publisher.

This restored confidence will allow teachers to utilize assessments such as CBM (Deno, 1985) and rubrics designed to measure all components of reading fluency (Caldwell, 2002; Rasinski, 1991, 2004). Through the use of contextualized measurements, teachers will also ensure students are reading a high volume of materials rather than focusing on word lists and isolated word skills.

Although standardized assessments are useful in comparing a student to a group of his or her peers (Markell & Deno, 1997), such tests do not offer teachers sufficiently reliable and valid information to provide meaningful and effective instruction to individual students. The lack of training available to teachers for understanding what the results of such tests represent is another issue relating to standardized assessments, but we save that discussion for another time.

## REFERENCES

Alexander, P., & Fox, E. (2004). A historical perspective on reading research and practice. In R. Ruddell & N. Unrau (Eds.), *Theoretical models and processes of reading* (pp. 33–68). Newark, DE: International Reading Association.

Allington, R. L. (1977). If they don't read much, how are they ever gonna get good? *Journal of Reading, 21,* 57–61.

Allington, R. L. (1983). Fluency: The neglected reading goal. *The Reading Teacher, 36*(6), 556–561.

Allington, R. L. (2002). You can't learn much from books you can't read. *Educational Leadership, 60*(3), 16–19.

Allington, R. L. (2009). *What really matters in fluency: From research to practice.* New York: Pearson/Allyn & Bacon.

Caldwell, J. S. (2002). *Reading assessment: A primer for teachers and tutors.* New York: Guilford Press.

Dahl, K. L., & Freppon, P. A. (1995). A comparison of inner-city children's interpretations of reading and writing instruction in skills-based and whole language classrooms. *Reading Research Quarterly, 30,* 50–74.

Deno, S. (1992). The nature and development of curriculum-based measurement. *Preventing School Failure, 36*(2), 5–11.

Deno, S. (1985). Curriculum-based measurement: The emerging alternative. *Exceptional Children, 52,* 219–232.

Dowhower, S. (1991). Speaking of prosody: Fluency's unattended bedfellow. *Theory into Practice, 30*(3), 165–175.

Elliott, J., & Tollefson, N. (2001). A realiability and validity study of the Dynamic Indicators of Basic Early Literacy Skills—Modified. *School Psychology Review, 30*(1), 33–50.

Flurkey, A. D. (1998). *Reading as flow: A linguistic alternative to fluency.* Unpublished research monograph, Hofstra University.

Fuchs, L., Deno, S., & Mirrkin, P. (1984). The effects of frequent curriculum-based measurement and evaluation on pedagogy, student achievement, and student awareness of learning. *American Educational Research Journal, 21*(2), 449–460.

Fuchs, L., Fuchs, D., & Compton, D. (2004). Monitoring early reading development in first grade: Word identification fluency versus nonsense word fluency. *Exceptional Children, 71*(1), 7–21.

Fuchs, L., Fuchs, D., & Deno, S. (1982). Reliability and validity of curriculum-based informal reading inventories. *Reading Research Quarterly, 18*(1), 6–26.

Hintze, J., Ryan, A., & Stoner, G. (2003). Concurrent validity and diagnostic accuracy of the Dynamic Indicators of Basic Early Literacy Skills and the Comprehensive Test of Phonological Processing. *School Psychology Review, 32*(4), 541–556.

Ivey, G., & Baker, M. (2004). Phonics instruction for older students?: Just say no. *Educational Leadership, 61*(6), 35–39.

Jenkins, J., Fuchs, L., van den Broek, P., Espin, C., & Deno, S. (2003). Accuracy and fluency in list and context reading of skilled and RD groups: Absolute and relative performance levels. *Learning Disabilities Research and Practice, 18*(4), 237–245.

Johnston, P. (2000). *Running records.* York, ME: Stenhouse.

Koretz, D., Stecher, B., Klein, S., & McCaffrey, D. (1994). The Vermont Portfolio Assessment program: Findings and implications. *Educational Measurement, 13*(3), 5–16.

Kuhn, M. (2005a). Helping students become accurate, expressive readers: Fluency instruction for small groups. *The Reading Teacher, 58*(4), 338–344.

Kuhn, M. R. (2005b). A comparative study of small group fluency instruction. *Reading Psychology, 26*(2), 127–146.

Kuhn, M. R., Schwanenflugel, P., Morris, R. D., Morrow, L. M., Woo, D., Meisinger, B., et al. (2006). Teaching children to become fluent and automatic readers. *Journal of Literacy Research, 38*(4), 357–388.

Kuhn, M., & Stahl, S. (2003). Fluency: A review of developmental and remedial practices. In R. Ruddell & N. Unrau (Eds.), *Theoretical models and processes of reading* (pp. 412–453). Newark, DE: International Reading Association.

LaBerge, D., & Samuels, S. J. (1974). Toward a theory of automatic processing in reading. *Cognitive Psychology, 6,* 293–323.

Leahey, T., & Harris, R. (2001). *Learning and cognition*. Upper Saddle River, NJ: Prentice Hall.

Markell, M., & Deno, S. (1997). Effects of increasing oral reading: Generalization across reading tasks. *Journal of Special Education, 31*(2), 233–250.

Nathan, R., & Stanovich, K. (1991). The causes and consequences of differences in reading fluency. *Theory Into Practice, 30*(3), 177–184.

National Reading Panel. (2000). *Teaching children to read: An evidence-based assessment of the scientific research literature on reading and its implications for reading instruction* (NIH Publication No. 00-4769). Washington, DC: National Institute of Child Health and Human Development.

Park, B. (1992). *Junie B. Jones and the stupid smelly bus*. New York: Scholastic.

Pinnell, G. S., Pikulski, J., Wixon, K. K., Campbell, J. R. Gough, P. B., & Beatty, A. S. (1995). *Listening to children read aloud* (Research Report No. ED 378550). Washington, DC: National Center for Education Statistics.

Rashotte, C., & Torgeson, J. (1985). Repeated reading fluency in learning disabled children. *Reading Research Quarterly, 20*, 180–189.

Rasinski, T. (1999). Exploring a method for estimating independent, instructional, and frustration reading rates. *Journal of Reading Psychology, 20*, 61–99.

Rasinski, T. (2004). Creating fluent readers. *Educational Leadership, 61*(6), 46–51.

Rasinski, T., & Hoffman, J. (2003). Oral reading in the school literacy curriculum. *Reading Research Quarterly, 38*(4), 510–522.

Rowling, J. K. (1998). *Harry Potter and the sorcerer's stone*. New York: Arthur Levine.

Sacks, C. H., & Mergendoller, J. R. (1997). The relationship between teachers' theoretical orientation toward reading and students' outcomes in kindergarten children with different initial reading abilities. *American Education Research Journal, 34*(4), 721–740.

Samuels, S. J. (1979). The method of repeated reading. *The Reading Teacher, 32*, 403–408.

Samuels, S. J. (1987). Information processing abilities and reading. *Journal of Learning Disabilities, 20*, 18–22.

Samuels, S. J. (1994). Toward a theory of automatic information processing in reading, revised. In R. Ruddell & N. Unrau (Eds.), *Theoretical Models and Processes of Reading* (pp. 1127–1148). Newark, DE, International Reading Association.

Samuels, S. J. (2007). The DIBELS tests: Is speed of barking at print what we mean by reading fluency? *Reading Research Quarterly, 42*(4), 563–566.

Schreiber, P. (1991). Understanding prosody's role in reading acquisition. *Theory into Practice, 30*(3), 158–164.

Schwanenflugel, P., Hamilton, A., Melanie, K., Wisenbaker, J., & Stahl, S. (2004). Becoming a fluent reader: Reading skill and prosodic features in the oral reading of young readers. *Journal of Educational Psychology, 96*(1), 119–129.

Zutell, J., & Rasinski, T. (1991). Training teachers to attend to their students' oral reading fluency. *Theory into Practice, 30*(3), 211–217.

# PART III

## SPECIAL TOPICS, SPECIAL POPULATIONS

# 14

## Teaching Fluency (and Decoding) through Fast Start

*An Early Childhood Parental Involvement Program*

Timothy Rasinski
Nancy Padak
Bruce Stevenson

The National Reading Panel (2000) identified word decoding (phonics) and reading fluency as two key components of successful early reading instructional programs. Clearly, the ability to decode words accurately (phonics and decoding) and effortlessly (fluency) is essential to success in learning to read. Readers who experience difficulty in decoding words, or who must invest too much effort into decoding words, cannot be considered proficient readers who adequately comprehend what they read. The critical and essential nature of decoding and fluency makes them strong candidates for instruction early in the school reading curriculum.

Given the time constraints to school-based instruction, any opportunity to expand instruction beyond the confines of the school is welcome. Home involvement is clearly one area in which reading instruction can be expanded. Indeed, the theory and research supporting the inclusion of parents in children's school learning, especially in the early years of school, are deep and compelling (Chavkin, 1993; Christenson, 1995; Crimm, 1992; Durkin, 1966; Eccles & Harold, 1993; Epstein, 1989, 1994, 2001; Henderson, 1988; Henderson & Berla, 1994; Neidermeyer, 1970; Postlethwaite

& Ross, 1992; Pressley, 2002; Rasinski, 1989, 2003; Topping, 1996; U.S. Department of Education, 1994).

## DESIGN CHARACTERISTICS FOR PARENT TUTORING PROGRAMS

To be effective, parent tutoring programs in reading for early childhood must adhere to certain design characteristics (Rasinski, Padak, & Fawcett, 2010). The characteristics can be used as guidelines to design programs to meet specific needs or to evaluate existing programs.

### Use Proven and Effective Strategies

Parents often have limited time to devote to working with their children. Therefore, at-home activities must be based on proven and appropriate methods for achieving success in reading. Too often at-home activities have questionable value for improving academic performance. Drawing and coloring pictures or cutting out photographs from magazines may not be the best use of parents' and children's time together at home. In this chapter, we look at the design components of a parent literacy program created to develop fluency.

### Provide Ongoing Training, Communication, and Support

Most parents are not teachers. They need training that includes demonstrations and opportunities for discussion and questions. Someone who is enthusiastic about and committed to parent involvement should provide the training.

School personnel need to understand the realities of busy family life and be sensitive to educational barriers that may impede parent–child reading activity. Some parents may not feel comfortable reading aloud to their children because of their own real or perceived lack of reading ability. Parents of English language learners may not themselves be fluent readers of English. Parents whose own educational experiences were negative may hesitate to attend or participate in school functions. Yet all these parents want to help their children succeed. The teacher's challenge, then, is to find meaningful ways for all families to be involved in at-home reading activities. With some thoughtful planning, resourceful teachers can find meaningful and effective ways to involve parents in their children's literacy development.

Continuing communication and support can provide parents with timely feedback about their questions and concerns, and can encourage persistence with the at-home reading activities. Support can be in the form of a regular informative newsletter, monthly sessions in the school, or offers of personal contact by phone or e-mail. Ongoing communication and collaboration build bonds of mutual support between home and school.

## Use Authentic Reading Texts

Years of research have demonstrated that one of the best things that parents can do for children of any age is to read to them. Reading aloud provides children with a model of fluent reading and offers parents natural opportunities to point out text features for young children. Similarly, when parents read with their children or listen to their children read, children grow as readers. Texts for these activities should be authentic (e.g., stories, poems, song lyrics, jokes, jump rope rhymes); children should be able to read them successfully with enough support from parents. These simple activities—reading to, reading with, and listening to children—are powerful ways to promote student growth in reading.

Some parent involvement plans fail because parents lack appropriate texts or the time or resources to acquire them. Although periodic trips to the public library are advisable, requiring them as a condition of participation in at-home reading activities may discourage parental involvement. The easiest solution is to provide parents and children with reading materials. When the materials are provided, parents are more likely to engage in reading with their children. The materials themselves act as reminders to parents to get the job done.

## Make Activities Easy, Enjoyable, Consistent, and Long Term

Parents tell us that parent involvement activities don't work if they are too complex, take inordinate amounts of time, or change in nature from day to day or week to week. They say it's hard to develop a routine of working with their children under such conditions. Therefore, at-home reading activities need to reflect this reality. At-home activities for young children should be relatively brief (10–15 minutes several times each week), simple routines, with some variation to keep interest high. Such activities make it easier for parents and children to develop predictable, time-efficient routines. These, in turn, increase the likelihood that the at-home activities will be conducted regularly and successfully.

Consistency is important as well. Once an effective instructional routine is introduced, major changes or disruptions in the parent–child routine should be avoided. Rather, families should be able to develop a level of comfort with the routines. Variety can be introduced by changing the texts and the ways in which parents and children respond to what they read.

For parents and children to persist in academic tasks over the long term, the instructional activities must be enjoyable for everyone. A sense of informality and playfulness infused into the activities can help achieve this goal. Parents should be reminded to be enthusiastic, to provide positive encouragement, and to support their children's attempts to read. Allowing children some control over activities also lends enjoyment and personal ownership to the sessions. If the reading is followed by some word games, for example, children can choose the games, as well as the words, to include.

When home and school collaborate to provide regular, enjoyable, and authentic reading experiences over the long term, students benefit because they have multiple daily opportunities to grow as readers.

## Provide Ways to Document Home Activities

Documenting at-home activity permits teachers and schools to monitor parent–child involvement and evaluate the program's success in achieving its goal. More importantly, perhaps, documentation gives parents tacit encouragement to continue reading with their children. Parents can use a log sheet to record their work with their children over a specified period of time. Parents tell us that posting the sheet in a prominent place reminds them to engage in the learning activity. At the end of the time period, the log sheets are returned to the school and used to monitor and evaluate participation.

## FAST START: COMBINING EARLY LITERACY INSTRUCTION WITH HOME INVOLVEMENT

We used these design characteristics to develop and refine Fast Start, a simple home-involvement program that has shown remarkable results. Fast Start (Padak & Rasinski, 2004a, 2005; Rasinski, 1995), an adaptation of the Fluency Development Lesson (Rasinski, Padak, Linek, & Sturtevant, 1994), is a parental involvement in reading program for primary grade students designed to get children off to a successful start through intensive and systematic parental involvement in word decoding and fluency instruction that uses authentic texts and is coordinated through the school. The program involves a 10- to 15-minute daily instructional routine in which parents repeatedly read a brief text to and with their children (Dowhower, 1994), proactively listen to their children read the text to them, and engage in a brief word study activity with their children. Specifically, Fast Start procedures include the following:

- Parent and child work with a daily passage. The passage is short (50–200 words), usually high in predictability (patterned texts with rhyming words), and age appropriate in terms of content. Age-appropriate verse poems and song lyrics work particularly well for grades K–2.

- Parent and child sit side by side in a quiet area or room. The parent reads the text to the child several times, until the child is familiar with the passage. The parent draws the child's attention to the text by pointing to the appropriate lines and words as they are read.

- Parent and child discuss the content of the passage and also point out text features such as repeated words, rhymes, alliterative lines, patterns of text, and so on.

- Next, parent and child simultaneously read the passage together. The passage is again read several times, until the child feels willing and comfortable with reading the passage on his or her own.

- The child reads the text alone, with the parent providing backup or shadow reading support. The child is encouraged to point to the words as they are read to ensure voice-to-print matching. The child reads the text several times.

- Finally, the parent engages in phonemic awareness and/or word study activities with the child. These activities may include, but are not limited to, the following:
  - The parent and child may choose words from the text that are of interest; this may include rhyming words, content words, high-frequency words, and so on. The words are printed on cards and added to word cards from previous days. This word bank is used for word practice, sentence building, word sorts, and other informal word games and activities.
  - The parent draws the child's attention to various sounds that are salient in the passage and may help the child make the letter-to-sound match. For example, the parent may say two words from the text and ask the child to clap if the words begin with the same sound.
  - The parent chooses a word that contains a common word family (i.e., rime or phonogram) that is salient in the text (e.g., *ock* in *Hickory Dickory Dock*). The word is written on a sheet of paper, with the word family underlined or highlighted in some fashion. Then the parent and child brainstorm other words that rhyme and that contain the same word family (e.g., *sock, lock, rock, clock, tock*). These words are written in list form under the original word and then practiced.

The beauty of Fast Start is its simplicity, brevity, and effectiveness. It is a simple routine that can be used every day. Indeed, the expectation is that parents use the routine on a daily basis with their children, essentially altering only the passage to be read. Similarly, the lesson routine is quick to implement.

The entire lesson can be implemented in less than 15 minutes. However, in that brief period of time, a large number of words, both in meaningful context and in isolation for detailed analysis, are read and reread.

## EVIDENCE OF FAST START SUCCESS

Fast Start has been implemented in a number of settings, and the results have been remarkably and universally positive.

### In a Clinical Reading Program

In a 5-week pilot implementation of an adapted version of Fast Start with struggling readers in a university summer reading clinic, Rasinski (1995) reported strong correlations (.60–.79) between degree of parent participation in Fast Start and various measures of reading growth. Parents were introduced to Fast Start in an orientation meeting at the beginning of the clinical program and were asked to implement it daily with their children. Materials for parents were provided by clinic staff members. Students were pre- and posttested on various measures of reading proficiency. Results indicated that students who regularly participated in Fast Start lessons with their parents made substantially greater gains in word decoding and reading fluency than children who did Fast Start less consistently or not at all. These results held for children in the primary through middle grades.

### In Literacy Acquisition

Another study examined the implementation of Fast Start at the critical initial stage of literacy development—the beginning of first grade (Rasinski & Stevenson, 2005). Thirty beginning first-grade students, representing a wide range of reading abilities, were randomly assigned to experimental or control conditions for a period of 11 weeks. Parents and students in the experimental group received Fast Start training, weekly materials packets, and weekly telephone support. They were asked to implement Fast Start daily with their children over the 11-week trial. The time for implementation ranged from 10 to 12 minutes per day. Control group parents and students received alternative parent involvement opportunities typical for their family and classroom.

Significant main effects for those students considered most at risk in reading (as measured by the pretest) were found on measures of letter/word recognition and reading fluency. Indeed, among at-risk first graders, the Fast Start students made twice the progress in letter and word recognition and two and a half times the progress in fluency (words read correctly per minute on a grade-appropriate passage) made by students in the control group, who received more traditional home involvement opportunities from the school.

Verbal and written survey information collected from the experimental group indicated generally positive perceptions of the program by parents. Comments from all Fast Start parents during the weekly telephone conferences indicated very little negative feeling toward the program. Most comments were quite positive or reflected minor concerns that were easily rectified.

## School-Based Implementation of Fast Start

Padak and Rasinski (2004a, 2004b) worked with K–1 teachers in an implementation of Fast Start in 18 elementary schools in an urban school district over the course of the 2002–2003 school year.

Kindergarten students were pre- and posttested using Clay's (2002) observational survey. Results indicated that children who were involved in Fast Start had significantly greater word vocabulary growth, attained concepts about print more quickly, and learned to identify uppercase and lowercase letters more quickly than students who did not participate in Fast Start.

First graders were pre- and posttested with the Developmental Reading Assessment (Beaver, 1997), a measure that incorporates authentic reading experiences. Analysis of scores for these children showed that students who were at least somewhat involved in Fast Start significantly outperformed their non–Fast Start counterparts. These results indicate that the Fast Start program was effective in increasing children's reading abilities, regardless of their measured ability at the beginning of the year. Remarkably, even being "somewhat" involved in Fast Start was enough to lead to significant achievement gains.

Analyses of surveys and interviews showed that children who participated in Fast Start were overwhelmingly positive about the experience. Children noted that they liked the content of the texts and enjoyed working with family members. Regarding content, one child said, "The poems were not hard or easy—they were just right." Children also enjoyed the word play activities.

Children firmly believed that Fast Start helped them become better readers. Their reasons for this belief centered in three areas:

- Challenging content: "Because they had lots of words I didn't know"; "The words were hard but now I'm reading."
- Encouraged reading development: "The harder it gets, the better you get"; "Because I couldn't read that much before and now I'm reading

a lot of stuff"; "Because they have hard words, and the more I read, the more I know."

- Encouraged interest in reading: "Because all of a sudden I sat down and started reading"; "I read them every day after school. Sometimes I write poems myself."

Parents' perceptions about Fast Start, gathered through surveys, were also very positive. Many parents commented about their children's and their own positive response to Fast Start: "The one-on-one time was nice"; "It gave him something to look forward to every night"; "I have always loved poetry. I see the same excitement in [my child] now"; "It brought us closer together."

Parents were also very positive about the impact that Fast Start had on their children's reading ability and on whether the time they devoted to Fast Start was well spent. With regard to the former, parents commented, "[My child] is eager to read now and without assistance"; "It seemed to help him with his fluency and expression"; "It has helped him recognize words and build confidence in reading." And about spending time in Fast Start, sample parent comments include the following: "To see your child read and want to read is priceless"; "This is a nice way for the family to spend time together"; "It allows for quality time."

In general, teachers believed that Fast Start time was well spent and that their students enjoyed the activity. Although teachers were less sure about academic benefits or about parents' responses, the empirical evidence suggested that they need not be concerned. Parents in this urban district found Fast Start worthwhile, and its value was validated in the children's growth in reading.

More recent implementations of Fast Start have demonstrated its effectiveness to school personnel. Reading specialist Frances Imperato (2009, 2011) has used Fast Start as the parent involvement program for kindergarten students in her school for 5 years. The Martin Luther King Elementary School in Edison, New Jersey, has a large population of students who are English language learners. Imperato's initial use of Fast Start with students was a success. All kindergarten classes had an increase in the number of students actually reading at the end of the school year over previous years. Moreover, classrooms with the highest level of participation in Fast Start had three times the number of students making significant gains in reading over classrooms where participation levels were lower. Based on 5 years of implementation, Imperato concludes that "without doubt, this family instructional routine, as well as others that involve real reading and word play between parents and children, have had a positive influence for literacy in my school" (Imperato, 2009, p. 344).

In the most recent year of Fast Start implementation Imperato (2010) found that 82% of kindergarten students ended the school year as readers. "Of particular note, parents of kindergarten students continue to stop me in the halls to let me know how much fun this program is and how it is helping them help their own children" (Imperato, 2010, p. 2).

## CONCLUSIONS

Our work with Fast Start convinces us that intensive and systematic parental involvement programs at the early childhood level and focused on critical areas of the reading are possible. In every implementation of Fast Start, students made progress in their reading achievement beyond what would normally have been expected. Moreover, the research we review here suggests that parents, children, and, to a lesser extent, teachers feel that Fast Start is an engaging activity for children and parents and a valuable tool for improving students' literacy. In an era in which parental involvement is widely advocated but poorly implemented in a systematic and ongoing manner, Fast Start presents schools and teachers with a wonderful opportunity to make strong inroads into the literacy achievement of children considered most at risk for failure in reading.

Fast Start is a program that does indeed work with children. It is not, however, the only program that might be developed and implemented with parents and children. Its design is based on an analysis of fundamental and critical aspects of literacy for beginning readers (i.e., decoding and fluency) and a consideration of features that are important for parental involvement. Fast Start is based on sound theory, research, and principles of instruction in literacy. Conceivably, other instructional programs for other groups of children and other areas of curriculum can be developed through a similar developmental process.

The essential question now is how to scale up Fast Start and other such promising programs to a level at which they will have a measurable and large-scale impact on the students' literacy development. This is not so much a question that can be answered through empirical research; rather, educational curriculum and policy development professionals must become advocates for home involvement programs.

Other questions regarding fluency and decoding instruction and home involvement deserve exploration. Can similar parental involvement programs be developed and implemented successfully beyond the primary grades? Would a program similar to Fast Start be successful as a summer education program, where the coordination with and support of the school may be less than optimal?

We also see important empirical questions related to the immediate application of Fast Start in the manifestations described in this chapter.

First, does Fast Start implementation in the primary grades have long-term consequences for student literacy development? Theoretically, the answer is "yes." Students who more quickly master the basic aspects of literacy development (word decoding and fluency) should be more ready to deal with the higher, more complex aspects of literacy (vocabulary and comprehension). Although theoretically compelling, such consequences have not been empirically tested.

A second question relates to the notion of teacher buy-in of a program such as Fast Start. Results from previous work highlighted in this chapter suggest that teachers have not been as enthusiastic about Fast Start as parents and students. This finding is troubling in that we are convinced that teachers are critical to the success of home involvement programs such as Fast Start. Teachers who are less committed to the successful implementation of programs such as Fast Start are less likely to realize the full potential of the program. We suspect that many teachers have not been fully prepared in their preservice and in-service education programs to work with parents, and that many have been frustrated by past experiences in trying to involve parents. Nevertheless, home involvement programs require the proactive support of teachers. We need to learn more about the impediments to teacher involvement and ways to support teachers in their work with parents in programs such as Fast Start.

In summary, it appears that Fast Start holds great promise for both parental involvement in reading and significant improvements in reading achievement for early childhood readers. For educators wishing to use Fast Start, we suggest a focus on those students who have minimal sight word vocabularies and minimal reading fluency development or who have experienced difficulty in acquiring these skills.

Since Fast Start seems quite effective for those students most at risk for reading failure, its use in kindergarten, first, and second grades may alleviate more serious reading difficulties and preclude the use of more costly reading interventions at higher grades. It may also help school districts comply with parent involvement and reading achievement mandates.

## REFERENCES

Beaver, J. (1997). *Developmental reading assessment*. Upper Saddle River, NJ: Pearson.

Chavkin, N. F. (Ed.). (1993). *Families and schools in a pluralistic society*. Albany: State University of New York Press.

Christenson, S. L. (1995). Best practices in supporting home collaboration. In A. Thomas & J. Grimes (Eds.), *Best practices in school psychology III* (pp. 253–267). Washington, DC: National Association of School Psychologists.

Clay, M. M. (2002). *An observational survey of early literacy in achievement* (2nd ed.). Portsmouth, NH: Heinemann.

Crimm, J. A. (1992). *Parent involvement and academic achievement: A meta-analysis.* Doctoral dissertation, University of Georgia, Athens.

Dowhower, S. L. (1994). Repeated reading revisited: Research into practice. *Reading and Writing Quarterly, 10,* 343–358.

Durkin, D. (1966). *Children who read early.* New York: Teachers College Press.

Eccles, J. S., & Harold, R. D. (1993). Parent–school involvement during the early adolescent years. *Teachers College Record, 94,* 568–587.

Epstein, J. L. (1989). Family structures and student motivation: A developmental perspective. In C. Ames & R. Ames (Eds.), *Research on motivation in education: Vol. 3. Goals and cognitions* (pp. 259–295). New York: Academic Press.

Epstein, J. L. (1994, October–November). *Perspectives and previews on research and policy for school, family, and community partnerships.* Paper presented at the Family–School Links Conference, Pennsylvania State University, University Park.

Epstein, J. L. (2001). Effect on student achievement of teacher's practices of parent involvement. In J. L. Epstein (Ed.), *School, family, and community partnerships: Preparing educators and improving schools* (pp. 221–235). Boulder, CO: Westview Press.

Henderson, A. (1988). Parents are a school's best friends. *Phi Delta Kappan, 70,* 148–153.

Henderson, A., & Berla, N. (Eds.). (1994). *A new generation of evidence: The family is critical to student achievement.* Washington, DC: National Committee for Citizens in Education.

Imperato, F. (2009). Getting parents and children off to a strong start in reading. *The Reading Teacher, 63*(4), 342–344.

Imperato, F. (2011). *2010–2011 Fast Start analysis.* Unpublished manuscript.

National Reading Panel. (2000). *Report of the National Reading Panel: Teaching children to read: Report of the subgroups.* Washington, DC: U.S. Department of Health and Human Services, National Institutes of Health.

Neidermeyer, F. C. (1970). Parents teach kindergartners at home. *Elementary School Journal, 70,* 439–445.

Padak, N., & Rasinski, T. (2004). Fast Start: A promising practice for family literacy programs. *Family Literacy Forum, 3*(2), 3–9.

Padak, N., & Rasinski, T. (2004). Fast Start: Successful literacy instruction that connects schools and homes. In J. A. R. Dugan, P. Linder, M. B. Sampson, & B. A. Brancato (Eds.), *Celebrating the power of literacy: Twenty-sixth yearbook of the College Reading Association yearbook* (pp. 11–23). Commerce, TX: College Reading Association.

Postlethwaite, T. N., & Ross, K. N. (1992). *Effective schools in reading: Implications for policy planners.* The Hague: International Association for the Evaluation of Educational Achievement.

Pressley, M. (2002). Effective beginning reading instruction. *Journal of Literacy Research, 34,* 165–188.

Rasinski, T. V. (1989). Reading and the empowerment of parents. *Reading Teacher, 34*, 226–231.

Rasinski, T. V. (1995). Fast Start: A parental involvement reading program for primary grade students. In W. M. Linek & E. G. Sturtevant (Eds.), *Generations of literacy: Seventeenth yearbook of the College Reading Association.* Harrisonburg, VA: College Reading Association.

Rasinski, T. V. (2003). Parental involvement: Key to leaving no child behind in reading. *New England Reading Association Journal, 39*, 1–5.

Rasinski, T. V.,, Padak, N., & Fawcett, G. (2010). *Teaching children who find reading difficult* (4th ed.). Upper Saddle River, NJ: Prentice-Hall.

Rasinski, T. V., Padak, N. D., Linek, W. L., & Sturtevant, E. (1994). Effects of fluency development on urban second-grade readers. *Journal of Educational Research, 87*, 158–165.

Rasinski, T. V., & Stevenson, B. (2005). The effects of Fast Start reading: A fluency-based home involvement reading program, on the reading achievement of beginning readers. *Reading Psychology, 26*, 109–125.

Topping, K. J. (1996). Tutoring systems for family literacy. In S. Wolfendale & K. Topping (Eds.), *Family involvement in literacy: Effective partnerships in education.* London: Cassel.

U.S. Department of Education. (1994). *Strong families, strong schools: Building community partnerships for learning.* Washington, DC: Author.

# 15

# Reading Fluency and Comprehension in English Language Learners

Kristin Lems

The phrase "the same, but different" (Lems, Miller, & Soro, 2010) aptly captures the complexity of the fluency construct for English language learners (ELLs). On the one hand, research establishing the validity of oral reading performance scores for ELLs is inconsistent; on the other hand, there is abundant support for using fluency instruction to support ELL reading development (e.g., Pluck, 2006; Taguchi, Takayasu-Maass, & Gorsuch, 2004). In addition, there are benefits to implementing fluency practice for ELLs, such as increases in confidence, understanding of prosody and chunking, increases in reading rate, and enhanced phonological awareness as well as implicit learning. These go well beyond the abundant benefits enjoyed by native speakers of English.

Because literacy is developing side by side with English language acquisition, fluency is situated somewhat differently in the literacy development of ELLs, but it is still consequential. This chapter explores the ways in which fluency in the context of teaching ELLs parallels or differs from fluency with native English speakers and ways in which fluency reflects and supports ELL literacy development.

## FLUENCY AND COMPREHENSION

We know very well by now that oral reading fluency scores have a robust relationship with silent reading comprehension for native speakers of English (e.g., Deno, Marston, Shinn, & Tindal, 1983; Deno, Mirkin, & Chiang, 1982; Fuchs, Fuchs, & Maxwell, 1988; Hintze, Shapiro, & Conte, 1997; Kuhn & Stahl, 2003; Shinn, Knutson, Good, Tilly, & Collins, 1992). There is also research to support the validity of using oral reading scores of ELLs as a measure of their reading comprehension. Baker and Good (1995), for example, found curriculum-based oral reading scores of second-grade bilingual Hispanic students correlated as well as the scores of native English speakers with reading comprehension measures. Ramirez (2001) found higher correlations between oral reading and silent reading comprehension measures for fifth-grade Spanish-speaking ELLs than for silent reading comprehension and several other measures. Vanderwood, Linklater, and Healy (2008) found correlations of .60 ($p \leq .01$) for 134 third-grade native Spanish-speaking ELLs for 1-minute oral readings and scores on a California statewide reading test.

However, other studies report lower levels of correlation. McTague, Lems, Butler, and Carmona (Chapter 17, this volume) found correlations of .359 ($p \leq .01$) between elementary Spanish-speaking ELL oral reading scores and their performance on an Illinois standardized reading test. And Lems (2004) found only a moderate correlation between the oral reading and silent reading comprehension of literate adults from a variety of first-language backgrounds. These studies are small, however, and reliability and validity studies of ELL students have not been disaggregated on large-scale oral reading assessment studies such as the AIMSweb (Shinn & Shinn, 2002) and Read Naturally (*www.readnaturally.com*), although both programs state that ELL performance was included in their research.

Regardless of these differences, a parallel that runs across all the data is that, consistently, increases in reading level are matched by increases in oral reading scores for both native English speakers and ELLs (e.g., Fuchs, Fuchs, Hosp, & Jenkins, 2001; Lems, 2004).

## AFFECTIVE FILTER

Oral reading has been a component of literacy instruction in the classroom setting for many years, but its use is fraught with complexities, and oral reading in the classroom has long been controversial (Allington, 1984). One of the main reasons for the controversy is the stressful atmosphere it creates for some students. For all students, but especially for ELLs, being asked to read a passage out loud, particularly one that has not been seen before, can be traumatic. This is exacerbated if the reading is also being used as an assessment (for example, when a teacher is standing by with a stopwatch). Other problems may be that passages considered to be at the reader's grade level may be at his or her frustration level instead, ensuring failure. Also, learners may be self-conscious in the presence of their peers.

In addition to these universally unnerving features, ELLs have the anxiety of having to pronounce words in a language they are just learning. In the field of second-language teaching, a key concept is the importance of lowering the affective filter, or anxiety level (Krashen, 1985). In fact, learner self-consciousness about saying words in a new language may be part of a silent period (Krashen, 1985), which learners often go through in the early stages of second-language acquisition, but which might also extend into prolonged reticence to speak.

In addition, ELLs can easily get tripped up by lack of background knowledge about something in the passage. Teachers report that oral reading passages often make cultural assumptions about family structure, vacations, holidays, pets, and other topics that are difficult for some ELLs to infer (Lems, personal communication, April 24, 2011). Proper nouns that ELLs have never heard in spoken form can be especially problematic. Adult ELL students in one oral reading study, for example, repeatedly miscued on the word "Indianapolis," often making four or five attempts before moving on. Usually, after multiple tries, the word was still finally deducted as a miscue (Lems, 2004).

In addition, even when ELLs get to the point that they can decode and pronounce well and understand the words they are reading, the mental engagement required is considerably heavier than it would be for native speakers because processing the words has not reached a level of automaticity. The combination of self-consciousness and the mental strenuousness involved in decoding and pronouncing words from an unfamiliar passage can create a "perfect storm" and turn students' affective filters into an impenetrable barricade. With that in mind, therefore, the benefits that may come from taking measures of ELLs' oral reading, at least in the early stages, may be offset by the additional stresses on their affective filter.

In addition to these variations, there are three confounding features that affect the validity of assessment scores of ELLs' oral reading: foreign accent, first-language writing system, and difficulty performing several tasks simultaneously. These three factors may help account for the lower correlations found in a number of studies of ELL oral reading.

## FOREIGN ACCENT

Linguists Labov and Baker (2010) studied the reading miscues of diverse urban children in several U.S. states, and found that word readings judged as incorrect were sometimes based on interference from dialect or foreign accent and not necessarily true reading errors. When an English sound is not found in students' first languages, they may mispronounce an English word even though they know it. For example, an Urdu-speaking ELL may pronounce the word *went* as *vent* because the /w/ sound isn't found in Urdu and the /v/ sound is the phoneme closest to it. Most miscue rubrics would count that word as a substitution and deduct it from the number of correct words read; however, the rubric fails to capture the possibility that the student knows the word but pronounces it in an accent or dialect. Raters need training in both linguistics and reading to be able to distinguish true reading errors from mispronunciations when listening to the oral reading of ELLs. In fact, some very proficient ELLs will never lose their foreign accents, and some will also never read aloud expressively.

## FIRST-LANGUAGE WRITING SYSTEM

When students are literate in languages that use a different writing system from the Roman alphabet, which is used for English, their oral reading rate, accuracy, and expression are likely to be affected. Lems (2004) found no correlation between English oral and silent reading scores for native speakers of Mandarin, which has a logographic writing system, but moderate correlations for Spanish- and Polish-speaking students, whose languages share an alphabet with English, even though the students' silent reading comprehension levels were in the same range. The study supported the notion that the proximity of the first-language writing system to the English writing system influences how easily students learn to read aloud in English. If the first-language writing system resembles English, it will have a facilitating effect on English oral reading, but if the writing system is dissimilar to English or has a different correspondence of sounds and letters, there may be interference. As a result, the oral reading of these learners may not be a good proxy for their silent reading comprehension.

## PERFORMING SEVERAL TASKS SIMULTANEOUSLY

Rasinski notes, in a fluency article not focused on ELLs, that, during oral reading, "readers often channel their attention and cognitive energy into decoding and allocate little attention to understanding the passage" (1990, p. 41). This is especially true for a cold reading of a previously unseen passage. Because of this channeling of attention, it is hard to get an accurate idea of readers' comprehension after they have performed a cold oral reading. The researchers in the 1980s and 1990s who developed curriculum-based measures of oral reading in hopes of finding quick, classroom-centered ways to check on reading processes of young readers never used oral reading performances to assess reading comprehension (e.g., Deno, 1985; Deno et al., 1982, 1983). The comprehension measures were taken from completely separate sources, such as reading tests, cloze exercises, or written or oral retellings of silently read passages. Students were never asked to answer questions about a passage they had just read aloud. Nevertheless, the practice of asking students to read a passage aloud and then answer questions about it—sometimes referred to as "fluency practice"—has become common in many schools. Such lessons may consist of asking children to read an unknown passage aloud, often without regard to their reading level, timing them, and then asking them to immediately answer comprehension questions about it. Sometimes they are even rated for "expressiveness" at the same time!

This does not conform to the literature validating fluency assessment and is not based on the same assumptions as the original research. When fluency instructional methods contain a comprehension component, using such techniques as paired reading or repeated reading, there can be positive effects on reading proficiency (Topping, 2001). However, using fluency as an instructional technique is not the same as using it as a reading test.

It is important to understand this distinction because teachers of ELLs express surprise that their students are able to accurately read a passage aloud but are not able to demonstrate comprehension of what they have just read. This is a remarkably normal phenomenon, especially for students whose English reading comprehension is still developing. Although some comprehension may be constructed during oral reading of a passage, the primary focus is on performing the oral reading. Even if students can grasp the general topic of the reading, they are not likely to be able to easily construct answers to the questions on the spot (Lems, Miller, & Soro, 2010).

The salient point here is not that students should never read aloud or that they should never be expected to answer questions about a passage they have just read aloud. Rather, it is that reading aloud will look different for ELLs, both in the performance of the reading and in their ability to answer questions about it, and care should be taken in interpreting oral reading by ELLs using the same assumptions as for native English speakers.

## FLUENCY INSTRUCTION: BENEFITS FOR ELLs AND CLASSROOM IMPLEMENTATION

With all the cautions about oral reading assessment of ELLs taken into consideration, we move to the other branch of the topic: fluency instruction. Fluency practice offers a number of distinct benefits for ELLs, and some of these even surpass the benefits enjoyed by native speakers (Hiebert & Fisher, 2006; Pluck, 2006). In addition to benefits to the students, teachers can gain valuable insights about an ELL's current English acquisition level from listening to him or her read aloud and can then differentiate instruction accordingly. If there is consistent vowel interference from the learner's first language heard in the reading, for example, the teacher can provide a targeted mini-lesson to practice the selected English vowel sounds.

Specific benefits to engaging in fluency instruction with ELLs, with suggestions for classroom instruction that addresses each of the benefits are discussed in the following sections.

## Confidence and Motivation

Fluency practice builds self-confidence. Children who have the opportunity to listen to or practice passages multiple times, whether for a performance, a home-school program with audiotapes, or through partner reading (Goldsmith-Conley & Barbour, 2004), develop more self-confidence as readers (Koskinen, Blum, Tennant, Parker, Straub, & Curry, 1995). Fluency practice is especially helpful to students for whom decoding in English is still an unfamiliar enterprise. The sheer repetition of the words builds automaticity, and this increases confidence. Practicing and then successfully performing an oral reading passage can build the habit of success and help lower the affective filter, which, in so doing, opens the gate to greater learning (Krashen, 1985).

### Classroom Implementation

To build self-confidence, students might sing along chorally with the karaoke version of a song, perform a poem, or engage in Readers Theatre (Rasinski, Ackland, Fawcett, & Lems, 2011). Readers Theatre is a natural way to build confidence because it involves repeated reading and mastery of a script. The characters in Readers Theatre scripts are often colorful, with short, dramatic lines perfect for ELLs. The short, dramatic parts allow students to focus on developing expressive reading rather than worrying about decoding a lot of words, and they also contain a lot of lively language, such as idioms, figures of speech, and humor. Knowing these phrases and practicing saying them builds learner confidence.

## Chunking and Prosody

Fluency activities give ELL readers practice in developing two important reading competencies: chunking and prosody. Chunking (sometimes called parsing) is the ability to separate and combine words into meaningful phrase units. It requires knowledge of syntax, and it is part of the language system native speakers acquire beginning in infancy through immersion in a language. When children begin to learn to read, they apply their mental framework about how words are supposed to sound when they are grouped together in phrases to the reading of written words. When children have not been immersed in a language they are learning to read, they need additional practice in hearing, seeing, and saying the phrases of the new language. The more they hear, read, and say the phrases, the better they will be able to follow complex sentence patterns in English and ultimately write them. Fluency activities provide a great medium to do that.

Prosody is slightly different from chunking. Chunking is the ability to group words together into grammatically logical phrases, whereas prosody involves expressing the nuances of the phrases through voice tone. Prosody includes the set of vocal patterns and inflections that people use when speaking and reading aloud. Each language has a different set of prosodic patterns. In English, the most important words in a phrase are longer, louder, and higher pitched, and this underscores their importance. Prosody also includes pausing, intonation patterns, word lengthening, and interpretive features such as "getting into character" for certain roles through varying intonation, pausing for emphasis, or altering pronunciation to provide sociocultural information about the character. The interpretive features are often referred to as "expressive" features. Although it is difficult to evaluate the exact components of expressiveness in oral reading because of its subjective nature, Johnson and Moore (1997) found a moderate but significant relationship between the reading comprehension scores of ELLs and how native-like their pausing behaviors sounded when reading English text aloud.

### Classroom Implementation

ELLs may lack background knowledge about how the expressive features of a written text might sound. To help bridge the gap, teachers of ELLs need to do extensive modeling of expressive reading through interactive read-alouds (Trelease, 2006). Furthermore, recorded books, with a variety of reader voices, can help supplement teacher modeling. When students read along silently with a text that is being read orally, it helps them create associations between the look and sound of the words, phrases, and punctuation marks. Hearing multiple voices also helps train the reader in understanding English spoken in several different styles and dialects. Modeling and oral reading practice may also exert a positive influence on ELLs' overall pronunciation and speaking fluency.

## Reading Rate

People read more slowly in a second language than in their first language, and below a certain rate, it is next to impossible for readers to keep up with an academic curriculum (Anderson, 1999; Birch, 2007; Rasinski, 2000). Anderson calls this slow journey through text a "marathon of frustration" (p. 4). Such frustration can deter readers from persevering to the point of becoming proficient enough in reading to succeed in their academic goals. ELLs benefit from opportunities to learn to increase their reading rate so that they can function successfully in school and in the workplace. In addition, being able to read at a faster rate allows more text to be held in working memory—the temporary storage area we use to hold images and sounds as we move across text (Breznitz & Share, 1992). As more words are able to be held in working memory, comprehension of larger phrase units can occur, and reading comprehension increases.

### Classroom Implementation

Rate practices might involve doing timed repeated readings, both oral or silent, charting progress on a graph, or rereading until reaching a certain target rate. Anderson (1999) enumerates a number of rate-building activities for adolescent and adult learners. For younger learners, fluency centers can be set up in classrooms. Each station of the fluency center contains a set of graded readings at different difficulty levels with numbered lines, blank rate charts for students to complete on which they record the name of each passage and their beginning and ending scores in words read per minute, a folder to hold their charts, and a stopwatch. Children visit the fluency center regularly, read each passage four times, and mark their progress for each successive reading on a chart. Students enjoy charting their own scores and seeing their progress. Older learners can also chart their fluency progress and may use readings from their subject expertise for practice. In addition, computer-scored passages are now available for not only assessment but also rate-building instructional purposes (e.g., Rainbow Reading Programme: *www.rainbowreading.co.nz*, Read Naturally: *www.readnaturally.com*). Of course, a fluency instructional program should never focus on rate building as a replacement for comprehension; it is only one part, similar to practicing scales in music as a component of larger musicianship.

## Phonological Decoding

Pronouncing written words, or phonological decoding, is a vital skill for beginning readers. The ability to decode and pronounce words is one of the most powerful predictors of reading success, even as early as first grade (e.g., Share & Stanovich, 1995; Torgeson & Burgess, 1998; Wagner, Torgeson, & Rashotte, 1994). In fact, this core competence crosses languages and includes languages with many kinds of orthographies. Second-language acquisition researcher Koda calls phonological decoding "the most indispensable competence for reading acquisition in all languages" (2005, p. 34) because even for proficient readers, having a good phonological representation of a word helps us retrieve it from working memory. Phonological decoding is a core literacy skill (Koda, 2005).

### Classroom Implementation

Audio-assisted reading is a great way to practice phonological decoding for ELLs because they can use both sight and sound to figure out the appearance, sound, and meaning of words. Also, texts can be divided into lines to show phrase boundaries, the way a poem looks on a page. This method provides visual assistance for students at an emergent level as they become familiar with how phrases are divided. Later, students can read along quietly with a CD or quietly mumble read (read below their breath). The technique of audio-assisted repeated reading has shown dramatic results in fluency programs for ELLs in Australia and beyond (Pluck, 2006).

## Implicit Learning

Finally, fluency instruction fosters implicit learning (Nation, 2007). Implicit learning can be considered the gradual accretion of important literacy concepts over time. It might be considered the mortar that holds the individual skills together. It is nurtured by practicing language "form and process over a long period of time" (Grabe, 2010, p. 73). Like any very important indirect skill, it is not easily captured with one kind of metric. However, implicit learning may be the tipping point that determines a syndrome of success or failure. Implicit learning is a byproduct of a well-organized, language-rich classroom.

### Classroom Implementation

A program of fluency instruction that fosters implicit learning takes place over a period of time, implemented at the beginning of the academic year and conducted faithfully throughout. The most important fluency instruction for this metaskill is not oral reading but rather extensive reading, which is silent reading practice (Krashen, 2004). Fluency instruction can be incorporated into silent reading through repeated reading and comprehension-checking activities (Grabe, 2010, p. 73). Repeated reading (Samuels, 1979) is a widely-used and effective reading strategy that has been shown to have positive benefits on both the rate and comprehension of ELLs (Grabe, 2010; Taguchi et al., 2004). Each time they reread, students figure out a few more words and phrases and have a deeper understanding of the meaning of the text. When repeated reading is structured into classroom fluency instruction, whether orally or silently, it positively affects rate, vocabulary development, and reading comprehension. Additionally, it helps build stamina in the reader.

## FINAL THOUGHTS

Because the oral reading of ELLs provides different information about their English language reading development than it does for native speakers of English, oral reading scores should be considered as formative assessments and used for progress monitoring only. It is especially important not to hold ELLs to native speaker expectations for prosody, or expressive reading. When fluency measures are taken for ELLs, they should be assessed using scales that factor in their level of English language acquisition, not scales used for native speakers (Birch, 2007). It is also important to check passages for hidden cultural assumptions. At the same time, ELLs' oral reading rate and accuracy should improve over time, just as it does for native speakers, and lack of oral reading progress in English should be carefully noted. Teachers with a class of students from mixed language backgrounds should plan to provide greater opportunities for those students who need more practice in English decoding in order to get their reading to a level of automaticity comparable to that of their classmates.

Fluency practice in the classroom is compatible with all of the best practices for ELL pedagogy, so long as it provides for adequate modeling, plenty of practice time, and keeping the affective filter low. The best thing about fluency instruction is that there are many ways to structure in student success, and success builds on itself, creating a positive feedback cycle. Whether one chooses audio-assisted reading, self-timed repeated reading, partner reading, Readers' Theatre, karaoke, poetry, or song performances, there is something for everyone to enjoy, a real win–win situation. Good luck!

## REFERENCES

Allington, R. (1984). Oral reading. In P. D. Pearson, R. Barr, M. L. Kamil, & P. Mosenthal (Eds.), *Handbook of reading research* (pp. 829–864). Mahwah, NJ: Erlbaum.

Anderson, N. (1999). *Exploring second language reading: Issues and strategies.* Boston: Heinle & Heinle.

Baker, S. K., & Good, R. (1995). Curriculum-based measurement of English reading with bilingual Hispanic students: A validation study with second-grade students. *School Psychology Review, 24*(4), 561–578.

Birch, B. M. (2007). *English L2 reading: Getting to the bottom* (2nd ed.). Mahwah, NJ: Erlbaum.

Breznitz, Z., & Share, D. L. (1992). The effects on accelerated reading rate on memory of text. *Journal of Educational Psychology, 87,* 193–197.

Deno, S. L. (1985). Curriculum-based measurement: The emerging alternative. *Exceptional Children, 52,* 219–232.

Deno, S. L., Marston, D., Shinn, M., & Tindal, G. (1983). Oral reading fluency: A simple datum for scaling reading disability. *Topics in Learning and Learning Disabilities, 2,* 53–59.

Deno, S. L., Mirkin, P. K., & Chiang, B. (1982). Identifying valid measures of reading. *Exceptional Children, 49,* 36–45.

Fuchs, L. S., Fuchs, D., Hosp, M., & Jenkins, J. R. (2001). Oral reading fluency as an indicator of reading competence: A theoretical, empirical, and historical analysis. *Scientific Studies of Reading, 5*(3), 239–256.

Fuchs, L. S., Fuchs, D., & Maxwell, L. (1988). The validity of informal reading comprehension measures. *Remedial and Special Education, 9*(2), 20–29.

Goldsmith-Conley, E., & Barbour, J. (2004). Timed partner reading: A practical technique for fluency instruction? *Illinois Reading Council Journal, 36*(3), 33–41.

Grabe, W. (2010). Fluency in reading—thirty five years late. *Reading in a Foreign Language, 22*(1), 71–83.

Hiebert, E. H., & Fisher, C. W. (2006). Fluency from the first: What works with first graders. In T. Rasinski, C. Blachowicz, & K. Lems (Eds.), *Fluency instruction: Research-based best practices* (pp. 279–294). New York: Guilford Press.

Hintze, J., Shapiro, E., & Conte, K. L. (1997). Oral reading fluency and authentic reading material: Criterion validity of the technical features of CBM survey-level assessment. *School Psychology Review, 26*(4), 535–553.

Johnson, R., & Moore, R. (1997). A link between reading proficiency and native-like use of pausing in speaking. *Applied Language Learning, 8*(1), 25–42.

Koda, K. (2005). *Insights into second language reading: A cross linguistic approach.* Cambridge, UK: Cambridge University Press.

Koskinen, P. S., Blum, I. H., Tennant, N., Parker, E. M., Straub, M. W., & Curry, C. (1995). Have you heard any good books lately?: Encouraging shared reading at home with books and audiotapes. In L. M. Morrow (Ed.), *Family literacy: Connections in schools and communities* (pp. 87–103). Newark, DE: International Reading Association.

Krashen, S. (1985). *The input hypothesis.* Beverly Hills, CA: Laredo.

Krashen, S. (2004). *The power of reading: Insights from the research* (2nd ed.). Portsmouth, NH: Heinemann.

Kuhn, M. R., & Stahl, S. (2003). Fluency: A review of developmental and remedial practices. *Journal of Educational Psychology, 95*(1), 3–21.

Labov, W., & Baker, B. (2010). What is a reading error? *Applied Psycholinguistics, 31*(4), 735–757.

Lems, K. (2004). *Adult ESL oral reading fluency and silent reading comprehension.* Unpublished doctoral dissertation, National College of Education.

Lems, K., Miller, L. D., & Soro, T. S. (2010). *Reading in a new language: Linguistic considerations.* New York: Guilford Press.

Nation, I. S. P. (2007). The four strands. *Innovation in Language Learning and Teaching, 1*(1), 1–12.

Pluck, M. (2006). "Jonathon is 11 but reads like a struggling 7-year-old": Providing assistance for struggling readers with a tape-assisted reading program. In T. Rasinski, C. Blachowicz, & K. Lems (Eds.), *Fluency instruction: Research-based best practices* (pp. 192–208). New York: Guilford Press.

Ramirez, C. M. (2001). *An investigation of English language and reading skills on reading comprehension for Spanish-speaking English language learners.* Unpublished doctoral dissertation, University of Oregon.

Rasinski, T. V. (1990). Investigating measures of reading fluency. *Educational Research Quarterly, 14*(3), 37–44.

Rasinski, T. V. (2000). Speed does matter in reading. *The Reading Teacher, 54*(2), 146–151.

Rasinski, T. V., Ackland, R., Fawcett, G., & Lems, K. (2011). *The fluent reader in action: A close-up look into 15 diverse classrooms, grades 5 and up.* New York: Scholastic.

Samuels, S. J. (1979). The method of repeated readings. *The Reading Teacher, 32,* 403–408.

Share, D. L., & Stanovich, K. E. (1995). Cognitive processes in early reading development: Accommodating individual differences into a model of acquisition. In J. S. Carlson (Ed.), *Issues in education: Contributions from psychology* (Vol. I, pp. 1–57). Greenwich, CT: JAI Press.

Shinn, M. R., Knutson, N., Good, R. H., Tilly, W. D., & Collins, V. (1992). Curriculum-based measurement of oral reading fluency: A confirmatory analysis of its relation to reading. *School Psychology Review, 21,* 459–479.

Shinn, M. R., & Shinn, M. M. (2002). *AIMSweb training notebook.* Eden Prairie, MN: Edformation.

Taguchi, E., Takayasu-Maass, M., & Gorsuch, G. J. (2004). Developing reading fluency in EFL: How assisted repeated reading and extensive reading affect fluency development. *Reading in a Foreign Language, 16*(2) 70–96.

Topping, K. J. (2001). *Thinking reading writing: A practical guide to paired learning with peers, parents and volunteers.* New York: Continuum.

Torgeson, J. K., & Burgess, S. R. (1998). In J. L. Metsala & L. C. Ehri (Eds.), *Word recognition in beginning literacy* (pp. 3–40). Mahwah, NJ: Erlbaum.

Trelease, J. (2006). *The read-aloud handbook* (6th ed.). New York: Penguin.

Vanderwood, M. L., Linklater, D., & Healy, K. (2008). Nonsense word fluency and future literacy performance for English language learners. *School Psychology Review, 37*(1), 5–17.

Wagner, R. G., Torgeson, J. K., & Rashotte, C. A. (1994). The development of reading-related phonological processing abilities: New evidence of biodirectional causality from a latent variable longitudinal study. *Developmental Psychology, 30,* 73–87.

# 16

# Fluency Instruction in Reading in a Second or Foreign Language

Etsuo Taguchi
Greta Gorsuch

## WHAT FLUENCY IS AND WHY IT IS CRITICAL FOR SUCCESSFUL READING

For the past decade, reading fluency has been a focal issue in English as a first language (L1) settings (e.g., Kuhn & Stahl, 2003; National Reading Panel, 2000; Rasinski, Blachowicz, & Lems, 2006; Samuels & Farstrup, 2006). More recently, it has also become one of the main topics in English as a second language (L2) settings (e.g., Grabe, 2009, 2010; Grabe & Stoller, 2002; Nation, 2009). There seems to be an increasing consensus among reading researchers and educators that the basic constituents of reading fluency are accuracy, automaticity, and use of appropriate prosody (e.g., Dowhower, 1989, 1994; Herman, 1985; Kuhn & Stahl, 2003), though some differences remain in how much emphasis is put on each of these elements (Kuhn, Schwanenflugel, & Meisinger, 2010).

Two major characteristics of the fluency construct that we wish to focus on in the context of L2 or foreign language (FL) settings are accuracy and automaticity. At the beginning stage of reading skills development, readers tend to sacrifice speed in order to be as accurate as possible in identifying letters, letter combinations, and words. That process of form identification, however, gradually gets faster and more accurate as learners' skills develop. Processes are considered to be automatic when they possess four properties: speed, effortlessness, autonomy, and unconsciousness (Kuhn et al., 2010, pp. 231–232; Schneider, Dumais, & Shiffrin, 1984, p. 1; Segalowitz, 2003, 2010, p. 78). That is, a cognitive process that is automatic is performed accurately and fast. At the same time, readers who engage in automatic processes feel no sense of struggle while performing automaticity-related tasks such as word recognition. A process can be said to run automatically when readers start to perform it without realizing, and it is even difficult for them to stop doing it once it gets started. At a movie theater, for example, learners may watch a foreign movie with subtitles in their native language. They will often find themselves reading the subtitles of that movie at the bottom of a screen as soon as they are displayed, and this happens even when they themselves are not aware that they are reading the subtitles. Reading the subtitles is automatic in the sense that learners cannot stop themselves from starting reading them once displayed on the screen, and also that they are not aware that they are engaged in reading them.

Automatic word recognition is vital to the construct of fluency and to the role fluency plays in the comprehension of text (e.g., Samuels, 2004, 2006). Fluent readers with automatic word recognition skills recognize almost every word in the text rapidly, accurately, and effortlessly. They are able to direct ample cognitive attentional resources to comprehension by liberating themselves from word recognition tasks. In contrast, disfluent readers have to expend most of their cognitive attention on identifying words, and the remaining cognitive resources available to be allocated to comprehension are accordingly limited. As a result, such readers' comprehension suffers (e.g., LaBerge & Samuels, 1974; Samuels, 1994, 2004, 2006; Perfetti, 1985; Stanovich, 1991, 1992).

## DIFFERENCES IN WORD RECOGNITION IN READING IN A FIRST AND A SECOND LANGUAGE

Generally, readers' word recognition skills are faster in a first language than in an L2 or FL, and such a gap reflects the degree of automaticity they have achieved in each language through exposure to print. For complex cognitive skills such as are involved in language use, achieving a recognized level of expertise may require up to 10,000 hours of practice (Charness, Krampe, & Mayr, 1996; Ericsson & Charness, 1994; Ericsson, Krampe, & Tesch-Römer, 1993). In the case of L1 development, a child will have performed such an amount of communication activity by age 4 or 5 as a native speaker of a language. That much time for communication practice, however, is rarely available to more mature L2 or FL learners unless they are fully immersed in an L2 environment (Segalowitz, 2003, p. 401). This limitation of practice or exposure time is usually the case with adult or adolescent L2, and particularly FL, learners across the globe.

Evidence for the detrimental effect of this paucity of practice can be found in the results of early studies that investigated a lack of automaticity in lower identification skills of letter and word recognition processes in L2 and FL learners. Oller and Tullius (1973), for example, compared the mean duration of eye fixation between L1 and L2 readers and found that English L2 readers with more than 70% comprehension on their levelwise reading materials fixate longer than English L1 readers. The L1 readers' norms were taken from an earlier study by Taylor (1966) involving over 12,000 native speakers of English. Since the duration of eye fixation presumably represents information-processing time (Rayner, 1978), L2 readers needed more time to process textual information than L1 readers. Moreover, Hatch, Polin, and Part (1974) found that, whereas English L1 readers paid more selective attention to content words, L2 readers equally attended to content *and* grammatical function words such as prepositions. They also found that L2 readers were more likely to miss graphic cues that carry prosodic information, such as commas and periods.

In a series of studies on bilingual processing, Segalowitz and his colleagues have shown two characteristics that are specific to automatic processes: the ballistic (unstoppable) nature of automaticity and the stable nature of automaticity. To demonstrate; Favreau and Segalowitz (1983) compared two groups of English and French L1 bilingual individuals who were learning French and English as an L2, respectively, using a lexical decision task. The two groups were reconstituted as one group whose reading rate difference between their L1 and L2 was less than 10% (262 vs. 275 words per minute) and a second group whose reading rate difference was more than 10% between their L1 and L2 (318 vs. 234 words per minute). While differing in reading rate, both reading rate difference groups nonetheless had equal listening and reading comprehension skills. Favreau and Segalowitz found that, in the L1 condition and in short prime-target intervals of 200 milliseconds, both the equal-reading-rate bilingual group and the unequal-reading-rate bilingual group exhibited a facilitation effect for semantically related words (e.g., *BIRD-ROBIN*). In addition, in the L2 condition and in the short prime-target intervals, a facilitation effect was found for both groups, although the effect was weaker for the unequal-reading-rate bilingual group than for the equal-reading-rate bilingual group. This shows the strong contribution of the unstoppable nature of automaticity in the processing of L2 targets by the equal-reading-rate group and the significantly weaker contribution in the processing of L2 targets by the unequal-reading-rate group.

In addition, Segalowitz, Poulsen, and Komoda (1991) found that some highly fluent adult French–English bilingual individuals read at a rate that was as much as 30% slower in their L2 than in their L1. The findings from these two studies indicated that even bilingual individuals who had good listening and comprehension skills in both L1 and L2 still lacked automaticity in word recognition skills in their L2, which further suggests that it takes a considerable amount of time for L2 readers to achieve automaticity.

Moreover, Segalowitz and Segalowitz (1993; see also Segalowitz, Segalowitz, & Wood, 1998) have further proposed the use of an index that assesses the degree of automaticity development. As a skill develops, its execution becomes faster and the variability with which the skill is executed is reduced. The coefficient of variability (CV) is defined as the ratio of the standard deviation to the mean reaction time for each individual. Segalowitz and Segalowitz suggested that the index can be used to assess whether skill processing is undergoing qualitative change. This is because with simple speeding up of skill processing the CV score does not change. But with the qualitative restructuring that accompanies both speeding up and decreased variability it will change to show the development of a stable automaticity.

Obviously, efficient word identification processing and other such lower level skills cannot be the sole foundation of good reading comprehension. Background knowledge and higher order comprehension skills also facilitate readers' good comprehension performance (e.g., Anderson & Pearson, 1984; Carrell & Eisterhold, 1983). Still, building automaticity in the lower level processes of reading is essential because it is unlikely that good readers lack well-developed word recognition skills (e.g., LaBerge & Samuels, 1974; Perfetti, 1985; Samuels, 2004, 2006; Segalowitz et al., 1998; Stanovich, 1986, Stanovich, Cunningham, & West, 1981). Efficient lower level processing skills are essential for L2 or FL readers. Because of inefficiency in these skills, reading in an L2 or FL is usually slow and laborious (Anderson, 1999; Jensen, 1986; Segalowitz et al., 1991). Furthermore, this dilemma may create motivational problems for L2 and FL learners in regard to utilizing reading as a significant source of linguistic input, a critical issue in settings where reading may constitute the sole source of linguistic input available to learners in a non-English-speaking setting (Gebhard, 1996; Redfield, 1999; see further discussion on this topic later). Day and Bamford (1998) note that it is only through the actual reading experience that L2 and FL readers can acquire the complex linguistic, world, and topical knowledge needed to improve their reading skills (p. 19). Therefore, for theoretical and pedagogical reasons, L2 and FL researchers and educators indicate the need to find effective methods to help L2 and FL learners develop their reading fluency (Day & Bamford, 1998; Grabe, 1991, 2004, 2009, 2010; Nation, 2009; Silberstein, 1994).

## PEDAGOGICAL RESPONSES OF L2 AND FL EDUCATION TO READING FLUENCY

It can be argued that fluency development has not been a priority in L2 and FL education globally. Until fairly recently, "reading" in L2 and FL settings has been construed as a means to introduce and practice vocabulary and grammar, often at the sentence level (Bernhardt, 1991, 2011; Carr & Pauwels, 2006). If longer texts were used in English as a foreign language (EFL) and other L2/FL classes both abroad and in the United States, it would be in an intensive reading situation, in which, for even high-proficiency beginning students, difficult literary or expository texts might be dissected or translated into the first language for discussion of the finer points of their vocabulary, grammar, and cultural content (Amer, 1997; Chen, 2006; Nation, 2009). Arguably, the situation is not much changed today. Many current FL textbooks in the United States have "reading" texts, which are carefully contrived from the vocabulary and grammar and themes of a given chapter and which are largely ignored by instructors and students alike (Bernhardt, 2011; Swaffar & Arens, 2005). Needless to say, the reading processes and practices and habits we try to encourage in L1 readers are not central components of many FL and L2 adult classes, as in Bell (2001, p. 3): "Texts are often treated as vehicles for the presentation, practice, manipulation, and consolidation of language points, rather than the encouragement of reading itself."

This is not to say that there has been a lack of interest on the part of L2/FL pedagogues and researchers to promote reading for enjoyment, sustained silent reading, independent reading, or whatever label is used (e.g., Bell, 2001; Mason & Krashen, 1997; Masuhara, Kimura, Fukada, & Takeuchi, 1996; Robb & Susser, 1989; Yang, 2007). Part of this impetus has been the highly publicized theory that comprehensible input in the target language is necessary for acquisition (Bochner & Bochner, 2009; Krashen, 1985, 1987, 1988, 1995). For many, particularly those working in EFL settings, the lack of L2 input was critical in that young Japanese, Chinese, or Moroccan learners of English would rarely meet English-speaking foreigners, or hear English, or have access to authentic English texts to be read for realistic purposes (other than practicing sentence-level grammar) (Al-Homoud & Schmitt, 2009; Chen, 2006; Redfield, 1999). And even when learners had access to input, it might not be comprehensible, as in Krashen (1987, p. 63): "When the acquirer does not understand the message, there will be no acquisition ... a monolingual English speaker, for example, hearing Polish on the radio, would acquire nothing, because the input would be only 'noise.'"

Thus, some in the field suggested reading programs using graded readers, young adult fiction, children's stories, or other linguistically simple texts as a viable means of engaging L2 learners in comprehensible input in an otherwise input-poor environment (Chen, 2006; Redfield, 1999). The most common, and commented-on, program has been extensive reading (ER) (e.g., Al-Homoud & Schmitt, 2009; Cirocki, 2009a; Day & Bamford, 1998; Iwahori, 2008; Nation, 2009; Paran, 1996). ER programs involve secondary-level or higher learners choosing a specified number of graded readers to read for pleasure during a given semester or similar time frame and perhaps completing book reports after reading a reader. One goal of ER is to reach specified target amounts of silent sustained reading (Donnes, 1999; Hill, 1997), suggesting the objective of increasing learners' reading fluency (e.g., Grabe, 2010; Iwahori, 2008).

ER is seen as means of reaching other important language learning goals: "Reading can establish previously learned vocabulary and grammar ... and through success in language use it can encourage learners to learn more and continue with their language study" (Nation, 2009, p. 49).

Graded readers, which have become more numerous and varied in content in recent years (Edinburgh Project on Extensive Reading, 2008; Nation, 2009), are adapted from authentic literary texts or are original stories, written with an eye to restricting the grammatical structures and the vocabulary range used while still maintaining the exciting narratives and interesting characters of good, authentic writing (Gorsuch & Taguchi, 2009). An important stipulation of ER programs is that learners choose readers at or just below their level of comprehension (Day & Bamford, 1998). As graded readers are written with specific vocabulary ranges in mind, it is implied that vocabulary knowledge in learners is one determining factor of how easily a reader might access a text, develop reading fluency, and learn to engage in purposeful reading.

## RESEARCH RESPONSES OF L2 AND FL EDUCATION TO READING FLUENCY

As noted, pedagogical responses to the perceived need for reading fluency have been robust. However, research responses have been less so, particularly concerning automaticity for lower order word identification (Birch, 2006; Gorsuch & Taguchi, 2009; Grabe, 1991, 2004; Silberstein, 1994). For the purposes of this chapter, research responses can be characterized in two general categories: repeated reading (RR) and extensive reading (ER). (Two other research responses—speed reading and word recognition training—will not be commented on because of space limitations. Interested readers are referred to Akamatsu, 2008; Chang, 2010, Cushing-Weigle & Jensen, 1996; Fukkink, Hulstijn, & Simis, 2005; Koda, 1996; Muljani, Koda, & Moates, 1998; Segalowitz & Segalowitz, 1993; Segalowitz et al., 1998; and Yamashita & Ichikawa, 2010.)

## Repeated Reading

RR is a relatively new approach in the L2 and FL field. Like ER described in the previous section, RR also uses relatively easy texts but differs in that L2 learners read specified passages from these texts repeatedly and often with audio support (assisted repeated reading). In one RR study (Taguchi, Takayasu-Maass, & Gorsuch, 2004), a group of college-level Japanese learners of English participated in 42 RR sessions over a 17-week period. A graded reader was segmented into passages of 400–600 words for each treatment, which followed this procedure:

1. Students silently read the previous passage to remember what they had read in the last session. This step was skipped only when they started a new graded reader.
2. Students timed their first reading of a passage with a stopwatch.
3. Students read the passage two times while listening to the exact audiotaped version with headphones.
4. Students read the passage silently two more times and timed each of their readings with a stopwatch.
5. Students wrote a book report about what they had read in the story passage.

Other studies done by Taguchi and others varied in the number of repetitions used, but always included the audio component. Thus, they used assisted RR in their research.

RR is an instantiation of automaticity theory (LaBerge & Samuels, 1974) into practice for L1 readers (Samuels, 1979), and aims to develop automaticity in word recognition skills. Automaticity would be seen in the transfer of practice effects to new, unpracticed passages. Moreover, increases in automaticity would mean increased reading rates and comprehension of practiced and new, unpracticed passages. Taguchi (1997) examined the effects of assisted RR in English on oral and silent reading rates of 15 Japanese university students in a 10-week, 28-session RR treatment, and found that learners' silent reading rates increased within practiced passages. This practice effect did not seem to transfer significantly to silent and oral reading rates for new, unpracticed passages, however. A later study by Taguchi and Gorsuch (2002) found that a 10-week, 28-session RR treatment facilitated Japanese university-level English learners' reading rates from a pretest reading passage to a different posttest reading passage. Aiming to intensify the treatment and further explore comprehension gains, Taguchi et al. (2004) extended the RR period to 17 weeks, totaling 42 sessions. It was not possible to make the treatments more frequent because the researchers had to work within the schedule of English language class meetings in the Japanese university where the study took place. Taguchi et al. found that assisted RR treatments significantly improved learners' silent reading rates from the first to the last RR session. Moreover, while learners' comprehension of passages did not drop from pretest to posttest, it did not seem to increase significantly either. Taguchi et al. speculated that learners probably did increase their comprehension, but that the comprehension measures may not have been sensitive enough to catch subtle but important changes.

Working with low-intermediate Vietnamese learners of English, and with newly developed, text-specific comprehension measures, Gorsuch and Taguchi (2008) found that with an 11-week, 16-session assisted RR intervention learners experienced steady increases in reading rates of new, unpracticed passages and significant increases in posttreatment reading comprehension, as measured by a recall protocol and a short answer test, compared with a control group. Even though the intervention could only be termed moderate in intensity (because of the course schedule offered at the university), learners' silent reading rates increased and comprehension significantly improved. Becase the texts contained 40–60% vocabulary in common and grammatical structures were limited in variety, it was reasonable to posit that there had been growth in automaticity in word recognition. Further, in a longitudinal, qualitative analysis of posttreatment reports written in Vietnamese (the learners' L1), learners reported using fewer instances of word-level processing strategies (such as translation) over time and using more top-down and metacognitive reading comprehension strategies (Gorsuch & Taguchi, 2010).

Working outside regularly scheduled language classes, Blum et al. (1995) and also Dlugosz (2000) found that assisted RR was an effective supplement to L2 literacy programs. Both studies concluded that RR along with audio cassette tapes improved readers' ability to read books fluently and accurately and enhanced their motivation to read. The issue of whether to include RR as part of regular classes or as a supplementary task outside of class is a salient one, and is taken up again later in the "Practical Suggestions for RR implementation in L2/FL Settings" section.

## Extensive Reading

ER, as noted, has multiple goals, and until recently had a basis more in principled pedagogy than in research. Research on ER is as varied in scope and methodology as its multiple goals. One overarching theory is that as a means of increasing comprehensible input, learners' engagement with ER will generally increase their L2 proficiency (Nation, 2009; see also Day & Bamford, 1998, for a review of ER research on increases in learners' L2 proficiency). Thus, there is a research interest in gains in vocabulary (e.g., Waring & Takaki, 2003), often using standardized vocabulary measures as opposed to vocabulary measures specific to the texts used by learners (e.g., Yamashita, 2008). This may be partly because in ER learners' self-select graded readers, and thus it would be difficult for researchers to track vocabulary in texts used by learners and then create vocabulary measures generalizable to all learners in a study. Using a series of vocabulary tests (unfortunately, not fully described), Cirocki (2009b) found gains in vocabulary knowledge for teenage Polish learners of English engaged in an ER program. Al-Homoud and Schmitt (2009), using a more transparently validated standardized vocabulary measure, found gains in male Saudi English language learners' vocabulary knowledge after learners engaged in ER for 10 weeks, reading on average one graded reader per week. These learners showed as much vocabulary knowledge growth as a similar group of learners in a traditional intensive reading course.

ER researchers are also interested in tracking changes in L2 and FL learners' motivation to read L2 texts as a result of engaging in regular programs of ER. Takase (2009), working with Japanese learners of English, found gains in learner motivation to read in English and higher self-perceptions of English ability. These university-level learners engaged in 20 minutes of ER twice a week for an unknown period of time (presumably 4–8 months, the length of Japanese university semesters or full-year courses). Poulshock (2010) also found similar learner-reported gains in motivation to read texts in the liberal arts and sciences after Japanese English learners at the college level engaged in a semester-long program of ER.

Finally, increasing reading fluency is a goal of ER, and thus some researchers focus on learners' gains in reading speed through increased vocabulary knowledge and in some cases speed-reading training (Nation, 2009; see also Fujigaki, 2009). Iwahori (2008), working with Japanese high school learners of English, found increases in silent reading rate after learners engaged in a 7-week ER treatment in which learners read 28 graded readers. Bell (2001) compared two groups of Yemeni learners of English at a language study center over a two-semester period. The 14 learners engaged in an ER program increased their silent reading rate and reading comprehension more than a control group engaged in an intensive reading course.

## EXPLORING THE ISSUES FOR EFFECTIVE RR IMPLEMENTATION IN L2/FL SETTINGS

### What Role Does Oral Reading Play in Facilitating the Effects of RR?

The role of oral reading (reading aloud) in implementing RR is a rather unexplored issue in past L2 RR research. In a meta-analysis of English L1 RR studies that focused on the effects of RR with participants in grades 2 through 9, it was found that oral RR was effective in increasing reading fluency and comprehension (National Reading Panel, 2000). The RR studies that have been carried out in L2 and FL settings (as mentioned previously) have not been strictly comparable because they mostly involved mature students, who were engaged in silent RR of texts. A study by Lems (2006), however, was a rare attempt to investigate how oral reading fluency affects reading comprehension. She found that the higher students' L2 proficiency goes up, the higher the correlation between their oral reading fluency and reading comprehension is. Using 1-minute oral reading recordings from 232 postsecondary students at an academic English as a second language (ESL) program, Lems found that the better a reader's oral fluency was, measured in terms of words correct per minute and miscue ratio, the better the reader's comprehension. Gorsuch (2011), in an attempt to improve the oral expressiveness of advanced-level ESL learners in the United States, had graduate students from China, India, and other countries engage in 20 silent, audio-supported, and optional oral reading RR treatments. In addition to changed oral fluency, the 28 participants read new, unpracticed passages significantly faster and with better comprehension at the end of the treatments. As reading aloud is a fairly common pedagogical practice in L2/FL settings (unfortunately without silent or oral repetition), further research should explore the effects of oral reading on various outcome measures such as reading fluency and comprehension. Further, it may be possible to encourage the use of RR by embedding it into the practice of oral reading in some classes.

## What Is the Relationship between Reading Fluency and Comprehension?

In L2 and FL settings, it remains to be demonstrated whether improved word recognition alone leads to improved comprehension or is simply one of a number of enabling components (e.g., Fukkink et al., 2005). Automaticity theory, the theoretical backbone of RR, suggests that automatic word recognition frees readers from expending their attentional resources on word recognition tasks. Readers trained to a level of automaticity in word recognition should, as a result, be able to direct most of their attention to resource-demanding comprehension processes. The National Reading Panel (2000) found that, in terms of the effect of RR on reading comprehension, the mean weight effect size for 49 comparisons drawn from 12 studies was a moderate 0.35, which may be interpreted as indicating a causal relationship between improved fluency and better comprehension. The National Reading Panel's findings for L1 learners have been corroborated by several subsequent meta-analyses (Chard, Vaughn, & Tyler, 2002; Therrien, 2004).

However, the relationship between automatized word recognition (construed as reading fluency) and comprehension is not so clear in L2/FL settings, and it still remains to be consistently demonstrated. It is not clear whether automated word recognition skills are a sufficient condition for successful reading comprehension or whether they are a necessary, but also not sufficient, condition for good reading comprehension. No research to date has resoundingly shown a causal relationship between improved word recognition skills and enhanced reading comprehension in L2 and FL settings (Fukkink et al., 2005; Taguchi & Gorsuch, 2002; Taguchi et al., 2004; Gorsuch & Taguchi, 2008).

Nonetheless, it is known that good readers engage in automatic prelexical letter and word recognition alongside efficient postlexical phrasal and sentential processes, such as syntactic parsing and proposition integration (e.g., Grabe, 1988; Rumelhart, 1977). These readers use higher order comprehension-fostering strategies such as previewing headings and subheadings and attending to topic sentences and other important elements in the text to get a macrostructure of a passage to aid their comprehension. We surmise that readers with improved word recognition skills but without attendant basic comprehension skills such as grammatical parsing and proposition integration are not able to utilize the attentional resources they have successfully freed up as a result of greater automaticity in their word recognition to assist their comprehension. Fukkink et al. (2005) suggested a possible, supportive explanation for the absence of a clear transfer effect: They speculated "that the role of automatic word recognition in L2 reading is too small to expect significant changes in higher order reading comprehension in view of the complex nature of the reading process" (p. 71).

## What Role Does Audio Support Play in Fostering Reading Comprehension?

Several studies in L2 settings have suggested a beneficial role for audio support in fostering reading comprehension in RR treatments (Taguchi, 1997; Taguchi & Gorsuch, 2002, Taguchi et al., 2004; Gorsuch & Taguchi, 2008). It seems that prosodic information contained in the oral reading model helps readers parse grammatically intact phrases and sentences, which leads to better comprehension. Studies have shown that readers comprehend better when provided with texts segmented by phrase units (larger discoursal units than single words) (e.g., Cromer, 1970; O'Shea & Sindelar, 1983). According to Kuhn and Stahl (2003), both RR and parsing (chunking) texts into phrase units seem to facilitate readers' comprehension, but fast isolated word recognition does not (e.g., Fukkink et al., 2005). It is likely that more is needed to contribute to successful reading comprehension than automaticity and accuracy in word recognition skills (as measured by faster reaction times to single isolated words). On the basis of this argument, Kuhn and Stahl (2003, p. 18) emphasized the role of prosody in achieving better comprehension. The prosodic models were provided by audio-assisted RR, in which an exact audio model of the text was simultaneously provided to readers while they read text.

This "necessary but not sufficient" position is also favored by L2 and FL reading researchers. Grabe and Stoller (2002), for example, suggested that, in addition to lexical-level word recognition, fast and automatic syntactic parsing (which may be aided by audio input) is an important lower level subcomponent of L2 reading. That is, L2 readers' ability to recognize grammatical structures in sentences, and identify what pronouns and definite articles refer to, is important to comprehension (pp. 22–23). They also claimed that L2 readers must be exposed to print both extensively and intensively in order to develop automatic syntactic parsing skills. We argue that audio-supported RR has the potential to develop such skills for L2 and FL learners. Unlike English L1 readers, who have tacit grammar knowledge, knowledge of how the language sounds as it is spoken in phrase groups, and a tremendous amount of vocabulary knowledge through exposure to print even before they start learning to read, L2 and FL readers are exposed to much less input during their language-learning careers. Thus, automatic word recognition and basic postlexical comprehension skills together play a salient role in reading comprehension (Grabe & Stoller, 2002; Koda, 1996; Segalowitz, 2010). We are curious as to how audio-supported RR contributes to these processes.

## PRACTICAL SUGGESTIONS FOR RR IMPLEMENTATION IN L2/FL SETTINGS

In this section, we focus on RR as one of the most viable means of increasing reading fluency. For those interested in ER, we recommend consulting the many sources cited previously in the "Pedagogical Responses of L2 and FL Education to Reading Fluency" section.

### Use RR within Regular Course Schedules and Structures

Given what we know about reading fluency in L2 and FL settings globally, we suggest using RR treatments on a regular basis *within* existing course schedules and structures. We have demonstrated in the past decade that effective, moderate intensity RR treatments can be achieved with a modest commitment of 30 minutes twice a week. We believe RR works best when the treatments are consistent and extended over time. It may be more difficult to incorporate RR in its most effective form, with sufficient repetitions and audio support, if simply left to the unsupervised efforts of learners working on their own (Gorsuch, 2011). When learners comprehend a text well as a result of engaging in RR, the text itself can be used to create additional tasks to bring about desired language-learning outcomes, such as pair interaction, negotiation of meaning in the L2, and learner-centered discussion about vocabulary and content (Gorsuch, 2007). Finally, using a single well-chosen class reader is one of the side benefits of using RR. It may be easier in the long run to have two or three sets of excellent class readers that everyone uses and that can be reused for 2 or more years (Gorsuch & Taguchi, 2009). Learners at different levels of ability benefit in different ways when engaged in RR; nevertheless, all benefit in some way.

## Student Record Keeping in RR

We have found many benefits from having learners keep their own time logs, timing their reading and recording it using inexpensive stopwatches and then writing brief postreading reports. First, having students keep their own time logs helps avoid confusion in the RR procedure. By so doing, students can follow and check each RR step easily without making mistakes (see Figure 16.1 for a sample log sheet). A second important reason for keeping a time log is that learners can see that with each repetition of reading of a given text their reading times generally go down. This is very motivating, although learners should never be encouraged to read fast just for the sake of reading fast. Learners also see their initial reading times of new, unpracticed texts go down as the RR treatments extend into weeks and months. Finally, writing postreading reports presents an important counterpoint to the reading log times. The postreading reports encourage learners to comment after the fact about comprehension or reading issues that arose while reading (see Figure 16.2 for a sample postreading report sheet). We believe this may be key to developing learners' metacognition, which is thought to be a necessary step in becoming an independent, life-long reader. For instance, some learners' times increase between repetitions within a single RR session. They notice this when completing their time logs, and some of these learners will then actually reflect in their postreading logs on what slowed them down. More often than not, they mention being intrigued by some aspect of the text that they had noticed only after one or two repetitions. In this way, learners become aware of the trade-off between reading speed and comprehension, which is itself an important metacognitive discovery.

## Selecting and Preparing Texts

In RR implementation, we find it useful to locate a short story or longer text that is rather easy for students. We then segment the longer text at relevant points into short portions to be used for each RR session. We suggest

Student ID: _____
Name: _____

268

| Number of RR Session (Number of words) | Ex. (365) | 1 ( ) | 2 ( ) | 3 ( ) | 4 ( ) | 5 ( ) |
|---|---|---|---|---|---|---|
| Date (month/day) | Sept. 8 | | | | | |
| Text information (Page & line numbers) | p 3 L 12 <br> p 4 L 15 | | | | | |
| Finishing time (RR working time) | 2:10 (30 mins) | ( : mins) | ( : mins) | ( : mins) | ( : mins) | ( : mins) |
| Starting time | 1:40 | : | : | : | : | : |
| Reading previous part Check (✓) or write NA* | ✓ | | | | | |
| Reading time (1) | 2 mins 55 s | mins s | mins s | mins s | mins s | mins s |
| Reading with tape (2) Check (✓) | ✓ | | | | | |
| Reading with tape (3) Check (✓) | ✓ | | | | | |
| Reading time (4) | 2 mins 29 s | mins s | mins s | mins s | mins s | mins s |
| Reading time (5) | 2 mins 13 s | mins s | mins s | mins s | mins s | mins s |
| Write report Check (✓) | ✓ | | | | | |

**FIGURE 16.1.** Sample log sheet.

* Check the box after you read the previous part of text or write NA (nonapplicable) when you read a new story.

Date: _____

Repeated reading session number: _____

Name: _____

Title of the book: _____

Today's part of the book: From: page _____ line _____ To: page _____ line _____

- - - - - - - - - - - - - - - - - - - - - - - - - - - - - - - - - - - - - - - - - - - - - - -
In the space below, write about today's reading session. Please write anything that came to mind. For example, how do you like reading with the tape? What is difficult about reading in English? How does this method help you? Or how does it not help you? How do you think your reading has changed? You can write freely here.
- - - - - - - - - - - - - - - - - - - - - - - - - - - - - - - - - - - - - - - - - - - - - - -

**FIGURE 16.2.** Sample report form.

lengths for RR session passages varying from 100 to 500 or more words, depending on the passage content, students' reading levels, or time constraints regarding when RR is able to be performed in class. In general, even more advanced readers find longer passages harder to process during an RR session. Many readers in our past studies have commented in postreading reports that shorter passages are easier to read. At the same time, they are sensitive to passages that end or begin at "clumsy" points in a discoursal sense. Some readers have reported they enjoy passages that stop at some point of suspense, because it makes them eager to resume reading the text at the next session. Also, we prepare an audio recording of those text passages to be used in the RR procedure. Some publishers or graded-reader publishers provide CDs or audio files. In other cases, we record someone reading the text aloud or practice ahead of time and provide a live reading (Gorsuch & Taguchi, 2008).

While Gorsuch (2011) has used popular science texts written with an expository discourse structure and at the seventh-grade level for RR sessions with graduate-level scientists from China, India, and Korea, our other RR programs have used graded readers from the genres of mystery, science fiction, crime, and family drama. Texts useful in RR treatments can be obtained from many sources, including *www.sciencenewsforkids.org* for basic science texts in English; *www.ials.ed.ac.uk/postgraduate/research/EPER.html* for ESL/EFL texts; *thejapanshop.com/home.php* for Japanese books; *germanbookshop.co.uk* for German; and *www.continentalbook.com* for Arabic, Chinese, English, and other languages.

## How to Select Texts Appropriate to Students' Level for Fluency Development

It is important to choose texts that do not have more than a few unknown words. One way is to construct and administer a cloze test (e.g., Madsen, 1983; Mikulecky, 1990). This can be done by taking one or two portions of a passage from a promising text, keeping the first sentence intact and then deleting every fifth or seventh word in the passage, creating 50 blanks in total. There are two ways to score the students' answers. The exact scoring method only gives credit for exact words from the passage, and the semantically acceptable scoring method allows credit for words that are semantically equivalent to the deleted words (Madsen, 1983; Mikulecky, 1990). The criterion score used to assess students' independent reading level in the exact scoring method varies among researchers/practitioners, ranging from 44% (Bormuth, 1967, p. 18) to 50% (Allerson & Grabe, 1986, p. 176) to greater than 60% (Mikulecky, 1990, p. 150). When learners attain or surpass the set criterion score, the text can then be considered suitable for use in fluency building. For the more liberal semantically acceptable scoring method, the criterion for independent reading should be 65% (15% more than that for exact scoring) (Allerson & Grabe, 1986, p. 176). However, teachers should revise the criterion based on student feedback in order to approximate their reading level. This is yet another way in which postreading reports can inform an RR program.

A quick and rather blunt method for checking the readability of promising RR texts is to use readability formulas such as the Flesch–Kincaid Grade Level, which are available in Word software. Such readability formulas can give a pragmatic "ballpark" estimate in helping teachers match texts to learners in their classes (Greenfield, 2004), and are based on multiple measures of text-based characteristics, such as syllables per sentence, letters per word, and words per sentence in the case of English L2 learner readability formulas (Greenfield, 2004; see also Shokrpour, 2005). The Flesch–Kincaid Grade Level results in a score from 0.00 to 12.00, which represents what is thought to be the appropriate reading level by grade level and month for students in first through 12th grades in the American education system. We have used texts ranging from 0.8 (pre-first grade) to 4.3 (fourth grade, third month) in our studies with beginning and preintermediate participants.

A final way to assign appropriate texts to a group of learners is to check the number of unknown words in the text. Simply have students read a given passage and ask them to circle the words they do not understand. Some studies indicate that L2 English readers should know about 98% of word tokens in the passage (Hirsh & Nation, 1992; Hu & Nation, 2000) for reading without external support. Thus, one criterion for estimating passage appropriateness is that approximately two unknown words for every 100 words is acceptable for independent reading.

## What Is the Optimal Number of Repetitions for RR Treatments?

Finally, we consider the optimal number of repetitions for each text in RR treatments. We believe it is best to strike a workable balance between the number of repetitions within each session and the effect of the repetition on students' motivation. Past studies (e.g., Taguchi & Gorsuch, 2002; Taguchi et al., 2004) suggest that excessive repetitions (six or more) may discourage learners from fully engaging in rereading texts. However, as reported in many postreading reports we have collected over the years, learners seem to become aware that through repetitions they become more able to catch the details and development of a text. In RR in L1 English settings, between three to five repetitive readings are reported to be effective in increasing reading rates and comprehension (e.g., O'Shea, Sindelar, & O'Shea, 1985; Samuels, 2006, p. 17). For the time being, L2 and FL teachers could use the precedent of three to five repetitions from the just-mentioned L1 RR studies but still use learner feedback to explore the number of repetitions that will best aid learners' fluency and comprehension building while remaining motivating.

## REFERENCES

Akamatsu, N. (2008). The effects of training on automatization of word recognition in English as a foreign language. *Applied Psycholinguistics, 29,* 175–193.

Al-Homoud, F., & Schmitt, N. (2009). Extensive reading in a challenging environment: A comparison of extensive and intensive approaches. *Language Teaching Research, 13,* 383–401.

Allerson, S., & Grabe, W. (1986). Reading assessment. In F. Dubin, D. E. Eskey, & W. Grabe (Eds.), *Teaching second language reading for academic purposes* (pp. 161–181). Reading, MA: Addison-Wesley.

Amer, A. (1997). The effect of the teacher's reading aloud on the reading comprehension of EFL students. *ELT Journal, 51,* 43–47.

Anderson, N. J. (1999). *Exploring second language reading: Issues and strategies.* Boston: Heinle & Heinle.

Anderson, R. C., & Pearson, P. D. (1984). A schema-theoretic view of basic processes in reading comprehension. In P. D. Pearson (Ed.), *Handbook of reading research* (pp. 255–292). New York: Longman.

Bell, T. (2001). Extensive reading: Speed and comprehension. *The Reading Matrix, 1*(1), 3–15.

Bernhardt, E. (1991). *Reading development in a second language: Theoretical, empirical, and classroom perspectives.* Norwood, NJ: Ablex.

Bernhardt, E. (2011). *Understanding advanced second-language learning.* New York: Routledge.

Birch, B. (2006). *English L2 reading: Getting to the bottom* (2nd ed.). Mahwah, NJ: Erlbaum.

Blum, I., Koskinen, P. A., Tennant, N., Parker, E. M., Straub, M., & Curry, C. (1995). Using audiotaped books to extend classroom literacy instruction into the homes of second-language learners. *Journal of Reading Behavior, 27,* 535–563.

Bochner, J., & Bochner, A. (2009). A limitation on reading as a source of linguistic input: Evidence from deaf learners. *Reading in a Foreign Language, 21,* 143–158.

Bormuth, J. (1967, February). Cloze readability procedure (Report No. CSEIF-OR-1). Los Angeles: Center for the Study of Evaluation of Instructional Programs. (ERIC Document Reproduction Service No. ED010983)

Carr, J., & Pauwels, A. (2006). *Boys and foreign language learning: Real boys don't do languages.* Houndmills, UK: Palgrove Macmillan.

Carrell, P. L., & Eisterhold, J. C. (1983). Schema theory and ESL reading pedagogy. *TESOL Quarterly, 17,* 553–573.

Chang, A. (2010). The effect of a timed reading activity on EFL learners: Speed, comprehension, and perceptions. *Reading in a Foreign Language, 22,* 284–303.

Chard, D., Vaughn, S., & Tyler, B. (2002). A synthesis of research on effective interventions for building reading fluency with elementary students with learning disabilities. *Journal of Learning Disabilities, 35,* 386–406.

Charness, N., Krampe, R., & Mayr, U. (1996). The role of practice and coaching in entrepreneurial skill domains: An international comparison of life-span chess skill acquisition. In K. A. Ericsson (Ed.), *The road to excellence: The acquisition of expert performance in the arts and sciences, sports, and games* (pp. 51–80). Mahwah, NJ: Erlbaum.

Chen, Y. M. (2006). Using children's literature for reading and writing stories. *Asian EFL Journal, 8*(4). Retrieved February 24, 2011, from *www.asian-efl-journal.com/Dec_06_ymc.php.*

Cirocki, A. (Ed.). (2009a). *Extensive reading in English language teaching.* Munich, Germany: Lincom Europa.

Cirocki, A. (2009b). Implementing the ER approach to literature in the EFL secondary school classroom: An action research study. In A. Cirocki (Ed.) *Extensive reading in English language teaching* (pp. 521–545). Munich, Germany: Lincom. Europa.

Cromer, W. (1970). The difference model: A new explanation for some reading difficulties. *Journal of Educational Psychology, 61,* 471–483.

Cushing-Weigle, S., & Jensen, L. (1996). Reading rate improvement in university ESL classes. *CATESOL Journal, 9,* 55–71.

Day, R. R., & Bamford, J. (1998). *Extensive reading in the second language classroom.* New York: Cambridge University Press.

Dlugosz, D. W. (2000). Rethinking the role of reading in teaching a foreign language to young learners. *English Language Teaching Journal, 54,* 284–290.

Donnes, T. (1999). Extensive reading revisited: An interview with Richard Day and Julian Bamford. *Language Teacher, 23*(7), 4–7.

Dowhower, S. L. (1989). Repeated reading: Research into practice. *The Reading Teacher, 42,* 502–507.

Dowhower, S. L. (1994). Repeated reading revisited: Research into practice. *Reading and Writing Quarterly: Overcoming Learning Difficulties, 10,* 343–358.

Edinburgh Project on Extensive Reading. (2008). *Postgraduate study and research.* Retrieved March 5, 2011, from *www.ials.ed.ac.uk/postgraduate/research/EPER.html.*

Ericsson, K. A., & Charness, N. (1994). Expert performance: Its structure and acquisition. *American Psychologist, 49,* 725–747.

Ericsson, K. A., Krampe, R., & Tesch-Römer, C. (1993). The role of deliberate practice in the acquisition of expert performance. *Psychological Review, 100,* 363–406.

Favreau, M., & Segalowitz, N. (1983). Automatic and controlled processes in the first and second language reading of fluent bilinguals. *Memory and Cognition, 11,* 565–574.

Fujigaki, E. (2009). Extensive reading for weak readers: Developing reading fluency in the EFL/ESL context. In A. Cirocki (Ed.), *Extensive reading in English language teaching* (pp. 273–293). Munich, Germany: Lincom Europa.

Fukkink, R., Hulstijn, J., & Simis, A. (2005). Does training in second-language word recognition skills affect reading comprehension? An experimental study. *Modern Language Journal, 89,* 54–75.

Gebhard, J. G. (1996). *Teaching English as a foreign or second language.* Ann Arbor: University of Michigan Press.

Gorsuch, G. J. (2007). Developing "the course" for college level EFL learners and faculty members in Vietnam. *Asian EFL Journal Quarterly, 9*(1), 195–226.

Gorsuch, G. J. (2011). Improving speaking fluency for international teaching assistants by increasing input. *TESL-EJ, 14*(4), 1–25. Retrieved March 30, 2011, from *www.tesl-ej.org/wordpress/issues/volume14/ej56/ej56a1.*

Gorsuch, G. J., & Taguchi, E. (2008). Repeated reading for developing reading fluency and reading comprehension: The case of EFL learners in Vietnam. *System, 36,* 253–278.

Gorsuch, G. J., & Taguchi, E. (2009). Repeated reading and its role in an extensive reading program. In A. Cirocki (Ed.) *Extensive reading in English language teaching* (pp. 249–271). Munich, Germany: Lincom Europa.

Gorsuch, G. J., & Taguchi, E. (2010). Developing reading fluency and comprehension using repeated reading: Evidence from longitudinal student reports. *Language Teaching Research, 14*(1), 27–59.

Grabe, W. (1988). Reassessing the term "interactive." In P. Carrell, J. Devine, & D. Eskey (Eds.), *Interactive approaches to second language reading* (pp. 56–70). New York: Cambridge University Press.

Grabe, W. (1991). Current developments in second language reading research. *TESOL Quarterly, 25,* 375–406.

Grabe, W. (2004). Research on teaching reading. *Annual Review of Applied Linguistics, 24,* 44–69.

Grabe, W. (2009). *Reading in a second language.* Cambridge, UK: Cambridge University Press.

Grabe, W. (2010). Fluency in reading: Thirty-five years later. *Reading in a Foreign Language, 22,* 71–83.

Grabe, W., & Stoller, F. L. (2002). *Teaching and researching reading.* Harlow, UK: Pearson Education.

Greenfield, J. (2004). Readability formulas for EFL. *JALT Journal, 26*(1), 5–24. Retrieved October 30, 2011, from *www.jalt-publications.org/jj/issues/2004-05_26.1.*

Han, Z. H., & Chen, C. A. (2010). Repeated-reading-based instructional strategy and vocabulary acquisition: A case study of a heritage speaker of Chinese. *Reading in a Foreign Language, 22,* 242–262.

Hatch, E., Polin, P., & Part, S. (1974). Acoustic scanning and syntactic processing: Three reading experiments with first and second language learners. *Journal of Reading Behavior, 6,* 275–285.

Herman, P. A. (1985). The effect of repeated readings on reading rate, speech pauses, and word recognition accuracy. *Reading Research Quarterly, 20,* 553–564.

Hill, D. (1997). Survey review: Graded readers. *English Language Teaching Journal, 51*(1), 57–79.

Hirsh, D., & Nation, P. (1992). What vocabulary size is needed to read unsimplified texts for pleasure? *Reading in a Foreign Language, 8,* 689–696.

Hu, H. M., & Nation, P. (2000). Unknown vocabulary density and reading comprehension. *Reading in a Foreign Language, 13,* 403–430.

Iwahori, Y. (2008). Developing reading fluency: A study of extensive reading in EFL. *Reading in a Foreign Language, 20,* 70–91.

Jensen, L. (1986). Advanced reading skills in a comprehensive course. In F. Dubin, D. E. Eskey, & W. Grabe (Eds.), *Teaching second language reading for academic purposes* (pp. 103–124). Reading, MA: Addison-Wesley.

Koda, K. (1996). L2 word recognition research: A critical review. *The Modern Language Journal, 80,* 450–460.

Krashen, S. (1985). *The input hypothesis: Issues and implications.* Torrrance, CA: Laredo.

Krashen, S. (1987). *Principles and practice in second language acquisition.* New York: Prentice Hall.

Krashen, S. (1988). *Second language acquisition and second language learning.* New York: Prentice Hall.

Krashen, S. (1995). Free voluntary reading: Linguistic and affective arguments and some new applications. In F. R. Eckman, D. Highland, P. W. Lee, J. Mileham, & R. R. Weber (Eds.), *Second language acquisition theory and pedagogy* (pp. 187–202). Mahwah, NJ: Erlbaum.

Kuhn, M. R., Schwanenflugel, P. J., & Meisinger, E. B. (2010). Aligning theory and assessment of reading fluency: Automaticity, prosody, and definitions of fluency. *Reading Research Quarterly, 45,* 230–251.

Kuhn, M. R., & Stahl, S. A. (2003). Fluency: A review of developmental and remedial practices. *Journal of Educational Psychology, 95,* 3–21.

LaBerge, D., & Samuels, S. J. (1974). Toward a theory of automatic information processing in reading. *Cognitive Psychology, 6,* 293–323.

Lems, K. (2006). Reading fluency and comprehension in adult English language learners. In T. Rasinski, C. Blachowicz, & K. Lems (Eds.), *Fluency instruction: Research-based best practices* (pp. 231–252). New York: Guilford Press.

Madsen, H. (1983). *Techniques in testing.* New York: Oxford University Press.

Mason, B., & Krashen, S. (1997). Extensive reading in English as a foreign language. *System, 25,* 91–102.

Masuhara, H., Kimura, R., Fukada, A., & Takeuchi, M. (1996). Strategy training or/and extensive reading? In T. Hickey & J. Williams (Eds.), *Language, education, and society in a changing world* (pp. 263–274). Clevedon, UK: Multilingual Matters.

Mikulecky, B. (1990). *A short course in teaching reading skills.* Reading, MA: Addison-Wesley.

Muljani, D., Koda, K., & Moates, D. R. (1998). The development of word recognition in a second language. *Applied Psycholinguistics, 19,* 99–113.

Nation, I.S.P. (2009). *Teaching ESL/EFL reading and writing.* New York: Routledge.

National Reading Panel. (2000). *Teaching children to read. An evidence-based assessment of the scientific research literature on reading and its implications for reading instruction* (NIH Publication No. 00-4769). Washington, DC: National Institute of Child Health and Human Development.

Oller, J. W., & Tullius, J. R. (1973). Reading skills of non-native speakers of English. *International Review of Applied Linguistics, 11,* 69–79.

O'Shea, L. J., & Sindelar, P. T. (1983). The effects of segmenting written discourse on the reading comprehension of low- and high-performance readers. *Reading Research Quarterly, 18,* 458–465.

O'Shea, L. J., Sindelar, P. T., & O'Shea, D. J. (1985). The effects of repeated readings and attentional cues on reading fluency and comprehension. *Journal of Reading Behavior, 17,* 129–142.

Paran, A. (1996). Reading in EFL: Facts and fictions. *ELT Journal, 50,* 25–34.

Perfetti, C. (1985). *Reading ability.* New York: Oxford University Press.

Poulshock, J. (2010). Extensive graded reading in the liberal arts and sciences. *Reading in a Foreign Language, 22,* 304–322.

Rasinski, T., Blachowicz, C., & Lems, K. (Eds.). (2006). *Fluency instruction: Research-based best practices.* New York: Guilford Press.

Rayner, K. (1978). Eye movements in reading and information processing. *Psychological Bulletin, 85,* 618–660.

Redfield, M. (1999). Massive input through eiga shosetsu: A pilot study with Japanese learners. *JALT Journal, 21*(1), 51–65.

Robb, R., & Susser, B. (1989). Extensive reading vs. skills building in an EFL context. *Reading in a Foreign Language, 5,* 239–251.

Rumelhart, D. E. (1977). Toward an interactive model of reading. In S. Dornic (Ed.), *Attention and performance* (Vol. 6, pp. 573–603). New York: Academic Press.

Samuels, S. J. (1979). The method of repeated readings. *The Reading Teacher, 32,* 403–408.

Samuels, S. J. (1994). Toward a theory of automatic information processing in reading, revisited. In R. B. Ruddell, M. R. Ruddell, & H. Singer (Eds.), *Theo-*

*retical models and processes of reading* (4th ed., pp. 816–837). Newark, DE: International Reading Association.

Samuels, S. J. (2004). Toward a theory of automatic information processing in reading, revisited. In R. B. Ruddell & N. J. Unrau (Eds.), *Theoretical models and processes* of reading (5th ed., pp. 1127–1148). Newark, DE: International Reading Association.

Samuels, S. J. (2006). Reading fluency: Its past, present, and future. In T. Rasinski, C. Blachowicz, & K. Lems (Eds.), *Fluency instruction: Research-based best practices* (pp. 7–20). New York: Guilford Press.

Samuels, S. J., & Farstrup, A. E. (Eds.). (2006). *What research has to say about fluency instruction.* Newark, DE: International Reading Association.

Schneider, W., Dumais, S. T., & Shiffrin, R. M. (1984). Automatic and control processing and attention. In R. Parasuraman & R. Davies (Eds.), *Varieties of attention* (pp. 1–27). New York: Academic Press.

Segalowitz, N. (2003) Automaticity and second language acquisition. In C. Doughty & M. Long (Eds.), *The handbook of second language acquisition* (pp. 382–408). Oxford, UK: Blackwell.

Segalowitz, N. (2010). *Cognitive bases of second language fluency.* New York: Routledge.

Segalowitz, N., Poulsen, C., & Komoda, M. (1991). Lower level components of reading skill in higher level bilinguals: Implications for reading instruction. *AILA Review, 8,* 15–30.

Segalowitz, N., & Segalowitz, S. (1993). Skilled performance, practice, and the differentiation of speed-up from automatization effects: Evidence from second language word recognition. *Applied Psycholinguistics, 14,* 369–385.

Segalowitz, S., Segalowitz, N., & Wood, A. (1998). Assessing the development of automaticity in second language word recognition. *Applied Psycholinguistics, 19,* 53–67.

Shokrpour, N. (2005). Comparison of three methods of assessing difficulty. *Asian EFL Journal Quarterly, 6,* 159–167.

Silberstein, S. (1994). *Techniques and resources in teaching reading.* New York: Oxford University Press.

Stanovich, K. E. (1986). Matthew effects in reading: Some consequences of individual differences in the acquisition of literacy. *Reading Research Quarterly, 21,* 360–407.

Stanovich, K. E. (1991). Changing models of reading and reading acquisition. In L. Rieben & C. A. Perfetti (Eds.), *Learning to read: Basic research and its implications* (pp. 19–31). Hillsdale, NJ: Erlbaum.

Stanovich, K. E. (1992). The psychology of reading: Evolutionary and revolutionary developments. *Annual Review of Applied Linguistics, 12,* 3–30.

Stanovich, K. E., Cunningham, A. E., & West, R. F. (1981). A longitudinal study of the development of automatic recognition skills in first graders. *Journal of Reading Behavior, 13,* 57–74.

Swaffar, J., & Arens, K. (2005). *Remapping the foreign language curriculum: An approach through multiple literacies.* New York: Modern Language Associates.

Taguchi, E. (1997). The effects of repeated readings on the development of lower identification skills of FL readers. *Reading in a Foreign Language, 11,* 97–119.

Taguchi, E., & Gorsuch, G. J. (2002). Transfer effects of repeated EFL reading on reading new passages: Silent reading rate and comprehension. *Reading in a Foreign Language, 14,* 1–18.

Taguchi, E., Takayasu-Maass, M., & Gorsuch, G. J. (2004). Developing reading fluency in EFL: How assisted repeated reading and extensive reading affect fluency development. *Reading in a Foreign Language, 16,* 1–19.

Takase, A. (2009). The effects of SSR on learners' reading attitudes, motivation, and achievement: A quantitative study. In A. Cirocki (Ed.), *Extensive reading in English language teaching* (pp. 547–559). Munich, Germany: Lincom Europa.

Taylor, E. A. (1966). *The fundamental reading skill.* Springfield, IL: Charles C Thomas.

Therrien, W. (2004). Fluency and comprehension gains as a result of repeated reading: A metaanalysis. *Remedial and Special Education, 25,* 252–261.

Waring, R., & Takaki, M. (2003). At what rate do learners learn and retain new vocabulary from reading a graded reader? *Reading in a Foreign Language, 15,* 130–163.

Yamashita, J. (2008). Extensive reading and development of different aspects of L2 proficiency. *System, 36,* 661–672.

Yamashita, J., & Ichikawa, S. (2010). Examining reading fluency in a foreign language: Effects of text segmentation on L2 readers. *Reading in a Foreign Language, 22,* 263–283.

Yang, A. (2007). Cultivating a reading habit: Silent reading at school. *Asian EFL Journal, 9*(2). Retrieved February 24, 2011, from *www.asian-efl-journal. com/June_07_ay.php.*

# 17

# Fluency Scores
# of English Language Learners
## *What Can They Tell Us?*

Becky McTague
Kristin Lems
Dana Butler
Elsa Carmona

English language learners (ELLs) abound in public schools around the country, where they are enrolled in a wide variety of programs and services. These students range from having no educational preparation in their first language to being literate in their native language but knowing limited English or having conversational English skills but no academic language in English. ELLs come from every ethnic, racial, and national background, and a majority of them are born in the United States. They come to the American school system from a vast range of prior experiences and from a large number of first languages, which vary in their similarity to English. For all of these reasons, it is challenging to assess their literacy needs and achievements.

Although oral reading is not a part of the all-important state achievement exams at either the elementary or the secondary level, it is an integral part of a number of programs for students identified as needing academic support in the response-to-intervention (RTI) framework. This framework has been widely implemented across the United States as a way to detect and respond to academic concerns at the earliest possible stage of a student's time in school, and many ELLs are enrolled in RTI interventions. One prominent test, the Dynamic Indicators of Basic Early Literacy Skills (Good, Kaminski, Simmons, & Kame'enui, 2001), uses oral reading assessments to check progress in literacy growth. In this assessment, students are asked to do cold oral readings of an unknown passage at their grade level as a teacher records their scores of words correct per minute. The scores can be used to predict the likelihood that students will meet the reading proficiency levels of the standardized tests that will come later in the year. Thus, oral reading scores, although not of great consequence for grades or district reporting, are important measures for "taking the temperature" of a reader and, in some cases, deciding whether or not an intervention should begin or continue.

Federal literacy legislation required that ELLs take standardized tests along with their native English-speaking classmates, even if they have been enrolled in the school for only 1 day. The tests are written in English, and there are few accommodations for ELLs. As their English language bilingual skills are developing, many ELLs do not meet the standards and benchmarks designed for native English-speaking children of the same age. This is of concern to educators, especially because if progress in English literacy levels out, these students may not be able to perform at grade level in middle school and in ninth grade, thus becoming candidates for failure to earn a high school diploma and all its ensuing serious consequences.

We do not know exactly how oral reading fluency reflects the English reading comprehension of ELLs. A number of studies have shown correlations between ELLs' oral and silent reading in English (e.g., Lems, 2004), but statistics are not available on large-scale studies. We know that, like native speakers of English, ELLs' scores on words correct per minute assessments rise when their silent reading comprehension rates rise; however, there are many details of the relationship, related to both second-language literacy and language acquisition, that have not yet been made clear.

With this background in mind, we took a look at the oral reading fluency scores of ELLs in four Chicago public schools and asked the following questions:

1. How do the oral reading fluency scores of ELLs compare with the benchmarks used for native speakers of English?
2. What kind of relationship can be found between ELLs' oral reading fluency scores and their performance on the reading section of the Illinois Standards of Achievement test (ISAT), given to all Illinois public school children in grades 3, 5, and 8?
3. What place might fluency instruction have in a broader program of language and literacy instruction for ELLs?

# THE CONTEXT

The data were collected as part of the Chicago Literacy Initiative Partnership (CLIP), an 8-year effort cosponsored by the Chicago Community Trust and the Chicago Public Schools (Hanson, DeStefano, Blachowicz, Mueller, & Eason-Watkin, 2006) to improve literacy instruction and outcomes. In the CLIP project, several universities worked in separate subprojects, each forming a partnership with a group of low-performing elementary schools (Ogle, 2008; Teale, 2008). The subproject we describe here, called the Literacy Project, involved one university and several public schools, including those in the data collection.

The four schools were part of the Literacy Project during the 2008–2009 academic year, in which the data were collected. The schools, all housed in large, old buildings, are within 2 square miles of each other, in two adjoining Hispanic neighborhoods in Chicago, and are all classified as 99% low income. School A serves a K–8 population of about 980 students, 97% of whom are from Mexican Spanish-speaking households; School B, named for one of Chicago's most historic Mexican American neighborhoods, serves about 800 K–8 students of overwhelmingly Mexican descent. School C, a grade 3–8 school, has 1,200 children distributed among one main building and several portable classrooms and a 99% Hispanic population. School D houses 939 children in grades K–8 and is also 99% Hispanic (2011 statistics).

Prior to their coming into the Literacy Project, the four schools had done only minimal work with schoolwide strategic reading assessments, and fluency had been neither an instructional priority nor part of data collection. Data on student progress were drawn mainly from large-scale achievement tests, such as the ISAT, given yearly in the spring to all students in reading, writing, and math, and used by the state to determine each district's and each school's annual yearly progress, or unit testing based on basal readers.

Teachers in schools involved with the Literacy Project were asked to assess their students with a fluency snapshot (Blachowicz, Sullivan, & Cieply, 2001) in order to evaluate their reading instruction and make better and more responsive teaching decisions. The Literacy Project initially chose to have only one classroom perform the fluency snapshot for each grade level for grades 3–8. In time, however, the school principals and literacy coaches chose to extend use of the fluency snapshot to all classrooms in those grades. They felt it was an easy and effective tool that could give teachers information about what was happening in their classrooms and also provide an overview of reading progress throughout the school. The value of fluency in capturing reading progress has been widely validated (Shinn, 1989; Strecker, Roser, & Martinez, 1998).

## METHODOLOGY

Teachers were given a fluency packet that contained grade-level passages, conventions for marking the passages, procedures for administration, and fluency norms by grade level (Johns, 2005). The fluency snapshot assessment was administered in the fall and spring. The classroom teachers took students to a quiet area and timed their reading of a grade-level passage for 1 minute. They recorded the miscues on a numbered separate copy of the reading, brought the students back to their seats, and then calculated the words read correctly in 1 minute. The teachers plotted student scores on a chart with columns for each fluency snapshot so that they could see students' development across time and view a ranking of fluency scores. Students were tested within the first 5 weeks and in the last 5 weeks of the school year.

Training for the fluency snapshot was done through a "train the trainer" model. First, the university coaches trained the school literacy coaches, and then the coaches trained the teachers. Over the years, the school literacy coaches offered refresher and review sessions for teachers at the schools. Teachers were also provided hand-held timers so that the 1-minute timing could be standardized.

## DATA ANALYSIS

In order to address our first question posed earlier, students' oral reading scores were compared with two sets of fluency norms: the mean scores of English readers at the 50th percentile for Hasbrouck and Tindal (2006) ratings, which are widely used as norms in grades 3–8, and the Ditkowsky (2011) norms, correlating oral reading scores from RTI assessments with student performance on the reading portion of the ISAT. As with the Hasbrouck and Tindal norms, we chose the cut scores considered "proficient" level for grades 3–8. We compared the spring oral reading scores for all three sets of data.

We also calculated the difference between the ELLs' mean fluency scores and the Ditkowsky proficiency cutpoints. In addition, we calculated the number of points in words correct per minute gained by (different groups of) students in our sample, going from one grade level to the next. Finally, we calculated how many words correct per minute students would need to gain from one year to the next to achieve the proficiency level of "reaching" the reading standard for the ISAT test.

To answer our second question, we obtained scores on the reading section of the ISAT for 190 of the original students from two of the schools. The scores were reported in one of four categories based on the percentage of answers correct: warning, below, meets, or exceeds the standards. We performed a Pearson correlation to compare the students' oral reading scores with their ISAT reading scores. We wanted to see how they would compare with Ditkowsky's correlations of oral reading fluency scores and scores on the reading section of the ISAT, established from a set of more than 4,000 English-speaking students.

## RESULTS AND DISCUSSION

Table 17.1 shows the mean fluency scores in words correct per minute for 589 Spanish-speaking ELLs in grades 3–8, taken in spring 2009. It can be seen that the mean fluency scores of the ELL students were consistently below both sets of norms for native speakers, except in seventh grade, when the scores were within one word of each other. However, after nearly converging in seventh grade, there was sizable drop in words correct per minute for the ELLs in eighth grade, leaving a large gap between the mean score of the ELLs and the mean score needed to be likely to reach the standard on the reading portion of ISAT. In fact, the mean score of 124 words correct per minute for 107 eighth-grade ELLs reaches only the "proficient" level for fourth graders (127 words correct per minute) in the Ditkowsky norms. Of course, the students at each grade level are different people, and cohorts of students can vary greatly year by year. In addition, the number of students,

**TABLE 17.1. Descriptive Statistics for Oral Reading in Grades 3–8**

|  | Mean score | SD | Hasbrouck–Tindal mean fluency scores, spring, median level | Ditkowsky cutpoints, spring, for proficient level | Difference from Ditkowsky cutpoints | Gain by grade (different cohorts) | Gain needed to reach Ditkowsky cutpoint |
|---|---|---|---|---|---|---|---|
| Grade 3 (n = 95) | 83 | 25.7 | 107 | 119 | 36 |  |  |
| Grade 4 (n = 102) | 106 | 38.4 | 123 | 127 | 21 | 23 | 44 |
| Grade 5 (n = 83) | 128 | 34.7 | 139 | 141 | 13 | 22 | 35 |
| Grade 6 (n = 99) | 124 | 33.4 | 150 | 143 | 19 | −4 | 19 |
| Grade 7 (n = 103) | 151 | 34.1 | 150 | 152 | 1 | 27 | 1 |
| Grade 8 (n = 107) | 124 | 25.4 | 151 | 140 | 16 | −26 | 16 |

589, is still modest compared with that in the two other sets of norms, which number in the thousands. One interesting similarity is that for all three sets of scores, the mean fluency score for eighth-graders is lower than that for seventh graders.

Still, on the basis of the available data, it can be seen that the oral reading scores of the ELLs remain at a lower rate of words correct per minute compared with native English speakers, and that they do not reach the cutpoints that are correlated with successful scores on the reading portion of the ISAT at any grade. Notably, the average oral reading scores of these ELLs do not reach the mean oral reading levels of native speakers by the end of eighth grade. This has implications for high school performance.

The second question pertains to how closely the oral reading scores of the ELL students correlated with their own performance levels on the reading portion of the ISAT. The correlation for the 190 students was .359 ($p \leq 0.01$). However, Ditkowsky found a very robust correlation of .70 in his data set (Ditkowsky, 2011). Although based on a small sample of ELLs, the discrepancy between the correlations for ELLs versus native speakers suggests that native English speakers' fluency scores tell more about their performance on the ISAT than those of ELLs. Although there is clearly a relationship between ELL's oral reading and silent reading, it may be confounded by a panoply of other factors related to second-language acquisition. A study of the oral and silent reading of postsecondary ELLs had similar results and reached a similar conclusion (Lems, 2004).

## FLUENCY AS PART OF A STRONG LITERACY CONTEXT

The third question of our study pertained to how fluency instruction might be part of a program of enriched literacy instruction for ELLs. Establishing quality classroom instruction and robust literacy environments has been the focus of many reform movements and model initiatives (Allington, 2002). It is known that one important factor for improving literacy outcomes is excellent literacy instruction for all students for optimum achievement in this area (Snow, 1998).

The Literacy Project was designed to improve classroom practices in literacy, especially as they affected comprehension, accuracy, and reading rate. Although fluency was included as a goal, it was a small piece of a program that included other broad objectives: (1) developing a school literacy infrastructure with a multiple-team approach among school principals, literacy coaches, and literacy teams; (2) providing intense on-site staff development with access to university coursework in reading and teacher-to-teacher visits within schools; (3) creating more access to books through the establishment of "bookrooms," with book sets for guided reading, novels for book clubs, read-alouds, professional titles for teachers, and books to send home with families (access to books is a significant predictor of reading achievement, according to Lindsay's 2010 metastudy; and (4) setting up regular grade-level meetings to discuss instructional strategies, including fluency.

Prior to developing the bookroom, teachers had primarily used basal materials. Read-aloud material was usually selected from teachers' resources, discarded materials, or contributions from families and had not been part of a regular routine of classroom instruction. With the development of the bookrooms, students were exposed to more highly engaging material as well as more appropriate books for instruction. With the implementation of grade-level meetings and connections to better literacy choices, the teachers started using read-alouds for modeling fluency, and the professional development library was available as a resource for strategies and ideas about fluency. Teachers were able to go to the bookroom and select materials for their classroom, small-group, or individual instruction. Whole-group instruction was replaced with guided reading and book clubs.

Another read-aloud activity used by many of the teachers was "mystery reader." The idea is simply that parents were encouraged to come to school to read their favorite picture book to the students. The teachers would create a schedule for parents to come to the student's classroom and read a book from the classroom library, the parent library, or their home. This activity became very important because many of the students were so proud to see their family members modeling fluent reading.

Similar to other schools, fluency had been a forgotten element of reading. With the implementation of the fluency assessment, it became a more visible and essential part of the curriculum. During the grade-level meetings, best practice methods that build fluency, such as reciprocal teaching (Palinscar & Brown, 1984), Readers Theatre (Griffith & Rasinski, 2004), and repeated reading (Samuels, 1979), were explained and discussed. The strategies were discussed not only at grade-level meetings, but at after-school in-services in which teachers were shown how to assess fluency with 1-minute snapshots and running records.

Some of the other teachers started using Readers Theatre as part of their reading curriculum. Teachers found scripts from the bookroom books and on the Internet for their students to read and reread for Readers Theatre. The Reader's Theater usually began as a whole-class activity, but some teachers set up read-aloud centers using the Readers Theatre scripts.

With in-service workshops given by the university coaches and the school literacy coaches, instructional practices moved from whole class to small group and then to the individual students. Independent reading was not a new idea; however, many of the teachers were reluctant to try it because of the lack of student accountability. However, coaches presented new ideas and practices evolving from professional development, and ideas from individual teachers surfaced and were adopted by other teachers.

One teacher taught the students to engage in paired reading (Topping, 2006). During the interaction, one child would read aloud as the second child timed the reading with a stopwatch, recorded the score, and then summarized what the other child had read. Then the children would change roles and repeat these steps with the next passage.

Another teacher varied her implementation of independent reading workshop (IRW). Her students chose books, read silently, and wrote responses in the form of letters to their reading teacher and then the teacher would have individual reading conferences with each child during the week. Along with the letter writing, she encouraged students to read different genres so that they could broaden their literary tastes. In addition, the students were asked to recommend other genres to their classmates during class meetings and read a short excerpt from the suggested genre. This form of IRW enabled the students to practice oral reading for an audience.

Quality instruction and the establishment of a strong literacy context are enough to create gains in literacy outcomes, but other factors are needed to accelerate progress with large ELL populations. Many ELL students in these two schools received bilingual services through some form of bilingual education, but these programs usually end for students after the third grade. In fact, at the schools in our study, 50% of students in third grade were receiving bilingual instruction compared with only 10% eighth grade. Perhaps the program ended too soon for many students to derive the full benefit of bilingual instruction. In addition, other instructional factors may slow down literacy learning for ELL students: A focus on vocabulary and story development during early literacy instruction could be the catalyst for greater progress in literacy learning.

## VOCABULARY AND STORY DEVELOPMENT AS FACTORS

Hart and Risley (1995) have found that children living in poverty hear significantly fewer words per minute than middle class and professional families. Perhaps the students of these impoverished schools not only heard less vocabulary in their formative years, but also hear less at home and around the neighborhood on a daily basis. It is known that a robust vocabulary is a strong predictor of reading comprehension (Beck, McKeown, & Kucan, 2002). Fluency is connected to accurate reading, and accurate reading is connected to vocabulary. For example, in one simple listening assessment using the book *The Carrot Seed* (Krauss, 1945), we ask students to retell the story of a boy planting a seed, watering it, believing the seed would grow, and then discovering that his seed does grow into a big carrot. We found that many of the primary children in these schools could not retell the story (in Spanish or English), or explain some of the vocabulary used. This trend continued in the upper grades, when students were asked to retell stories and nonfiction articles. The retellings from many students were vague and lacked details. This lack of full-bodied story retelling was noted in an annual report on the project (DeStefano, Hanson, Kallemeyn, & Johnson, 2006).

In the early grades, we found that word recognition would increase over the three grade levels of our literacy assessment, but storybook listening and story development always stayed under the 50th percentile, even in the spring scores for kindergarten and first grade, whether the assessment was given in Spanish or English. ELL students may need more intense vocabulary development and immersion in story structure to make a bridge to reading. Students who are somewhat proficient in two languages may still lack the substantial vocabulary and story structure development needed to support robust word learning, fluency, and comprehension.

At this time teachers need to think about expanded factors as to why ELL students do not reach the level of native English speakers on fluency assessments by eighth grade. Thomas and Collier (1997, 2002) conducted a large-scale study of ELLs enrolled in different program models to discover how many years were needed for this population to reach grade-level proficiency in English. They found that achieving academic language parity with native speakers takes ELLs somewhere in the range of 5–7 years, and that language learning programs, generally, are advantageous to this development. It is possible that some students are exited from first-language support programs too soon or that such programs are not available to them, and other factors, including limited knowledge of vocabulary or story structure, may also impede the development of reading fluency. This might suggest a basis for instruction that would boost decoding, fluency, and comprehension. Providing a more robust foundation in the development of both language and literacy conventions may be a direction to explore to help ELL students progress further in fluency, with all of the benefits that brings.

## REFERENCES

Allington, R. (2002). What I've learned about effective reading instruction from a decade of studying exemplary classroom teachers. *Phi Delta Kappan, 83*(10), 740–747.

Beck, I., McKeown, M., & Kucan, L. (2002). *Bringing words to life: Robust vocabulary instruction.* New York: Guilford Press.

Blachowicz, C., Sullivan, D., & Cieply, C. (2001). Fluency snapshots: A quick screening tool for your classroom. *Reading Psychology, 22,* 95–109.

DeStefano, L., Hanson, M., Kallemeyn, L., & Johnson, J. (2006). *Fourth year evaluation report for ARDDP for Chicago Community Trust.* Chicago: Chicago Community Trust.

Ditkowksy, B. (2011). *Cut scores to Illinois Standards Achievement Test based on 2010 scores.* Retrieved from *www.measuredeffects.com/UserFiles/modules/file_upload_library/Full%202010%20Cut%20Scores.pdf.*

Fountas, I. C., & Pinnell, G. S. (2001). *Guiding readers and writers: Grades 3–6.* Portsmouth, NH: Heinemann.

Good, R. H., III, Kaminski, R. A., Simmons, D., & Kame'enui, E. J. (2001). Using Dynamic Indicators of Basic Early Literacy Skills (DIBELS) in an outcomes-driven model: Steps to reading outcomes. *OSSC Bulletin, 44*(1).

Griffith, L., & Rasinski, T. V. (2004). A focus on fluency: How one teacher incorporated fluency with her reading curriculum. *The Reading Teacher, 58*(2), 126–137.

Hanson, M., DeStefano, L., Blachowicz, C., Mueller, P., & Eason-Watkin, B. (2006, April). *Development, validation and use of indicator of high literacy performance: A framework for use in school literacy programs.* Paper presented at the annual conference of the American Educational Research Association, San Francisco, CA.

Hart, E., & Risley, T. R. (1995). *Meaningful differences in the everyday experience of young American children.* Baltimore, MD: Brookes.

Hasbrouck, J., & Tindal, G. A. (2006). Oral reading fluency norms: A valuable assessment tool for reading teachers. *The Reading Teacher, 59*(7), 636–644.

Johns, J. (2005). Fluency norms for students in grades one through eight. *Illinois Reading Council Journal, 34*(4), 3–8.

Krauss, R. (1945). *The carrot seed.* New York: Harper & Row.

Lems, K. (2004). A study of adult ESL oral reading fluency and silent reading comprehension. In E. Maloch, J. V. Hoffman, D. L. Schallert, C. M. Fairbanks, & J. Worthy (Eds.), *54th yearbook of the National Reading Conference* (pp. 240–256). Oak Creek, WI: National Reading Conference.

Lindsay, J. (2010). *Children's access to print material and education-related outcomes: Findings from a meta-analytic review.* Naperville, IL: Learning Point Associates.

Ogle, D., M. (2008). Teacher education and professional development in reading: 50 years of learning. In M. J. Fresch (Ed.), *An essential history of current reading practices* (pp. 207–228). Newark, DE: International Reading Association.

Palinscar, A. S., & Brown, A. L. (1984). Reciprocal teaching of comprehension-fostering and comprehension-monitoring activities. *Cognition and Instruction, 2,* 117–175.

Samuels, S. J. (1979). The method of repeated readings. *Reading Teacher, 32,* 403–408.

Shinn, M. R. (1989). *Curriculum-based measurement: Assessing special children.* New York: Guilford Press.

Snow, C. (1998). *Presenting reading difficulties in young children.* Washington, DC: National Academy Press.

Strecker, S. K., Roser, N. L., & Martinez, M. G. (1998). Toward understanding oral reading fluency. In T. Shanahan & F. V. Rodriquez-Brown (Eds.), *Forty-*

*seventh yearbook of the National Reading Conference* (pp. 295–310). Chicago: National Reading Conference.

Teale, W., H., (2008). Partnerships for improving literacy in urban schools. *The Reading Teacher, 61*(8), 674–680.

Thomas, W., & Collier, V. (2002). *A national study of school effectiveness for language minority students' long-term academic achievement final report: Prohect 1.1.* Berkeley, CA: Center for Research, Education, Diversity and Excellence. Retrieved from *crede.berkeley.edu/research/llaa/1.1_final.html.*

Thomas, W. P., & Collier, V. P. (1997). *School effectiveness for language minority students.* Washington, DC: National Clearinghouse for Bilingual Education.

Topping, K. J. (2006). Paired reading: Impact of a tutoring method on reading accuracy, comprehension, and fluency. In T. Rasinski, C. Blachowicz, & K. Lems (Eds.), *Fluency instruction: Research-based best practices* (pp. 173–191). New York: Guilford Press.

# 18

# Curious George and Rosetta Stone

## The Role of Texts in Supporting Automaticity in Beginning Reading

Elfrieda H. Hiebert

Through my early teens, I lived in a dual-language—German and English—environment, but my use of German fell off rapidly once I began third grade in a large, urban school. Unlike the students in the small village school that I had attended to that point, my new classmates were all native English speakers. And as often happens with children from immigrant homes, I became adamant that I would fit in by only speaking English too. As I approached my 60th birthday, however, my lifelong interest in literacy and language (and of gerontology) convinced me that I would like to recapture my first language and become proficient in German.

I began by getting a set of German language children's books. My reasoning was that reading these books could be a focus of frequent phone conversations with *meine Mutti*, a fluent German speaker. I selected books that were easily obtained in the United States, one of which was *Coco fährt Rad* (*Curious George Rides a Bike*; Rey, 1980). Putting into practice what I have learned and even written about the appropriate pedagogy for building fluency (see, e.g., Hiebert, 2007), I practiced repeated reading of the book. My mother and I had the same version of the text, and several times a week I would read a section to her repeatedly. These read-aloud sessions were painful. Why? Consider the section *Coco fährt Rad* in Table 18.1. I knew the meaning of the words in this section, since I assume that automaticity and comprehension are inseparable. Consequently, I began each session with a translation of the text. But there were so many words to pronounce!

**TABLE 18.1. Examples of Texts for Beginning Reading in German**

| *Coco fährt Rad* | Modeled after Rosetta Stone | |
|---|---|---|
| Das ist Coco. Er wohnte bei seinem Freund, dem Mann mit dem gelben Hut. Er war ein lieber kleiner Afe, und er war immer neugierig. An diesem Morgen war Coco schon neugierig, als er aufwachte, denn er wusste, dass heute ein besonderer Tag war. | rot | einen rotten Apfel |
| | grün | einen grünen Apfel |
| | | rote und grüne Äpfel |

I was fast with the high-frequency words such as *das, ist, er, bei, dem,* and *mit.* However, multisyllabic words such as *neugierig, aufwachte,* and *besonderer* were not so easy, especially when the next paragraph had a new set of challenging multisyllabic words—in this case, *Frühstück, Dschungel,* and *Überraschung.*

After the first several weeks of these repeated reading sessions, I was convinced that I was developing a reading disability in German. I would see a big word coming up in the text and start making errors with the little words.

At this point, I decided to try a new approach. I bought the first levels of the language-learning software program Rosetta Stone. I moved quickly through the first lessons that focus on colors, numbers, and simple objects, as illustrated by red and green apples in the sample text in Table 18.1.[1] In lessons such as these, I was learning the German letter–sound correspondences, the ways in which German adjectives function, and a variety of other dimensions of orthography, morphology, and syntax. I soon abandoned the German children's books to concentrate on Rosetta Stone, and I applied my skills in conversations with my mother about simple topics, although there is only so far one can go in talking about apples, leaves, or balloons.

I had not planned for my German-learning experience to be a case study of the research that I have conducted over the past 15 years. After all, I am an adult language learner who has substantial metalinguistic awareness of three elements that most young children do not have: (1) the oral language of instructional text, (2) learning pedagogy, and (3) language systems. But there were elements of the experience that did resonate with my research. For novices (even adult ones) to become automatic in reading (or speaking) a language requires that there be at least a modicum of repetition

---

[1] Because of copyright restrictions, the text in column 2 of Table 18.1 illustrates, rather than duplicates, a Rosetta Stone beginning lesson.

of the critical and consistent patterns of language. The children's books, while interesting and containing instances of critical and consistent language patterns, also contained many multisyllabic words with new, challenging patterns. Even with my expert knowledge of language and prior experience with German, I failed to become automatic with any but the most frequent words when confronted with the large amount of new and complex information in the children's books. Rosetta Stone, however, provided critical and consistent data without substantial amounts of diverting information.

The theme of this chapter is straightforward but often overlooked in beginning reading instruction: Beginning reading texts need to give young children many opportunities to apply their emerging knowledge of written words. Opportunities to focus on increasing reading speed occur in subsequent levels, but this later proficiency is built on the early foundation. If children's early experiences have not built that foundation, fluent reading is difficult to develop (Torgesen et al., 2001).

The theme is sufficiently important to bear elaboration. Specifically, the kinds of experiences that support fluency in beginning readers differ from those that other authors in this volume describe for students who are not novices, even if they are struggling readers. Chall (1983) described a stage of reading development—Stage 0—that precedes formal reading instruction. It is in this stage that children learn about texts, letters, words, sounds, and the act of reading through read-alouds, scribbling on paper, moving preformed letters to form words, and a host of other activities that should occur in preschools and kindergarten. For students who have not had such Stage 0 experiences but are placed in kindergartens and first grades that have Stage 1 expectations (learning to break the code quickly), texts that provide consistent information about critical word features in manageable chunks are fundamental.

Over a 15-year period, my colleagues and I (e.g., Hiebert, 1999; Hiebert & Fisher, 2006b; Hiebert, Martin, & Menon, 2005) have worked to refine a curriculum for creating texts that support a foundation of automaticity, meaningfulness, and engagement. In this chapter, I call this curriculum by the name of the digital system it uses to analyze texts: TABB (text analysis: beginning books). The chapter describes the curriculum and summarizes evidence that exposure to TABB-based texts supports a fluent start for beginning readers. It concludes with text selection guidelines for educators.

I stress that this work is aimed at supporting the reading development of children who depend on schools to become literate. For children from low-income homes and immigrant backgrounds where languages other than English are spoken in home and community, the quality of school reading experiences will determine whether they learn to read well. These are the students for whom the match between proficiency and texts matters most.

## TABB: A ROAD MAP FOR SUPPORTING AUTOMATICITY IN BEGINNING READERS

A good curriculum can be thought of as a road map—a way to show us how to get from where we are now to where we want to be. For teachers, *where* they want their students to be is reading proficiently. But setting the goal of "wanting my students to be good readers" is not enough to make it happen. Although this goal is laudable, helping a classroom of 25 young children whose literacy learning occurs primarily in school attain it requires a substantial amount of teacher knowledge and effort. Without a strong curriculum to provide that knowledge and guidance, teachers will have a hard time assisting students in becoming good readers.

At the same time, a road map that has been generated for every teacher to follow with every single child in the United States presents problems. The use of the same reading program teachers' guide across thousands of classrooms assumes that all children are starting from the same location and will move at the same pace. If the assumption that one map works for all were accurate, then chapters such as this one would not be necessary. Indeed, if the same lesson plan presented at the same pace works for all, it should be possible to have a digitally generated voice (much like a GPS) to guide children through the reading process and get them all to the desired destination: proficient reading. Even with more than a decade of federal, state, and district mandates stipulating that teachers use scripted lessons and follow the same instructional pacing (e.g., Esquith, 2004; Gunn, 2004), an appreciable difference has not been evident in the end-of-grade 3 reading achievement of American students (Gamse, Jacob, Horst, Boulay, & Unlu, 2008).

The Common Core State Standards (Common Core State Standards Initiative, 2010) illustrate a perspective between the extremes of "get my kids to love reading" and a scripted set of lessons. The standards do not provide guidelines for beginning reading because they are aimed at the reading proficiencies necessary for college and careers (and so assume a foundation of reading proficiency). They, however, do set benchmark goals for particular points along the way and *always* maintain the vision of the overall goal: proficient reading of literary and informational text. This presentation of benchmarks that foster an end goal also is the direction represented in TABB—a curriculum with enough specificity that students are supported in expanding their capacity but not with so much specificity that teachers must march students lockstep through a set of lessons.

The TABB curriculum focuses specifically on word recognition. Of course, other dimensions such as syntax and genre are central to the design of efficacious texts that support reading success (Mesmer, Cunningham, & Hiebert, 2010). But without the ability to recognize written vocabulary, beginning readers will find the message of texts (at least those messages that do not depend on illustrations for interpretation) inaccessible.

## The Focus of the TABB Curriculum

To obtain an index of the number of words in a text that are predicted to be critical for readers with particular levels of knowledge, the TABB approach focuses on two areas: (1) the features of individual words and (2) the distribution of words within a text or a set of texts.

### Features of Individual Words

To beginning readers, as for adults, a word is a multifaceted entity (Nagy & Scott, 2000). The essence of a word is its meaning. For young children, the initial interest lies in recognizing their own names, the name of a pet or best friend, or words such as *Mommy, Daddy,* and *love* (Hiebert, 1983). The recognition of such highly personal words, often by the idiosyncratic shapes of their graphic representation, may support initiation into literacy, but it is not sufficient for independent word recognition (Ehri, 1991). Four features contribute to the ease or difficulty with which a word is recognized and remembered: (1) frequency in written language, (2) morphology, (3) vowel and syllabic structure, and (4) concreteness.

*Frequency in Written Language.* The frequency with which a word occurs is not an inherent quality of the word. Rather, it reflects the word's function in written language. The most frequent word in written English— *the*—is predicted to occur 68,000 times in every 1 million words of text (Zeno, Ivens, Millard, & Duvvuri, 1995). Words that are among the first spoken by young children—*cookie* and *juice*—occur with considerably less frequency in written text: four and 19 times per million words, respectively. This contrast illustrates that frequency cannot be used as a proxy for word familiarity in learning to read. Even so, most of the words that occur with high frequency in written language—the ubiquitous high-function words such as *the, of, a, and, was*—are also a frequent part of oral language.

*Morphology.* A second feature of words that contributes to their ease of recognition pertains to their morphological or meaning units. The word *into,* for example, is made up of two base meaning units: *in* and *to.* Another highly frequent word—*others*—is made up of a base meaning unit—*other*—and *s*, which is called a bound morpheme because it never appears on its own. Such morphological changes in words are often given short shrift in beginning reading programs, even though words that share a root word but have an inflection (i.e., *ed, ing, s/es, 's, s'*) or a derivation (e.g., prefix or suffix) are frequent in written English. Nagy and Anderson (1984) estimate that approximately 40% of the words in written English are derivative or inflected forms of other words.

In oral language, the inflected forms that typically appear in beginning reading programs (i.e., *ride, rides, riding*) are known by native English language learners when they start school. Typically, these children also know some derivational suffixes such as *-er* (e.g., *runner, teacher*) (Anglin, 1993; Tyler & Nagy, 1989). The manner in which children are able to draw on this knowledge as they encounter new words in texts is less certain. Even more uncertain is the task posed by inflections and derivations for children who speak unique dialects of English or who speak native languages that have different morphological forms and rules than English. It is typically assumed that children transfer their morphological knowledge in speech to the recognition of simple written endings (i.e., inflected forms, simple derivational suffixes such as *-er* and *-ly/-y*). Instruction on endings does not typically appear in the scope and sequence of core reading programs until second grade, even though numerous words with inflected endings and simple derivational suffixes appear (without instructional focus) in the first-grade texts.

*Vowel and Syllabic Structure.* The third category of words that contributes to their ease of recognition is their common, consistent vowel patterns. English words, even those that include irregular letter–sound correspondences, are alphabetic. To develop automaticity in reading requires generalization and application of knowledge about the relationships between written letters and their oral language sounds. Scholars may argue the interpretations of research findings as to the weight that should be placed on teaching letter–sound correspondences at different times in the learning-to-read process, but there can be no doubt that learning how letters represent the sounds of the oral language that they know is what distinguishes readers from nonreaders (Adams, 1990; National Reading Panel, 2000).

*Imagery Value.* The fourth feature contributing to word recognition is the word's imageability, or the ease with which it arouses a mental image (Paivio, Yuille, & Madigan, 1968). Most, but not all, words that have a high imagery value are concrete nouns. Some verbs, however, create strong images (e.g., *running*), and some nouns that are highly concrete may not be known to young children (e.g., *carburetor*). Consequently, the term *imagery value* is used to describe the degree to which a word is memorable because of its meaning.

Within the currently most prominent text-leveling system (Fountas & Pinnell, 1999), the texts viewed to be most appropriate for beginning readers are those with a strong picture–text match. That is, children can figure out at least some of the words on a page by looking at the accompanying illustrations. Relying on illustrations, however, can diminish beginning readers' attention to critical features of words (Samuels, 1970). Highly imageable words that appear consistently in a program, on the other hand, can support reading acquisition. Even among words chosen for a decoding curriculum, the imagery value of words influences word recognition. Primary-level students (Kolker & Terwilliger, 1981) and even kindergartners (Hargis & Gickling, 1978) learn high-imagery words more efficaciously than low-imagery words. When the decodability of words has been manipulated along with imagery value, high-imagery, decodable words are learned more quickly than other groups of words, including high-imagery, less decodable words (Laing & Hulme, 1999).

## Features of a Reading Program

No matter how many times a parent or kindergarten teacher rereads a favorite text to children, a single text does not make up an instructional program. Children learn to read well as a result of exposure to many texts. A precise number for the volume of the needed texts will never be possible. However, especially in classrooms where the majority of beginning readers do not have a long history with books, texts need to be plentiful and, for particular parts of a school day, provide the scaffolding needed for children to work with critical information about reading.

When classes contain many children who depend on appropriate school experiences—and when time is of the essence—there are two primary characteristics that go into the design of a program of texts: (1) sequence of critical information and (2) amount of new information in a single unit (i.e., a text). We describe these elements as influencing the "cognitive load"—the amount of information that young children can process at any given time.

In teaching novices, whether the domain is piano or quantum physics, optimal learning requires that information be presented in a logical sequence. Numerous theories, schemes, recommendations, and even governmental policies exist about how best to initiate children into reading written English. But amid all of this theory and rhetoric, a surprisingly small amount of research has validated specific sequences in introducing critical features of written words to children. Empirical validation exists only for the phonics sequence, and even this work is limited in scope (Guthrie & Seifert, 1977; Pirani-McGurl, 2009).

It was only after extensive reviews of research were conducted that choices were made about the sequence of words within the TABB curriculum. The content of the TABB curriculum that resulted from this review and decision-making process is illustrated in Table 18.2.

The content of the curriculum has been parsed into nine levels. For three of the dimensions—frequency, decodability, and morphology—each new level adds additional information (as can be seen with the illustrative levels in Table 18.2). For the fourth variable of imagery value, all 1,000 high-imagery words that have been identified through analyses of concept books (e.g., DK Publishing, 2008; Scarry, 1985 ) and corpora of children's oral and written language reception and production (Johnson, Moe, & Baumann, 1983) are viewed as equally appropriate for inclusion in children's texts at the first level. It is at the first level where high-imagery words would be expected to be most prominent, and these words would be expected to steadily consume less and less of the percentage of texts in higher levels.

## Using TABB to Establish the Difficulty of Texts

The information on the features of words and the number of different words within a book is matched to the levels of the curriculum to get a measure we call the *critical word factor* (CWF; Hiebert & Fisher, 2007). The CWF tells a teacher how many words in a particular text fall outside a specific level of the curriculum. That is, the critical words are the words that do not fit any of the four criteria—frequency, decodability, morphology, and concreteness—at whichever of the nine levels of the curriculum is the focus (see example levels in Table 18.2). Students may be able to use decoding or context skills to get a word's meaning, but the word contains new information that may require them to attend to the word and not recognize it automatically.

A text does not have a single CWF. A single text can be matched against numerous levels of the curriculum (or even different curricula for that matter), and for each level the result can be a different CWF. To illustrate how the CWF is computed, the words in sets of four types of texts have been analyzed according to levels 3, 5, and 7 of the TABB curriculum. These four text types represent reading programs that are currently in use in beginning reading instruction in American classrooms and that have been used in the studies described in the next section of this chapter. The words for each text type came from six books that appear sequentially within the same point in the program.

**TABLE 18.2. Progression of the TABB curriculum: Tasks from Emergent to Independent Reading**

| Level | Frequency | Decodability | Morphology | Imagery value |
|-------|-----------|--------------|------------|---------------|
| 1 | 25 most frequent | • VC<br>CV<br>CVC[1] | [No new content] | • High percentage of highly imageable words from familiar categories (e.g., home, animals) |
| 3 | 75 most frequent | • CVCC(C) and CCVC | Plural es[2] | [No new content] |
| 5 | 300 most frequent | • Consonant-controlled vowels in high-frequency groups (e.g., *call, old, bright*) | *ed* | • Moderate percentage of highly imageable words from familiar categories |
| 7 | 500 most frequent | • *ow* as long *o*; *r*-controlled (*air, ear*) | [No new content] | [No new content] |
| 9 | 930 most frequent | • Two-syllable words with consistent vowels in first syllable (e.g., *table, happy*) | Compound words where the head word is among the most frequent 750 words (e.g., *uphill, upset; outside/ outdoor*) | • Imageable words come from moderately familiar categories (e.g., animal homes) and account for smaller percent of total words. |

*Note.* V, vowel; C, consonant.
[1]Plural with *s* and possessive ('s) have been added in level 2.
[2]Remaining CVC patterns (*e, i, o, u*) are added in level 2.

When analyzed according to the criteria of level 3 of the TABB curriculum, the four sets of texts have CWFs that range from 6 (NEARStar; Pacific Resources for Education and Learning, 2003) to 20 (anthology; Cooper et al., 2002). What does this mean for young readers? If students are not yet automatic with the 75 most frequent words and with consonant clusters at the beginning and/or end of words, six of every 100 words in the NEARStar texts will require them to figure out words that have additional features. In the anthology, they will be confronted with 20 new words in every 100 words of text.

If students have knowledge that aligns with level 5 of the curriculum, however, one word for every 100 within the NEARStar texts is predicted to be critical or hard. In the anthology, 13 of every 100 words will have information that level 5 readers are unlikely to know. For students with facility with the 500 most frequent words and knowledge of consonant-controlled vowels (level 7 skills), none of the words in the set of NEARStar texts is predicted to be critical or hard. Within the anthology, however, there will continue to be a fairly critical number of words that could challenge even level 7 readers—nine for every 100 words.

In examining the information in Table 18.3, remember that all of the texts were presented by their publishers as appropriate for approximately the same point in reading development: the end of the first trimester of first grade. The differences across the four sets of texts at this first level, how-ever, are substantial. In the next section, we explore how these different profiles influence students' reading acquisition.

**TABLE 18.3. Comparison of the CWFs for Three Programs at Mid-First-Grade Level**

|  |  |  | Curriculum | | |
| --- | --- | --- | --- | --- | --- |
| Study | Program | Sample text | 3 | 5 | 7 |
| Hiebert & Fisher (2006a, 2006b) | NEARStar designed according to TABB curriculum (Pacific Resources for Education & Learning, 2003) | Dan sees the man. He stops. The dog sees the man too. It stops. The school van stops, too. Can Dan and the dog go to school now?.06 | .01 | .01 | 0 |
|  | Decodable (Adams et al. 2000) | Can I help? Ham, Sam Clam? Called Fred. Not ham, clicked Sam Clam. Grab a top hat, Bill Bat, said Fred. No top hats, snapped Bill Bat. | .11 | .07 | .06 |
| Menon & Hiebert (2005) | Leveled readers selected according to TABB curriculum (Juel, Hiebert, & Englebretson, 1997) | Lost! said the dog. Oh, no! said the frog. Help! said the hog. The dog, the frog, and the hog sat on a log. | .09 | .03 | .01 |
|  | Lionni (1975) from anthology core reading program (Cooper et al., 2002) | Parrots are green. Goldfish are red. Elephants are gray. Pigs are pink. All animals have a color of their own except for chameleons. They change color wherever they go. | .20 | .13 | .09 |

## EXAMINATIONS OF TABB-BASED TEXTS

Three experiments have been conducted with texts based on the TABB curriculum. In the first one, existing reading program texts were reorganized to comply, as best as possible, with the parameters of the curriculum. The second and third experiments used a set of texts that had been written according to the sequence of the curriculum. The first study has an "implicit match" to the TABB curriculum, while the second and third studies exemplify texts with explicit matches to the curriculum.

### Implicit Match

The first study (Menon & Hiebert, 2005) was a classroom-based investigation of students' reading performances as a function of reading texts from anthologies in the district's core reading program or a set of "little books" that had been organized to represent key elements of the TABB curriculum. With two first-grade classes, teachers used anthology texts in their typical patterns. In the other two first-grade classes, teachers were asked to substitute the TABB-based texts for those in the anthologies. The only change that teachers were requested to make had to do with the books that they used for their lessons and students' reading, whether that reading was in the whole class, small groups, or independent.

The instruction that extended over a 16-week period began at the point where many students were ready for the content of TABB curriculum 3 (see Table 18.2). The features of the two types of texts used in the study—the core reading anthology and the little books—are summarized in Table 18.3. A primary difference between the two sets of texts was that the anthology had substantially more hard words per 100 words of text than did the little books. Even though the little books had been reordered according to the TABB criteria, it was not possible to obtain a level of repetition of individual words to achieve the approximately three to four critical words per 100 that has been identified within the framework as likely appropriate for efficacious beginning reading development.

Even though it was not possible to create optimal word–density ratios with the existing leveled texts according to the TABB curriculum, a higher percentage of words was repeated in the little books than in the anthology texts: between 85 and 90% of all words in the former relative to 65–70% in the latter. In particular, fewer words appeared a single time in the little book curriculum than in the anthology curriculum: 20% compared with 30–35%. Although the little book program did not provide a built-in, consistent progression in word–density ratios across time and groups, the program did provide a greater degree of word repetition during a specific week than did the anthology texts read during a comparable period.

Students' performances on the Qualitative Reading Inventory word lists and texts from the beginning to the end of the intervention period were used to establish the effectiveness of the two conditions. Students in the TABB condition had higher means on both the word list and passage measures than did students in the anthology condition during the posttest assessments. The group reading little books improved by 2.8 text levels as a result of the intervention, while the group reading from anthology selections improved by 1.8 text levels during the same period. At the end of the 15 weeks, intervention group students were reading, on average, second-grade-level passages, while comparison students were reading first-grade-level passages.

The results of this study suggest that even a moderate amount of scaffolding of texts can make a difference in the word recognition skills of first graders. Whether of initially struggling, average, or high reading achievement, students in the intervention group read at one level of text higher than the students in the anthology group by the end of first grade. After 15 weeks of reading from the little books, most of the students were leaving first grade able to be successful with the second-grade texts, while their peers who had read from the anthology did not have this extra advantage. Further, 33% of the comparison group students had not attained the level of first-grade reading, in contrast to 10% of the students in the little book group who failed to attain this level.

## Explicit Match

Except for the length of the intervention, the design of the two studies that Hiebert and Fisher (2006a, 2006b) considered the *explicit match* of the curriculum was similar, in terms of type of students, research design, instructional procedures, and texts. Instruction in Study 1 (Hiebert & Fisher, 2006b) lasted for 12 hours over an 8-week period and Study 2 (Hiebert & Fisher, 2006a) lasted for 20 hours over 12 weeks.

In both studies, students were English language learners during the final trimester of first grade. They attended schools in which the majority of students were native Spanish speakers (94–97%). The students were administered a timed word recognition task that included both phonetically regular and high-frequency words. On the basis of the results of this assessment, students from a particular class who had adequate but not proficient levels of fluency (defined as fewer than 50 words correct per minute) were randomly assigned to one of three groups: (1) the TABB-based texts, (2) decodable texts on the state's list of approved books (but not adopted by the district), and (3) a control group that used the decodable texts in the district's core reading program. At least nine students from a class were needed to ensure that three students could be randomly assigned to each of the three groups.

Students met in small groups with a project teacher for half-hour sessions. Project teachers were provided with lesson plans, developed by the investigators, for each text. Time allocations were provided for each of four activities: (1) word card activities that used two words with particular letter–sound correspondences from a text (6 minutes); (2) three readings of a new book—teacher-led read-aloud with a retelling of the story by students, paired reading, and choral reading (10 minutes); (3) writing words on individual chalkboards (5 minutes); and (4) reading an additional book or rereading of books from previous lessons (9 minutes).

The content and focus of the lesson were the same (i.e., the students in the comparison group received information about the same phonics elements and high-frequency words). During that time, one group read from texts that were written to comply with the TABB curriculum (Pacific Resources for Education and Learning, 2003), illustrated in the first row of Table 18.3. The other group read from the decodable books of the Open Court Reading program (Adams et al., 2000). The total number of words per text was kept equivalent by selecting particular decodable texts and particular TABB-based texts within each respective program. The texts for the decodable group were also sorted to emphasize the features of the curriculum as best as possible. However, the decodables had not been written to include elements of high-frequency and high-imagery words. As can be seen in Table 18.3, there were differences between the TABB-based texts and the decodable texts. The decodable text had significantly more words that fell outside of the level-appropriate curriculum. Also evident in Table 18.3 is that the decodable curriculum moves very quickly to emphasize inflected endings. In the case of the inflected ending -ing, this addition means that some words are increased in size substantially when the final consonant is doubled (e.g., run/running). The TABB-based texts did not make similar demands at this point in the sequence. Further, the decodable texts had many more unique words than did the TABB-based texts— almost 100 in the same number of total words.

Eight assessments of two types were given to individual students before and after the intervention: Four assessed students' reading of words in text and four assessed their knowledge of words without textual context. The text-reading measures yielded information on rate of reading, accuracy, and comprehension on first-grade passages of the Texas Primary Reading Inventory (TPRI; Texas Education Agency, 2002) and the 40th texts of each of the two programs that were used in the intervention. Word-level assessments consisted of two measures from the Test of Word Reading Efficiency (Torgesen, Wagner, & Rashotte, 1999) as well as the two experimenter-developed measures of phonetically regular and high-frequency words that were used for identifying the sample.

Results of both studies are summarized in Table 18.4 as effect sizes. Remember that the differences between the two groups were fairly subtle. That is, the curriculum sequence was kept the same and the activities in which students were involved were the same. The primary difference lay in the repetition of words that represented particular patterns in the TABB-based curriculum. An examination of Table 18.4 effect sizes reveals three key findings:

1. The longer the intervention, the greater the difference between the TABB and the decodable group.
2. Both of the intervention groups that received texts with the well-paced, sequential curriculum did substantially better than the class-room group. A question that should be raised is the degree to which these differences were due to the whole-class format rather than the curriculum. The answer is that with nine children in the intervention, the number of students in particular classes, which had class sizes of about 17 to 19, is actually quite small. Therefore, all of this difference cannot be attributed to class size.
3. Students did much better in the TABB-based group on their own text. In other words, a sequence was supporting students, which was not the case with the decodable text group. In fact, the TABB group students also did just a little bit better than the students in the decodable group on the assessment text from the decodable program. So we can conclude that the TABB-designed text was supporting progression along a curriculum, and that it was moving at a pace that allowed beginning readers to become more automatic in their reading.

## WHAT TEACHERS CAN DO

The theme of this chapter has been that beginning readers become fluent by reading many texts in which they recognize most of the words. Put another way, texts that match students' word knowledge allow them to develop a habit of fluent, meaningful reading from the start. Texts that require beginning readers to stop and figure out large numbers of words hinder such a habit.

I have used the TABB curriculum to illustrate how texts can be identified to support automaticity in beginning readers. This curriculum should

**TABLE 18.4. Effect Sizes for Two Interventions of TABB-Based and Decodable Texts**

| Comparison | TPRI 1st text | TPRI 3rd text | TABB 40th text | Decodable 40th text | High freq. | Sight | Phon. reg. | Phon. decod. |
|---|---|---|---|---|---|---|---|---|
| | | | Study 1 | | | | | |
| TABB—Decodable | .05 | −.05 | .7 | .06 | −.1 | .04 | −.04 | −.26 |
| TABB—Control | .39 | −.02 | .64 | .44 | .13 | .27 | .29 | .28 |
| Decodable—Control | .36 | .01 | .25 | .80 | .19 | .25 | .33 | .43 |
| | | | Study 2 | | | | | |
| TABB—Decodable | .08 | .25 | .43 | .01 | .29 | .05 | .22 | .05 |
| TABB—Control | .42 | .22 | .7 | .05 | .43 | .21 | .26 | .33 |
| Decodable—Control | .32 | −.01 | .26 | .04 | .15 | .16 | .03 | .27 |

*Note.* .5+: dark gray; .33–.49: medium gray; .20–.32: light gray.

by no means be regarded as a be-all and end-all of beginning reading curricula. In fact, at this time, the TABB software is in the experimental phase and available for research use only. The underlying principles of the text selection process, however, are applicable to any venue for teaching beginning readers. Specifically, teachers need a road map that lets them know what the goals are at particular points along the way in beginning reading acquisition and where students are in this progression. Once they have this information, they need to identify the books that are a good match for students and determine how quickly to move them through a set of books.

## Knowing What Students Need to Know

Teaching children to read requires that teachers understand the linguistic knowledge base of written English. At various points in the past century, scholars have focused attention on various parts of this base: high-frequency words, high-interest words and predictable syntactic structure, and, currently, letter–sound correspondences. The stance of this chapter has been that the words that make up written English are multifaceted, and that the benchmarks and goals within a beginning reading curriculum need to address several quite different features of words simultaneously. But even in contexts that emphasize a single criterion, such as letter–sound correspondences, teachers need to be vigilant in keeping in mind what students need to learn and the kinds of texts that support and move them forward in acquiring that knowledge.

## Knowing What Students Know

To understand where students are in the progression of reading acquisition, teachers need valid assessments that match the curriculum and give the kind of information they can use to select appropriate texts. Often there is a mismatch between the assessment and the texts. Take, for example, a common situation: In many schools and districts during the Reading First era, decodable texts were used for reading instruction, and the Dynamic Indicators of Basic Early Literacy Skills (DIBELS; Good & Kaminski, 2002) was used for assessment. The reputation of DIBELS as a phonics-first measure reflects the nonsense word subtest and the domination of 1-minute reading in the assessment of text fluency. The means of validating the sequencing of texts for the 1-minute assessment, however, was the Spache (1953) readability formula, which establishes difficulty on the basis of sentence length and a list of primarily high-frequency words (Good & Kaminski, 2002). A readability formula that evaluates the length of sentences and the presence of high-frequency words (Spache, 1953) was the basis for validating the DIBELS test passages (Good & Kaminski, 2002), but the DIBELS assesses students' reading according to quite a different model. The assessment data, then, are not highly useful in aiding teachers in selecting appropriate texts within a decodable program.

If teachers find themselves in situations in which there is a mismatch between instructional texts and assessments, they may wish to draw on a technique used in the explicit match studies of the TABB curriculum. In these studies, Hiebert and Fisher (2006a, 2006b) selected texts from strategic points in the program, made certain that the texts were not used for instruction, and used them to assess students' progress. Such a procedure also ensures that teachers have sufficient numbers of texts to use for assessment. Young children's development as readers can be in jumps and starts, and assessments that occur only at the beginning, middle, and end of the year may not capture growth sufficiently. The use of texts from the instructional program that represent strategic benchmarks gives teachers an accurate and current view of children's movement along the beginning reading progression.

## Matching Students with Texts

Language and learners are both idiosyncratic. No amount of engineering (even with digital, hand-held, on-the-spot assessments) will ever produce an exact match between readers and texts. However, texts should have at least some words that have features with which children are facile and other words that have features that they are learning. A rule of thumb in reading education for almost a century has been that successful reading requires that approximately 95% of the words in a text need to be known to readers in instructional contexts and 98–99% in independent ones (Betts, 1946). At the beginning levels, finding texts in which students know all but a handful of words can be challenging. At the very least, students should know at least a core group of words in a text, and teachers should be able to support students in focusing on the features of the unknown words. Remember that in the implicit match TABB study, the differences between the little books and the selections in the core reading anthology were of degree, not of kind. Even with the little books, in which students did substantially better than in the core reading anthologies, the percentage of phonetically regular words did not achieve the critical mass that policy-makers mandate in the textbook adoptions of California (California State Board of Education, 2006) and Texas (Texas Education Agency, 2000). The majority of the words in the texts, however, did have patterns that students either knew or were learning.

One feature that did make a difference in the little book treatment condition was the amount of time that teachers spent on particular levels of texts. The intervention had been set up so that teachers had numerous texts with the linguistic content of a particular level. From among the available texts, teachers made choices about the number of texts given to different groups of students with similar needs. Teachers were making the decisions about the pace at which new content was provided. These decisions were based on teachers' decision making, not the decisions made by a group of reading program editors or authors at a different point in time and at a geographic location far from these classrooms and reflected in a teacher's guide as to what generic children *should* be able to do at particular points in time. The curriculum (i.e., an emphasis on high-frequency words, picture–text match, or decodable words) may be determined by the texts that a district or school has purchased. How long individual children spend with texts at particular levels, however, is within a teacher's purview. The presentation of lessons and pacing guides within published programs may appear "official," especially when the programs are offered as research based.

In some school districts (Esquith, 2004), policies have been implemented to mandate that teachers move all students through texts at the same pace. But even in the same class, students move at remarkably different paces in grasping particular patterns within words. When teachers have relevant and accurate information about what students know, they can make informed choices about how many texts students require at particular levels. One group of first graders may need to read dozens and dozens of texts at one benchmark level, while another group may only need a handful of books at that same benchmark level and be ready to move to the next level.

Over the last decade, a prominent perspective has been that the predetermined pace identified within the teacher's guide of a core reading program should be followed for all (e.g., Gunn, 2004). However, if some students can only read a handful of the words in a text, repeated reading of the text and movement to the next text will do very little good. Evidence that many first graders are simply moved through texts without learning the critical information can be seen in the explicit match studies (Hiebert & Fisher, 2006a, 2006b). Prior to the interventions (as well as during the intervention for the students in the control groups), all students proceeded through a designated set of texts at the mandated rate in kindergarten and the first half or more of first grade. Most students had little, if any, fluency with a core group of words. Their teachers had presented the lessons. The children had gone through the books, but the pace at which new information was presented was so discrepant from children's foundational knowledge that little had been gained from the experience.

Instructional choices on the part of teachers regarding pace do not mean that a lower bar is set for the students who are currently reading texts that are "easier" than the "one size fits all" track. The destination—proficient reading by third grade—is the same for all. Some students may be starting out at a different point than others. But the vast majority of students will attain the destination provided that they are given appropriate information in appropriate increments over time.

A second decision that goes hand in hand with pace is the amount of repetition with critical content that students have. Automaticity with content comes from repeated exposure to it. The aim of the interventions described in this chapter is not to get beginning readers to "read faster" but rather to read more. Observations of classrooms indicate that the amount that students read in classrooms is critically related to their reading achievements. From the best available information, the amount that low-performing first graders typically read per hour during classroom reading instruction is approximately 54 words (Allington, 1984). In both groups in the explicit match studies, students read approximately 270 words per half-hour, or 540 words per hour. The interventions increased by 10-fold the amount that students were reading as part of instruction. Keeping an estimate of the number of words that students are reading can be an important activity for teachers. Once a baseline has been established, teachers can focus on how to increase the amount of time that students are reading.

To get them solidly on the road to successful and engaged reading, young children require immersion in instruction where the texts make it possible for them to become automatic with the most critical features of written language. Matching appropriate texts with readers requires an understanding of the critical features and children's existing automaticity with these features. When teachers select appropriate texts and give students sufficient exposure to and repetition of critical features, students will develop the fluency in recognizing words that serves as a foundation for successful reading.

## REFERENCES

Adams, M. J. (1990). *Beginning to read: Thinking and learning about print.* Cambridge, MA: MIT Press.

Adams, M. J., Bereiter, C., McKeough, A., Case, R., Roit, M., Hirschberg, J., et al. (2000). *Open Court Reading.* Columbus, OH: SRA/McGraw-Hill.

Allington, R. L. (1984). Content coverage and contextual reading in reading groups. *Journal of Reading Behavior, 16,* 85–96.

Anglin, J. M. (1993). Vocabulary development: A morphological analysis. *Monographs of the Society for Research in Child Development, 58*(10, Serial No. 238).

Betts, E. A. (1946). *Foundations of reading instruction.* New York: American Book.

California State Board of Education. (2006). *Reading/language arts framework for California's public schools: Kindergarten through grade twelve.* Sacramento: California Department of Education.

Chall, J. S. (1983). *Stages of reading development.* New York: McGraw-Hill.

Common Core State Standards Initiative. (2010). *Common core state standards for English language arts & literacy in history/social studies, science, and technical subjects.* Washington, DC: CCSSO & National Governors Association.

Cooper, J. D., Pikulski, J. J., Ackerman, P. A., Au, K. H., Chard, D. J., Garcia, G. G., et al. (2002). *Houghton Mifflin reading.* Boston: Houghton Mifflin.

DK Publishing. (2008). *My first words: Let's get talking.* New York: DK Preschool.

Ehri, L. (1991). Development of the ability to read words. In R. Barr, M. L. Kamil, P. B. Mosenthal, & P. D. Pearson (Eds.), *Handbook of reading research* (Vol. II, pp. 383–417). New York: Longman.

Esquith, R. (2004). *There are no shortcuts.* New York: Anchor.

Fountas, I. C., & Pinnell, G. S. (1999). *Matching books to readers: Using leveled books in guided reading, K–3.* Portsmouth, NH: Heinemann.

Gamse, B. C., Jacob, R. T., Horst, M., Boulay, B., & Unlu, F. (2008). *Reading First impact study final report.* Washington, DC: National Center for Education Evaluation and Regional Assistance, Institute of Education Sciences, U.S. Department of Education.

Good, R. H., & Kaminski, R. A. (2002). *DIBELS oral reading fluency passages for first through third grades* (Technical Report No. 10). Eugene: University of Oregon.

Gunn, B. (2004, July). *Fidelity of implementation: Developing structures for improving the implementation of core, supplemental, and intervention programs.* Paper presented at the Reading First National conference, Minneapolis, MN. *Implementation_Fidelity-Developing_Structures.ppt.*

Guthrie, J. T., & Seifert, M. (1977). Letter-sound complexity in learning to identify words. *Journal of Educational Psychology, 69*(6), 686–696.

Hargis, C. H., & Gickling, E. E. (1978). The function of imagery in word recognition development. *Reading Teacher, 31,* 870–874.

Hiebert, E. H. (1983). A comparison of young children's self-selected reading words and basal reading words. *Reading Improvement, 20,* 41–44.

Hiebert, E. H. (1999). Text matters in learning to read (distinguished educators series). *The Reading Teacher, 52,* 552–568.

Hiebert, E. H. (2007). The word zone fluency curriculum: An alternative approach. In M. Kuhn & P. Schwanenflugel (Eds.), *Fluency in the classroom* (pp. 154–170). New York: Guilford Press.

Hiebert, E. H., & Fisher, C. W. (2006a, July). *A comparison of two types of text on the fluency of first-grade English language learners.* Paper presented at the annual meeting of the Society for the Scientific Study of Reading, Vancouver, BC.

Hiebert, E. H., & Fisher, C. W. (2006b). Fluency from the first: What works with first graders. In T. Rasinski, C. Blachowicz, & K. Lems (Eds.), *Fluency instruction: Reasearch-based best practices* (pp. 279–294). New York: Guilford Press.

Hiebert, E. H., & Fisher, C. W. (2007). The critical word factor in texts for beginning readers. *Journal of Educational Research, 101*(1), 3–11.

Hiebert, E. H., Martin, L. A., & Menon, S. (2005). Are there alternatives in reading textbooks? An examination of three beginning reading programs. *Reading and Writing Quarterly, 21*(1), 7–32.

Johnson, D., Moe, A., & Baumann, J.F. (1983). *The Ginn word book for teachers: A basic lexicon.* Boston: Ginn.

Juel, C., Hiebert, E. H., & Englebretson, R. (1997). *Ready readers.* Parsipanny, NJ: Modern Curriculum Press.

Kolker, B., & Terwilliger, P. N. (1981). Sight vocabulary learning of first and second graders. *Reading World, 20*(4), 251–258.

Laing, E., & Hulme, C. (1999). Phonological and semantic processes influence beginning readers' ability to learn to read words. *Journal of Experimental Child Psychology, 73,* 183–207.

Lionni, L. (1975). *A color of his own.* New York: Knopf.

Menon, S., & Hiebert, E. H. (2005). A comparison of first graders' reading with little books or literature-based basal anthologies. *Reading Research Quarterly, 40*(1), 12–38.

Mesmer, H. A., Cunningham, J. W., & Hiebert, E. H. (2010, December). *Toward a model of beginning reading text complexity.* Paper presented at the annual meeting of the National Reading Conference, Fort Worth, TX.

Nagy, W. E., & Anderson, R. C. (1984). How many words are there in printed school English? *Reading Research Quarterly, 19*(3), 304–330.

Nagy, W. E., & Scott, J. A. (2000). Vocabulary processes. In M. L. Kamil, P.

Mosenthal, P. D. Pearson, & R. Barr (Eds.), *Handbook of reading research* (Vol. III, pp. 269–284). Mahwah, NJ: Erlbaum.

National Reading Panel. (2000). *Teaching children to read: An evidence-based assessment of the scientific research literature on reading and its implications for reading instruction: Reports of the subgroups* (NIH Publication No. 00-4754). Washington, DC: National Institute of Child Health and Human Development.

Pacific Resources for Education and Learning. (2003). *NEARStar* (levels 1–3). Honolulu: Author.

Paivio, A., Yuille, J. C., & Madigan, S. (1968). Concreteness, imagery, and meaningfulness values of 925 nouns. *Journal of Experimental Psychology, 76,* 1–25.

Pirani-McGurl, C. A. (2009). *The use of item response theory in developing a phonics diagnostic inventory.* Retrieved November 2, 2011, from *scholarworks. umass.edu/open_access_dissertations/68.*

Rey, H. A. (1980). *Coco fährt rad.* Boston: Diogenes.

Samuels, S. J. (1970). Effects of pictures on learning to read, comprehension, and attitudes. *Review of Educational Research, 40,* 397–407.

Scarry, R. (1985). *Richard Scarry's biggest word book ever!* New York: Random House.

Spache, G. (1953). A new readability formula for primary-grade reading materials. *Elementary School Journal, 53* (7), 410–413.

Texas Education Agency. (2000). *Proclamation of the State Board of Education advertising for bids on textbooks.* Austin, TX: Author.

Texas Education Agency. (2002). *Texas Primary Reading Inventory.* Austin, TX: Author.

Torgesen, J. K., Alexander, A. W., Wagner, R. K., Rashotte, C. A., Voeller, K., Conway, T., et al. (2001). Intensive remedial instruction for children with severe reading disabilities: Immediate and long-term outcomes from two instructional approaches. *Journal of Learning Disabilities, 34,* 33–58.

Torgesen, J. K., Wagner, R. K., & Rashotte, C. A. (1999). *Test of word reading efficiency.* Austin, TX: PRO-ED.

Tyler, A., & Nagy, W. (1989). The acquisition of English derivational morphology. *Journal of Memory and Language, 28,* 649–667.

Zeno, S. M., Ivens, S. H., Millard, R. T., & Duvvuri, R. (1995). *The educator's word frequency guide.* New York: Touchstone Applied Science Associates.

# 19

# Building a Focus on Oral Reading Fluency into Individual Instruction for Struggling Readers

Jerry Zutell
Randal Donelson
Jessica Mangelson
Patsy Todt

In his seminal article, Allington (1983) discussed fluency as a forgotten goal of reading instruction. Interest in this dimension of proficient reading was slow to develop (for an exception, see Zutell & Rasinski, 1991a), but research such as the National Assessment of Educational Progress (NAEP) study, as reported by Pinnell and colleagues (1995), and reviews such as the report of the National Reading Panel (2000) have, over the last two decades, generated considerable focus on fluency assessment and building fluency instruction into the literacy curriculum. The extent and significance of these activities have led to the inclusion of a comprehensive review of reading fluency (Rasinski, Reutzel, Chard, & Linan-Thompson, 2011) in the most recent volume of the *Handbook of Reading Research* (Kamil, Pearson, Moje, & Afflerbach, 2011).

The NAEP study, in particular, found that fluency serves as a much better predictor of comprehension than oral reading accuracy, the traditional measure of reading instructional level. Our experiences working with struggling readers have been consistent with these findings. We find that a large majority of students who come to us for assistance are relatively slow, laborious readers, even on materials on which they are able to score at the independent level for accuracy. Furthermore, they are often able to maintain reasonable oral reading accuracy on more difficult materials, although their reading rates are well below expectations for students at their age and/or ability level. Struggling readers at beginning levels, with minimal sight vocabularies, often read even simple, well-known, and rehearsed texts in a word-by-word manner, with little sense of meaningful language.

In this chapter we describe how we address these issues in our clinical instruction. The approach and procedures we use in working with struggling readers were first formulated and applied when we worked as a team during the time Jerry Zutell served as Director of The Ohio State University Reading Clinic. Thus, we begin with a brief description of that instructional setting. Then we describe the general components of our program, present our beliefs about the nature of fluent reading, and discuss in more detail the instructional components that specifically address improving fluency. We conclude with a discussion of characteristics of tutors who deliver effective fluency instruction based upon our observations and experiences.

## THE CLINICAL SETTING

As with many university clinics, our program had two main objectives: (1) to provide careful, research-based, one-on-one instruction to improve the reading and writing abilities of struggling readers and (2) to provide a supervised clinical experience for preservice and practicing teachers in order to prepare them to work with students who have difficulty in learning to read and write. The course credit associated with the clinic was (and still is) one means of meeting requirements for initial licensure as an Intervention Specialist and for Reading Endorsement on an existing teaching certificate or license. Tutors typically had taken several reading courses, including a required course on assessment and remedial instruction, before beginning their clinical work. Very few had direct previous experience working one on one with a struggling reader.

Tutoring was done in individual carrels, under the direct supervision of a faculty instructor and an experienced graduate assistant. Sessions were approximately 50 minutes, and were done three times a week for 9 weeks during regular academic quarters and five times a week for 5½ weeks during summer session. Tutors changed each quarter. Tutors attended class, carried out initial assessments, developed and delivered lesson plans, wrote personal reflections, and constructed an in-depth case study report as part of course requirements.

Students with reading difficulties were referred for tutoring in a variety of ways, including by classroom teachers, school psychologists, and other school personnel; through "word of mouth" from parent to parent; and from calls to the university and visits to the clinic website. It was not unusual to have more than one child from the same family attending, and we even had children of former students receiving services. We charged a fee by quarter but used a sliding scale, so that no one was excluded because of inability to pay. We kept a list of applicants organized by date of application and moved through the list as openings became available. Students remained in the clinic as long as the staff determined they were in need of further support and as long as the family was willing and able to maintain regular attendance. We did not serve students who had additional circumstances that we did not have the expertise to address—for example, students with severe loss of hearing or vision or with minimal knowledge of English. However, at any given time, a significant number of our students may have been diagnosed as having learning disabilities, attention deficits, and/or hyperactivity. We tended to have a mix of students in terms of gender, socioeconomic status, and ethnicity (European American and African American).

## INSTRUCTIONAL APPROACH

### Assessment

In our approach, initial assessments are used to determine instructional materials and activities, and ongoing assessments are used to adjust materials and instruction as student needs and abilities change. At the beginning of each quarter or semester, students are tested with an informal word identification inventory (immediate and total scores) and a developmental spelling inventory (e.g., Schlagal, 1989). The results are used to make initial placements in instructional-level reading texts and in appropriate word study activities. Throughout their enrollment in tutoring, students are assessed for speed and accuracy to determine whether they should be kept at the same level or moved to easier or harder texts. Brief spelling tests at the end of each word study cycle help the tutor decide on the content for the next set of lessons. At the end of the quarter or semester, an informal reading inventory (e.g., Woods & Moe, 2010) is administered to measure achievement. Results of all assessments are included in the case study report, which is used by the next tutor in conjunction with his or her own findings to make initial placements in appropriate materials.

### Instruction

Although instruction is adjusted to meet the literacy learning needs of each individual, plans follow a basic format consistent with the comprehensive developmental approach used at the clinic. There are several essential components to each plan of study.

Each student is engaged in reading materials at his or her instructional level. Depending on ability level, this reading is done orally (beginning readers), as a mix of oral and silent reading (transitional readers), or mostly silently (more advanced readers). Guided reading and discussion about these materials follow a before–during–after approach. Techniques consistent with this approach, such as the Directed Reading–Thinking Activity (Stauffer, 1980), "what we know, what we want to find out, what we have learned" (K-W-L; Ogle, 1986), and story mapping are used to frame discussion. (For beginning readers such activities aimed at maintaining and developing comprehension are often done as listening activities because their level of understanding typically exceeds the conceptual demands of beginning reading materials.)

Each student is regularly engaged in writing. Often this writing is directly connected to reading, by way of note-taking, graphic organizers, summaries, and/or responses. Writing activities follow a process model that includes brainstorming, note-taking, drafting, revising, editing, and publishing.

Each student spends time working in developmentally appropriate word study activities. These typically involve manipulatives, including magnetic letters; letter tiles; onset-rime slides, wheels, or cards; picture cards; and word cards for word sorting (Bear, Invernizzi, Templeton, & Johnston, 2008). For students with a sufficient sight word vocabulary, instruction follows a modified version of the Directed Spelling Thinking Activity (Rasinski & Zutell, 2010). Patterns for study are chosen based on assessment results and analyses of word attack/spelling attempts during reading and writing activities. The cycle of instruction begins with high tutor input through demonstration and verbalization of decision making. Over time the student assumes more independence, and the requirements of the sorts become more demanding. Combinations of collaborative sorts, independent sorts, visual sorts, blind sorts, speed sorts, word hunting, and writing-to-the-sort activities are used. A spelling test on the final day of the cycle assesses student knowledge of the patterns studied and informs the choice for the next word study activity.

We expect these essential components to be incorporated into lesson plans on a regular schedule, though the time devoted to each may vary from session to session depending on circumstances and the needs of individual students. Work on word attack strategies, spelling strategies, and meaning vocabulary is also regularly addressed during reading and writing activities. Word games, free reading, and reading to the student are optional activities that are regularly incorporated during time remaining in the tutoring session. This framework forms the context into which an additional component—direct instruction on reading fluency—is also often incorporated.

## PERSPECTIVES ON FLUENCY

Following Zutell and Rasinski (1991b), we view fluency as having three major components: phrasing, smoothness, and pace. We believe phrasing is at the heart of fluency. Fluent readers chunk words into meaningful phrases and/or clauses. They focus on ideas. They use pitch, stress, and intonation appropriately to convey the meanings and feelings clearly intended by the author. For fluent readers, reading also appears fairly effortless, or automatic, and occurs minimally at a conversational pace. Thus, behaviors that indicate a lack of fluency include inappropriate or extensive pauses; monotonic, word-by-word, and/or choppy reading; inappropriate prosody; run-ons; multiple attempts at words or phrases; and a slow, laborious pace.

Here we also offer our own views on some aspects of fluency that we believe need to be addressed and clarified.

First is the issue of reading with expression. Certainly, fluent readers do often read with expression, as may be appropriate for certain texts, most clearly those related to feelings, emotions, characters, and/or dialogue. And we do often use such texts as a means to illustrate the connections between fluent reading and accessing meaning. But we also recognize that many written texts are meant to be read in a "matter-of-fact" way—for example, expository texts, content textbooks, explanations, and directions. Some students working on fluency exclusively in stories may conclude that all texts are to be read "expressively" and may, therefore, generate readings that do not match the tone and intent of the author and may even interfere with full understanding. For this reason, we try to incorporate nonfiction texts into fluency instruction, even with our beginning readers, so they develop an understanding of the importance of appropriate phrasing and prosody for comprehending all manner of reading materials.

Second, we treat accuracy as a separate aspect of overall reading performance. All word errors do not have the same impact on fluency. They can be made quickly, and not be attended to, possibly not recognized as errors, or take away time and energy during word attack, even if they are corrected. While a high degree of automatic word recognition is necessary for proficient reading and supports fluency, it is not sufficient. We have found that readers can be accurate without being fluent and can be orally fluent without being highly accurate. This is not to say that proficient readers are inaccurate! Of course, they are fluent and accurate and have strong comprehension. But we consider fluency, accuracy, and understanding to be integrated but separate aspects of reading performance that can be sources of strengths or weaknesses for individual students. We attempt to control the issues of word identification and word attack by focusing our fluency instruction on texts that are on independent level or are well known and/or rehearsed.

Third, our use of the term "pace" rather than "speed" is purposeful. Speed is an average, quantitative measure that may possibly reflect a mix of overly fast, unphrased reading with time-consuming word attack. We define "pace" as the typical rate of reading during periods of minimal disruption.

Thus, when working closely with an individual, struggling reader in an instructional context, we are wary of focusing exclusively on words correct per minute, a fluency measure now so popular in large-group assessments, because it may mask the interactions of various aspects of the reader's behavior. We believe that attending to how a student gets to such a score is as important as the score itself. For this reason, we keep track of speed and accuracy separately rather than combine them in a single measure. Moreover, we contend that, for instructional purposes, appropriate speed and accuracy should be viewed as an outcome of a focus on ideas, as manifested in reading in meaningful units, and of automatic word recognition, not as the goal itself.

So while we see the usefulness in having a student chart speed and accuracy for motivational purposes and as a concrete indication of fluency progress, we believe that effective fluency instruction is more than blind practice at improving the number of words correct per minute. It includes modeling and practice of phrased reading in otherwise easily managed texts. At the same time, effective fluency instruction must be supported by a strong word study program (as outlined earlier) in order to develop the extensive sight vocabulary and automatic word recognition that help students manage progressively more difficult texts more easily.

## ACTIVITIES SPECIFICALLY FOCUSED ON IMPROVING ORAL READING FLUENCY

In this section we describe the specific practices and procedures that we have found effective in increasing students' oral reading fluency and that we believe have a positive impact on overall reading achievement. In their comprehensive review of fluency, Rasinski et al. (2011) include an extensive discussion of research on instructional practices. Our approach includes many of the positive elements they describe, woven into our own situation (clinical work), perspectives, and understandings.

### Fluency Instruction for Beginning Readers

In our clinical work we encounter a number of primary grade students who have very limited sight vocabularies, such that they are unable to read all but the simplest texts on their own. They may not yet have internalized the voice–print match and need direction in tracking print, matching the spoken word with the written one. Others may be "glued to the print" (Chall, 1996), proceeding word by word through simple, predictable picture books. On the other hand, some struggling readers in this range may use predictability and memorization as a means to avoid text rather than to engage it. The challenge at this stage is for students to become word oriented and to develop an expanding sight vocabulary while maintaining a sense of language, meaning, and ideas in their reading.

We address this issue with a cycle of instruction combining elements of Reading Recovery (Clay, 1993) and the Language-Experience Approach (Stauffer, 1975). In this cycle we use leveled books, beginning with simple, highly memorable texts and progressing to more complex, less predictable ones (Peterson, 1991), so that students must gradually rely less on memory and more on the text and their own word knowledge.

Day 1 begins with an introduction to the book using an informal predict–read–confirm/revise structure. The tutor usually does the first reading but may encourage the student to participate through choral or shared reading. After this reading, the tutor and student discuss the characters, events, outcomes, vocabulary, and illustrations as relevant to understanding and enjoyment. Then the student reads the text at least once, with support from the tutor as necessary. The purpose of this day is to provide the student with a thorough knowledge of the text that will support future readings and free the student's attention to examine the details of words in those readings (Morris, 1993).

Day 2 begins with a brief review of text content followed by student independent reading and rereading. Here the student may need to use word attack skills and strategies discussed beforehand and receive tutor encouragement and support to solve unknown words. The tutor now also begins to move words out of context by creating sentence strips to be matched back to the text and by cutting the strips into individual words to be identified and reassembled into text sentences and new ones. Previously unknown words that are now more easily identified are marked as candidates for the student's word bank. The tutor may also ask the student questions about particular word features to encourage attention to detail (e.g., "Find the two words on this page that have double letters").

On Days 3 and 4 the student rereads the text with a specific focus on reading fluently. The tutor encourages and supports this by reminding the student of the qualities of fluent reading, possibly demonstrating on a section or sections of text. The tutor may also engage the student in echo reading, in which the student reads a phrase, clause, or sentence immediately after the tutor, echoing his or her phrasing and prosody. Attention to words continues with more work assembling sentences, identifying and matching words in and out of context, and reviewing words in the word bank. Unknown, difficult words are typically discarded. Games such as

Concentration and Go Fish played with words from the word bank may be used to reinforce word learning.

For Day 5, the final day of the cycle, the tutor types a copy of the text on plain paper, and the student reads the text independently from that copy. The tutor times the reading and keeps track of errors and self-corrections. Reading the text away from its book format serves several purposes. Some students depend on picture cues and split their attention between text and pictures, well beyond the point at which this strategy is productive. Removing this source of information encourages them to become text oriented. Many young, struggling readers initially lack confidence in their ability to read text without picture support and resist doing so. This procedure helps them build confidence in their ability to read longer sections of text independently. It, therefore, prepares them for the way text is presented in traditional testing situations, including the informal reading inventory at the end of the quarter or semester. Additionally, using this standardized format at the end of the cycle enables the tutor to obtain more reliable information about the student's speed and accuracy and his or her readiness to move to slightly more complex and demanding texts.

On this day, the tutor also presents the new words learned from the story in isolation for quick identification. Those easily identified words are added to the student's word bank. As the student becomes more proficient in word learning, a larger proportion of new words is learned and kept.

When tutors and students are working with easier texts in this range, daily activities go quickly because of the simple, brief nature of the texts. In these circumstances, they may be working with three different texts within a session, with cycles for each started on different days. As levels increase and activities with them take more time, students may work with only one or two texts. At the upper range (approximately Reading Recovery levels 14–16), only selected sections of the text may be used for fluency practice and the speed and accuracy checks.

When students read with at least 95% accuracy and reasonable fluency by the end of the cycle, and they are adding many new words to their word banks, they are working in texts that are appropriately challenging. When students are reading with independent-level word accuracy (97%) with clearly comfortable fluency and are adding almost every new word to their word banks, the tutor should move them to more demanding texts. Regular checks of speed and accuracy at the end of the cycle provide ongoing assessment data for tutors to use in best matching students and materials.

## Fluency Instruction beyond Beginning Stages

Students at the equivalent of Reading Recovery levels 16–20 or above (approximately early second-grade level) have sufficient sight vocabularies to read instructional-level texts without the extensive support of the beginning reading cycle. They are also able to read easier texts independently, though these are often at a considerably lower level than age- and/or grade-level expectations. Still, they often read even independent-level texts slowly and laboriously. They need direct instruction in reading fluently. For these students, we include two separate components in their instructional plan.

They read materials at their instructional level to provide an appropriate challenge, a chance to accelerate their instructional level, and the opportunity to work on word attack strategies in context.

For a direct focus on fluency, the tutor and student select a manageable section of a text at high instructional or independent level. This may be a new text or a favorite one that was used earlier as an instructional selection. Texts should have natural language patterns that are reasonably familiar to the student.

On Day 1 the tutor begins by reminding the student about the specific purpose of the activity. Together, they review the aims of fluency practice: to develop quick and easy reading, to produce reading that "sounds like talking," and/or to read in phrases and clauses to support understanding. They may also focus on specific aspects of fluency that the reader struggles with (e.g., choppy reading, slow pace). The student then previews the material silently to locate and resolve any meaning or sight word difficulties (with the help of the tutor as necessary). Next, the student begins to read the text orally. During this reading, the tutor may decide to model fluency directly in several ways: by taking turns reading parts of the selection, by modeling a section and then having the student read that section, and/or by focused echo reading, in which the tutor breaks the text into phrases, clauses, or sentences, and the student reads each, immediately following the tutor, maintaining direct visual focus on the text (as opposed to simply repeating what the tutor has said). On this day the student may also listen to a taped professional, or to the tutor reading, as he or she follows a written copy of the text. Finally, a "more formal" independent student reading may be done for taping and for charting speed and accuracy. This forms a baseline of comparison for later readings.

On Day 2 the tutor and student briefly review Day 1 activities and performance. They listen to the taped reading from the previous lesson, discussing the strengths of the student reading and improvements that might be made. The tutor may decide to provide further modeling of specific sections, again using listening to a model, shared, choral, and/or echo reading as appropriate. When the student feels ready, a reading is taped and charted, as on Day 1. The tutor and student then compare performances across the lessons. Depending on the results and individual motivation, the student may decide to do a second taped reading and charting.

Day 3 may include some activities similar to those on Day 2, but in an abbreviated form and with the primary focus on reading and assessment. Then performances across multiple days and readings are compared and discussed. Comparisons may also be made between performances across texts in order to focus on progress and motivate the student to continued effort.

These two cycles of instruction for building fluency are different according to the needs of readers at different stages of development. In the first, a focus on fluency is integrated into heavily supported instructional-level reading, because students at this level are not yet in control of the sight vocabulary necessary for independent reading. In the second, fluency is addressed separately from instructional-level reading in order to minimize the need for word attack and to free students' attention to focus specifically on qualities directly related to fluency.

But there are also essential components common to both formats. Both are built around multiple readings combined with teacher modeling and discussion to clarify the concept and make it concrete and specific for the student. Both begin with high teacher support and move to more student control and independent performance by the end of the cycle. While the beginning cycle tends to be longer because of its multiple purposes, in both situations tutors are encouraged to use their judgment in adding or reducing the number of days in the cycle, depending on student performance and attitude.

It should be noted that one way in which both cycles differ from some other approaches to fluency instruction is that the end of the cycle typically does not depend upon the reader reaching a predetermined speed or number of words correct per minute. A tutor does have the option to extend the length of a cycle if he or she judges that the additional time will add significantly to the student's performance. The tutor may also suggest targets within a cycle to give the student manageable and concrete goals. But having a fixed goal can be unrealistic and not account for individual differences in vocabulary, structure, and match to the student, even though the texts are judged comparable by a readability formula and/or tutor judgment. Spending too much time on a text often leads to boredom, decreased motivation, and a loss of focus. Furthermore, requiring an inflexible level of "mastery" for each individual text is likely to limit the number and variety of texts with which a student can work.

We believe that variety contributes significantly to student interest, experience, learning, and transfer. So we find it more productive in the long run to work a significant but limited amount of time with a single text, allowing tutors to incorporate a greater variety of texts into their students' experience. Similarly, for the beginning cycle, we do not require students to learn all new words from each text before moving to a new one. We are less concerned about specific words than with the overall growth of known words. By definition, high-frequency words tend to repeat across texts, which provides additional opportunities for them to be learned. We are confident that the number of words and the rate of growth will increase as students develop an understanding of how words work. This development is supported by the range of moderately frequent words encountered across a variety of texts (Henderson, Estes, & Stonecash, 1972).

## CHARACTERISTICS OF EFFECTIVE TUTORS WHEN WORKING ON FLUENCY

While the cycles of instruction described earlier provide clear structures for fluency instruction, they involve more than simply carrying out a specific set of procedures. Their successful implementation depends considerably on the skillfulness and judgment of the tutor, who makes ongoing decisions about text selection, when to provide feedback, and what kind of feedback to provide. In our work with tutors and students, we have observed that tutors who are more successful in delivering fluency instruction often have several characteristics in common. Here we offer a brief discussion of some of those characteristics.

• Inexperienced tutors often tolerate less fluent reading than more seasoned tutors. Effective tutors have a clear sense of what fluent reading should sound like. They are attentive and not reluctant to intervene when the reading begins to break down. They focus on positive behaviors, and they do so in specific, explicit ways. They avoid vague or blanket positive support and are careful not only to discuss but also to demonstrate differences between fluent and less fluent readings. In particular, effective tutors recognize appropriate and inappropriate pitch, stress, and intonation and provide explicit and specific models and comparisons between appropriate and inappropriate prosody. They notice and intervene when students are reading faster but not more prosodically.

• Effective tutors are aware of the importance of matching the difficulty of the text to the purpose of the instructional activity. They are vigilant in monitoring student performance to insure that fluency work is done in texts that require minimal word attack. On the other hand, they work to increase the level of texts their students can read at an instructional level in order to accelerate reading development.

• Effective tutors also match their response to word errors differently when working on fluency as opposed to when focused on word work in instructional-level texts. For fluency, they provide difficult words quickly and in a low-key manner so as not to disrupt the flow of the reading.

- Effective tutors include narrative and expository texts in fluency practice and illustrate/coach how to read in idea units in these texts. Beginning tutors often tend to focus exclusively on texts with dialogue for practice on expression. But, overall, a limited number of the texts that students need to read contain large stretches of such dialogue. Effective tutors understand the importance of developing and maintaining fluency across a variety of texts and writing styles by focusing on ideas as the units of processing.

- Effective tutors rely more on demonstration than on telling, but they also explain clearly what students should be attending to in their demonstrations and in listening to tapes of their reading. They use taping, charting, and reviewing performance as a means both to focus students' attention on specific aspects of their behavior and to illustrate student improvement.

- On the other hand, effective tutors try to avoid making readers too self-conscious. Struggling readers are typically anxious about their ability and performance. If they are nervous and overly focused on how well they are doing, they may not be able to engage the text fully in the very ways that support fluent reading. Ideally, effective tutors create situations in which students get so "wrapped up" or "lost" in a text that they are focused on discovering and understanding rather than on individual words and how they are reading.

- When using buddy and echo-reading techniques, effective tutors move from a focus on individual phrases, clauses, and sentences to larger, manageable chunks (e.g., two to three sentences). They are sensitive to students losing focus if chunks become too long or unmanageable, but they understand that their goal is to stretch students' efforts to use larger chunks and to maintain fluent reading over large sections of text.

- Some students read fluently enough during instruction that focuses their attention directly on fluency but revert to the slow and/or choppy reading to which they have become accustomed in other reading situations. Effective tutors encourage students to maintain focus and pace across reading activities, so that fluent reading becomes the natural, automatic way in which they engage texts.

## CONCLUSION

Both current research and clinical experience indicate that fluency is an essential component of proficient reading. In our program for struggling readers, fluency instruction is embedded in a comprehensive program that also includes instructional-level reading, developmentally appropriate word study, writing, and comprehension instruction. Within such a framework, fluency is addressed specifically and directly through cycles of instruction that include clear and explicit explanations of the concept, demonstrations and modeling, independent-level reading, repeated readings, and feedback. The specific tutor characteristics and behaviors discussed in this chapter have a direct impact on the effectiveness of instruction. Reading educators would be well advised to address these qualities directly when preparing tutors to work with struggling readers.

## REFERENCES

Allington, R. L. (1983). Fluency: The neglected reading goal. *The Reading Teacher, 37,* 556–561.

Bear, D. R., Invernizzi, M., Templeton, S., & Johnston, F. (2008). *Words their way: Word study for phonics, vocabulary, and spelling instruction* (4th ed.). New York: Allyn & Bacon.

Chall, J. S. (1996). *Stages of reading development* (2nd ed.). Fort Worth, TX: Harcourt Brace.

Clay, M. M. (1993). *Reading Recovery: A guidebook for teachers in training.* Portsmouth, NH: Heinemann.

Henderson, E., Estes, T., & Stonecash, S. (1972). An exploratory study of word acquisition among first graders in a language-experience approach. *Journal of Reading Behavior, 4,* 21–30.

Kamil, M. L., Pearson, P. D., Moje, E. B., & Afflerbach, P. (Eds.). (2011). *Handbook of reading research* (Vol. IV). New York: Routledge.

Morris, D. (1993). The relationship between children's concept of word in text and phoneme awareness in learning to read: A longitudinal study. *Research in the Teaching of English, 27*(2), 133–154.

National Reading Panel. (2000). *Teaching children to read: An evidence-based assessment of of the scientific research literature on reading and its implications for reading instruction: Reports of the subgroups* (NIH Publication No. 00-4754). Washington, DC: National Institute of Child Health and Development.

Ogle, D. (1986). K-W-L: A teaching model that develops active reading of expository text. *Reading Teacher, 39,* 564–570.

Peterson, B. (1991). Selecting books for beginning readers. In D. DeFord, C. Lyons, & G. Pinnell (Eds.), *Bridges to literacy: Learning from Reading Recovery* (pp. 119–147). Portsmouth, NH: Heinemann.

Pinnell, G. S., Pikulski, J. J., Wixson, K. K., Campbell, P. J. R., Gough, P. B., & Beatty, A. S. (1995). *Listening to children read aloud: Data from NAEP's integrated reading performance record (IRIP) at grade 4* (Report No. 23-FR-04, prepared by the Educational Testing Service). Washington, DC: Office of Educational Research and Improvement, U.S. Department of Education.

Rasinski, T., & Zutell, J. (2010). *Essential strategies for word study: Effective methods for improving decoding, spelling, and vocabulary.* New York: Scholastic.

Rasinski, T. V., Reutzel, C. R., Chard, D., & Linan-Thompson, S. (2011). Reading fluency. In M. L. Kamil, P. D. Pearson, E. B. Moje, & P. Afflerbach (Eds.), *Handbook of reading research* (Vol. IV, pp. 286–319). New York: Routledge.

Schlagal, R. (1989). Constancy and change in spelling development. *Reading Psychology, 10*(3), 207–232.

Stauffer, R. G. (1975). *Directing the thinking process.* New York: Harper & Row.

Stauffer, R. G. (1980). *The language-experience approach to the teaching of reading* (2nd ed.). New York: Harper & Row.

Woods, M., & Moe, A. (2010). *Analytical Reading Inventory: Comprehensive standards-based assessment for all students including gifted and remedial* (9th ed.). New York: Allyn & Bacon.

Zutell, J., & Rasinski, T. (Eds.). (1991a). Fluency in oral reading. *Theory into Practice, 30*(3), 142–227.

Zutell, J., & Rasinski, T. (1991b). Training teachers to attend to their students' oral reading fluency. *Theory into Practice, 30*(3), 211–217.

# Index

Page numbers followed by an *f* or a *t* indicate figures or tables.